Collin College
CENTRAL PARK CAMPUS
McKinney, Texas 75070

D0143110

WITHDRAWN

CPC

The Music Business and Recording Industry

The Music Business and Recording Industry is a comprehensive, introductory textbook focused on the three income streams in the music industry: music publishing, live entertainment, and recordings. The book provides a sound foundation for understanding key issues while presenting the latest research in the field. It covers the changes in the industry brought about by the digital age, such as changing methods of distributing and accessing music, and new approaches in marketing with the Internet and mobile applications. New developments in copyright law are also examined, along with the global and regional differences in the music business.

This new edition introduces a co-authorship, as well as a number of pedagogical features:

- **Key Concepts** are outlined at the beginning of each chapter
- **"Do it Yourself" Activities** promote a more interactive, hands-on experience
- **Internet Activities** present guided opportunities to use Web resources to enhance understanding of how things run in the music business
- **Case Studies** illustrate specific instances of how real people have succeeded in the music business
- The **Companion Website** includes instructor and student resources including multiple choice quizzes and slides.

As new methods of distribution change, new revenue sources are created, and the industry evolves. *The Music Business and Recording Industry* sets the economic and historical framework for understanding where the business has been and where it is going.

Geoffrey P. Hull is Professor Emeritus in the Recording Industry department at Middle Tennessee State University. He has 36 years experience teaching music business and recording classes. He has JD, MBA, and BS degrees and is a licensed attorney in the state of Tennessee.

Thomas Hutchison is Professor of Marketing and Music Business Internship Coordinator at Middle Tennessee State University. He has over 20 years experience in the music business as a marketing research consultant. Hutchison holds a MS and PhD from the Florida State University.

Richard Strasser is an Associate Professor of Music Industry at Northeastern University. A graduate from the Australian National University and Manhattan School of Music, Strasser is a recipient of Northeastern University's Excellence in Teaching Award and a member of the NASM Working Group that established standards and guidelines for music industry education accreditation.

ML
3790
H84
2011

Hull, Geoffrey P.

The music business
and recording
industry.

$58.95

Collin College Library
CENTRAL PARK CAMPUS
McKinney, Texas
WITHDRAWN

The Music Business and Recording Industry: Delivering Music in the 21st Century

Third Edition

Geoffrey P. Hull
Middle Tennessee State University

Thomas Hutchison
Middle Tennessee State University

Richard Strasser
Northeastern University

Routledge
Taylor & Francis Group

NEW YORK AND LONDON

Second edition published 2004
by Routledge

This edition published 2011
by Routledge
270 Madison Avenue, New York, NY 10016

Simultaneously published in the UK
by Routledge
2 Park Square, Milton Park, Abingdon, Oxon OX14 4RN

Routledge is an imprint of the Taylor & Francis Group, an informa business

© 1998, 2004 Geoffrey P. Hull
© 2011 Taylor & Francis

Typeset in Janson and Akzidenz Grotesk by
Florence Production Ltd, Stoodleigh, Devon
Printed and bound in the United States of America on acid-free paper by
Sheridan Books, Inc.

All rights reserved. No part of this book may be reprinted
or reproduced or utilised in any form or by any electronic,
mechanical, or other means, now known or hereafter invented,
including photocopying and recording, or in any information
storage or retrieval system, without permission in writing from
the publishers.

Trademark Notice: Product or corporate names may be trademarks
or registered trademarks, and are used only for identification and
explanation without intent to infringe.

Library of Congress Cataloging in Publication Data
Hull, Geoffrey P.
 The music and recording business : delivering music in the 21st century/
 Geoffrey P. Hull, Thomas Hutchison, Richard Strasser. — 3rd ed.
  p. cm.
  Previous ed. published under title: Recording industry.
  Includes index.
 1. Sound recording industry. 2. Music trade. I. Hutchison, Thomas W.
 (Thomas William) II. Strasser, Richard, 1966– III. Hull, Geoffrey P.
 Recording industry. IV. Title.
 ML3790.H84 2011
 338.4'7780973–dc22   2010019432

ISBN13: 978-0-415-87560-8 (hbk)
ISBN13: 978-0-415-87561-5 (pbk)
ISBN13: 978-0-203-84319-2 (ebk)

Contents

Preface

Is the sky really falling on the music and recording business? Is it the end of their world as they knew it? Or is it just another manic decade? Truly the decade of the 2000s brought more turmoil to the music business than probably any other decade since the 1950s or the 1930s, and maybe the most ever. Record stores closed in droves. Millions of people downloaded many millions of unauthorized copies of songs and recordings. Concert ticket prices soared to over $100 for some shows. New sources of revenue from ringtones, downloads, and digital performances appeared. So, the answers to our questions are: (1) not really, (2) to a certain extent yes, and (3) surely. Those are three good reasons for a reexamination of the music and recording business at this time.

The Music Business and Recording Industry, Third Edition, is not simply a revision of *The Recording Industry, Second Edition*. Routledge's Senior Music Editor, Constance Ditzel, and I decided it was time for a major makeover and to turn the book into a true textbook with pedagogical features and a website, in addition to some much-needed updates. As much trouble as the music business has been in at this point, there are hundreds of students of the business who want to make popular music, make their livings making it, or want to participate in the process as recording engineers, arrangers, producers, music publishers, or label "insiders." You are the people we hope to talk to and inspire with this book. To that end, "we" are three authors now. The strengths of Thomas Hutchison and Richard Strasser complement original author Geoffrey Hull well, and add fresh perspectives. It is a different book, with a different title—but with the same basic theme.

Organization and Changes to the Third Edition

The book *does* attempt to put everything about music and recordings into a context, whether that is historical or economic or both. Simply describing what is going on is not adequate for understanding why things are unfolding the way that they are. The "Three Income Streams" approach of the earlier versions is a great organizing approach and accurately explains a lot of what the music business is all about. It is a central theme. We have compiled a lot of information about copyright law, because if there were no copyrights, there would be almost no music business. To reflect the changed nature of the business we have expanded marketing into two chapters (Chapters Eleven and Twelve), and combined retailing with the second marketing chapter (Chapter Twelve). We have positioned the music business into a context of the overall entertainment industry in Chapter One because it competes for leisure time and dollars with all those other entertainment choices. "New media" (internet, mobile, and such) are not really all that new to most of you who are reading this book so they have been integrated into all the chapters in the book. They are a fact of life now. The music business is global, so Chapter Thirteen is on international aspects of the business. To provide updates on things that are changing rapidly, there is a companion website that we will update with new cases, new statistics, and new content in general.

It was tempting to try to be "all things to all people," but we did not cover everything—and can't really be "all things to all people" anyway. Specifically, we have omitted coverage of "art music." That is because that business functions very much differently from the popular music business and would seem to fit better in a course on "Arts Management" or "The Business of Art Music." Also, there are no sample contracts in the book because they add greatly to length and are more appropriate for an advanced course, not a survey course, which is the target of this book. Nor is this a book about all the cultural implications of music; those are also better left to courses where the concepts can be more deeply explored.

Features

We are trying to engage you more in the process, with "DIY (Do it Yourself) Activities" to help get you started in the right direction. We have "Internet Activities" to provide guided opportunities to use web resources that will enhance your understanding of how things run in the music business. We have "Case Studies" to bring in specific instances of how real people have succeeded in the music business. We have a running glossary in every chapter, as well as a full glossary at the end of the book because this crazy business has a lot of specific terminology that must be understood. There are illustrations and tables in every chapter to aid in understanding. As you will discover, there are several pedagogical features that emphasize key points and help to retain what is read, but also make the subject matter more interesting.

To summarize the pedagogical elements and ancillaries described above, they are:

- DIY (Do it Yourself) Activities
- Internet Activities
- Case Studies
- Running Glossary
- Companion website: **www.routledge.com/textbooks/9780415875615** with Multiple-Choice Quizzes, Suggestions for Further Reading, Links to Online Resources, Author Blog and PowerPoint Slides for Instructors

To the Professor

Your most daunting job is to decide how much to leave in and how much to leave out. We have targeted this book at students who have some experience in college. A sophomore or higher-level student should have no trouble with the concepts and explanations. The devil is in the detail—how much do you want them to know at the end of the semester. I've always thought that no one should be able to pass an undergraduate survey music business course if they could not explain what a mechanical license is or what a music or sound recording performance license is. Make sure the students do the DIY and Internet Activities. They are fertile leads for discussion and understanding as are the Case Studies in each chapter.

To the Student

We hope you find this book both interesting and educational. You are in this class because you want to know more about the business that you seek to become a part of. Even if you want to be an audio engineer, producer, or performer you need to know how the business works because that is the source of your income. Use the DIY Activities and Internet Activities to look beyond the pages of the book and into the workings of this dynamic business. Ask lots of questions of your teacher. Look for answers in the book, on the Internet, and on the website for the book. Get involved. If the book seems dry at times remind yourself that even the people in the real world music business sometimes have to put up with the mundane in order to get to the exciting. You have to dream big and really *want* to be in the music business because your first job will probably be hard to get, and not pay very well.

You have to love music because that is what makes it all worthwhile.

Geoff Hull, Tom Hutchison, and Richard Strasser
May 2010

Acknowledgments

A number of people, places, and organizations have provided invaluable support in the preparation of this book. Industry organizations providing a wealth of information include the National Association of Recording Merchandisers (NARM), the Recording Industry Association of America (RIAA), the National Music Publishers' Association (NMPA), the American Federation of Musicians (AFM) Local 257, the National Association of Music Merchandisers (NAMM), and the International Federation of the Phonographic Industry (IFPI).

The greatest industry source is *Billboard*. Thanks for reporting over 100 years of recording and entertainment industry news and events. One must also include more recent publications such as *Pollstar*, and organizations like SoundScan and SoundExchange as important sources of information. Thanks to the Internet and everybody's websites for a wealth of information.

I found a great deal of research support and resources on the campus of Middle Tennessee State University. Probably the greatest resource was the Center for Popular Music. Thanks especially to director Paul Wells, and the rest of the staff of the Center. How else could I have found a copy of "Payola Blues" or hundreds of other publications about the recording industry without the Center's collection? I don't want to think about it. The Walker Library's *Billboard* and *Variety* collection and its online databases, especially General OneFile and Lexis-Nexis Academic Universe, proved most helpful. MTSU's commitment to fiber optics and computers made surfing the World Wide Web a breeze and brought a wealth of information right to my desktop. Administrative thanks to my department Chair, Chris Haseleu, for letting me "do my thing," and to the Dean of the College of Mass Communication, Dr. Roy Moore. Thanks to all my colleagues in the Recording Industry Department for being, well, collegial.

Just as most recording artists would not be very successful without record companies, most authors would not be very successful without publishers. So, thanks to Senior Music Editor at Routledge, Constance Ditzel, for picking up on the challenge of turning out a high caliber survey of the music business textbook. Thanks to the many reviewers who spent hours poring over manuscript and making suggestions about how to improve it. We couldn't always do everything you suggested, but a lot of it has made its way into these pages.

Thanks especially to my wife, Patty, for all her support and for putting up with my long hours.

Geoff Hull

1 The Entertainment Industry and the Music Business

Introduction

The pursuit of leisure is an ubiquitous activity that has been part of the human experience since the time we first strolled on this planet. In fact, the act of escaping every day stresses, whether they be hunting and gathering, or mastering quantum mechanics, for the purpose of relaxation and enjoyment transcends time, location, and culture. Often **leisure activities** came with obligations towards festivals, celebrations, feasts, or other special occasions. In many parts of the world, the development of entertainment coincided with the creation of a ruling class. In early advanced cultures, with clearly differentiated working roles, leisure activities were associated with those in an elite class or of high political standing. For example, the Egyptian civilization, the Assyrian and Babylonian cultures included many "leisure" activities but these were primarily activities of the upper strata in society. The ancient Greek civilization (around 500 B.C.) had a professionalization of sport and public entertainment, such as theater. To the Greeks, leisure was part of good citizenship.

Fast forwarding to the eighteenth and nineteen centuries, the industrial revolution led to profound changes in leisure time. With the development of factories, populations were uprooted from their agrarian existence in small villages and moved to large, overpopulated cities. Within this environment, opportunities for leisure were limited, especially for children. A reform movement not only dealt with the conditions of an urban life bereft of basic human rights, but one without adequate leisure. At the turn of the twentieth century, an interest in leisure as it relates to industrial societies was developed. In fact, leisure time is so important that many governments provide facilities for certain leisure activities for the "good" of people in general, including performing arts centers, parks, and recreation centers.

> **Leisure activities**
> Those things that people do that are not required by work or normal day to day activities such as sleeping or eating.

KEY CONCEPTS

- Entertainment Industry is the monetized function of leisure time.
- Entertainment companies are influenced by external variables such as the economy, politics, social trends, and technology.
- Generally, all sectors within the entertainment industry exhibit similar characteristics including high capitalization, advanced intellectual property protection requirements, globalization tendencies, and oligopolistic tendencies.

Continued

- Three important sectors that highlight these trends and have an impact on the music industry include the:
  - Motion picture industry
  - Broadcast industry
  - Video game industry.

Today, people have more free time than they did several decades ago, although actual gain is sometimes overstated. Equally, there are now more diverse ways of spending leisure time: more facilities, indoor and outdoor, provided by private companies and public authorities; a greater range of activities from group participatory events, such as sports and musical concerts; and a range of activities within the financial reach of every economic class. Due to the diversity of entertainment/leisure activities, it is hard to estimate accurately the total annual expenditure on leisure. One metric used as a measure of economic stature is the amount of recreation available to citizens. Developed countries, such as the United States, allow employees a certain amount of "free time." Even with the general increase of leisure time in industrially developed countries, competitive pressures require entertainment companies to create multifunctional products. For example, Apple's *iPhone* is not only a mobile telephone; it is an MP3 player, games console, GPS, video player, and more (see Figure 1.1).

Defining leisure is not so much about identifying a specific activity but rather describing a state of mind. For example, leisure includes diverse activities such as lying on a beach, watching television, listening to Indian ragas, or playing the latest version of *Halo*. To that effect, the concept of entertainment permits a

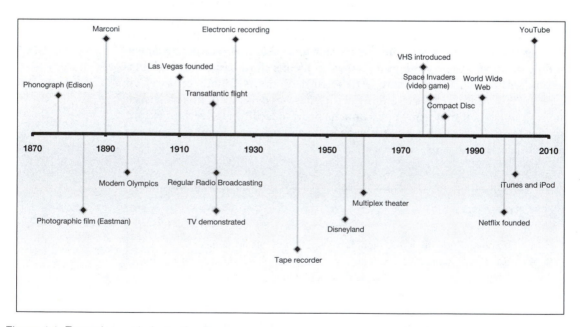

Figure 1.1 Entertainment industry timeline

variety of definitions and forms. From the voluminous literature on the subject, five general, although overlapping, definitions of leisure exist:

1. Leisure as time (free time after practical necessities of life have been addressed)
2. Leisure as a state of being (leisure not as a means to an end, but rather an end in itself)
3. Leisure as a way of life (entertainment is part of a person's life rather than an alternative to work)
4. Leisure as an all-pervading "holistic concept" (leisure seen in all actions, e.g. family activities, home decorating, etc.)
5. Leisure as activity (leisure made up of activities, ranging from passive to active e.g. watching TV to do-it-yourself home repairs).

The entertainment industry today clearly exhibits leisure activities on all five levels. Furthermore, many experts categorize the entertainment industry according to four states of involvement: passive, emotional, active, and creative.[1] Passive entertainment does not require the participant to be involved in the unfolding of an activity. For example, listening to music performed by a band does not affect the creation of the music or how it will sound. Active participation, on the other hand, requires an individual to contribute in the production of the entertainment. For example, activities such as performing in a band or participating in an MMORPG (Massively Multiplayer Online Role-playing Game) affect the outcome of the product. Creative entertainment activities range from being actively part of an entertainment event (e.g. role playing in a video game) to the creation of a commercial or noncommercial product (e.g. painting, sculpting, woodworking).

While there is the general view that leisure has been increasing, there are many studies that indicate that the amount of free time available to Americans has been decreasing over the past few years. In fact, when broken down, studies show that the amount of leisure time available varies by career, demographic characteristics (age, gender, etc.), and socioeconomic class. According to the Harris Poll, "the number of hours spent working (including housekeeping and studying) has not changed significantly"[2] over the past decade (see Figure 1.2).

The Intersection between Media Companies and the Music Industry

Today, the music industry is intrinsically part of the greater entertainment industry in terms of products, structures, and ownership. Artists and music companies have embraced a wider array of revenue generation opportunities beyond the traditional music outlets, such as recording and live performance. Nontraditional entertainment sectors are now an important source of revenue, be it for performances, recordings, or licenses, and are essential in developing an artist's brand. For example, the motion picture and television industry has been a media outlet for the music industry to exploit songs, both as background music and via sound tracks. Now both media have become important for the development of artists as actors, thereby extending their brand equity.

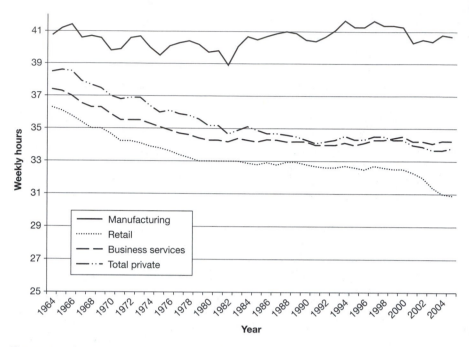

Figure 1.2 Average weekly hours worked

Entertainment Economics

As an industrial sector, the entertainment industry is similar to other industries that manufacture and produce products for profit. As with other industrial sectors, each division within the entertainment industry creates a product that is unique to that industry. For example, each movie created is unique, with a different set of circumstances, deals, and actors. As an economic sector, the entertainment industry consists of a large number of sub-industries that are devoted to specific forms of entertainment. Although there are numerous sub-industries, the entertainment industry as a whole can be broken down into eight major divisions:

1. Motion Picture Industry
2. Music Industry (recording, publishing, and live performance)
3. Broadcasting (television, radio, and Internet)
4. Publishing (books, magazines, and newspapers)
5. Games (video and computer games and toys)
6. Sports
7. Exhibition Entertainment (museums, amusement parks, and theater)
8. Gambling.

Throughout the late 1990s and into the new millennium, the entertainment industry went through an intense strategic restructuring that resulted in the presence of large corporations dominating specific markets. Internationally, the

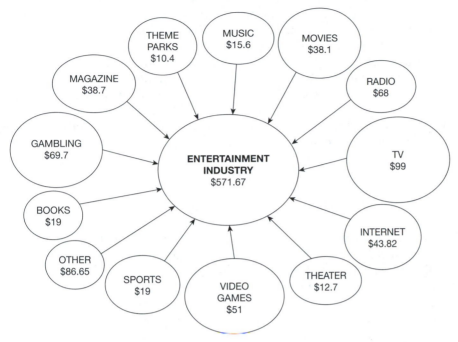

Figure 1.3 Spending on entertainment in billions
Source: Pricewaterhousecoopers

entertainment industry is collectively worth over US$2.2 trillion and is growing at an annual rate of 5 percent (see Figure 1.3).[3] Based on this projection, it is likely that by the year 2020, the entertainment industry would be worth as much as US$6.1 trillion. This growth is in part due to a global free market economy (aided by international trade institutions such as the World Trade Organization (WTO)), international competition, and the convergence of technology between media and other industries. The result is the growth of multinational entertainment **conglomerates** that exploit existing economies of scale and scope by joining forces through takeovers, mergers, and other strategic alliances. With the continued erosion of traditional market boundaries, market concentration, and cross-industry ownership, the entertainment industry has truly become an international business. Nonetheless, even in this diverse global area, there are several characteristics that are common to all sectors within the entertainment industry.

Unique Creative Products for Profit

In general, the entertainment industry provides products used during free or leisure time. Each sector within the entertainment industry provides a unique product that is distinct to that sector. In many respects, this uniqueness acts as a protective measure that prohibits other companies making identical products for sale. Nonetheless, the profit motive within the entertainment industry, especially with large multinational corporations, has implications in the type of

Conglomerate
A business corporation that is formed by the ownership of a number of other businesses or divisions operating in a wide variety of areas. For example, Sony Corp. owns record companies, music publishing companies, film production and distribution, and consumer electronics hardware manufacturing.

products created. In the entertainment industry, especially the recording, motion picture, network-television, and video game industry, profits from a few highly popular products offset losses from many mediocre commodities. This tends to make the entertainment industry a high risk sector, as no formula can predict the success of a product. In fact, the failure rate of recorded music (albums that do not make a profit) is over 90 percent. Furthermore, like many other industrial sectors, the entertainment industry is sensitive to external variables that affect the production and type of products. For example, the global financial crisis in 2008–2010 had a profound effect on the entertainment industry, especially for sectors dependent on advertising and consumer spending.

High Up-front Capital Costs

Capital costs
The up-front costs of creating, distributing, and marketing the product.

A feature of the entertainment industry, especially within the global environment, is the financial cost of creating, distributing, and marketing entertainment products (see Figure 1.4). **Capital costs** associated with entertainment products have increased exponentially in recent years. Compounding this fact is that many entertainment products have very short life cycles, requiring companies to produce new products on a regular basis to meet consumer demand. For example, a major US movie will cost up to several hundreds of millions of dollars to produce, market, and distribute. A full national theatrical release may only last a few weeks or not at all. Furthermore, marketing expenditures within the entertainment industry tend to be large relative to the cost of operation and production, placing greater financial pressure on initial capitalization of entertainment commodities. In fact, entertainment companies spend more per product in advertising than other sectors in the economy. The need for large amounts of capital has also contributed to the domination of the entertainment industry by a few large companies that have access to large pools of capital. In addition, globalization has created further consolidation as companies must have access to large amounts of money and resources to promote products in the international market.

Protection of Intellectual Property

Intellectual property
Copyrights, patents, trademarks, and trade secrets are all intellectual property, which means they are not physical property like land or books, but rather are rights associated with the use of works, inventions, marks, and information.

The entertainment industry is dependent on the creative output of individuals (e.g. artists, producers, writers, and programmers) and companies. The process of creation utilizes time, raw material, and labor in a combined effort to deliver

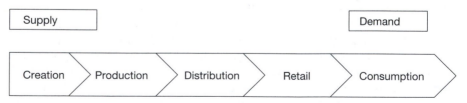

Figure 1.4 Entertainment industry value chain

unique products to a specific audience. In an effort to protect the monetization of this commodity, entertainment companies must obtain legal protection that inhibits others from copying and selling replicas of the product. Intellectual property rights, such as copyrights, trademarks, and patents, secure the economic/ commercial value of entertainment commodities. Copyright not only protects the inherent right of intellectual property, it safeguards the production, distribution, and consumption of entertainment products. Thus, at every stage of the creation and distribution of entertainment, especially within new technologies, intellectual property protection has become a primary competitive resource and the basis of competitive advantage in the entertainment industry. The music industry has undergone redefinition, having moved from "an industry primarily selling [manufactured] commodities," to becoming an industry of services, which exploit a "basket of rights."[4] In 2007, copyright industries contributed as much as US$1.52 trillion or 11.05 percent of the US gross domestic product (GDP), with "core" copyright industries reaching $889 billion or 6.44 percent of GDP.[5]

Conglomeration of Global Producers

During the 1990s, the growth of the global economy had a profound impact on the entertainment industry. Not only has this opened up markets and profits for companies, it has resulted in consolidation of producers and products. For example, between 1990 and 1995 there were 557 media business acquisitions.[6] By 2000, the international entertainment industry consisted of six corporations accounting for 70 percent of the global market with sales totaling US$165.94 billion and a collective net income of approximately US$26 billion.[7]

The "Big Six" (Time Warner, Disney, Vivendi Universal, Viacom, Bertelsmann, and News Corp.)[8] have also attained global dominance through **horizontal integration** across the entertainment industry spectrum, in areas such as motion pictures, television, magazines, music, and retail merchandise. This not only allows them to maintain their top position in the entertainment industry, but also forms a formidable barrier against competing firms trying to enter the global entertainment market. The dissemination of entertainment by mainly US media corporations has also led to the domination of US entertainment products in foreign markets. In this environment, demand for domestically produced entertainment is limited without aggressive funding, often from government agencies. Thus, international exposure for non-US entertainment products, especially within America, is restricted to niche markets.

Horizontal integration
An economic term describing the actions of a firm to buy out competing companies at the same level, such as one record store chain acquiring another record store chain.

Growth through Technology

Technology has not only spurred tremendous growth in the entertainment industry, but has been the main driver of transformation within the industry. In particular, digitalization (digitization) has created a range of opportunities for creative expression, production, and distribution and has propelled new modes of entertainment business. **Digitization** has not only facilitated the development

Digitization
The turning of some analog work, such as a recording, book, or map, into a digital format that can be stored and transmitted via computers.

of new entertainment industries ("new media"), but it continues to stimulate growth in other industries such as computer software, telecommunications, and advertising. According to Standard & Poor's "Industry Survey on Movies and Home Entertainment," "the convergence of media platforms, combined with the expansion in media outlets and the expansion of ways to package and format content, are providing both opportunities and challenges"[9] to industry participants. For example, the explosion in social networking and user-content sites is not only accelerating content fragmentation, but also moving a large degree of control away from businesses into the hands of consumers.

Furthermore, the growth in digital formats has sharply boosted competitive conditions in the entertainment industry. The motion picture and home entertainment industry are undergoing long-term changes as technological developments have altered and expanded distribution channels. Hollywood movie studios and television networks are actively seeking to exploit the direct-to-consumer online distribution channels of their content. Although the entertainment industry has made great strides in the utilization of technology as a new media, the proliferation of reproduction equipment, especially digital technology, has provided the means for piracy of entertainment products on a global scale. In its 2006 "Commercial Piracy Report," the International Federation of the Phonographic Industry (IFPI) estimated that the global pirate market for recorded music totaled some 1.2 billion units to a value of US$4.5 billion.[10] In response, governments have implemented stringent legislation and policies that allow local entertainment industries to defend their intellectual property. Furthermore, trade associations within the entertainment industry have reinforced government policy by taking an active role in the fight against piracy.

DIY Activities

- Obtaining data about industrial sectors is of vital importance to business leaders. Quantitative data is expensive or often difficult to find. The US Census Bureau is a government agency that is not only responsible for conducting the census, but collects data on the economy. Companies use the economic census for a variety of reasons including forecasting, analyzing competition within a region, or understanding the averages within a sector.
- Suppose you want to learn more about the arts, entertainment, and recreation industry in the US (you can filter any geographic region if needed).
- Go to the Census Bureau website (www.census.gov). Enter the Economic Census and click on the 2007 census tab and open the Economic Census data sets by sector (entertainment is sector 71).
- How many performing arts, spectator sports, and related industries establishments are found in the US in 2007?
- Has the entertainment sector improved since 2002?
- What is the average revenue for the entertainment industry in your home state?

Conclusion

The entertainment industry is a highly dynamic environment, where consumer demand is uncertain and infringement poses a severe challenge. Nevertheless, product/service development, creativity, and innovation remain the bedrock and impetus for continual growth in the entertainment industry. Technology aside, growth in the entertainment industry is contingent on brand appeal and effective marketing strategies, in spite of general market uncertainties.

Today, the US entertainment landscape is dominated by massive corporations that have concentrated their control over a range of entertainment products through vertical integration. These conglomerates have interests in TV, motion pictures, radio publishing, and the Internet. Nonetheless, the entertainment industry is one of constant renewal and innovation. The exponential growth of the video game industry has not only become a catalyst for the generation of revenue for music via licensing and original music, it has been a transformative medium for well established artists to capture a new audience for their music (e.g. the Beatles with *RockBand* and Aerosmith with *Guitar Hero*). In an effort to understand the economic dynamics of the entertainment industry, we will investigate three sectors (motion picture, television, and computer game industries) that characterize the entertainment industry and have a close relationship with the music industry.

Motion Picture Industry

Introduction

Beginning in cheap nickelodeons and patronized by poor immigrants of America's cities, the US motion picture industry quickly became a medium of mass entertainment and one of the most significant entertainment forms of the past century. Today, the motion picture industry, as with many other sectors within the entertainment industry, is experiencing rapid changes, owing to the industry's increasing dependence on technology and the changing entertainment environment. According to a recent Standard and Poor report, the US movie and home entertainment business is experiencing sustained growth due to expanding audiences, pipelines, and content. Industries in the motion picture industry provide products and services for audiences around the world, including new movies shown in theaters, video titles, and a wide range of television shows. Through differing distribution arrangements, content owners receive revenues from a variety of ancillary sources, such as the sale or rental of their products to consumers, advertising, and subscription services.

The motion picture industry has had a close relationship to the music industry since its inception. Music not only provides the background to a particular scene it helps define the character of a film, via the sound track. For the music industry, film soundtracks are a profitable genre (see Figure 1.5). For example, the sound track to *Saturday Night Fever* was certified 15x Platinum for shipments of over 15 million copies.[11]

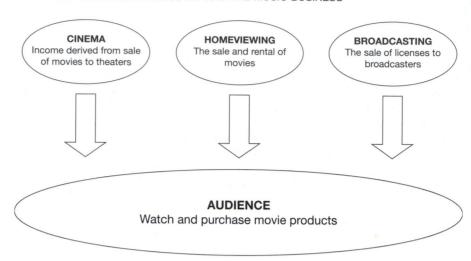

Figure 1.5 Film industry flowchart

Consolidation
The creation of larger and larger organizations as smaller ones are absorbed, purchased, or merged into larger ones.

Antitrust laws
Laws that attempt to control whether businesses unfairly compete by forming monopolies or fixing prices to the detriment of consumers.

Industry **consolidation** has also had a profound effect on the development of the motion picture industry in the new millennium. Unlike many other entertainment sectors, but similar to the music and recording industries, the motion picture industry has had a long history of a few companies dominating the production and distribution of movies. In the mid-1920s, the motion picture industry consisted of a consortium of five large corporations that owned the majority of movie studios, distribution divisions, and theaters. With the breakup of the major studios, due to **antitrust law** and the incursion of television, the major production companies gradually transformed into management structures that put teams together on a project-by-project basis. Further, these production companies began to rent studio space to other companies for the production of movies. Today, six major studios, many of which are international conglomerations, dominate the motion picture industry:

1. Warner Brothers (owned by Time Warner)
2. Paramount Pictures (owned by Viacom)
3. Walt Disney/Touchstone Pictures
4. Columbia Pictures (Sony)
5. Universal Studios (GE/Comcast)[12]
6. 20th Century Fox (News Corporation).

As with other entertainment sectors, technological advances have been an important impetus for change in the motion picture industry. Methods of viewing movies have changed many aspects of film making. For example, in the mid-1970s many considered the introduction of **VHS** and home recording as the death nail for theater exhibition. However, today motion picture companies have embraced this technology as an important income stream. Furthermore, the growth of home entertainment during the 1970s spurred the creation of large multiplex theaters in new suburban locations.

VHS The home video tape recording format (along with Betamax).

Motion Picture Production

Similar to other sectors in the entertainment industry, the motion picture industry has specific organizations, actors, and structures that produce and distribute products to the general public. From the creation of a movie script to theatrical release, this process may take up to two years and cost millions of dollars. During this time frame, raw materials and labor combine to create a motion picture. Today, movies are made under a contract signed by a major distributor, a production company, and a collection of freelance talent. With a major theatrical release, distributors typically fund a movie from start to finish or provide a portion of the financing in return for fees and a share of the proceeds. For motion picture companies, theater sales are no longer the principal source of revenue. Profitability often depends heavily on contributions from various home video and TV markets. The financial model for film production operates around the assemblage of ad hoc teams of freelancing creative actors (e.g. actors, director, scriptwriter, photography) in a project financed by a producer, who is in charge of the distribution and marketing of the film. Unlike the music industry, the financing of motion picture projects is not an advance, but rather an investment, with returns specified as a share of the revenues of box-office receipts, retail, and other ancillary products (e.g. merchandise). The role of distributors in this process is essential, with the major studios controlling larger markets and independent distributors focusing on niche or local markets. The process of creating and distributing motion pictures follows five stages (see Figure 1.6):

1. Development
2. Pre-production
3. Production and post-production
4. Distribution
5. Exhibition.

All motion pictures begin with an idea or script. Material comes from original ideas, works of fiction, or actual events. Sources of adaptations come from books, television programs, comics, plays, or remakes of other films. In fact, the adaptation as a script source accounts for over 50 percent of all Hollywood films. After approval of the initial script, there are two ways a script is developed. A studio may purchase the rights to a movie and develop the concept in-house. Alternatively, external agencies, such as **PACTs**, develop concepts. PACTs are individuals or production companies that have ongoing contracts (a pact) with specific studios for the development of a motion picture. This may take the form of a first-look deal, which may provide a producer with financing; an equity partnership under which the studio and a company's backers share in both the overheads and profits; or a distribution deal, under which a company is wholly financed by outside partners and utilizes the studio's distribution and marketing arms. Unlike the music industry, the film industry is not reliant on funding from profits. Funding comes from various sources. Major studios draw on corporate funds, while independent studios may draw on a wider variety of sources such as banks and other financial institutions that have specialized departments that deal with film financing.

PACTs
The organizations and agreements set up to fund the production of major motion pictures.

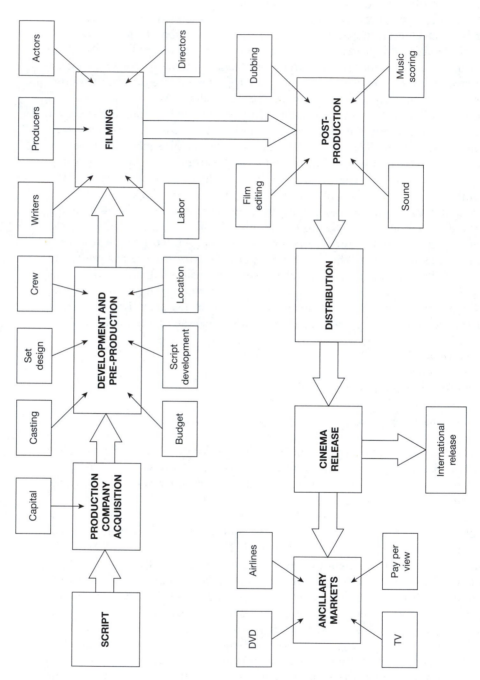

Figure 1.6 Motion picture industry flowchart

In many cases, a bank may enter into a distribution agreement with a studio for a percentage of future income. Other sources include merchandising and production placement arrangements (the inclusion of a product in a movie to gain exposure for that product), investment capital in the form of limited partnerships, and government and private foundations grants. This partnership is important as the cost of developing, marketing, and distributing films has grown in the past decade. According to Nash Information Services, the average feature film costs $65 million in pre-production, filming, and post-production, with some of the most expensive films exceeding $200 million. According to the Motion Picture Association of America (**MPAA**), location costs for a big budget film can reach as much as $225,000 per day.[13]

Movie exhibition today is controlled by major studios, with independent ("indies") studios reliant on the major studios for distribution through licensing agreements. Distributors decide on the release schedules for theatrical, television, pay-per-view (PPV), and video. Furthermore, distributors are in charge of accounting and collecting receipts from the exhibitors as well as developing a marketing strategy. The cost of promoting a feature film is often of the same magnitude as the production of the movie, with the average distributor spending $34.4 million in advertising.

Although large, diversified companies dominate the industry, barriers to entry in the filmmaking and distribution business are not high. As a result, the industry has seen a growth in recent years for independent films. Small companies can compete successfully by creating marketable movies, often directed to niche audiences, on low budgets. For distributors of motion pictures, revenues fall into five categories (theatrical exhibition, home video, broadcasters, foreign markets, and nontheatrical venues).

Theatrical exhibition includes a variety of venues, from single theaters to multiplexes and coverage, from regional to international markets. As a revenue source, distributors of motion pictures share of the total box office receipts can be as high as 90 percent of the box office gross. Box office receipts not only generate substantial income for studios, but are an indication of the popularity of a release. This in turn becomes an important marketing tool for developing value in other markets including television, home video, DVD, and foreign sales. Similarly, a movie that has good box office revenue often will have a longer life cycle. Those films that have poor box office sales are relinquished to ancillary markets, such as video and television. Blockbuster Hollywood releases (known as wide release) can involve 600–3,000 play dates. As with other aspects of the motion picture industry, the theater exhibition industry is dominated by a few companies (five major companies include Regal Entertainment Group, AMC Entertainment, Cinemark USA, Carmike Cinemas, and Cineplex Entertainment) that have the majority (over 60 percent) of the total screen share.[14]

The home video market includes exhibition on several platforms including DVD, Blue-ray Disc, and VHS. Studios receive a larger share, 45–50% of the rental fees, of their gross revenue from home video market than theatrical box office. Furthermore, with box office revenue dwindling, DVD sales and rental represent a larger share of the motion picture industry's revenue. This process of channel diversification has increased the "shelf-life" of feature films and contributed, to an extent, to reduce production and distribution risks. In an effort

MPAA The trade association (founded in 1922) that represents the producers and distributors of motion pictures, home video, and other television and cable entertainment programming. See also **RIAA (Recording Industry Association of America)** page 36.

to reduce the risk of releasing a feature film, studios are increasingly releasing movies directly to the DVD market. As a consequence, the role of large retailers has become increasingly important in the motion picture industry. Today, big box retailers such as Wal-Mart, Kmart, and Best Buy dominate the home video market in the US.

In 1986, a watershed year for the motion-picture industry, domestic wholesale gross revenues from home video sales ($2 billion) were greater than theatrical sources ($1.6 billion). Today, 87 percent of households have digital video disc players (DVDs) generating more than $16 billion in domestic retail revenues.[15] Not only is this an important revenue for manufacturers of DVD players, but video rental is extremely profitable for the rental store. A video chain-store operator (Blockbuster or Hollywood Video) buys a DVD from a studio for approximately $7. The studio shares between 30 percent and 40 percent of the rental revenue, with the percentage dropping to zero after 6 months. Then the store will sell the DVD for $7, totally recouping its initial investment. However, this profitable business model is transforming due to digitization and the advent of the Internet. Online companies such as Netflix not only offer physical distribution of videos through the Internet, but are now experimenting with electronic downloading.

Broadcasters, both cable and network television, are another important revenue source for the motion picture industry. License fees for domestic pay-TV are calculated on theatrical box office gross of a particular film. Studios also have output deals in which studios will guarantee that certain cable channels (HBO, Showtime, Cinemax, The Movie Channel) will air a specific film. Similarly, network television pays negotiated license fees to broadcast motion pictures.

Foreign markets are increasingly significant in the motion picture industry. These markets generate considerable income from theatrical, television, and home video sales. Distributors may use their own subsidiaries, foreign affiliates, or a sub-distributor to increase their share of the profits. Non-theatrical venues, such as airlines, schools, and hotels, represent a minor source of revenue for the industry. Most outlets pay a flat fee or specific amount per viewer. Finally, merchandising, video games, music, and publishing have licensing agreements with outside companies not related to a specific film (e.g. Lucasfilm Ltd and the *Star Wars* series). Most licensing involves the rights to characters, stories, and music that flow from the initial film product.

Conclusion

The motion picture industry, like other entertainment industry sectors, is currently in a state of flux. The scope and nature of technological change in the motion picture industry is bringing about a revolution to utilization of new media into a new age of digital convergence. Yet, the traditional theater exhibition still remains as one of society's most salient experiences of the motion picture industry. Nonetheless, "user" desires in controlling and engaging in a more interactive entertainment experience are changing the role of producers and distributors of the motion picture. For example, for the film *Snakes on a Plane* (2006) New Line Cinema incorporated feedback from online fans, via blogs, forums, and websites, to create the film's plot and language, which eventuated in the movie receiving an R rating. Although this new approach to motion picture creation did not result in higher box office returns, it represents a possible future direction for the motion picture industry.

Broadcasting Industry: Television

Introduction

Television has been a persuasive entertainment form for the past 50 years. In the first half of the 1950s, television expanded rapidly in the US as the new medium began to be adopted by the general public. Between 1950 and 1955, television set ownership grew nearly 700 percent, from 4.6 million receivers to 32 million.[16] This growth had an immediate impact on rival entertainment industries. In 1946, its peak year, the US motion picture industry grossed $17 billion ($680 million in 1946). By 1958, gross revenues from motion pictures were under $1 billion.[17] Through multiple purchases, takeovers, and mergers the television industry has begun to converge with global mega-corporations increasing their control over all aspects of television production and distribution. These corporations are consolidating their hold on other entertainment sectors, such as motion picture production, book and magazine publishing, the recording industry, and businesses associated with the delivery of leisure products. For example, telephone companies (Tel-Cos), which have provided video and data connection to commercial users, are now providing a range of products that are traditionally outside their original market, for example, the Cable TV market. Potential economic advantages associated with single corporation ownership of different aspects of an industry, or **synergies**, have been the cause of recent mergers between production studios and television networks. For example, Disney's acquisition of ABC for $19 billion gave it an outlet for its live and animated movies and television shows. Furthermore, the purchase of a television network enabled Disney to promote its theme parks, cruises, radio stations, and retail stores. Disney actors (such as Hilary Duff, Miley Cyrus, and the Jonas Brothers) now have their careers crossing multiple entertainment formats including movies, television, recordings, and merchandising. Television has not only been an important media for musical artists to reach a wider audience (as with MTV, VH1, and similar music cable stations), it has been an important income flow for music labels and artists through synchronized licenses.

> **Synergy**
> In business, the concept that says the combination of several organizations or systems into one can produce a higher output than they can independently of each other.

Within the last decade, the television industry has been rapidly changing. Much of this change is due to trends that have shaped US and international business as well as the entertainment industry, such as downsizing, mergers, globalization, and diversification. A major factor that has had a profound impact on broadcasting has been the deployment of new technologies for the delivery of content. During the 1950s, 1960s, and into the 1970s, three major broadcasters (ABC, CBS, and NBC) dominated the national television business. Most local stations were affiliates to specific major broadcasters, from which they derived the majority of their programming. In the 1970s, cable television began to eat into the major broadcaster's audience. Unlike the national broadcasters, which cater to the tastes of a mass audience, cable television was able to compete by aiming their programming (narrowcasting or niche broadcasting) to specific audience segments. Today, both forms of broadcasting, along with satellite television, are vying for audience attention in a highly competitive market.

Internet Activities

● With entertainment organizations merging it is often difficult to understand who owns what. Go to the *Columbia Journalism Review's* guide to companies at www.cjr.org/tools/owners/. Find the owner of your favorite radio station, TV station, cable service, and website. Any surprises? Are there conflicts of interest that possibly affect that ownership?

● Special effects are becoming more import in the motion picture industry. Many producers make changes to movies after the cameras have stopped rolling. Go to the website of Custom Film Effects at http://customfilmeffects.com. View before and after shots in the "Demo" tab. How does this capability change the planning and process of movie making? How does this affect the financing of movies?

Network Television

Although their market share has been eroding, the four major broadcast networks (ABC, CBS, NBC, and Fox) remain the largest force in US television programming. For national advertisers, these networks continue to provide household penetration and viewership levels not available elsewhere. The production of network TV shows is similar to the motion picture business. For example, good cash flow from program libraries help finance new shows. Larger companies often contract or jointly produce shows with smaller firms. Producers of television content will provide networks with a limited number (often two episodes) of material for broadcasting at a reduced price, often lower than production costs. If the network "picks up" the series, the producers will retain the rights to the show for exhibition in foreign markets, cable stations, or network reruns. As with other entertainment sectors the success of a few shows offsets the cost of producing shows that are not hits. Today, a handful of major motion picture studios supply both network and cable television (see Figure 1.7). These include Fox, Columbia, Disney, Paramount, Universal, Warner Brothers, and smaller independent companies. In-house production also exists, but at a much lower level.

Today, the four major US networks have over 300 affiliates throughout the country. These affiliates are either network affiliate stations or owned and operated stations (O&Os). Network affiliates and O&Os buy content from their parent network along with national advertising under a contractual agreement. Local affiliates are able to sell advertising (called spot advertising or spots) to

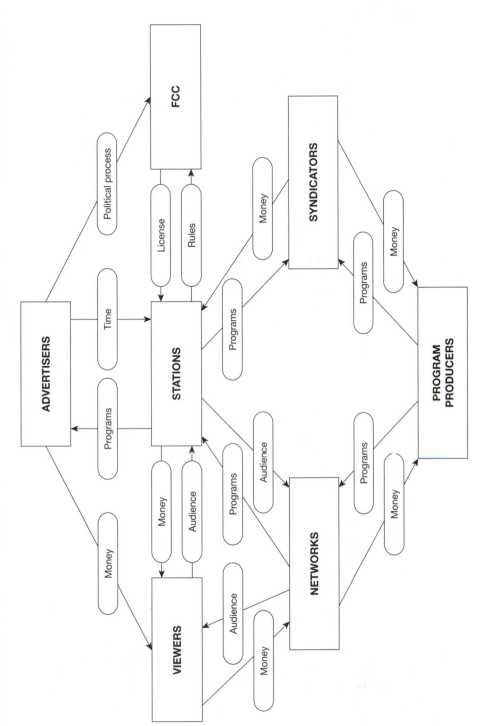

Figure 1.7 Organization of the TV industry

Syndication (television and radio) The licensing of programs for use at multiple local stations by independent agencies, not through the major networks.

CPB The private, non-profit organization set up by Congress in 1967 to promote the development of non-commercial broadcasting services and programs.

PBS The television network established to produce and distribute programming to non-commercial television stations.

merchants within their broadcasting range. On average, affiliates receive approximately 90 percent of their programming from national networks and **syndication**, with the remaining amount made up of local news broadcasting.

Public television in the US came about after the Public Broadcasting Act 1967 created the Corporation for Public Broadcasting (**CPB**) and led to the creation of the Public Broadcasting Service (**PBS**). Unlike networks, PBS does not produce programming. Instead, PBS helps member stations share programs produced by major stations within the system (e.g. WGBH in Boston). Ownership of public broadcasting stations is divided among four groups: states and municipalities (40 percent), community nonprofit foundations (33 percent), universities (25 percent), and public school boards (2 percent).

Cable Television

The cable system industry provides an economical and convenient delivery medium for entertainment. The industry consists of pipeline companies—multiple system operators (MSOs)—that deliver cable signals to consumers' homes via wired systems. Annual revenues for the cable industry total more than $75 billion, the bulk of which comes from viewer subscriptions. Nonetheless, narrowcasting is popular with adverting agencies, as it provides a homogenous audience based on age, class, income, ethnicity, and other demographic factors. In the television business, cable networks have been gaining a greater share of viewership and advertising dollars than the networks. Cable networks' production of high-profile original programming has increased their competitive position within the broadcasting market. In recent years, cable networks have increased their investment in major league sports events and made-for-TV movies. In fact, many cable stations are owned by major motion picture companies, which use the station as a means of distributing their products.

Income Generation

During the early development of television, broadcasters were interested in the sale of receiving equipment (hardware) such as television sets, as well as programming. But as television developed this trend gave way to the marketing and exploitation of broadcast content (software) itself. Today, network television derives most of its revenue from content or potential attention. In other words, television provides the audience and demographic that advertisers need to sell their products. Digital operators go one step further by combining channels into their platforms that are not reliant on the traditional revenue generating model. There are two models for revenue generation in television: a traditional system based on open access for the audience and financed through advertising, and a system that generates income from subscription or pay-per-play basis.

Major television networks adopted the advertising supported model from a pre-existing model established by radio. In fact, both CBS and NBC television networks grew out of identically named radio networks. Within the advertising model, production companies manufacture programs, rather than television stations. These production companies may be directly associated with a national network or with a specific Hollywood studio. Program content is in response to demands established by the networks based on their audiences and projected incomes. As previously mentioned, television broadcasters are not in the business of creating content, but rather supplying an audience or access to them to advertisers. The success of a television show is measured in dimensions of people and time (see Figure 1.8). This affects advertising prices which are quoted in dollars per thousand viewers per unit of commercial time, typically 20 or 30 seconds.

During the 1970s, cable operators discovered that viewers would pay extra to receive new program services not available on the national broadcast networks. Consumers were willing to pay a premium to view uncut, recently released theatrical films without commercials within a subscription system of payment. Like the advertising model, the subscription system begins with a production company selling rights to wholesalers who in turn sell them to distributors, in this case cable stations. Unlike the advertising based model, wholesalers cannot obtain funding via advertising companies. In an effort to subvert this system, advertisers rely on product placement as a means of selling goods directly to an audience. Cable stations supplement their advertising revenue by charging the system operator for each subscriber that carriers their signal (see Figure 1.9). This ranges between 20 and 50 cents per subscriber per month, with some stations charging more.

Today, most cable TV and direct broadcast satellite (DBS) systems offer a service that is actually a hybrid of the advertising and subscription models. Viewers who want access to non-advertising supported channels generally pay an additional premium. Retailers in turn pay wholesalers for the right to carry non-advertising supported channels. For example, PPV events offered by cable providers not only offer films, but also live telecasts of sporting events, such as boxing and the Olympics, and live rock concerts, such as Kiss and Eminem.

Conclusion

The broadcasting sector has enjoyed a long tenure as an important entertainment form for both consumers and businesses. However, like many other areas, this sector is facing increasing competition from new entertainment forms, such as video games and the introduction of technologies that have changed the way consumers use these media. For example, online delivery of content has become an alternative to the way in which consumers receive content. Networks now are streaming a wide variety of material to viewers on their computers. Unlike traditional platforms, which are susceptible to disruptive technology (such as TiVo), the online model uses imbedded advertising that, as of yet, cannot be scrambled. The online broadcasting system has also been a potential revenue generator. Record labels have been able to monetize music video clips on major online video channels such as YouTube.

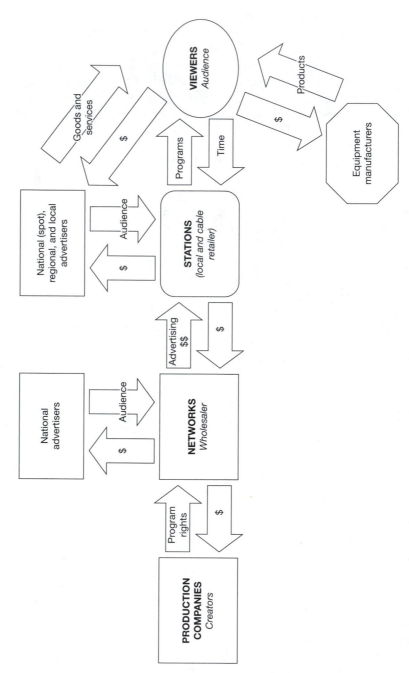

Figure 1.8 TV industry flowchart

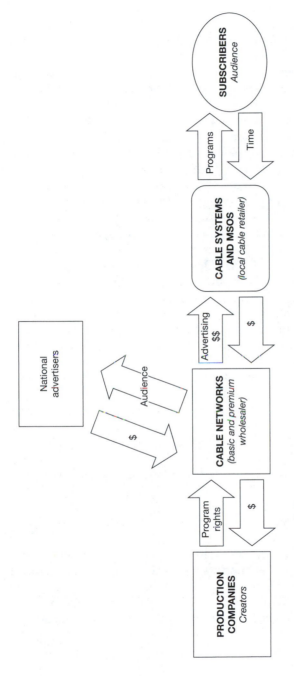

Figure 1.9 Cable TV system

Video Game Industry

Introduction

The video game industry, both in the US and globally, is one of the fastest growing sectors of the entertainment industry. From 2003 to 2006, the annual growth rate of gaming software exceeded 17 percent. Internationally, computer and video game companies sold 297.6 million units with $11.7 billion in revenue. Of the amount sold, game console software sales totaled $8.9 billion, computer game sales were $701.4 million, and portable software sales amounted to $2.1 billion.[18] In the United States, the video and computer game industry generates billions of dollars and employs thousands in the production, distribution, and sale of gaming equipment and software. On September 25, 2007, Microsoft's *Halo 3* earned $170 million within 24 hours of its release in the US. Within a week of its release, the game had grossed $300 million. One reason for the success of the gaming industry is its broad appeal to a large portion of society. According to the "Pew Internet and American Life Project Report," 53 percent of American adults over the age of 18 play video games, with over 97 percent of teens playing video games on a daily basis.[19] One of the fastest growing demographic sectors is women, especially those over the age of thirty-five, which represents 34 percent of the game-playing population.

As with many other sectors in the entertainment industry, the video game industry presents an industrial and business structure characterized by the central position of publishers as a source of funding for the creation, distribution, and marketing of video games. With games becoming increasingly more reliant on advanced graphics, the cost of development has increased exponentially over the past several years. This, together with the importance of marketing and third-party licensing, has contributed to the consolidation of game developers.

The music industry is forming closer ties with the video game industry (see Figure 1.10), both in terms of direct income via licensing music for use in games and more recently as a means of extending an artist's brand equity through games designed around music performance, such as *Guitar Hero*.

Video Game Industry Structure

According to the MobyGames database (an online encyclopedia), there are at least 49,000 different games that have been commercially released in the past thirty years.[20] Within this environment there are several sub-markets organized on specific hardware platforms and method of playing. Each sub-market has its own characteristics and structure, but collectively fall under four distinct categories:

1. Arcade games
2. Computer games
3. Console games
4. Online games.

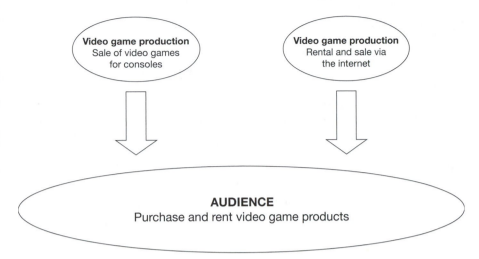

Figure 1.10 Video game flowchart

Arcade games are coin-operated games played on a specific machine, often in a physical location such as a video arcade, cinema, or restaurant. Players pay to play a game that usually lasts anywhere from a few minutes to an hour. Arcade games were initially responsible for the development of the gaming industry, but have been replaced by personal systems that can be used at home or outside of the home, as with smart phones.

Computer games (PC games) have the advantage over arcade games in that they are played online or independently with software provided by CD-ROMs and DVDs in a gamer's home. Unlike console games, the PC gaming market does not have a concentration of hardware providers, due to the commoditization of the personal computer. Since technical specifications of PCs are openly available, PC video game developers are not required to pay any royalties on game sales to PC manufacturers. This situation allows smaller development companies to compete against larger companies creating a market that is marked by innovative genres, playing modes, and models for interaction between developers and users. Similarly, many companies have developed to meet niche markets in hardware add-ons, including graphics and audio cards, as well as user interface devices.

Console games are a genre associated with specifically designed devices that use a cartridge or a connection to the Internet. As with other entertainment sectors, the console game market has a high degree of concentration, with domination by three companies (Microsoft, Nintendo, and Sony). This con-glomeration forms a considerable barrier against other companies entering the market from a hardware perspective. Nonetheless, the success of these manufacturers is dependent on the availability of a broad range of compatible video games. This opportunity allows for medium to small developers to gain a financial foothold. Unlike PC games, the business model of hardware providers relies on royalties from video game sales paid by video game publishers, as well as from sales of video games. With the majority of income generated from licensing, consoles are often sold at a loss. To guarantee that the console provider will gain a monetary advantage, companies tightly manage access to the tools necessary for the development of video games compatible with their platforms (see Figure 1.11). Due to the complexity of such games, development budgets range from $5 million to $60 million.

Portable device games are associated with the growth of the mobile phone industry and specific gaming devices. Currently, two operating systems, Symbian and Microsoft Mobile, dominate the mobile/portable market. This fragmentation increases development costs, as it makes it necessary to adapt games to a diversity of platforms. Furthermore, there are different business models regulating the interaction between game developers and software platform providers in this market. For example, in the case of Symbian, access to the platform is free for developers, while providers obtain royalty fees on the sale of handsets from manufacturers. Although this market has relatively lower development costs, telecommunication companies play an important role by selecting, collecting,

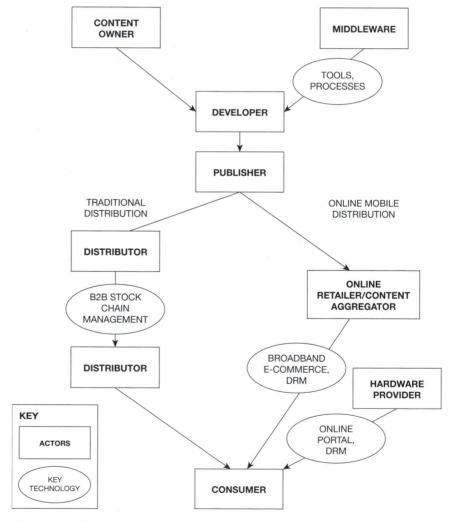

Figure 1.11 Video game value chain

and marketing groups of games in portals. Consumers can access these games by paying subscription fees or via a pay-per-download system. In some cases, games are complementary assets that increase the attractiveness of a carrier's services and provide high revenue margins through subscription.

An important development in the gaming industry has been the introduction of the Internet. This has not only assisted in the distribution of games to the public, but has spurred the creation of a new genre, the computer role playing game (CRPG) especially the MMOGs (Massive Multiplayer Online Games) or MMORPGs. In MMOGs, players create an online persona or avatar to interact with the environment or other players. This new model has been financially successful with US revenues exceeding $1 billion in 2005. Within the multiplayer game genre there are two different approaches to revenue generation. The most common method requires the portal site to act as a hosting and matchmaking website for players of these games. Portal sites offer either a free membership to players, which generates revenue through online advertising, or a premium membership that is free from advertising. Members pay to gain access to services for locating other players, scores, patches, and add-ons, and use of the portal's dedicated server machines for playing games. An example of such a portal is GameSpy.com, which maintains a subscription-based membership and provides information for a variety of games. Some game publishers run their own portal sites, dedicated to hosting their own games and ensuring a quality experience for the community of players. For example, *World of War Craft* has over 9 million subscribers who pay up to $15 per month to participate, as well as $50 to purchase the game. In 2007, the game generated $1.1 billion in revenue. Nonetheless, the high costs of developing and maintaining an MP's (multiple player's) infrastructure, along with the network externalities, has created a formidable barrier to entry in this genre.

MMORPGs, in contrast to console and PC games, use a hybrid revenue model. Consumers initially purchase or download the basic software necessary to run the game, as with the PC and console market. Once online, players pay a subscription fee for a persistent presence in the game environment. For a monthly fee, a player has access to a game character that can be developed over time by accruing additional features. The more rewards gained, the more powerful the character. Virtually all of these games have some kind of embedded trading mechanism that allows players to exchange wealth in the game world. For example, players in EverQuest (Sony Online) assume the roles of pseudo-medieval fantasy heroes, gaining magic and gold. Players are able to buy and sell their virtual property in exchange for virtual wealth. Although transactions are confined to the game, the success of virtual trading has the potential for the development of a third business model that is now emerging. This model will allow players to purchase or trade characters via the home portal or a secondary agent, such as eBay.

Conclusion

Although the video game industry is the fastest growing sector in the entertainment industry, it still is evolving in terms of business structures and revenue generation models. Nonetheless, this sector shows clear characteristics found in other entertainment sectors. These include high capital costs, a reliance on technology, and consolidation of companies, especially within the international market. With uncertainty surrounding profit generation in many entertainment sectors, companies have turned to video games as new means of revenue. For example, the *Guitar Hero* and the *RockBand* franchises have invigorated the music industry in important ways. Many bands featured in these video games have seen a resurgence in CD sales and downloads. Similarly, participants in the games have downloaded tens of thousands of songs for use in the games themselves.

Case Study: Disney

In 1928, a small Californian company released a 7-minute animated cartoon, *Steamboat Willie*. What made this film different from previous animated films was the inclusion of dialogue, sound effects, and a soundtrack. From that small beginning arose The Walt Disney Company, or Disney, the largest media and entertainment conglomerate. Disney's approach to entertainment began as the company realized the potential of its characters were more than merely actors in their motion pictures, but branded commodities that could be exploited in a variety of products and markets.

In 1936, Disney produced its first full-length animated feature *Snow White and the Seven Dwarfs*. The film not only received critical acclaim, it was a financial success that shaped the artistic direction of the company. Nonetheless, within 10 years Disney began to face financial ruin. By the early 1950s, Walt Disney realized that in order to remain financially solvent, he needed to diversify his motion picture company into other entities. This not only served as a barrier against the unpredictability of creative products, but as a means of generating revenues through ancillary markets. In 1954, Walt Disney entered into an agreement with ABC (which Disney bought in 1995 for $19 billion) to produce the *Disneyland Television Show*. A year later the company opened Disneyland in Anaheim, California.

Today, this corporate strategy is standard for entertainment companies, who employ one of three strategic techniques: horizontal integration, vertical integration, and diversification. Horizontal integration is the consolidation of ownership across a variety of industries or within a specific sector. Content may move between various sectors, such as movie characters exploited via television or video games. Vertical integration is the ownership of organizations that are engaged in the production and distribution of a product. Control of these intermediaries not only guarantees the production of goods, but provides the parent company revenues via each successive step in the supply chain. Finally, diversification is a strategy for companies to increase sales by obtaining new products in new markets. For the Walt Disney Company these three strategies allow the company to reach the widest possible audience through a multitude of products and markets.

At the core of the Walt Disney Company are its animated feature films. These films are not only revenue generators, but they also provide characters that are reproduced, repackaged, and re-marketed in virtually every article of clothing, stuffed animals, games, furniture, DVDs, compact discs, household appliances, jewelry, and other objects. These characters also allow Disney to create partnerships with companies outside the entertainment industry, such as McDonald's. For example, in 2002, Disney began marketing the release of *Lilo and Stitch*. Beginning with a primetime program that aired on Disney-owned ABC, the television special heavily promoted not only the movie, but also the soundtrack (produced by Walt Disney Records), Disney videos, Disney resorts, and toys available in the Happy Meals sold at McDonald's.

Although Disney is a corporation focused on "family entertainment," in 1983 the company created Walt Disney Pictures in an effort to create a "boldly diversified program of films aimed at significantly broadening the Disney audience."[21] Touchstone Pictures and Miramax Films allow Disney to present adult themed material, without damaging the Disney image. Similarly, in 2009 Disney announced the purchase of Marvel Comics for $4 billion. Many media analysts see this purchase as a means of capturing a greater share of the male audience, missing from its current line of female based characters (Cinderella, Sleeping Beauty, Snow White, as well as Hannah Montana).

Summary

The entertainment industry covers a broad array of activities and sectors. This diversity of forms is not hermetic, as each sector offers the opportunity for revenue generation for multiple entertainment forms. As such, music is an inherent part of several entertainment sectors beyond its traditional boundaries. From the more traditional relationships, such as the motion picture, broadcast and performing arts industries, to the growing gaming industry, to the not so obvious entertainment sectors such as sports (one can never imagine a Super bowl half-time show without music) and the gambling industry, especially with casinos catering now to families rather than using music as a loss leader to attract high rollers.

Although there are intersections between entertainment sectors, there are still unique business models that do not transcend sectarian boundaries. The motion picture industry, for example, has a clear distinction between production and distribution. Due to anti-trust laws, studios cannot own or operate movie exhibitors. This dynamic is not present in the music industry, which relies on vertical integration (even more so with 360 deals) as a means of maximizing revenues. The result is that music companies can generate revenue from the production side of the film industry, not exhibition. Understanding the role of music in divergent entertainment sectors is essential in a global entertainment industry.

QUESTIONS FOR REVIEW

- Explain how the increase in leisure time has affected the type of entertainment products created today.
- There are eight divisions within the entertainment industry. Be able to name them and the various sub-divisions within them.
- There are several common economic characteristics of entertainment sectors. Be able to explain these characteristics and how they affect certain industries.
- Explain how the movie, television, and video game industry intersect with the music industry.

2 Understanding the Music and Recording Business

Introduction

This chapter explores the nature of the music business in the early twenty-first century, its relation to the external environment, and the industry's place as a medium of mass communication. Then, taking a closer look, the industry is explained as a system that is composed of the three primary income streams: the sale and use of songs (the music publishing industry), live entertainment, and the sale and use of recordings (the recording industry).

"Change is the law of life. And those who look only to the past or the present are certain to miss the future" John F. Kennedy.[1]

Turmoil in the 2000s

Ch-ch-changes. As the recording industry entered the twenty-first century it appeared to be undergoing another one of the dramatic changes in direction that occur in the industry about every 20 years. A general downturn in the economy in the early 2000s and again in 2007–2008 affected the recording industry more than at any time since the Great Depression of the 1930s. Downloading of digital recordings via the Internet, both authorized and unauthorized, clearly curtailed physical sales of the all-important hit recordings. Record stores, buoyed by the apparently insatiable appetite for recordings that appeared in the 1980s and 1990s, had overbuilt and were closing by the score. Sales of recordings dropped from a high of $14.6 billion in 1999 back to $8.5 billion in 2008 (a decrease of over 40 percent) and appeared to be heading even lower. The major labels were laying off employees, cutting rosters, downsizing, and even closing at a frantic pace. By 2010 the labels were trying desperately to come up with a business model for successfully distributing recordings via the Internet and other means that would restore the "good old days."

KEY CONCEPTS

- The music and recording industries are in a period of turmoil brought about by changes in the way people access and consume music.
- The music business is a system of delivering music to consumers. Like any system, it creates and delivers things that have value to consumers (songs, recordings, and performances) but must do so within a dynamic external environment.
- The music business revolves almost entirely around three creative events: the writing of a song, the live performance of a song, and the making of a recording of a song.
- Three separate, but interrelated, revenue streams exist for the song, the live performance, and the recording.
- A host of music business middle people exists in each revenue stream between the writer, performer, or recording artist, and the ultimate public consumer.

Broadly speaking, the music and recording industries were moving out of the industrial age and into the new "digital age." About a millennium further back, the music business moved from the agricultural age into the industrial age (see Figure 2.1). During the agricultural age, music was consumed entirely through live performances. Those performances were from folk musicians, from more professional traveling troubadours, and from professional composers (such as Bach, Hayden, and Mozart) and orchestras maintained by the churches and the wealthy. Early industrialization included the large scale manufacturing of instruments, most importantly pianos, which found their way into private homes, and by the late 1800s, the music printing and publishing business. The most industrial product, recordings, became the mainstay of the business as we moved out of the Depression and into the middle part of the twentieth century. But the digital age, perhaps more aptly the **information age**, a system that derived most of its revenue from the manufacture and sale of physical products, simply had to evolve or die.

Information age Social and economic theories state that society has entered a new stage of development where society and development will be characterized not by the production of products, such as CDs or pianos, but by the production of content and the distribution and use of information.

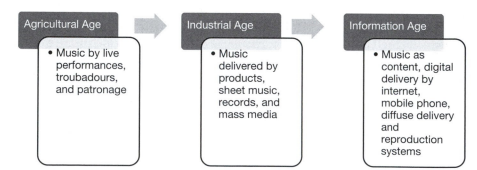

Figure 2.1 The three ages of the music business

Taking a closer look, as difficult as the times appeared to be, change was really nothing new to the recording industry. Figure 2.2 shows that the history of the business has unfolded in cycles of about 20 years. The first period of introduction and growth began in 1889 with the introduction of the first commercial musical recordings. The 1909 Copyright Act ushered in the next era by creating the mechanical right for music publishers, setting a statutory "limit" to royalties to be paid by labels to publishers, and by *not* providing a sound recording copyright. By 1929 the industry had evolved into a consumer business with sales of about 100 million units ($75 million), mostly records. The next period saw the near demise of the industry in the Great Depression of the 1930s, and then its rebirth in the 1940s and early 1950s. Pent-up postwar consumer demand for everything spurred the sale of playback equipment and recordings. The LP and **45** were introduced. Sales grew back from a mere 3 million units ($5.5 million) in 1933 to $189 million in 1950.

45 The 45 rpm single with one song recorded on each side.

The next phase began in the mid-1950s with the birth of rock and roll. Younger consumers had more money to spend on the songs, artists, and recordings that helped them define their lifestyles. New labels and new sounds emerged. Sales tripled to about $600 million by 1960. Stereo recording was introduced and the 78 single finally died in 1957. Stereo and the Beatles convinced young consumers that they should buy albums instead of singles. Profits rose and the major labels' distribution system emerged. This phase, a transition to a mass market with heavy concentration, lasted until the early 1980s. The introduction of the Compact Disc (CD) in 1982 drove the industry to new heights for another almost 20 more years. Sales grew to $14.6 billion (1.2 billion units) by the end of the century (1999). Labels consolidated and the four major recording and entertainment conglomerates of today emerged. Note that these are somewhat different from the larger Entertainment Conglomerates referred to in Chapter 1 because these all have music and recordings as a major component. Record retail, especially chains, saw unparalleled growth. But 20 years had come and gone and the industry entered the twenty-first century trying to re-invent itself in order to survive in the new digital and content-oriented environment.

Whatever the music business is changing into, it is clear that there is still a strong demand for songs, live performances, and recordings of those songs and performances. Though some of the means of accessing those had changed and new means were created, the content that still has value to consumers and lovers of music are songs, performances, and recordings.

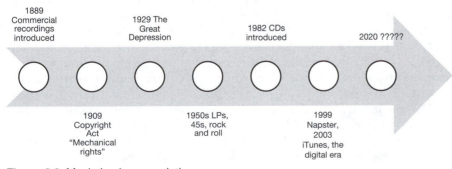

Figure 2.2 Music business evolution

Internet Activities

- Use an Internet search engine such as Google or Yahoo and search for your favorite recording artist. How many "hits" did you get? Look at four of the sites. On how many of them can you listen to and watch a performance, or buy a copy of the artist's performance?
- Go to the official website of your favorite artist. What are the different things that you can do there? Can you watch video? Listen to recordings? Download recordings? Buy tickets to a show? What else?
- Try an Internet search for the title of your favorite song from last year (just to be sure it has been out there long enough). How many different ways do you find of accessing that song? Videos? Print lyrics or guitar tablature? Recordings? Performances?

Ways of Understanding the Music Business

There are several useful models for examining the music business. Systems theory is useful for exploring the industry from a broader perspective, including its relations to the business environment, and overall processes. **Cultural theory** is of some use in examining the relationship of the outputs of the industry, recordings and popular music, to society. Economics, and the three income stream model, is most useful in examining the inner workings of the industry and its components.

Cultural theory
A communications theory stating that the meaning of a communication is understood in a variety of ways that are influenced by the culture into which that communication is sent. The focus of this theory is then on the recipient(s) of the communication instead of the sender(s).

Systems theory
A business theory stating that any business organization is a system of converting inputs into outputs and that the organization exists in an environment that influences its processes.

A Systems Approach

Systems theory is a business management tool used to develop an understanding of how an enterprise functions. Systems theory stresses that there are five components of any business system: inputs; some transformation process; outputs (the products which are the results of the transformation process); a feedback process which will influence the selection of inputs into the next round of processing; and an external environment within which the organization carries out its processes (see Figure 2.3). Looking at the music business in this way, one would conclude that some of the inputs are songwriters, songs, musicians, engineers, producers, studios, plastic, paper, performances, and technology. The transformation processes are the recording of masters, duplicating of the masters into physical copies and electronic copies, marketing, and performances. Outputs of the music industry are songs, CDs and other recorded configurations as products and as cultural artifacts, concerts and other performances, profits and losses for the owners and participants, and employee (including the artists and writers) satisfaction. Feedback occurs primarily when consumers purchase recordings and live performances, and listen to or view the broadcast media or the Internet.

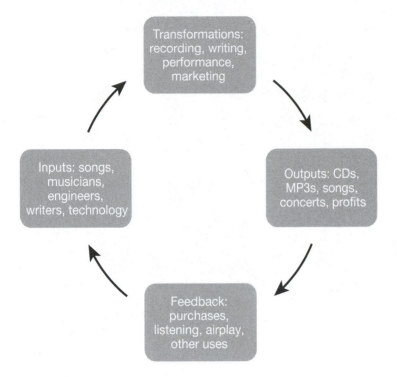

Figure 2.3 The music and recording business systems view

But the music business does not exist in a vacuum. There is an external environment containing the social, political, legal, technological, and economic forces that exist outside of the organization (see Figure 2.4). The music business interacts with those forces and is influenced by them. It depends upon popular tastes and culture and consumer activity to purchase or access the music, and upon technology to deliver that access. This interaction makes the music business an **open system**. By comparison, a **closed system** does not need to interact with the environment to survive.

A final systems concept, **entropy** refers to the tendency of any organized system to eventually decay into disorganization. If a business does not receive new energy from its environment and inputs it will cease to exist. The music industry must constantly seek new creative inputs from the artists and songwriters or it will stagnate. For example, the entropy concept explains that more product diversity is associated with more entropy in the music industry. That might indicate that a less highly structured industry with more independent labels and alternative distribution methods is more likely to be accompanied with a greater diversity of recorded product for consumers. That was certainly the situation in the music business in the first decade of the twenty-first century. With less control by major labels, more releases by all labels, rampant unauthorized downloading of recordings and videos, and the industry scrambling for a profitable business model, the state of entropy was high.

Open system
An organization that receives input from its external environment and interacts with that environment.

Closed system
A business system that does not have to interact with its external environment.

Entropy A state of business or physics in which there is total disorganization and chaos.

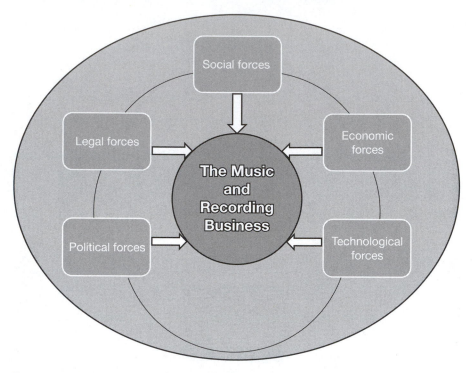

Figure 2.4 The external environment of the music and recording business

The External Environment

Society

The external environment is extremely important to the music business because its products are largely consumed on the basis of taste preferences. These tastes include particular songs, kinds of music, performers, and performances, and how and where access is obtained to those songs, performers, and performances. As the tastes and desires of consumers change, the record companies, music publishers, writers, and artists must be aware and alter their products. The history of the industry is full of examples where a particular label or even the entire industry failed to keep in touch with consumer tastes.

Probably the most famous example is the birth and growth of the popularity of rock and roll, when the major labels of the day either did not even know it existed, or chose to ignore it. A similar explosion of consumer interest in rap and hip-hop in the 1990s caught the major labels by surprise. In the late 1990s the industry failed to understand consumers' desire to access music in the form of MP3 files. By 2010 consumers wanted more access to music through their mobile phones and other mobile devices. Keeping up with consumer tastes and new trends in music is one job of the artist and repertoire (A&R) department of a label. The A&R department is also charged with finding new creative inputs in terms of songs and performers. If the A&R department has too many failures, the label will be in serious danger of dying. Chapter 9 discusses the A&R function in detail.

Popular music, the mainstay of the recording industry, clearly interfaces with society. It both influences society and is influenced by it. Certainly it influences fashion of dress when recording artists appear on stage or in videos in certain attire, such as when pre- and early-teen girls imitated Madonna's or Hannah Montana's style of dress.[2] Social themes are often mirrored in the music, either because that makes the music more acceptable to people or because the recording artist wants to convey a viewpoint on those themes.

Songwriters and recording artists attempt to engage in social dialog with consumers through their songs and recordings, and sometimes cause social controversies. Did Ozzy Osbourne's recording "Suicide Solution" *cause* some teens to commit suicide or did it *reflect* the despair that some teens felt that drove them to commit suicide? Most researchers have concluded that the relationships between popular music, its performers, and consumers, are complex and not easily reduced to simple statements. For instance, was Madonna in the mid- and late 1980s suggesting that girls should become "Boy Toys" or was she instilling a new sense of liberation for young women?[3] Popular music researcher Simon Frith concludes, "The political meaning of *all* popular music . . . is a matter of negotiation."[4] So, the exact nature of the influence of the music business on society, or vice-versa, is highly debatable.

Whatever the nature of its influence, pre-recorded music has become a significant component of nearly everyone's life. Half or more of the adult population purchases or illegally downloads recorded music in some form every year. Americans spend hundreds of hours every year listening to copies of recordings on MP3 players and stereo systems, and to recordings being played on the radio or Internet. Recorded music provides opportunities and frameworks for social interchange and expression through dance, karaoke, and "sharing" of favorite music on social networking sites or "tweeting" the latest music news or hottest songs. Respondents in one national survey rated the importance of music in their lives as 6.96 on a ten-point scale. Music buyers rated it 7.89 and classical music buyers 10.00.

On an international basis, trade agreements such as North American Free Trade Agreement (**NAFTA**) and the World Trade Organization (**WTO**) take into consideration the free exchange of cultural products, such as recordings and movies. They cause nations to discuss and debate the cultural impact of "outside" cultural products on local culture. They attempt to provide protection for the copyrights embodied in these local cultural products on a global basis so that no one can steal the work of artists, writers, and producers of any nation and sell it as pirate merchandise around the world.

Political environment

Usually the political environment is not as important to the music business as other external factors. However, every now and then it becomes extremely important. The political/social reactions against rock and roll in the late 1950s

NAFTA A treaty among nations in the northern part of the western hemisphere that promotes free trade among these nations by reducing tariffs, quotas, and other trade barriers.

WTO The international trade organization created in 1995 by the General Agreement on Tariffs and Trade treaty of 1994. WTO members promise to reduce trade barriers and to provide "Berne Level" protection to copyrights.

brought about the payola law and caused serious economic losses to a number of industry figures at the time, most notably Dick Clark. Many elements of the peace movement during the late 1960s found expression in popular music. The political establishment reacted by attacking popular music that had "drug-related" lyrics. In the late 1980s feminists reacted against rap lyrics that they perceived to be misogynist and caused a number of labels and radio stations to quit programming certain artists.

During that same time period there was a political reaction to violence and profanity in lyrics and music videos. This lead to the formation of the "Parents' Music Resource Center" (**PMRC**) backed by Tipper Gore (then *Senator* Al Gore, Jr.'s wife). Congressional hearings ultimately led the industry to self-regulate and begin identifying some recordings with a warning label that said "Parental Advisory Explicit Content." Prior to the labeling program some states passed laws forbidding the sale of material "harmful to persons under eighteen" and some sales clerks in retail stores were even arrested.

Later, some states sought to prohibit sales to minors of recordings with "Parental Advisory" labels. Some stores stopped carrying recordings by artists such as rap act "2 Live Crew" and others. One retailer said, "We're not trying to play God, promote censorship, or anything like that. We're just looking out for our image."[5] As late as 2009 the National Association of Recording Merchandisers (**NARM**) and the **RIAA** were still promoting awareness of the parental advisory labeling program. At the same time these two organizations successfully lobbied against passage of some state obscenity laws that would prohibit sale of "parental advisory" albums to minors. Similar concerns were raised about "Death Metal" acts such as Judas Priest. They successfully fought a lawsuit claiming that a subliminal message of "do it, do it" in one of their songs caused two men (18 and 20 years old) to commit suicide after listening to the album.

The overall significance of these attacks on popular music is debatable. Communication researchers DeFleur and Dennis conclude, "a number of popular music forms have been charged with being the cause of moral collapse when they came on the scene, yet our society has somehow held together. Undoubtedly it will survive whatever is in store."[6] The current debate over whether recordings should be available without restraint through peer-to-peer networks contains both political and legal issues.

PMRC An organization dedicated to getting record labels to identify the content of their music as potentially harmful to minors.

NARM The trade association for all record retailers and distributors. The labels are associate members.

RIAA The trade association for record labels and manufacturers.

Legal environment

The legal environment of the music business is similar to that of most businesses in terms of labor laws, environmental regulations, and tax laws. Copyright law, however, is a special legal environment that conveys significant benefits for the industry. It enables the industry to protect its main outputs, songs and recordings, from unauthorized duplication, thereby helping insure profitability. Unauthorized downloading through file sharing indicated that changes were needed in the law to balance the interests of consumers, content providers, and content distributors. Sound recording copyright owners and recordings artists sought a broader right to be compensated for the performances of their recordings on radio and television.

Copyright (or at least a related right) enables performers to protect their live performances from unauthorized recording, distribution, or broadcast. Payola laws limit the extent of control that the labels have over a very important avenue of promotion—radio airplay. Anti-trust laws and regulations limit the industry's attempts to control prices and may limit consolidation. International trade treaties protect audio and video recordings throughout the world. Chapters 3, 4, and 5 discuss the copyright aspects of the recording industry in detail.

Economic environment

As explained in Chapter 1, the music business is a leisure time/entertainment industry, relying on the use of discretionary time and income from consumers for listening to and watching music performances and for the purchases of recordings and live performance tickets. In times of serious economic downturn, when people have less discretionary income and perhaps less free time, the consumption of recordings and live music declines. The National Music Publishers' Association (**NMPA**) has observed the importance of the overall economy to the recording industry internationally: music publishing revenues are probably more sensitive to per capita GNP than to age or population. During the depression in the 1930s in the United States the record industry survived, barely, on performance revenues from radio airplay and on the sale of recordings to jukeboxes. During the end of the twentieth century and 2007–2009, an economic downturn, combined with rampant downloading, spelled hard times for many labels and artists. That is one reason why, in the political arena, the artists and labels pushed Congress to create a broad performance right for recordings, in addition to the one that already existed for songs. Such a right would create revenues for the artists, labels, and producers based on television and radio airplay of recordings.

NMPA A trade organization for music publishers; formerly known as the Music Publishers' Protective Association.

The world economy is moving in many areas from international to **transnational**. There is not just a market in France and a market in Brazil and a market in China; there is a global market and individual sub-markets. The same recordings by the same artists are major hits across a large number of countries. Management guru and futurist Peter Drucker tells us, "[T]he goal of management in a transnational enterprise that operates in one world market is *maximization of market share*, not the traditional short-term "profit maximization" of the old-style corporation."[7]

Transnational A situation where businesses, culture, and even governance may be shared across many national boundaries.

Chapter 13 discusses the international aspects of the music business in detail, but for now we can explore the implications of the maximization of market share philosophy on the music business. What we used to call the "**majors**," those record labels that owned their own distribution system, operated on this philosophy. The four international entertainment powerhouses rapidly divided up the world recording market. The IFPI estimates market shares as follows: Universal about 24 percent; Sony/BMG about 23 percent; EMI 13 percent; Warner, 12 percent. As noted earlier, independent labels garner about 28 percent of the world's market for recordings.

Majors The four main recording/entertainment conglomerates: Universal Music Group, Sony Entertainment, Warner Music Group, and EMI Music Group.

However, the "big four" were buying out independent labels in countries all over the world and creating transnational manufacturing and distribution systems.

Media economist Harold Vogel attributes this need for large distribution systems to high wastage (many products will not succeed) and the short life cycles of the "hit" recordings (usually less than a year). He says, "[B]ecause efficiency in this area requires that retailers located over a wide geographic swath have their inventories quickly replenished, most records are distributed by large organizations with sufficient capital to stock and ship hundreds of thousands of units at a moment's notice."[8] They are selling recordings from their different labels and from local labels all over the world. They were integrating horizontally and vertically, controlling more music publishing, film production, television production, audio and video hardware manufacturing, and radio, television, and cable broadcasting. They had learned that there is money to be made in many small successes, as well as blockbuster hits. There is good reason to own a label that sells gospel music or new age music even though those recordings may sell fewer than a hundred thousand units, because they can be profitable sales. The majors were willing to let people who know the markets for that kind of music make the creative and production decisions and they, the big four, supplied the distribution. The only problem is that distribution in a digital age is not as easily controlled and the digital distribution system(s) have not yet evolved into structures that can be bought and owned by the majors. The other question in the content-driven information age is whether physical distribution could continue to be the organizing factor for the music business.

Even from a more narrow perspective, examining only music business organizations and structures, one cannot help but be struck by fact that there are major influences on how the industry functions from other industries and segments of the economy. The most notable interfaces with other industries are with the Internet and with broadcasting. These are the two primary means that the recording industry uses to promote its products to potential consumers.

Unlike radio and television, which attempt to reach large numbers of listeners with a single broadcast, the Internet allows global access to music that can be tailored to individual tastes, one listener or transmission at a time. With streaming Internet "radio" that is customizable at the listener level, Pandora and other programs let the listener choose some favorite recordings, then suggest other recordings that the listener might like. A play list is then tailored to the particular listener's individual tastes. So the number of "formats" is limitless. On the other hand, how does the Internet listener know what recordings they might like in the first place? Where did they first hear them? On old-fashioned terrestrial radio, a friend's MP3 player, or on a cell phone? (Chapters 11 and 12 examine the relationship of the recording and broadcast industries in detail.)

Radio continues to change. While music programming accounts for about 75 percent of radio listening, no single format like Top 40 dominates the promotion and sale of all recordings. From 1986 to 1995 the number of radio stations reporting predominantly music formats increased by over 2,000 and the number of different formats reported nearly doubled, going from 12 to 23.[9] Even as concentration of radio station ownership increased in the 1990s at a mind-numbing rate after the deregulation of ownership rules with the Communications Act 1996, broadcasting executives were predicting further diversity in radio formats. But major radio chains were consolidating programming. In 2009 the nation's largest radio chain, Clear Channel, announced more corporate-level music programming and less local decision making on which recordings to play. Is that kind of industrial model, which is kind of like Henry Ford's, "You can have any color car you want, as long as it is black," likely to be successful in the information age?

The technological environment

Technology has affected all segments of the music business. The recording industry portion of the music business owes its very existence to technology. On the input side of the system, it is easier for musicians and writers to make high quality recordings and the quality that can be made is higher. In the transformation process, sophisticated control over recording and advances in reproduction have made more recordings available at lower production costs and enabled more sophisticated and lower cost distribution of that product. More methods of exposure are available thanks to the Internet, cable and satellite television, home video, and mobile phones. On the output side the availability of high quality, lower cost, and more portable playback systems has stimulated demand. The feedback loop has improved with more accurate and faster data gathering mechanisms.

What Thomas Edison did not know is that his "talking machine" invention in 1877 would lay the groundwork for a "music machine." Emile Berliner's disc recording system made this even more likely because the original recordings were easier to replicate into copies, thereby opening up much greater possibility for a mass produced item for the general population. Advances in player and recording technology through the 1940s made the music reproduced even more life-like. Stereo proved that consumers wanted their music to sound even better and more like a real performance. Cassette tapes made the medium more portable so that it could go with Americans in their ubiquitous automobiles, even without playing it on the radio. Smaller amplifiers and players soon meant that pre-recorded music could go to the beach, for a jog, for a walk in the park, or to the gymnasium for a work out.

The development of MP3 player systems, particularly the iPod, made more music even more portable. The CD and digital recording propelled the quality of sound available and the ease of use and durability to higher levels. Digital transmission and the Internet made new delivery systems possible so that people have an almost bewildering diversity of recordings to choose from. Reductions in the costs of manufacturing recordings and in the playback systems led to further market penetration for the players and the recordings. High quality, inexpensive recordings and playback systems were within the reach of nearly everybody. The subsequent greater demand for recordings infused more revenues into the industry and made an even greater diversity of product available. Large labels could afford to take more chances on a wider variety of artists. Small labels could find new artists with niche or emerging markets, make smaller investments, and still earn a profit on a relatively small sales base.

The same digital technology that created the CD and the Internet delivery systems also proved a curse for the industry. Every hour of every day hundreds of thousands of music fans illegally download copies of their favorite recordings

UPC or Bar code
A series of vertical black and white bars on a product identifying the specific product and its manufacturer.

SoundScan
The company that collects point-of-sale information from the UPC bar code scanners at a variety of record retail outlets and sells sales pattern information to the labels or other parties.

BDS The company that monitors radio airplay with computers that identify what records are being played by comparing the broadcast to identifiable "signature" parts of the recording stored in the computer's memory. BDS can deliver the actual count of the number of times a particular record is played.

SoundExchange
The organization formed by the RIAA that is in charge of distribution of royalties collected for the digital performance of sound recordings. It also negotiates royalty rates for Webcasters and others not subject to the compulsory license for digital audio performance of sound recordings.

from a variety of peer-to-peer networks. While the labels struggled to make paid downloads a profitable venture they fought the free, unauthorized downloads with a barrage of lawsuits.

The electronic revolution also had a significant impact on the creative inputs for the industry. As the sophistication of "home" recording equipment improved it became possible for creative musicians and writers to have more control over the process of recording. Digital quality recordings could be made in small studios. MIDI (Musical Instrument Digital Interface), synthesis, and digital audio workstations gave musicians and writers nearly total control over the creation of complex musical arrangements and works. Lower production costs meant that more people could make music and market it. With digital delivery, any musician capable of making a recording could at least get that recording out on the World Wide Web for people to hear if they wanted to. Stand-alone and computer CD burners made the replication of very small numbers of CD copies practical for almost any musician, or pirate.

Electronic data gathering mechanisms improved market research for record companies, broadcasters, music publishers, record distributors, and retailers. The Universal Product Code (**UPC**) led to better inventory management systems for retail and distribution. Ultimately, the **SoundScan** system of gathering sales information on a national basis allowed the development of sophisticated marketing plans and test marketing. Broadcast Data Systems' (**BDS**) and **SoundExchange**'s electronic monitoring of radio and television stations and the Internet led to more accurate airplay information for labels and performing rights organizations. The IFPI's International Standard Recording Code (**ISRC**) and Global Release Identifier (**GRid**) systems allow electronic tracking of streaming and downloads.

Ironically, an external environmental force like technology can bring both organizing factors, such as through the creation of mass production and delivery processes and the mass media, and disorganizing factors, such as individual recording gear and rapid dispersion of unauthorized copies, through the Internet.

The Recording Industry as a Mass Medium

Popular music, the primary content of the recording industry, can be partially understood as communication and the recording industry (as a part of the music business) as a mass medium. The main activity of the recording industry is the production and distribution of symbolic content to widely dispersed heterogeneous audiences. It uses several technologies to do this, including digital recording and reproduction, analog recording and reproduction, video recording and reproduction, and the Internet. Media theorist Dennis McQuail characterized the recording industry as a medium having:

- multiple technologies of recording and dissemination
- low degree of regulation
- high degree of internationalization
- younger audience
- subversive potential

- organizational fragmentation
- diversity of reception possibilities.[10]

This would appear to be a fair characterization except that the nature of the audience, at least those who purchase physical recordings, appears to be growing older.

Popular music communicates in many ways, some intended by the artist and songwriter, some not. Consumers form social groups based on their likes and dislikes of certain genres or artists. Music is one of the primary links on social networking sites like Facebook. Some music is consumed privately to soothe ravaged psyches or to excite them. Music may be used for social activities such as dancing. Music communicates through physical activities, cognitive activities, and emotion. Popular culture analysts often comment on the power of popular music. James Lull writes, "Music promotes experiences of the extreme for its makers and listeners, turning the perilous emotional edges, vulnerabilities, triumphs, celebrations, and antagonisms of life into hypnotic, reflective tempos that can be experienced privately or shared with others."[11] Similarly, Richard Campbell comments, "The music that helps to shape our identities and comfort us during the transition from childhood to adulthood resonates throughout our lives."[12] That may explain the staying power of "oldies" radio formats.

It is clear that music and recordings fit a model of communication that allows for different meanings to be constructed by the message sender(s) and receiver(s). They also fit a model that includes gatekeepers—individuals through whom the intended message must pass on its way to the receiver. The **gatekeeper** "determines what information is passed and how faithfully it is reproduced."[13] Some consider gatekeepers to be only those that mediate between the industry and its consumers. From the broader perspective of the earlier definition above, if the sender is the artist and the receiver is the listener or consumer then there are other gatekeepers as well. If the artist is not also the songwriter, then the writer must get through the music publisher's gate. The publisher must get through the producer's gate. The producer must get through the label A&R department's gate. The recording must get through the radio, video, and Internet gates, unless those gates can be held open with payola or other paid promotion or advertising.

Gatekeeper theory is useful in explaining the desire of the various players to use any device they can to keep the gates open so their communication can pass. The problem with this approach is that it tends to assume that the gatekeepers care which recordings pass through the gates. A given label does not care which of its recordings become hits, unless they have invested substantial amounts in some superstar artist. It takes *some* hits to sustain a large label but not usually any particular hit. A small label that has a small roster of artists who make recordings on small budgets may not need hits so much as it needs consistent sales in order to survive.

Dedication to the music and sufficient sales may be enough to sustain a small indie label. Radio stations program recordings they think their listeners will like (or at least not *dislike*) but that is usually without regard to the artist or label. Retailers care that they sell recordings, but as long as the profit on any two given recordings is equal it does not really matter which one a customer purchases.

IFPI An international trade organization for record labels, composed of the trade associations from individual countries, such as the RIAA in the US. The offices are in London, UK.

ISRC The international identification system for sound recordings and music video recordings, created through the IFPI. Each ISRC is a unique and permanent identifier for a specific recording which can be permanently encoded into a product as its digital fingerprint.

GRid The IFPI's GRid provides a system for the unique identification of "Releases" of music over electronic networks so that they can be managed efficiently.

Gatekeeper In communication theory, a person who decides which messages will be communicated from one channel to another. Thus, radio music directors are gatekeepers, deciding which recordings will be communicated through radio.

If one considers the artist or songwriter as the communicator, then she or he is so far removed from most of the gatekeepers that they have little contact or influence.

Does the Internet change the gatekeeper theory? Because virtually anyone can have space on the Internet to operate web pages, a MySpace or other **social network** site, or a blog there are almost no gatekeepers for that medium. The problem is that the lack of gatekeepers means that a flood of music is available with almost no way that a consumer can sort out what style and quality of music suits that consumer's tastes. Chapters 11 and 12 have discussions of how artists and writers can use the Internet as a promotional tool.

Social network sites An Internet-based network such as Facebook, MySpace, or LinkedIn that allows users to define a group of "friends" and to connect to each other and follow each other.

DIY Activity

Each chapter will have a DIY activity. These are aimed at getting you, the reader, into ways to make it happen for yourself. Having dreams is good, but taking action to make them come true is even better.

● Lots of people want to be music performers or songwriters. However, there are many other careers in the music business and recording industry. Pick three other music business people from the "Who's Who in the Recording Industry" list that follows. Find out for each one how *you* might get started in that career. All information sources are fair game for this, but you must document your sources of information.

The Three Revenue Streams Model

While all of these viewpoints shed some light on the functions of the recording industry, it can best be understood in terms of an economic model. Media economist Alan Albarran notes that, "[T]he study of media economics is the most important [method], in that the ability to attract revenues (and ultimately profits) enables different producers to continue to operate in media markets."[14] Whether or not it is "all about the music," it is money that enables even hobby musicians to continue to write, play, perform, and record. As Music Business and Songwriting Professor Hal Newman puts it, "Most songwriters have to have a day job to support their music habit."

At the heart of the economic model are three **revenue streams**—one generated through the utilization of a song, one generated from live performances of that song, and one from the utilization of a particular recorded performance of that song (see Figure 2.5, page 10).

At the head of each revenue stream is a creative act—a song is written, a live performance given, or a recording is produced. True, the publisher exploits the composition, but it is the writer who creates it. These creative acts give rise to legal rights associated with the acts. The songwriter's creative act results in copyright in a musical composition. So this stream is referred to as the

Revenue stream The path through which money flows. In the music business these paths are from consumers back to the creators of musical compositions, live performances, and recordings.

songwriting stream. Performers have a right to keep others from recording or broadcasting their performances. The record label, producer, and recording artist's creative acts result in copyrights in sound recording. Three distinct legal rights, three distinct creative acts, and three distinct treatments of a song produce three distinct income streams.

Why three streams and not just two or one? One might argue that "the song is the thing" because it is included in all three streams. But it is really the recording that provides most of the cash flow in all three streams. Sales of recordings and performances of recordings account for most of the music publishing revenues. It is mostly the artists who are popular recording artists that generate most of the live performance revenues by performing the songs that they have recorded. Live performance is a separate revenue-generating act for the artist, aside from whether it generates any revenues for the music publisher or record label. Many artists make as much or more income from live performances than they do from the sale of recordings or the use of their musical compositions. Live performance needs to be included as a music business income stream because, well, music is what is being performed. Finally, including the live performance stream accounts for more points of interconnection between the various streams and leads to the development of a more complete model.

The presence of cash flow in three streams drives the major players in the industry to try to gain control over and participate in all three income streams with measures such as the "360 deal." In such a deal, an artist signs an agreement for *all* (or most) music business functions with the same entity, be it a label or other entertainment entity. (The "360 deal" is discussed in more detail in Chapter 9.)

Who's Who in the Recording Industry

Before launching into the construction of a model, one is always advised by the instructions to check the parts list to be sure that all the parts are included. Be sure that one knows what a component is before attempting to assemble it into the finished product. For that reason the basic function of all of the players in each of the three streams is defined below. The order is that in which they appear in the income stream in Figure 2.5. The simplicity of some of the definitions belies the complex relationships often set up by some individuals wearing more than one functional "hat" in the industry. Many recording artists, for example, also write songs, self produce the recordings, and perform at live concerts. The point is that the *function* is being performed by somebody.

The music publishing/songwriting stream

- *Songwriters* (including composers and lyricists): Obviously, these people write songs. The songwriter may be completely independent, but may also be the recording artist or producer.
- *Music publishers*: Publishers acquire rights to songs from songwriters and then license the uses of those songs. Most music publishers sign songwriters to

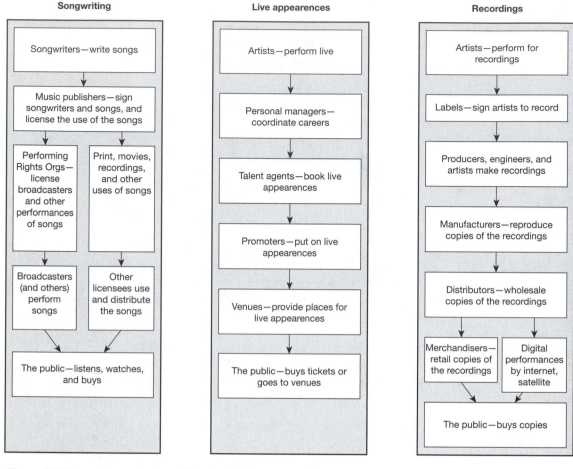

Figure 2.5 Three income streams: "Product" flow from creation to public

PRO A generic term, not a formal term, used for convenience in discussing any or all such organizations that license performance rights and pay performance royalties to songwriters, music publishers, and record labels. For example, ASCAP (American Society of Composers, Authors and Publishers), BMI (Broadcast Music, Inc), SESAC, and SoundExchange.

contracts agreeing to pay the writer a share of the royalties that the publisher makes from licensing the uses of the song.

- *Music performing rights organizations* (sometimes called "**PRO**s"): Such organizations license broadcasters, clubs, and others to perform songs, either live or from recordings.
- *Broadcasters*: These media perform songs by playing recordings of the songs or by broadcasting live performances of the songs. This term includes regular television and radio broadcasters as well as cable, satellite, and Internet transmitters.
- *The public (for the broadcasters)*: People listen and watch, usually with no charge other than serving as an audience, for the broadcaster's advertising messages.
- *Other media*: They create movies, print sheet music and song books, make recordings, and utilize the songs in other ways that create royalties for the publisher and songwriter.
- *The public (for the other media)*: People watch and buy these other uses of the songs.

The live performance stream

- *The musicians and singers*: The artists perform live for appearances primarily in concerts, in nightclubs, on television, and on radio. Not all live performers are recording artists, though most aspire to be, and not all recording artists are live performers, though most need to be.
- *Personal managers*: These people assist artists in the development and coordination of their careers as performing artists and as recording artists. They are shown in this income stream because most of their day-to-day functions revolve around live appearances, not around recordings.
- *Talent agents* (aka booking agents): Agents book live appearances for performers.
- *Promoters*: They put on live appearances by performers by arranging for the performer, the venue, the date, the production, and the marketing for the performance.
- *Venues*: These are the places for live appearances by artists, including clubs, concert halls, arenas, and stadiums.
- *The public*: People purchase tickets to, or otherwise attend, live artist performances.

The recording stream

- *Recording artists*: Sometimes referred to as "royalty artists," these are the people who perform for recordings by playing instruments and/or singing a particular performance that is recorded. The recording artist may or may not be a live performing artist, and may or may not be a songwriter. Most recording artists make money from this income stream by getting a royalty payment based on the sales of copies of the recordings that they make. Many lesser-known acts in all genres simply make and sell their own recordings at their performances or through the Internet by various methods with physical copies, downloads, or streaming.
- *Side musicians/vocalists*: Usually work on a per-job basis for the artist or producer to help create the desired recording. They are to be distinguished from the recording artists because side musicians do not receive royalties from the sale of recordings.
- *Record labels*: These organizations "hire" artists to make recordings that they plan on marketing in some way to the public. They usually sign the artist to a recording contract promising to pay the artist a royalty for recordings sold in return for the artist's promise to record exclusively for that particular label.
- *Record producers*: Are in charge of the process of creating the recording. They assist the artists by helping select material, studios, and assistants, and by helping the artists give their best performance. They assist the labels by taking care of the business aspects of the recording process and by delivering a marketable product.
- *Recording engineers*: Assist the producer and artist by running the equipment necessary first to capture the performance in a recording and to shape the final sound that the artist and producer ultimately want on the recording.

● *Studios*: Provide equipment and places for the artists to make their recordings. Although many large free-standing studios have closed, smaller "project" rooms and artist- or producer-owned studios have taken their place.

● *Record manufacturers*: Often (but not necessarily) the same as the label, these organizations make copies of the recordings (hard copies or electronic copies) suitable for sale in some manner to ultimate consumers.

● *Distributors*: Handle the copies of the recordings so that they can be conveyed to the ultimate consumer for purchase. For the most part, they wholesale the copies of the recordings made by the manufacturers to the retailers.

● *Merchandisers*: Retailers that sell copies of the recordings to the consuming public. This includes "bricks and mortar" stores as well as Internet retailers like iTunes or WalMart that sell electronic copies, or Amazon.com where one can also buy physical copies. Mobile telephone services may also serve as merchandisers selling ringtones and downloads.

● *Recording performing rights organizations*: These organizations monitor the performances of recordings (not to be confused with performances of the songs) and collect royalty payments for those performances for the artists and labels (see SoundExchange).

● *The public*: In this income stream these are the people who buy downloads or physical copies. This may be a different segment of the public from the one that buys tickets to live performances or listens to broadcasts or Internet streams.

In thinking about the music business it is important to always consider all three streams. The existence of the songwriting and live performance streams is important to the recordings stream because the artists and labels often have an economic stake in these other two streams. All of the major record industry conglomerates, and many individual labels, producers, and artists, have music publishing interests. Live performance is the crucible in which many new acts are formed. It may be an important medium to expose the public to the artists and their sound in order to promote the sale of recordings. Live performance may keep an artist's catalog of recordings selling long after the artist's recording career has peaked.

Figure 2.5 illustrates the most simplistic depiction of the three income streams as described above. Each stream has its own creative input from an initial source: songwriter, a performing artist, or a recording artist. Each stream ultimately ends up with the public consuming the output of the stream: the song, the live appearance, or the recording. Each stream has a primary control point through which the creative input is channeled: the music publisher, the personal manager, and the record label. Each stream has a "place" such as a favorite station to listen to, a concert hall or club, or a record store or Internet site, where the public has the opportunity to interface with the stream and cast an economic vote for their favorite music with their purchases or attention. Each stream has other parties between the creative person and the public who seek to profit from the income generated in the particular stream by performing some function useful to the completion of the flow of that stream.

Perhaps most significantly, it is public participation in each stream that generates the income. Unless the public either consumes the actual products.

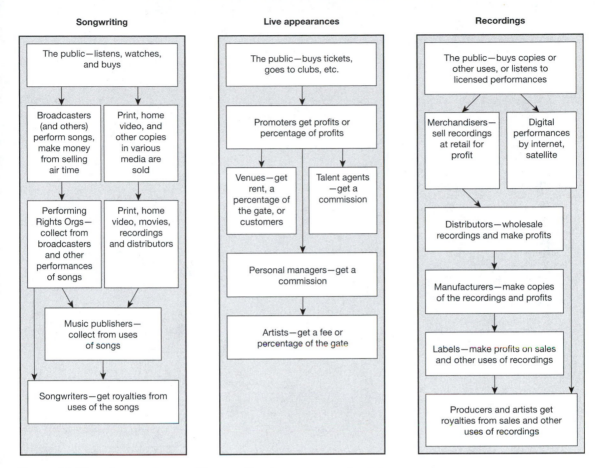

Figure 2.6 Three income streams: Revenue flow from consumer to source

such as sheet music or recordings, or attends movies, or provides an audience for the advertisers on radio or television, there is little or no money in the songwriting stream. Unless the public buys concert tickets or attends clubs and purchases food and drink, there is no source of revenue for the live appearance stream. Unless the public buys physical copies or downloads of recordings there is little revenue generated in the recordings stream. It is also the public that is the target in the communications model discussed earlier. Figure 2.6 illustrates the *income* flow downwards in each stream.

Three income streams the hard way

In order for a player in any stream to maximize security and profitability, participation in the other two streams is necessary. Figure 2.7 illustrates some of the many additional monetary and legal connections that exist between the various streams. These relationships between the three streams are examined in detail in Chapters 6, 7, and 8.

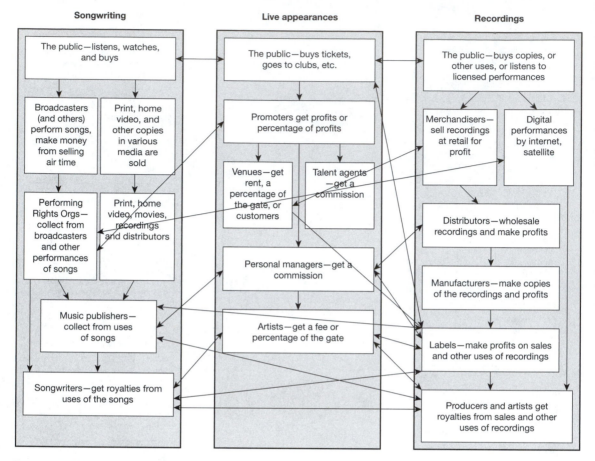

Figure 2.7 Three income streams: The hard way

Summary

The music business has changed and continues to change. Most of the recent changes have occurred because of the impact of digital technologies. The Internet has opened up new sales and distribution channels, as well as widespread piracy. Cell phone downloads, master ringtones, and ring backs have opened up new sources of revenue. The players in the music business are attempting to be involved in more revenue streams to compensate for the loss of sales of physical copies.

The business is best understood as a system that exists in an external environment of social, political, economic, and technological forces. This system transforms songs into performances and recordings, and generates revenue through the uses of those songs, performances, and recordings. Those acts form the three revenue streams for the music business: songwriting, live performance, and recording. Each of these streams starts with a creative event and ends with the consumption of that event (or product created by the event) by the public.

In turn, the public pays for its participation in the stream and that revenue then moves back through a host of players to those who initially created the song, performance, or recording.

Case Study: Ani DiFranco

Ani DiFranco is our case study in this chapter because she actively participates in all three income streams in often unique, yet sometimes predictable means. She is a truly independent artist who owns her own label. Unlike many "independent" artists, her Righteous Babe Records (RBR) label is not even distributed through a major label. She is truly outside of the mainstream of the major label music business, but participates in the music business to the fullest extent.

Ani was born in Buffalo, New York in 1970 and still makes that her home and the home of her record company. From a three income streams perspective:

- Songwriting: Ani wrote over 100 songs between her first live performances at the age of nine and her debut as a recording artist in 1989. Although she is essentially self-published, her catalog is administered by Bug Music, a significant independent music publishing company that began in the 1970s. (See Chapter 6 on music publishing administration deals.) Ani's performing rights organization is BMI. Even though she is "self-published" she still has her publishing company, Righteous Babe Music.

- Live Performance: It was Ani's constant touring and performing that built her fan base in the 1990s. She survived and began to prosper even without major radio exposure. But she is more than a performer. She is part owner of a concert venue. In 2000, DiFranco and her manager Scot Fisher purchased two decaying church buildings in downtown Buffalo, N.Y. With the help of the city, they worked on restoration and renovation of the buildings. Eventually the geothermally heated building penned as "Babeville" opened in 2006. It includes a concert hall (the old sanctuary), a club, an art gallery, and the offices of RBR. DiFranco's first performances in the new hall were made into a DVD, "Live at Babeville." Her talent agent is Jim Fleming (Fleming Artists).

- Recordings: Ani's RBR (Righteous Records until 1994) has released all of her 18 albums (through 2008). Distribution is through independent distribution on a national basis. Now the label boasts 13 other artists in addition to Ani. RBR engages in marketing in many of the same ways that the majors do. For example, RBR uses volunteer "Street Teams" to assist with marketing (read more about Street Teams in Chapter 12).

Want to know more? Visit www.righteousbabe.com, or read *Ani DiFranco: Righteous Babe Revisited*, Raffaelo Quipino (2004),[15] or *Small Giants* by Bo Burlingham (2007).[16]

QUESTIONS FOR REVIEW

- Describe how the music business has evolved from the industrial to the information age.
- Explain how the music business works as a system that must interface with an external environment of social, legal, political, economic, and technological forces.
- There are seven characteristics of the recording industry as a mass medium. Be able to briefly explain and give examples of each characteristic.
- Explain the three revenue streams in the music business and how each flows from a creative event to consumers.
- Be able to briefly describe the players and their functions in each of the three revenue streams.

3

Copyright Basics in the Music Business

Introduction

Copyrights play a critical role in the music business and an important role in the overall economy of the United States. The "copyright industries" (theatrical films, TV programs, home video, DVDs, business software, entertainment software, books, music and sound recordings) account for over 6 percent of the total US gross domestic product (gdp), employ nearly 5 million workers, and comprise one of the nation's largest exports. This chapter and the next two chapters, though not intended to be a complete summary of copyright law, do address the basics of copyright law as they apply to the music business and a number of specific copyright law provisions and issues of great importance to the music business.

Here is an important point. In the music business there are really two copyrights that exist in almost every recording: one for the song and one for the particular recorded performance of that song. That is a source of confusion about copyrights in the music business because when most people refer to a "song" they mean a recording of a particular song, not just the musical composition. But in "copyrightland" those two different works have distinct meanings and rights. That will be explained in detail in Chapters 4 and 5 but keep it in mind for this chapter, too.

The music business in general, and particularly the recording industry, runs on its copyrights. Songwriters create copyrightable songs to be performed by the recording artists. The recording artists perform for recording sessions and for live events. Record companies capture the performances of artists and producers on copyrightable sound recordings. All of these "products" are rather ephemeral and difficult to control. The problems with curtailing peer-to-peer distribution of unauthorized copies have proven that point.

Historically, the industry has been particularly prone to utilize legal methods in attempts to gain control over the production of its products, the supply of those products, the distribution of those products, and the income generated by those products in each of the three revenue streams. For example, a performing rights organization attempts to license a club in Wyoming. If the club does not buy a license, they are sued for copyright infringement. Record labels attempt to shut down illegal peer-to-peer networks and even individual users. The record labels or music publishers may ask the Justice Department to indict a pirate for criminal copyright infringement. Without the protection against unauthorized use of recordings and songs, two of the three income streams (sound recordings and music publishing) would be mere shadows even of their already diminished sizes.

The Statute of Anne, 1710; the first copyright act

Copyrights
A property right in a creative work which allows the author, and those who receive rights from the author, to control reproduction and other uses of the work. Copyrights are intangible personal property.

The Purpose of Copyright Law

Copyright law in the United States exists as a vehicle to encourage the creation of more literary and artistic works for the general benefit of society. By providing certain rights in their works the law makes it possible for the authors of those works to make a living, and thereby encourages them to create more works. So, it is for the benefit of society, not just the authors, that these laws exist. As the US Supreme Court put it:

> The copyright law, like the patent statutes, makes reward to the owner a secondary consideration. However, it is "intended definitely to grant valuable, enforceable rights to authors, publishers, etc., without burdensome requirements; 'to afford greater encouragement to the production of literary [or artistic] works of lasting benefit to the world.' The economic philosophy behind the clause empowering Congress to grant patents and copyrights is the conviction that encouragement of individual effort by personal gain is the best way to advance public welfare through the talents of authors and inventors in "Science and useful Arts." Sacrificial days devoted to such creative activities deserve rewards commensurate with the services rendered."[1]

KEY CONCEPTS

- The purpose of copyright law is to encourage authors to create more works to benefit society. This is done through balancing the interests of three groups, Creators, Consumers, and Commerce (i.e. publishers)—the "three Cs of Copyright."
- The basic rights of copyright are: making copies, making derivative works, distributing copies to the public, public performance, public display, and public performance of sound recordings by digital audio transmission.
- The duration of copyright protection is basically the life of the author plus 70 years.
- The copyright notice and registration of works are no longer required, but there are advantages to using them.
- Authors of most works can recapture their copyrights after a period of 35 to 40 years by a statutory termination of transfers.
- Many works in the music business are "joint works." Joint works imply equal ownership and equal rights in the works created.
- Fair use allows uses of works that are beneficial to society and not harmful to the copyright owner.
- In works made for hire the employer or hiring party owns the works with no right of termination for the author. But it is not easy for a work to be classified as a work made for hire.

The Three "Cs" of Copyright

That passage from the Supreme Court recognizes that there are really three interest groups, or communities, that are concerned with and that potentially benefit from copyright laws: the authors who create the works; the publishers (including record companies) who make copies and distribute the works to the public; and the members of the public who read, watch, listen to, and otherwise benefit from the existence of the works. A little creative labeling gets us a "C" name for each group (see Figure 3.1).

Creators

Copyright law gives them a way to make a living by creating works, thereby giving them incentive to create more works. Commerce makes the cash flow to the creators (i.e. authors).

Commerce

Commerce utilizes the works from the Creators by publishing them for the Consumers, and by investing in the Creators to encourage them to create more works. In so doing, they hope to make a profit.

Consumers

We benefit from the creation of more works by the Creators and the dissemination of those works to us by Commerce.

For example, the publishers and record labels benefit the writers and artists by providing them with financial support while the songs and recordings are

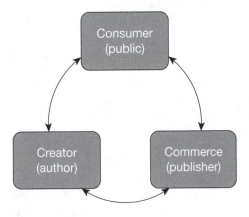

Figure 3.1 The three "C"s of copyright

being created. Then the publishers and labels collect for uses of the recordings and songs and pay royalties back to the writers and artists. The consumers benefit from the actions of the publishers and labels because those actions cause new songs and recordings to be available. It is then the consumers who send the money back through the income stream by making purchases that support the publishers, labels, songwriters, and artists.

In the United States, those purposes are written into the Constitutional authority for Congress to make copyright laws. Article I, Section 8, Clause 8 empowers Congress to make laws "To promote the Progress of Science and the useful Arts, by securing for limited Times to authors and Inventors the exclusive Right to their respective Writings and Discoveries." The laws are for the purpose of promoting the arts (for the sake of society and consumers), by protecting the rights of authors (creators). It was simply understood that commerce was the means of getting those works to the consumers. The 1790 Copyright Act protected the "assigns" of authors (those to whom authors would transfer the rights, i.e. the publishers).

Copyright laws passed by Congress reflect attempts to balance the interests of all three communities. The communities themselves also seek to balance their interests through contractual negotiations and other actions. The need to achieve a balance and to adjust that balance as times change is a fact to bear in mind when trying to understand the ins and outs of copyright law. If the system is out of balance then the needs of one or more of the parties is not being met. If that happens, then society will not benefit in the long run from the creation of more works. It is a bit like a three-legged stool. Each of the legs (one of the Cs) needs to be the same length, or the stool will become unbalanced and tip over.

The Rights of Copyright

In the United States, the rights of copyright are basically all statutory creations of the Copyright Act passed by Congress. The first federal Copyright Act was passed in 1790 by the First Congress. The laws have evolved through the years to cover more kinds of works, more rights, and to generally become more complicated. Although the basic rights may look simple on the surface, they are not.

Each of the rights is listed below along with a brief explanation of the statutory language. The current copyright law states that copyright owners have the exclusive rights to do and to authorize any of the following.[2]

1. **To reproduce the copyrighted work in copies or phonorecords**
   This is the most basic right. The right to make copies, right? Phonorecords are objects in which recordings are fixed and include digital files. Phonorecords are listed separately from other copies because of a 1908 Supreme Court case that said a piano roll was not a "copy" of a song because no one could look at the piano roll and play the song from it. We think of a "copy" a lot more broadly now.
2. **To prepare derivative works based upon the copyrighted work**
   A derivative work is a new version or edition of a work, like a movie made based on a book, or a particular recorded performance of a song.

3. **To distribute copies or phonorecords of the copyrighted work to the public by sale or other transfer of ownership, or by rental, lease, or lending**

   This right might be thought of as publication. Even giving away copies to the public would be a publication of the work. Note, however, that a *copy* must be transferred. So a performance of a work is not a publication because no copy is transferred.

4. **In the case of literary, musical, dramatic, and choreographic works, pantomimes, and motion pictures and other audiovisual works, to perform the copyrighted work publicly**

   The basic public performance right for musical works is discussed in detail in the next chapter. Of course, not all kinds of works can be "performed."

5. **In the case of literary, musical, dramatic, and choreographic works, pantomimes, and pictorial, graphic, or sculptural works, including the individual images of a motion picture or other audiovisual work, to display the copyrighted work publicly**

   Public display of a work is becoming more important with widespread use of visual images on the Internet. Again, not all kinds of works can be "displayed."

6. **In the case of sound recordings, to perform the copyrighted work publicly by means of a digital audio transmission**

   Note that this is separate and different from the basic public performance right. It is the *only* public performance right for sound recordings, and it is very narrow, as is discussed in Chapter 5.

All of the rights can be sold or licensed separately and may be broken down into even smaller pieces. For example, a record company may have the basic reproduction right for a sound recording, but may license iTunes to distribute digital copies; a game manufacturer to use it and reproduce it in a video game; and a movie company to use it in a motion picture, then reproduce that in DVDs or other copies; and a mobile phone provider to sell master ring tones of it. The multiple kinds of uses of a work create multiple sources of revenue for each work.

Duration of Copyrights

Copyrights in musical compositions and sound recordings last as long as those in any other works. The basic provisions currently allow for copyright protection for the life of the author plus 70 years. If there are multiple authors then the 70 years does not start to run until the death of the last surviving author.[3]

Most commercially released sound recordings are created as **"works made for hire"** for the record companies. At least that is what the labels claim. (More on that later.) In that case the label is considered the "author" for copyright purposes. Since businesses do not have a "life" that will meet a certain natural end, the duration of copyrights for works made for hire is stated as 95 years from the year of first publication, or 120 years from creation, whichever ends earlier. That means that sound recordings are protected in the United States for

Works made for hire In copyright law, a work made by an employee within the scope of employment, or a commissioned work of certain kinds if the parties agree in writing that the work is to be considered for hire. The employer or commissioning party owns the copyrights in works made for hire.

longer than most other nations protect them. The standard for WTO members is 50 years, while some countries protect sound recordings for only 25 years.

For works first published or registered with the Copyright Office before January 1, 1978, the rules for duration of copyrights are much more complex. Ever since the first copyright law was passed in the United States in 1790, until January 1, 1978 copyrights had been protected for a specific term of years. From 1909 to 1978 the duration was for 28 years and then for one additional **"renewal"** term of 28 years.

The 1976 Copyright Revision Act added 19 years to the renewal term of existing copyrights and changed the system to life of the author plus 50 years for works created on or after January 1, 1978. In 1998, Congress passed the Sonny Bono Copyright Term Extension Act, which added an additional 20 years to the renewal term, making it total 67 years. If the copyright in a pre-1978 work had not expired prior to 1998 it would have a total term of protection of 95 years. Table 3.1 summarizes the results.

When copyrights expire the work protected goes public domain (**PD**)—that is it becomes available for anyone to use without permission of the previous copyright owner.

Remember that one of the rationales underlying copyright law is to grant a "monopoly" to authors so they can make money and be encouraged to create

Renewal term
The second term of duration of copyright for works published prior to 1978. There was only one renewal term for pre-1978 copyrights.

PD A term of art regarding the status of works whose copyrights have expired or that were not subject to copyright protection. Public domain works may be used by anyone without obtaining licenses or clearances because PD works have no copyrights.

Table 3.1 Duration of copyright: Musical compositions (and all other works except sound recordings)

Date of Creation	Date Protection Begins	Duration*
January 1, 1978 and after	Date of fixation in a tangible medium.	Life of last surviving author + 70 years. If Work Made for Hire, a straight 95 years.
Published or registered 1964 through 1977	First publication with notice or Copyright registration (whichever is earlier).	28 years plus an *automatic* 67 year renewal = 95 years.
Published or registered 1923 through 1976	First publication with notice or Copyright registration (whichever is earlier).	28 years plus a 67 year renewal = 95 years IF renewed with the Copyright Office. Renewal was not automatic then.
Published or registered prior to 1923	First publication with notice or Copyright registration (whichever is earlier).	These works are all Public Domain now.**
Not published or registered before January 1, 1978	January 1, 1978.***	Life of last surviving author + 70 years.****

* Copyrights expire at the end of the calendar year, i.e. December 31, at midnight.
** Originally they had 28 years first term + one 28 year renewal. Those were extended by 19 years if renewals expired between 1962 and 1978 but did not get extended an additional 28 years in 1998.
*** Prior to 1978 these works were protected by Common Law copyright.
**** None of these works was allowed to expire before the end of 2002, no matter how long the author(s) had been dead. If published before the end of 2002, the protection ended at the end of 2047 unless life of the author + 70 would be later.

more works, but that monopoly will only last for a limited time. At the end of that time the public is served by the work becoming available to anyone, without need for a license, and therefore at a lower price. Thus, more of the arts are available to more people when the work goes public domain.

PD or not PD?

Musical works (songs) have had copyright protection since 1831, so calculating the status of a song is fairly straightforward. Any song published before 1923 is now public domain in the United States. Because the Copyright Term Extension act added 20 years to all existing copyrights in 1998, no more works will go public domain until 2019.

But the public domain status of **sound recordings** is a more complex matter. Prior to 1972 federal copyright law did not protect sound recordings (see Table 3.2 for a summary). They were protected under a patchwork of state laws. Most of the state laws do not contain a time when their protection ends. A 2007 decision by the highest court in New York State held that pre-1972 recordings were protected by common law copyright in New York (even though copies had been made and sold to the public). The federal law will not preempt common law copyright for pre-1972 sound recordings until 2067. So, in New York, even an Edison recording made in 1880 would be protected under state law until 2067—187 years!

Recordings created after February 15, 1972 (the effective date of the sound recording copyright amendment) are subject to federal protection and that federal protection preempts any state laws. For those recordings, the duration of copyright would be a 28 year original term, and a 67 year renewal term— a total of 95 years. Since none of the sound recording copyrights would have expired before renewal was made automatic in 1992, they will all get the full 95 years. So, none of the copyrights for recordings made between 1972 and 1978 will expire before the end of 2067. (Copyrights expire at the end of the calendar year in which they would otherwise expire.)

Sound recordings A kind of copyrightable work in which sounds created by various sources are captured, or "fixed," in some tangible medium such as tape or disc. These works are to be distinguished from the underlying works such as musical compositions or dramatic works which are recorded.

Table 3.2 Duration of copyright: Sound recordings

Date of Creation	Date Protection Begins	Duration
January 1, 1978 and after	Date of fixation in a tangible medium.	Life of last surviving author + 70 years. If Work Made for Hire, a straight 95 years.*
February 15, 1972 through 1977	First publication with notice or Copyright registration (whichever is earlier).	28 years plus an *automatic* 67 year renewal = 95 years.
Prior to February 15, 1972	Depends upon common law and various state laws.	Common law and state law protection for all these expires at the end of 2067.

* The labels consider most recordings to be works made for hire.

In 1978, the duration of copyright was changed to the life of the author plus 50 years, then in 1998 to life plus 70 years. If most sound recordings are works made for hire (a question discussed later in this chapter) their duration is 95 years from first publication, so the total term is the same as was for recordings created between 1972 and 1978. If they are not works made for hire, then they would be protected by the "life plus seventy" rules. Who the "authors" are of a sound recording is another question discussed later in this chapter.

Even when in 2068 copyrights in the sound recordings do begin to enter the public domain that does not mean that copyrights in the musical compositions recorded will necessarily be expired. Since one could not make a copy of a sound recording without also copying the musical composition, both copyrights must be considered. Most musical compositions, and any other literary or dramatic works likely to be recorded, will be operating under the "life plus seventy" rules. It would then be necessary to know who the authors and songwriters were and exactly when they died in order to know whether it was safe to copy a particular recording, even if the sound recording was clearly in the public domain.

Formalities: Notice and Registration

The current copyright laws recognize the existence of copyrights in works from the moment they are "created," (i.e. first fixed in some tangible medium of expression). That means a song would be protected by federal law as soon as the writer wrote it down or made a demo recording. Formalities, such as publication of the work with the appropriate copyright notice, and registration, are no longer necessary to secure basic copyright protection. That is the same standard used in most other nations, particularly those that have joined the **Berne Convention** for the Protection of Literary Property or the WTO.

Berne Convention
An international treaty in which over 160 countries have agreed to protect copyrights from each other.

The 1994 treaty that set up the WTO requires its members to apply Berne Convention standards in their copyright laws. There are, however, reasons why some formalities are still of importance to the recording industry, particularly in the United States.

Notice

There are two forms of copyright notice, one for most kinds of works, including musical works, and a different one for sound recordings. For most works that notice consists of (1) the symbol "©," or the word "Copyright," or the abbreviation "Copr."; (2) the year of first publication; and (3) the name of the copyright owner. For sound recordings the notice requirement is (1) the symbol "℗" (often referred to as the "circle P" notice); (2) the year of first publication of the *sound recording* (not the work recorded); and (3) the name of the sound recording copyright owner (usually a record label). The "circle P" notice is required by the Rome Convention for protection of sound recording copyrights on an international basis. One typically sees notices on albums, whatever their format, that have both the © and ℗ notices because the labels are claiming copyright in both the recording and the supplemental artwork, liner notes, and so forth, that are part of the packaging of the recording. Notices for the songs are not usually included unless the lyrics are reproduced in a booklet or in some manner accompanying the recording.[4]

The case of "Boogie Chillen"

A 1995 court decision regarding formality requirements for recordings of some pre-1978 works came close to casting a substantial number of songs into the public domain. The 1909 law required a copyright notice to be placed on copies of published works. Prior to publication, works were protected by common law copyright; some kinds of works, including musical compositions and dramatic works, could be protected by federal copyright registration even if unpublished. When a work was published it lost common law protection. If the publication was without the required notice, it lost federal protection. Without common law or federal protection the work then became public domain.

The 1908 case of *White-Smith Music Pub. Co. v. Apollo Co.* held that a piano roll, and by implication a phonorecord, was not a copy of a work because the work could not be visually perceived from that kind of device. Music publishers had therefore assumed that copyright notice for songs was not, therefore, required on phonorecords of the songs. In 1973 a federal district court in New York upheld that view. However, the Ninth Circuit Court of Appeals declined to follow that precedent. In *La Cienega Music Company v. Z .Z. Top*, that court held that distribution of recordings of John Lee Hooker's "Boogie Chillen" was a publication of the song and if the records did not contain a proper copyright notice for the song, the song would become public domain. The US Supreme Court refused to hear the case. Since literally thousands of recordings had been released without copyright notices for the songs recorded on them the music publishing companies were in uproar at the prospect of thousands of songs suddenly being public domain.

Congress came to the rescue in 1997 with an amendment to the Copyright Act that states, "The distribution before January 1, 1978, of a phonorecords shall not for any purpose constitute a publication of the musical work embodied therein." The notice dilemma is not a problem for recordings released between January 1, 1978 and March 1, 1989, since the copyright law at that time required notice only on "publicly distributed copies from which the work can be visually perceived." For the most part, then, there was no need for a notice for the song copyrights on the recordings unless the lyrics were reprinted on the sleeve, liner notes, or booklet. Even then, that notice would usually accompany the lyrics and still would not be on the label of the recording itself. Beginning March 1, 1989 notice was no longer required. That change was made in order for US copyright law to comply with the Berne Convention.

Registration

The statute specifically states, "registration is not a condition of copyright protection." However, registration is necessary in order to sue for infringement for works where the United States is the country of origin. The owner can register at any time, including after the discovery of an infringement; it is just that the suit cannot commence until there is a registration.

Registration soon after the creation of the work is also desirable for a number of other reasons. If the work is registered within 5 years of first publication the registration is considered as ***prima facie* evidence** of the validity of the copyright and the information contained on the registration form. That means the burden of proof would shift to the other party to prove that the copyright was not valid or that the label, publisher, or author was not the owner of the work—that might prove difficult to do. The Copyright Office now also allows pre-registration of works that are likely to be pirated prior to publication, such as songs, recordings, and movies. This is in addition to registration after the work is published. The Copyright Office website has additional information.

Perhaps more importantly, the copyright owner cannot get certain remedies for the infringement unless the work was registered *prior* to when the infringement began. Awards of statutory damages (see below) or attorney's fees cannot be made for published works unless registration is made within 3 months of publication or prior to the infringement if the infringement is later than 3 months after first publication.

In 2008 the Copyright Office began moving to a paperless and more automated registration system. Registration for all works is accomplished on form CO. If the work is to be published only electronically or is unpublished, the registration may be done by a "click through" form CO available online at the Copyright Office website. An electronic copy, such as an MP3, WAV, or other electronic file, can be submitted along with the registration. Payment of the registration fee of $35 may be made by credit card. If the work is published in hard copy, then the form is still filled out online, but a copy with machine readable coding is sent to the registrant, who then sends back to the Copyright Office the required two copies of the work with the form and $50 (see Figure 3.2). Be sure to check out the Copyright Office website (www.copyright.gov) before trying to use the Electronic Copyright Office (CO) registration system. The old paper forms, PA for musical works and SR for sound recordings, are still temporarily available, but are not really recommended to be used. For one thing, it costs $65 to register using these forms.

Although record companies fought a long battle for recognition of sound recording copyrights (see below), small labels, independent labels, and individual artists and songwriters with self-released recordings often do not take full advantage of the protection provided through registration. The lack of registration within 5 years of publication will mean that the registration, which would still be required in order to sue for infringement, will not be considered *prima facie* evidence establishing the validity of the copyright. In addition, the label or artist would not be able to collect attorney's fees or statutory damages if the recording was not registered prior to the infringement or within three months of publication/release. They would have to prove their exact losses and the infringer's exact profits, and pay their own attorney's fees.

Deposit of copies with the Library of Congress is required for all works published in the United States, even if the works are not registered. That is a particular problem because making a recording or song available for download or purchase

---

Prima facie evidence A legal term meaning evidence that is sufficient on its face to make a case or prove a point. A copyright registration is *prima facie* evidence of the validity of the copyright and other information on the registration form. It would then have to be up to the other party to prove otherwise.

UNITED STATES COPYRIGHT OFFICE
Form CO · Application for Copyright Registration

APPLICATION FOR COPYRIGHT REGISTRATION   PA

* Designates Required Fields

1 WORK BEING REGISTERED

1a. * Type of work being registered (*Fill in one only*)

☐ Literary work   ☒ Performing arts work

☐ Visual arts work   ☐ Motion picture/audiovisual work

☐ Sound recording   ☐ Single serial issue

ApplicationForCopyrightRegistration

1b. * Title of this work (*one title per space*)

My Song for the World

WorkTitles

1c. For a serial issue: Volume [   ] Number [   ] Issue [   ] ISSN [   ]

Frequency of publication: [   ]

1d. Previous or alternative title

[   ]

1e. * Year of completion [2 | 0 | 1 | 0]

Publication (*If this work has not been published, skip to section 2*)

1f. Date of publication [   ] (*mm/dd/yyyy*) **1g.** ISBN [   ]

1h. Nation of publication ☐ United States ☐ Other

1i. Published as a contribution in a larger work entitled

[   ]

1j. If line 1i above names a serial issue   Volume [   ] Number [   ] Issue [   ]

On pages [   ]

1k. If work was preregistered   Number PRE-[| | | | | | | |]

Privacy Act Notice
Sections 408-410 of title 17 of the *United States Code* authorize the Copyright Office to collect the personally identifying information requested on this form in order to process the application for copyright registration. By providing this information you are agreeing to routine uses of the information that include publication to give legal notice of your copyright claim as required by 17 U.S.C. § 705. It will appear in the Office's online catalog. If you do not provide the information requested, registration may be refused or delayed, and you may not be entitled to certain relief, remedies, and benefits under the copyright law.

Figure 3.2 Copyright registration form CO

on the Internet would be considered to be "publishing" the work. Most song-writers and artists are not aware of the deposit requirement.

Registration tips for unsigned bands and songwriters

A special feature of sound recording registration allows the owner to register both the recording and the underlying musical composition (or other work) recorded. The only catch is that the same person(s) must be the owners of the copyrights of both works. This is particularly useful to unsigned bands or songwriters who either publish their works on their own labels or who simply wish the comfort of a registration. The problem is that in a band it is likely that all the members of the band, and some additional persons including any audio engineers or producers, are all probably "authors" and owners of the copyright in the sound recording, whereas those same people are probably not the writers of all the individual songs on the album or demo recording. Using the band name as the "authors" of songs or recordings is not acceptable because the registration requires the names of individual persons.

A useful feature of both sound recording registration and musical composition registration (as well as other classes of works) is the registration of **collective works**. This feature can be turned to the advantage of the performing artist or songwriter who does not have a recording or publishing contract, hence a label, producer, or publisher, to look out for their copyrights. Provided that the copyright owners of all the works are the same, multiple works can be submitted in one registration as an unpublished collection, such as "The Songs of Geoff Hull, 2010." Whether on a demo CD or tape or in some sort of "folio," the single registration would protect all of the individual compositions or recordings in the collection. They would not be indexed by their individual titles in the Copyright Office records but even that could be accomplished by later filing a Supplementary Copyright Registration, form CA, which lists the individual titles and refers back to the previous collection registration. Even though the CA registration fee is substantially higher ($100 in 2010) than a basic registration fee, the typical unsigned band or songwriter could register, say, ten songs for the price of two registrations instead of ten—$135 instead of $350. In fact, the Copyright Office recommends this practice.

Collective works
A work (in copyright) formed by the assembly of a number of separate independent works into a collective whole, such as an anthology, periodical issue, or (perhaps) a record album.

Internet Activities

- Visit the International Intellectual Property Alliance website, www.iipa.com. What is the current value of Copyright Industries in the US? How do copyright exports compare with some other exports?
- Visit the Copyright Office website, www.copyright.gov. Find the form CO and download a copy of the form and instructions for a form CO.
- Still on the Copyright Office website, think of a song by one of your favorite artists. Search the records for the official PA registration number for that song or SR registration number for that recording. They will be indexed that way for all registrations prior to 2008. What problems did you have? Who is listed as the copyright "claimant" for the song or recording?
- Still on the Copyright Office website, find a song from the 1990s. Search the registration information to find out when it was transferred to a publisher. When could termination of that transfer take place? Be sure you look for the song (musical composition) and not the sound recording.

Ownership of Copyrights

Joint Authorship/Joint Works

It is common practice in the recording industry for people to collaborate on the songs they write or the recordings they create. The songwriting teams of Rogers and Hart, Lennon and McCartney, Ashford and Simpson, and many more are legendary. Popular groups work together to create the recordings that they make. Creative collaboration is one area where the synergy concept applies: the creative output of the group effort exceeds that which could be achieved by the individuals working alone. But the copyright law creates some presumptions about people who create works together that might not be what the authors have in mind.

If two or more authors create a work with the intention that their contributions be merged into a single unitary work, even if they create separate but interdependent parts, such as melody and lyrics, then their work is deemed to be a "joint work."[5] If a work is a joint work, then each author owns an equal, undivided share unless there is some agreement among the authors that otherwise spells out the ownership shares. So if one person writes a melody and another writes lyrics with the intention of creating a single song, then each owns half of the entire work (i.e. an undivided share) instead of one owning the rights to the lyrics and the other owning rights to the melody. Each author may authorize the use of the work, but is under a duty to account to the other authors for their fair shares of any royalties or revenues received.

These things are fine if they are what the authors intended. If they intend otherwise, they would have to have a written agreement spelling out their arrangement. For example, if one writer wanted a 60 percent share and the other a 40 percent share, they would have to have a written agreement to that effect because this would be a transfer of ownership.

The situation with bands becomes even more complicated. Suppose one band member comes up with the idea for a song, creates a verse and chorus, and basic melody. That member then presents the unfinished song to the other members of the band. Together they find a "groove" and work out an arrangement suitable for their musical style. Perhaps some of the other band members contribute a lyric, line, or make some suggestion to modify the melody. The bass player comes up with a bass part. The drummer works out a drum part to anchor the song rhythmically. How many authors are there of the song? How many authors are there of the sound recording that the band later makes as a demo? If the person who had the original idea and wrote some of the basic parts of the song intends all contributors to be equal authors, and if the other contributors intend to be equal authors then they have a joint work. Notice this has to be what *all* the parties intend, not just the people who later added small parts to the song.

There are also court decisions that hold that each person's contribution, to be deemed a joint author, must be at least copyrightable in and of itself. Generally, the **"head" arrangement** that a group of musicians makes for a popular song is not considered as copyrightable. So, unless the members of the group have made significant contributions to the melody and lyrics then they

Head arrangement A musical arrangement where the parts are not written out but simply made up on the spot by the musicians out of their heads. Such arrangements are usually more simplistic and probably not subject to copyright protection as derivative works.

are not "authors" of the song. Presumably they could have a written agreement that any songs created by the group were to be deemed joint works. Problems are likely to arise when there is no agreement and someone who thinks they are an author, such as the drummer, attempts to claim his or her share of the song after the group has split up (as it almost surely will).

Joint authorship in sound recording is a bit clearer. Under most circumstances all group members will have made a significant contribution to the recording because they made the sounds that were recorded. They are, therefore, all joint authors of the recording, because it is pretty clear that they fully intended to create a recording in which all had participated. The engineer who actually made the recording and the producer (if the producer contributed creatively to the recording process) may also be joint authors of the recording. If the recording is made for a label under a "standard" recording artist contract, the label will assert that the recording is a "work made for hire" and that it is the "author" for copyright purposes and copyright owner.

DIY Activities

- Find someone in the class who is a songwriter or who is in a band. Work with them to download and fill out the form CO for their song or recording. Note how the "bar code" sections change as new information is typed in! They may even want to actually register if they just got paid!
- With two other persons in the class, write a parody of a popular song. Use the "fair use" factors as discussed in the chapter and remember, your parody must make fun of the song itself, not just substitute funny lyrics.
- Assuming your parody is protectable, who owns the copyright? How is it split up? Is it a derivative work? Why?
- Now create a proper copyright notice for your new work. Assume that you record a demo, too. Create a notice for the sound recording.

Works Made For Hire

A significant issue for both record labels and music publishers, and the artists (and producers) and songwriters respectively who create the works for the labels and publishers, is whether the works created are "works made for hire." Generally, works made for hire are works created by employees within the scope of their employment, and certain kinds of **commissioned works** where the parties have agreed in writing that the work is a work for hire.

There are two significant results of a work being considered for hire. First, the employer, not the person who created the work, is deemed to be the author and owner for purposes of copyright. That means no further transfer of rights is necessary. It happens automatically. More importantly, the person who created the work does not have any termination rights in the work. Thus, in works for hire, the creator of the work does not have a right to "recapture" the copyrights

Commissioned works In copyright, a work that is created at the behest of some party other than the author, usually for pay and not as part of the author's job.

after a period of time (35 to 40 years). The employers can then be totally sure that they will own the copyrights for their entire duration (95 years from first publication or 120 from creation, whichever ends earlier). Simply put, can the recording artists recapture the rights to their masters from the labels? Can songwriters get their songs back from the music publishers? (See discussion below on termination rights.)

While that might seem simple enough on its face, the application has proven quite troublesome to the courts. The statute defines "work made for hire" as:

1. A work prepared by an employee within the scope of his or her employment; or
2. a work specially ordered or commissioned for use as a contribution to a collective work, as a part of a motion picture or other audiovisual work, as a translation, as a supplementary work, as a compilation, as an instructional text, as a test, as answer material for a test, or as an atlas, if the parties expressly agree in a written instrument signed by them that the work shall be considered a work made for hire.[6]

The case of the homeless statue

The Community for Creative Non-Violence (CCNV), an activist organization that promoted awareness of homelessness, contacted sculptor James Earl Reid to create a sculpture. The sculpture was for their December rally in Washington, D.C. Reid created the statue using materials paid for by CCNV, at his own studio. After the rally CCNV wanted to take the sculpture on tour. Reid objected saying that the inexpensive material used for the original casting would not withstand a road trip. CCNV asked for the return of the statue and Reid refused. Who did the sculpture and the copyrights in it belong to, Reid or CCNV? Was Reid CCNV's employee?

After reviewing the language and legislative history of the work made for hire provision, a unanimous Supreme Court concluded:

> Congress intended to provide two mutually exclusive ways for works to acquire work "for hire" status: one for employees and the other for independent contractors. Second, the legislative history underscores the clear import of the statutory language: only enumerated categories of commissioned works may be accorded work for hire status.

The Supreme Court decided that the appropriate test of whether someone was an employee or not under the works made for hire provisions of the Act were "principles of general common law agency." The Court referred to a "non-exhaustive" list of factors to be used in determining whether a worker is an employee or an independent contractor.

The Court specifically listed thirteen factors, including:

> the hiring party's right to control the manner and means by which the product is accomplished [. . .] the skill required; the source of the

instrumentalities and tools; the location of the work; the duration of the relationship between the parties; whether the hiring party has the right to assign additional projects to the hired party; the extent of the hired party's discretion over when and how long to work; the method of payment; the hired party's role in hiring and paying assistants; whether the work is part of the regular business of the hiring party; whether the hiring party is in business; the provision of employee benefits; and the tax treatment of the hired party.[Citations omitted]

The Court then cautioned, "No one of these factors is determinative."[7]

The answers to all of these questions depend upon the particular facts of the case being analyzed. In Reid's case, very few of the factors fell in favor of him being an employee. Because a sculpture is not one of the kinds of works that can be work made for hire by agreement, and because there was no agreement, the sculpture was not a work made for hire and Reid was determined to be the copyright owner. Even if there had been an agreement, they could not make the statue a work made for hire. They could not make him an employee, unless he in fact was an employee under the Supreme Court's test, and they could not make a sculpture one of the kinds of work made for hire by agreement because the statutory list of such works is quite specific and limited, and a sculpture simply is not on the list.

Works made for hire in music and recordings

Analyze the typical contractual and other working conditions of a "staff" songwriter, i.e. one under an exclusive writing contract with a music publisher (see Chapter 6), and of a recording artist with an exclusive contract with a label (see Chapter 9). You will probably conclude that in many instances it is probable that a recording artist, particularly one who is given freedom to create and even produce their own recordings, is probably not an "employee" of the record company. On the other hand, a songwriter who uses staff writing rooms, demo rooms, and recording facilities at the music publisher's place of business may very well be creating works for hire as an employee, without meaning to do so. Both of the situations have recently raised work for hire questions in the legal literature, but neither one has been litigated. Nor has a court determined the validity of the record labels' claim that the recordings are contributions to collective works and therefore may be work for hire by agreement, as their recording contracts say they are.

Termination Rights

In an effort to correct the many problems that had developed with copyright renewals under the 1909 copyright law, Congress created a new right for authors in the 1976 Copyright Act—the right of termination of transfers.[8] This right, as was the earlier renewal right, is designed to give authors, or their heirs, a right to recapture the copyrights after a period of time. The theory is that when

Termination rights Statutory rights of authors (or certain of their heirs) under copyright law to end transfers of copyrights and non-exclusive licenses during a 5-year period beginning after 35 years from the date of transfer and running through the fortieth year.

authors initially bargain away their copyrights for long periods of time, the value of the copyrights is not known because they have not stood the test of the marketplace and for that reason "beginner" authors are not in a very good bargaining position with publishers and labels. That certainly holds true for new recording artists, as discussed in Chapter 9. The statute, therefore, allows the authors to "recapture" their copyrights after a period of time during which the initial transferee, usually a publisher or label, has had ample time to exploit the work.

The termination "window" begins after 35 years after the transfer and runs for a 5-year period. (If the transfer includes the right to publish, the termination window begins after 40 years after transfer or after 35 years after first publication, whichever begins earlier.) During this time the termination may be effected by written notice to the transferee (owner) signed by a majority of the owners of the termination interest. Those people are the author(s) themselves, or if an author has died prior to serving the termination notice, the author's surviving spouse and children. The surviving spouse owns 50 percent and the children the other 50 percent. If a child has died, that child's children (the author's grandchildren of the deceased child) take that child's share. Only if there is not a surviving spouse, children, or grandchildren is the termination interest owned by the author's heirs by will or law.

The people owning a majority of the termination interest must agree to end the transfer. With multiple authors, where each author owns an equal share of the copyright, as with joint authors as discussed earlier, each author owns an equal share of the termination rights. So, if there were four authors, *three* would have to agree to terminate the transfer. A majority is 50 percent *plus one*, right? Figure 3.3 shows one example of how that might work.

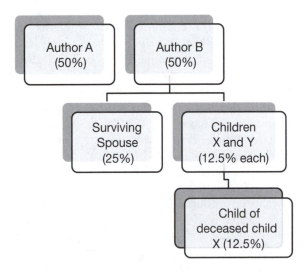

Figure 3.3 Termination rights shares with two authors (one of whom is deceased)

Whoever they are, the owners of the majority interest in the termination must notify the transferee no more than 10 and no less than 2 years before the effective date of termination that they are exercising their right to end the transfer and recapture the copyrights. If notice, number of people, and date of termination all fall within the requirements of the statute, then the authors or their heirs regain control of the copyrights. There is nothing that the transferee can do to prevent this. The statute even states that a termination may take place even if the author has contracted not to do it!

A very important point to keep in mind is that there are no termination rights in works made for hire. The original creators of the work cannot terminate a transfer to their employer, because technically speaking there was no transfer. The employer/"author" cannot terminate a transfer to anyone because they are not the people in need of protecting like the "poor starving authors who make bad deals" that Congress was originally trying to protect.

With that as background, here is the story of an interesting bit of legislative history. In 1999 Congress passed a "technical amendment" to the Copyright Act that added sound recordings to the list of kinds of works that can be works for hire by agreement. The amendment was tucked away in provisions of a bill that reworked the Satellite Home Viewers Act. There was an immediate hue and cry from the recording artist community and others. They claimed that the change was far from technical and that Congress should have held hearings on this important matter. Congress did hold hearings in 2000, and later that year, after the artists and RIAA representatives agreed, it rescinded the amendment, returning the law to the status quo, whatever that was. No court had ever ruled in a termination case whether a sound recording could be a work made for hire under the typical provisions of an artist–label relationship. Presumably the artists and labels will be litigating this issue in the near future.

Termination problems

For the record companies, the combination of problems with viewing the recordings as works made for hire and the existence of termination rights may mean that recording artists and/or producers can end the labels' rights to own the copyrights in the master recordings after 35 years. The value of masters that are 35 years old was illustrated in 1995 with the release of a collection of Beatles recordings from the 1960s. Capitol Records shipped more than 4 million units of the "Anthology" collection in late 1995. It debuted at number one in the *Billboard* album chart the next week with reported sales in the United States alone of over 800,000 copies in one week. In 2002 valuable old masters resurfaced again in the chart-topping Elvis Presley "Elv1s: 30 #1 Hits," and Rolling Stones' "Forty Licks" albums. Needless to say, the labels would not be pleased to lose the rights to such valuable products. The earliest termination date for recordings made and rights transferred in 1978 would be in 2013. The time for the earliest notice of termination of transfer for those recordings already passed in 2003. Artists and labels have a lot to gain or lose and both are likely to fight long and hard over the termination rights. This litigation will likely take a substantial time to resolve.

The record companies are putting lots of effort and language in their recording agreements to try to prevent the artists from recapturing, or more correctly terminating the transfers, of the sound recording copyrights. Particularly, the labels claim that the recordings are "contributions to collective works" under the second part of the work for hire definition above. The labels require artists to agree to that fact and state that the recordings are works made for hire. Again, while this may seem logical on its face, the statutory definitions of collective works, the legislative history of the statute, and court decisions interpreting the work for hire and other provisions cast doubt on the labels' claim. For example, in most artists' albums, who creates the collection of recordings and decides on what to include and the order of the songs—the artist, the producer, or the label? On the music publisher and songwriter side of the question, the litigation is likely to be when some unsuspecting songwriter attempts to terminate the transfer of copyrights to a music publisher only to find that the publisher counterclaims that the work was made for hire because the songwriter was really an employee of the publisher.

The "Fair Use" Limitation and Parody

The rights of copyright for all works are limited by a section of the Copyright Act generally referred to as "**fair use**." That section permits uses such as "criticism, comment, news reporting, teaching (including multiple copies for classroom use), scholarship or research" as fair uses, and not infringements provided they meet certain criteria (see Figure 3.4). Although an extended discussion of fair use is beyond the scope of this book, it is important to understand fair use in trying to answer questions of sampling, parody, and "file sharing" of musical works and sound recordings.

> Fair use A provision of the copyright law allowing some limited uses of works where the use is particularly beneficial to the public and does not do much harm to the copyright owner.

Figure 3.4 Fair use balance

Fair Use Factors

The Copyright Act lists four factors to be considered in determining whether a particular use is a fair use, and *all* of them must be considered in every case.[9] Just because a use is for educational purposes, for example, does not necessarily mean it is a fair use. How the use weighs on the other tests may tip the scales of justice towards infringement. See the "Fair Use Explained" box for the statutory language of each part of the test and a brief commentary.

Although there are certainly conceivable fair uses of sound recordings there have been few cases that have addressed that issue. One held that one candidate for governor of Maine who used a bit of another candidate's recording in a commercial was engaging in fair use. On the other hand, the Napster case and other file-sharing cases have repeatedly held that peer-to-peer "file sharing" is not fair use.

FAIR USE EXPLAINED

Each of the four fair use factors in the Copyright Act is listed below, with an explanation of how that factor tends to be applied by the courts.

1 *"The purpose and character of the use, including whether such use is of a commercial nature or is for nonprofit educational purposes."* Here the uses listed in the first part of the fair use section–criticism, comment, news reporting, teaching (including multiple copies for classroom use), scholarship, or research, plus parody (and maybe satire), and general private non-commercial use are more likely to be considered as fair uses. Uses which change, alter, or make the work into a new work or somehow "transform" the work are more likely to be considered "fair."

2 *"The nature of the copyrighted work."* Generally, factual works are less likely to receive protection than entirely creative works. Presumably, the reason one creates a factual work is to spread the information. Facts themselves are not protected by copyright. Also, it is generally less fair to make use of an unpublished work because the author has not yet exposed the work to the public for them to use.

3 *"The amount and substantiality of the portion used in relation to the copyrighted work as a whole."* This test has both a qualitative and a quantitative aspect. Taking the "hook" out of a song, even if only as short as eight notes, may be a significant taking. Taking only a few hundred words out of thousands may be significant if the words taken were a crucial part of a book.

4 *"The effect of the use upon the potential market for or value of the copyrighted work."* Fair use tries to balance the possible benefit to society (as opposed to the user of the protected work) that results from the use versus the potential harm to the copyright owner. Generally, harm is measured in economic terms such as lost sales, lost licensing revenues, and even lost opportunities. The more the work created by the claimed fair use provides a substitute for the original work, then the less likely the use is to be deemed "fair."

The case of "Oh, Pretty Woman!"

There are significant cases involving questions of fair use of musical compositions, most notably in the areas of satire and parody. In 1994 the US Supreme Court decided that parody of musical compositions could be a fair use in *Campbell v. Acuff-Rose Music, Inc.* Luther Campbell's "2 Live Crew" had made a parody rap version of the Roy Orbison/William Dees song, "Oh, Pretty Woman." Campbell's version used the famous guitar riff that introduces and is used throughout the song, portions of the melody, and a few lines of the lyrics of the original.

Although the Court did not definitively say Campbell's version was a fair use, they said:

> 2 Live Crew's song reasonably could be perceived as commenting on the original or criticizing it, to some degree. 2 Live Crew juxtaposes the romantic musings of a man whose fantasy comes true, with degrading taunts, a bawdy demand for sex, and a sigh of relief from parental responsibility. The later words can be taken as a comment on the naiveté of the original of an earlier day, as a rejection of its sentiment that ignores the ugliness of street life and the debasement that it signifies. It is this joinder of reference and ridicule that marks off the author's choice of parody from other types of comment and criticism that traditionally have had a claim to fair use protection as transformative works.[10]

The Court cautioned that "this is not to say that anyone who calls himself a parodist can skim the cream and get away scot free." To be a parody, the new work must directly comment on and criticize the original work. Thus, simply substituting funny new lyrics for the original would not be a fair use unless the new lyrics somehow poked fun at and commented on the original. The Court sent the case back to the district court to determine whether the repeated use of the bass/introductory riff was excessive and whether the parody version damaged the market for a straight rap version of the song. The parties ultimately settled the case at the District Court without further judicial decisions being rendered.

Poor Man's Copyright

It is not unusual to hear people, particularly musicians and songwriters, refer to "poor man's copyright." Prior to 1978 that was a **common law copyright** concept.

The notion of common law copyright is that the author of a work ought to be the first to be able to decide whether to disclose the work to the public. Until such time as a work was published, the rights in the work belonged to the author. So, common law copyright became generally known as the "right of first publication." Upon publication the work was eligible for statutory copyright protection if published with the copyright notice and/or registered (for dramatic and musical works whether published or not).

Since registration cost money, some people chose not to register their unpublished works (and some unpublished works could not be registered prior

Common law copyright Originally, the right of authors to be the first to publish their works as protected by common law, and not the federal copyright statute. Since 1978, common law copyright would generally only apply to works not fixed in a tangible medium of expression.

to 1978) but rather attempted to establish some kind of evidence of ownership and creation of the work by mailing it to themselves registered mail, depositing copies with some writers' protective organization, and so forth. This might then satisfy the burden of proof in a common law copyright infringement case that the work had been created by the author, as claimed. These non-statutory devices became known as "poor man's copyright." Whether "poor" should be taken to refer to the typical author's impoverished state or to the quality of evidence resulting from these practices is open to question.

Under the 1976 Copyright Act (which went into force on January 1, 1978), copyright in any work exists upon the first fixation of the work in a tangible medium of expression. Since common-law protection is specifically preempted upon first fixation, the only thing left for common law to protect is a work until it is first fixed. There would not be many works that would be "created" but not written down or recorded in some manner—perhaps a musical performance by some jazz musicians or a poem or song written and kept "in the head" of the author. Furthermore, registration is no longer a requirement for federal protection. If an impecunious author chooses not to register to save the registration fee, then the "poor man's" alternatives still exist as a means to attempt to create evidence of authorship and ownership. However, registration is *prima facie* evidence of the existence of the copyright and its validity as stated on the registration form. Registration prior to the infringing acts is necessary to get statutory damages and court costs and attorneys fees. Registration is required in any event, for US works or non-Berne country works, prior to any court action for infringement.

Here is a good rule of thumb to follow. If the author or copyright owner is going to distribute copies to the public or place the work where it is likely to be accessible to members of the public, or where the owner does not really know who will have access to the work, then registration is the best approach. If one were selling downloads or offering streams of the band's latest project on the band's website, then registration of those works is a good idea. Relying on "poor man's copyright" would be a bit risky in those circumstances, unless the writer or performer simply wants to give away their work.

Summary

This chapter has dealt with general aspects of the copyright law as they apply to sound recordings and musical compositions. For the most part, those general aspects apply to works in the recording industry the same as they apply to all works, regardless of their nature. Copyright laws exist to benefit society by encouraging authors to create more works and publishers to disseminate those works to the public. To do that, authors are given rights to reproduce their works, make derivative works, distribute copies to the public, perform the works publicly, display the works publicly, and to perform sound recordings publicly by means of digital audio transmission.

Generally, these copyrights last for the life of the author plus 70 years, but for works first published before 1978, the rules are more complicated. To improve protection of works, it is a good idea to register the work with the

Copyright Office. Multiple authors, who work together to create a work, are "joint authors" owning equal shares and having equal rights in the works created. Authors sometimes create works made for hire for their employers which automatically means the employers are treated as the "authors" and owners of the works. If a work is not a work made for hire, the authors (or some of their heirs) may recapture their copyrights by terminating the transfers of rights to publishers after 35 to 40 years. "Fair use" is a provision of the copyright law that allows certain uses of works what would otherwise be infringements, but which benefit the public and do not particularly harm the copyright owner.

Finally, "poor man's copyright," under the current law, is just a way to try to provide evidence of copyright creation and ownership without having to go to the expense and trouble of a formal copyright registration. However, registration is still recommended if a work is going to be exposed to the public. There are some particular twists of the copyright law specifically written to deal with some aspects of sound recordings and musical compositions that must be explored in some detail in order to understand how the recording industry attempts to mold the copyright laws to its advantage. They are discussed in the following chapters.

Case Study: Metro-Goldwyn-Mayer Studios, Inc. v. Grokster, Ltd

This is the real case of *Metro-Goldwyn-Mayer Studios, Inc. v. Grokster, Ltd*, 125 S. Ct. 2764 (2005). Unauthorized downloading and "file sharing" hit its first peak in the late 1990s with the Napster system. When a person used Napster, they would log on and the Napster computer would compile a list of songs on the person's computer that they wanted to "share" with other people. If they wanted to find a recording they would tell the Napster computer and it would search the files to find out which other computers that were on line had that recording, then send a link to the person looking for the song. When the record companies sued for infringement the courts held that Napster was liable for the infringements of its users because it was actively involved in the search process, did nothing to stop downloading of copyright protected materials, and profited from the infringements.

The Grokster system and software functioned differently. It did not maintain a central computer or list of recordings. It was simply search software that transformed various user's computers into "nodes" to facilitate the searches. Grokster was not directly involved in the downloading process at all. However, Grokster did tout itself as "The Next Napster" and did promote use of its software to engage in unauthorized downloads and "file sharing." Grokster made money by having people visit its website and download the free software.

In a rare unanimous decision, the US Supreme Court said Grokster could be liable for infringement because it actively promoted the direct infringements of the users. Grokster was "inducing" infringement and therefore could be held liable for the infringements of the users even though Grokster had no specific knowledge of what was being infringed at any given moment and even though the Grokster software could be used for lawful file sharing. (The Court noted, however, that 90 percent of the files downloaded through Grokster were copyright protected materials.) For a lot of reasons the court concluded, "The unlawful objective is unmistakable."

Continued

Want to know a lot more about Grokster? Read the Supreme Court's opinion. You can find it online at www.findlaw.com/casecode/supreme.html if you search by the name of a party as "Grokster." Or go to www.law.cornell.edu and look under the "opinions" bar for US Supreme Court. The case was decided in the 2004–2005 term and can be located using the parties' names. If your university has Westlaw or LEXISNEXIS it is even easier.

QUESTIONS FOR REVIEW

- What is the purpose of copyright law and how do the "Three Cs of Copyright" work together to achieve that purpose?
- What are the basic rights of copyright? What is one instance in which they are different for songs and for sound recordings?
- What is the duration of copyright for works created January 1, 1978 and after? What is it for works created before January 1, 1978?
- What is the copyright notice for songs? For sound recordings? Although no longer required, why are notice and registration still important?
- What are the laws regarding ownership and use of joint works? Why are they important to songwriters and band members?
- In what two ways can works be considered "works made for hire"? Why does it matter whether a work is a work made for hire?
- What are termination rights? Why are they important to songwriters, recording artists, music publishers, and record labels? What must be done to terminate a transfer according to the Copyright Act?
- What is "fair use" in copyright? What are the four factors to be considered in determining whether a use is a fair use? How would each of the four fair use factors come out in the typical "file sharing" case?
- What is "poor man's copyright"? Why is it no longer especially relevant?

4   Music Copyrights ©

Introduction

As mentioned in the previous chapter, the music and recording businesses depend to a large degree on the rights given to two important works: musical compositions (songs) and sound recordings. A source of confusion is that both of these copyrights exist at the same time in the recordings that are the driving force behind the music and recording businesses. A songwriter (who might also be a recording artist) composes a song and a recording artist makes a recording of that song. Whenever the recording is sold, downloaded, or played, both works are being used. That means that both copyright owners may be entitled to some compensation for the use of their works. This chapter focuses on the most important rights in musical compositions. Chapter 5 explores the rights in sound recordings. In this chapter, we pay special attention to those rights that generate revenues for the songwriters and music publishers; and in Chapter 5 to those for the artists and record companies.

KEY CONCEPTS

1. A sound recording is not a song.
2. An arrangement of a musical composition may be a copyrightable derivative work, but most performing groups who create "head" arrangements do not create a copyrightable arrangement.
3. The compulsory mechanical license sets the stage for the bulk of mechanical licenses, which are negotiated.
4. Public performance rights are probably the most important rights in songs.
5. Infringement of songs occurs in piracy, unauthorized downloading, sampling, and occasionally in plagiarism of songs.
6. There is no "four bar" rule in infringement (i.e. it probably is an infringement to take four bars of somebody's song and use it as your own).

Musical Compositions

Initial Copyright Ownership—a Song is a Song

Copyrights in musical compositions, or songs, usually belong to music publishers. The publishers acquire the rights from songwriters with a transfer of copyright ownership. Copyright initially belongs to the person who creates the work, the author, and that copyright begins from the moment the work is "fixed in a tangible medium of expression." That is to say, as soon as the song is written down, recorded, or otherwise put into some medium from which it can later be perceived or reproduced, the federal copyrights spring into existence. Only if the work is never "fixed" would it be protected under state or common law.

Copyright in Musical Arrangements

Compulsory mechanical license
A license that is granted by the copyright act to use a musical composition, sound recording, or other copyrighted work. It is "compulsory" because the copyright owner must permit the use if the user conforms to the requirements of the statute regarding payment of royalties, and so on.

Although it is quite clear that musical arrangements are generally copyrightable as derivative works, the situation is not as clear with the arrangements of songs that are often found on popular recordings. The "mechanical right" is the right to reproduce a musical composition "mechanically" using such things as recordings and piano rolls. The **compulsory mechanical license** (see below) gives the licensee, the record company, the right to create an arrangement "to the extent necessary to conform it to the style or manner of interpretation of the performance involved" but that arrangement cannot alter the basic melody or character of the song and is not copyrightable as a derivative work. So, one could take a rap and turn it into country or a rock song and turn it into a rap and not create the need to get a license to make a derivative work. Because the language in a typical negotiated mechanical license often tracks or incorporates by reference to the statutory language for the compulsory license, most recorded arrangements of pop songs would not be copyrightable. In order to create a copyrightable arrangement, the arrangers would have to have specific permission to create a derivative work. That might be found, for example, when a marching band arrangement is created based on a popular song.

The case of the "Satin Doll"

A court case testing copyrightability of arrangements involved the copyrights in the famous jazz composition and recording "Satin Doll" by Duke Ellington. Ellington originally wrote "Satin Doll" as an instrumental in 1953. That year a "lead sheet" showing the melody was registered with the Copyright Office. A version with harmony and revised melody was recorded by Ellington and released in 1953 on Capitol Records. Billy Strayhorn (actually his estate) claimed copyright in the arrangement as recorded. The court stopped short of holding that there could never be copyrightable arrangements of harmony. Instead the court sent on to trial the question of whether the particular harmony was sufficiently original to qualify for protection. The case was ultimately settled, but the terms of that settlement were undisclosed. An interesting PBS documentary in 2007 indicated that it may have been Strayhorn who actually composed many of the hits, including "Satin Doll," that had been attributed to Ellington.

The case of the "Red, Red Robin"

A case which *did* decide that the usual piano–vocal arrangements made by publishers, and by implication the usual arrangements made by musicians in a recording, were not copyrightable involved the 1926 song, "When the Red, Red Robin Comes Bob-Bob-Bobbin' Along." The Court concluded that even when the publisher worked from a simple lyric and melody "lead Sheet" from the songwriter there was not enough creativity in a "stock" piano–vocal arrangement to qualify it for copyright protection as a derivative work.

> There must be more than cocktail pianist variations of the piece that are standard fare in the music trade by any competent musician. There must be such things as unusual vocal treatment, additional lyrics of consequence, unusual altered harmonies, novel sequential uses of themes—something of substance added making the piece to some extent a new work with the old song embedded in it but from which the new has developed. It is not merely a stylized version of the original song where a major artist may take liberties with the lyrics or tempo, the listener hearing basically the original tune.[1]

This is not the sort of thing that members of bands who do not write the basic melody or lyrics of a song like to hear. It is, however, something that they, and the band members who *do* write the lyrics and melodies, should be aware of.

The Compulsory Mechanical License

A bit of historical background on the compulsory **mechanical license** is necessary here to understand how and why some of its terms exist. Phonorecords, the objects on which sounds are recorded, have been around in some form or another, cylinder or platter, since before the turn of the twentieth century. By 1899 they had become a significant commercial commodity with an estimated 3,750,000 copies being sold each year. That number reached 27,500,000 per year by 1909, the year of the copyright law revision that gave music publishers the mechanical right. At that time the estimated number of phonographs in the United States was put at 1,310,000 and total sales of phonograph recordings since 1889 were estimated at 97,845,000 units.

During the decade between 1899 and 1909 recordings had become a significant business, and the means of manufacturing had become widespread enough, that the labels had begun to feel the effects of unauthorized copying of their recordings. The labels sought relief from Congress in the form of legislation amending the copyright law that would allow copyright in their recordings.

Mechanical license Permission from the copyright owner of a musical composition to manufacture and distribute copies of the composition embodied in phonorecords intended for sale to the public.

At the same time, music publishers were complaining that the copies of their songs embodied in the phonorecords and piano rolls should not be sold without some compensation to the owners of the copyrights in the musical compositions—a proposition which the labels would have preferred to reject. The labels maintained, and the decision of the United States Supreme Court in *White-Smith Music Publishing Co. v. Apollo Co.* backed up their position, that a recording that utilized some mechanical device such as a piano roll or cylinder or disc recording to reproduce the song, was not a copy of that song, because the song could not be visually perceived from the mechanical reproduction. The difficulty with that position was that the labels could not very well maintain that the non-copy of the song (the recording) should be entitled to some copyright protection of its own. The labels became much more concerned over the prospect of having to negotiate a license for every song they recorded and abandoned the argument that sound recordings should be copyrightable. Then they could maintain, with straight faces, that recordings were not copies of songs and that, therefore, the music publishers and songwriters were not entitled to any right to object to those copies being sold. The labels said that unfair trade laws adequately protected their own rights in the recordings.

The state of the piano roll and player piano manufacturing industry posed an additional complication. In 1899 the Aeolian Organ Company, the largest manufacturer of player pianos, sold 75,000 mechanical pianos and pianolas. By 1921, near their peak of popularity, an estimated 342,000 such devices were sold. The Aeolian company was not only a manufacturer of the pianos, but also of the rolls of music needed to make them perform. As it became clear after the *White-Smith* case in 1908 that Congress was going to give music publishers a right to control mechanical reproductions of their songs, it was reported that the Aeolian company had begun to enter into arrangements with many of the largest music publishers to be the exclusive manufacturer of piano rolls of their compositions.

Fearing that they might create an Aeolian piano roll monopoly, Congress responded to pleas of the other piano roll manufacturers to make the mechanical right subject to a compulsory license. The effect of the license was to be that once a musical composition copyright owner had allowed one party to make a mechanical reproduction of the song, then anyone else might do the same thing provided the publisher was compensated. At the urging of Congress, the record companies, pianola manufacturers, music publishing companies, and authors' groups arrived at a compromise which became the compulsory mechanical licensing provision of the 1909 Copyright Act. Although the labels complained that the statutory rate of two cents per copy was too high, they were pleased to have a guaranteed way to be able to reproduce recordings of popular songs without having to negotiate over a royalty rate for every recording.

Today, even though the vast majority of mechanical licenses issued by music publishers in the United States are negotiated and not compulsory, it is important to understand the workings of the compulsory (a.k.a. "statutory") license. Many mechanical licenses are pegged to the statutory rate. And, the existence of certain features of the statutory license establishes the parameters around which many of the terms of a negotiated license are set.

Availability of the compulsory mechanical license

The compulsory mechanical license is available for the manufacturing and distribution of "phonorecords" of non-dramatic musical works to the public. (A license to do the same thing, but not for public distribution, would usually be referred to as a "transcription license.") The phonorecord is the material object, be it compact disc, vinyl disc, or other device, in which both the sound recording copyright and the musical composition copyright are fixed when a recording of a song is made and distributed. Though not specifically defined as such, the term also includes digital delivery of "copies", i.e. a **"digital phonorecord delivery**." In the United States, licenses for reproduction of songs in videos (motion pictures or music videos) are referred to as **"synchronization"** licenses. In many other places in the world, video or **"videogram"** licenses would also be called "mechanical licenses"—a source of some confusion.

A record company can obtain a compulsory mechanical license for a song once the music publisher has allowed a recording of the song to be made and distributed to the public. So, while a music publisher could control who made the first recording of a song, after that any record company or artist could make a "cover version" recording of the same song by using the compulsory license. Even when the compulsory license is available, its terms are not viewed with much favor by record companies. They would prefer to negotiate a lower rate, less frequent payments, and different accounting for returns. So, because the first time recording of a song requires a negotiated license, and because the labels desire to have terms more favorable than the compulsory license, there are not many actual *compulsory* mechanical licenses issued.

Statutory rates

When the compulsory mechanical license was created in the 1909 revision of the copyright law the rate was set in the statute as two cents per copy. It remained that way until 1978. Since 1978 the rate has been changed numerous times through procedures set up in the Copyright Act (see Table 4.1). Even though the rate is now determined by the Copyright Royalty Board (**CRB**), it is still referred to in the industry as the "statutory rate." Labels often "get a rate" below the statutory rate, most often 75 percent of the statutory rate.

But more than just physical copies are covered by the compulsory mechanical license. In the CRB 2009 decision, the publishers, labels, and Internet service providers agreed that full downloads, limited downloads, ring tunes, and other digital phonorecord deliveries were also covered. The CRB decided on those rates as indicated in Table 4.2.

Some of the terms of the new rates need further definition:

- *Permanent downloads* are those that may be retained and used indefinitely by the end user.
- *Limited downloads* include those where a copy of the song embodied in the recording is delivered to the users but is only accessible for a limited amount of time (as in a subscription service), or a limited number of times. This is

---

Digital phonorecord delivery A term in the Copyright Act for a download of a recording.

Synchronization The right of the owner of a musical composition copyright to use the composition in time relation to visual images, such as in movies or television shows, or perhaps in multimedia.

Videogram A video recording of a motion picture, music video, or other visual work. Usually the term refers to videograms that are manufactured and distributed for consumer purchase.

CRB The panel of three administrative judges established by Congress to adjust or set compulsory royalty rates for mechanical, digital performance of sound recordings, digital delivery of phonorecords and others.

Table 4.1 Compulsory mechanical license rate changes

Date(s)	Rate	Authority
1909–1977	2 cents per copy	Copyright Act of 1909, § 1(e)
January 1, 1978	2.5 cents per copy or 0.5 cents per minute	1976 Copyright Act, § 115
January 1, 1981	4 cents per copy or 0.75 cents per minute	1980 Copyright Royalty Tribunal rate adjustment proceeding
January 1, 1983	4.25 cents per copy or 0.8 cents per minute	1980 Copyright Royalty Tribunal rate adjustment proceeding
July 1, 1984	4.5 cents per copy or 0.8 cents per minute	1980 Copyright Royalty Tribunal rate adjustment proceeding
January 1, 1986	5 cents per copy or 0.85 cents per minute	1980 Copyright Royalty Tribunal rate adjustment proceeding
January 1, 1988 to December 31, 1989	5.25 cents per copy or 1 cent per minute	1980 Copyright Royalty Tribunal rate adjustment proceeding, based on consumer price index, December 1985 to September 1987.
January 1, 1990 to December 31, 1991	5.7 cents per copy or 1.1 cents per minute	Adjustment based on consumer price index, October 1987 to October 1989.
January 1, 1992 to December 31, 1993	6.25 cents per copy or 1.2 cents per minute	Adjustment based on consumer price index, October 1989 to October 1991.
January 1, 1994 to December 31, 1995	6.6 cents per copy or 1.25 cents per minute	Adjustment based on consumer price index, October 1991 to October 1993.
January 1, 1996 to December 31, 1997	6.95 cents per copy or 1.3 cents per minute	Adjustment based on consumer price index, September 1993 to October 1995.
January 1, 1998 to December 31,1999	7.1 cents per copy or 1.35 cents per minute	CARP Proceeding, 62 FR 63506, December 1, 1997.
January 1, 2000 to December 31, 2001	7.55 cents per copy or 1.45 cents per minute	CARP Proceeding, 62 FR 63506, December 1, 1997.
January 1, 2002 to December 31, 2003	8.0 cents per copy or 1.55 cents per minute	CARP Proceeding, 62 FR 63506, December 1, 1997.
January 1, 2004 to December 31, 2005	8.5 cents per copy or 1.65 cents per minute	CARP Proceeding, 62 FR 63506, December 1, 1997.
January 1, 2006 to December 31, 2007	9.1 cents per copy or 1.75 cents per minute	CARP Proceeding, 62 FR 63506, December 1, 1997.
January 1, 1998 to December 31, 1999	9.1 cents per copy or 1.75 cents per minute	CRB Decision, 74 FR 4529, January 26, 2009.

Source: Copyright Office, Licensing Division

Table 4.2 The compulsory mechanical license rates for other uses until 2013

Type of Use	Rate
Physical phonorecords	9.1 cents per copy or 1.75 cents per minute of playing time, whichever is larger.
Permanent downloads	Same as physical rate above.
Limited downloads	10.5 percent of service provider's revenues.
Ringtunes	24 cents per copy.
Interactive streaming	10.5 percent of service provider's revenues.*
Promotional uses	Zero.
Non-interactive streaming	Does not require a mechanical license.

Source : CRB Decision, 74 F.R. 4529, January 26, 2009

* There is also a minimum fee that allows small subscribers to an amount per subscriber per month.

to be distinguished from a stream where the user can only listen to the song during the stream and does not retain a copy on their computer.

- *Interactive streaming* is when the listener on the Web gets to choose which songs to listen to and when to listen to them. The publishers, labels, and CRB agreed that this use did require a mechanical license. The rate in Table 4.2 *includes* the musical composition performance royalty (ASCAP, BMI, SESAC) of about 5.5 percent.
- *Promotional uses* include uses by the label or others to promote the recording and song, generally less than 30-second clips. This may be an interactive stream, or a free trial time for streaming, or limited download services. These are covered by the compulsory mechanical license, but have a royalty of zero.
- *Non-interactive streaming* is when the listener does not get to choose which songs to listen to or when to hear them (outside of perhaps skipping the next song in the rotation). This is a performance of the song, but does not deliver a copy to the user, so it is not subject to the compulsory mechanical license.
- There are also minimum fees set that would allow small webcasters to pay a per use fee or an amount per subscriber per month.

Other compulsory mechanical provisions

The statute also requires that the compulsory licensee (the record label) file a notice of intention to obtain a compulsory license with the copyright owner. It requires that payment be made for each record "distributed," meaning the label has "voluntarily and permanently parted with its possession." To account for the fact that recordings are usually sold subject to return by the retailer, the Copyright Office has made regulations further defining "distributed" to mean the earlier of when revenue is recognized by the label from the sale of the record, or when nine months has passed from the date of shipment. The labels would prefer to be able to withhold some payments as a reserve against anticipated returns for a longer period and to make payments quarterly instead of monthly.

Performing Rights and Music

Public performance rights for songs are particularly important in the recording industry. Income from public performances is the largest source of revenue for music publishing (as discussed in Chapter 6). Public performance rights in musical compositions were first added to the copyright laws in 1897 but did not take on particular significance until the 1909 copyright revision, in part because minimum damages for unauthorized performances were so small, $100 for the first performance and $50 dollars for subsequent performances or "as to the court shall appear to be just." During the 1909 revision process the provision for civil liability for public performance was amended to apply to public performances "for profit," the idea being not to make church groups, school children, and other such groups liable for copyright infringement when they performed songs publicly. ASCAP was formed in 1914 to begin a systematic way for publishers and writers to collect for public performance and by 1917 had landed a test case in the US Supreme Court on the issue of just what constituted a "for profit" public performance.

The case of "Sweethearts"

Composer Victor Herbert, one of the ASCAP founders, found his songs from the operetta "Sweethearts" being performed in Shanley's restaurant by professional singers and musicians for the enjoyment of the diners. Shanley argued that he was not charging the patrons to hear the music so the music was not "for profit" within the meaning of the statute. In a brief opinion, Justice Holmes explained that the public performance right did, indeed, apply to such situations because the music really was being performed for the profit of the restaurant, regardless of whether an admission fee was charged. "The defendant's performances are not eleemosynary," said Justice Holmes.

> They are part of a total for which the public pays, and the fact that the price of the whole is attributed to a particular item which those present are expected to order, is not important. . . . If music did not pay it would be given up. If it pays it is out of the public's pocket. Whether it pays or not the purpose of employing it is profit and that is enough.[2]

Public performances exemptions

The current copyright law defines public performances broadly. To perform a work "publicly" means, "(1) . . . at a place open to the public or at any place where a substantial number of persons outside of a normal circle of a family and its social acquaintances is gathered; or (2) to transmit or otherwise communicate a performance . . . to a place specified in clause (1) or to the public . . ." So, private clubs and most broadcast, closed circuit, or cable transmissions are covered. Although the words "for profit" were dropped from the public performance right in the 1976 revision to broaden the application of the right, a number of specific exemptions were added, generally at the behest of groups representing the special interests who wanted exemptions. All of these exemptions apply at least to non-dramatic works—that is those where the songs are not used in some manner to accompany a dramatic presentation or to tell a story, such as an opera or Broadway musical. The list below paraphrases the statute and covers, out of the ten specific exemptions, those most interesting or most significant to the recording industry. For details on these and the other exemptions, refer to the statute.

- Performances by instructors or pupils in the course of face-to-face teaching at non-profit educational institutions, or in distance learning courses (applies to all works);
- Performances of non-dramatic literary or musical works in transmissions for educational broadcasting from government or non-profit educational institutions;
- Performances of non-dramatic literary or musical works in the course of religious services at a place of religious worship or assembly (also applies to dramatic musical works of religious nature);
- Non-commercial performances other than in transmissions where there is no payment to musicians or promoters, and either no admission charge, or the proceeds are used for charitable, religious, or educational purposes;
- Public reception of transmissions on single sets of the kinds of receiving devices commonly found in the home if there is no admission charge and no further transmission;
- Performances in stores selling recordings and musical works where the purpose is to promote sale of the recordings, or the hardware used to view or listen to the recordings, and there is no admission charge and no transmission.

In 1998, Congress bowed to the interests of restaurants and other merchants when it passed the "Fairness in Musical Licensing Act." That Act expanded exemption for the public reception of a broadcast transmission to cover most eating and drinking establishments of fewer than 3,750 square feet and most other establishments of fewer than 2,000 square feet. In 2000, the WTO ruled that the amendment was inconsistent with United States' treaty obligations under the Berne Convention and WTO treaties because it exempted too many establishments. Later, a WTO arbitrator ruled that the United States should bring its statutes into compliance by July, 2001. Failure to bring its laws into compliance could allow other members of the WTO to impose trade sanctions against the United States. By 2010, Congress had still not acted. There are frequently amendments proposed to the law to exempt other performances, usually by special interests that simply do not want to have to pay for performance licenses. Congress then finds it must balance the economic and political interests of the copyright owners with the economic and political interests of other groups.

Internet Activities

- Visit the Copyright Office website. Search the records to find out who owns the copyright in the Musical Composition, "My Sweet Lord." NOTE: You'll have to use the RE (Renewal) registration because this work was first registered before 1978. Who owns the copyright in that song?
- Visit two song lyrics or song tab sites. Is it clear whether they are licensed? What kinds of licenses should they have? Reproduction? Display? Performance? Should they be required to have a license at all? Why or why not?
- Visit two Internet music sites of any kind. What kinds of licenses should these sites have for the use of the musical compositions (songs)? Music performance? Reproduction? Distribution? Public display? Combine your list with the rest of the class.
- Not everybody likes copyright. Do a broad "Google" or other search to find opposing points of view. Try "copyright is good" or "copyright is bad" for your search. Make a pooled list of reasons pro and con with the rest of the class.

Copyright Infringement: "You Stole My Song!"

Every Songwriter's Nightmare

Copyright infringement in the music business is most likely to be either plagiarism of the song, unauthorized sampling of the song or recording, or unauthorized downloading. We will deal first with the plagiarism variety.

"Get a hit, get an infringement suit" is a common saying in the music business. Instances of alleged infringement are common for a number of reasons. (1) There are some charlatans who think they can make a quick buck off of someone else's success. There was not really an infringement, but they figure if they claimed that there was and sued, they might get a settlement and a few thousand dollars. (2) Lots of popular songs *do* sound a lot alike. There are form and style constraints in much of popular music. There are only so many ways to arrange notes in a melody that would be pleasing to most people. Given those two factors, it is quite possible that two composers could create works that did, indeed, have similarities, even without ever having seen or heard the other's work. In that case one composer is likely to think that the other has infringed.

It is rather difficult to prove infringement in court. The person claiming infringement must be able to prove several things:

1. That they are the author or owner of the copyrights in the work that is claimed to be infringed. That is usually not too difficult since a copyright registration form is *prima facie* evidence (i.e. sufficient by itself with no other evidence being necessary) of the validity and ownership of the copyright.

2. That the other party copied their work. To show this the plaintiff must prove that the other party (a) somehow had access to their work and (b) that the two works are "substantially" similar. The access is fairly easy to prove if the original work enjoyed widespread public distribution or performance but can be quite difficult if the plaintiff's work was unpublished. For writers who send out unsolicited demos, this is often a problem because it is difficult to say that a demo actually got to the alleged infringer, or had a reasonable chance of doing so. That is one reason why artists, producers, and publishers do not like to get unsolicited demos. So, if the demo is not addressed in the right way to the right party, then it is probably going into the trash without further review.

"Substantial similarity" means the two songs must be similar in more ways than simply style or an occasional few notes. There is an old saying that one can copy up to four bars of music and not be infringing. NOT SO! In the case of Saturday Night Live's parody of the "I Love New York" song and advertising campaign, the court said that the copying of only four notes of the original composition could be an infringement. NBC and Saturday Night Live were ultimately allowed to use the song because their use was deemed to be a fair use since it was a parody of the original. (See Fair Use discussion in Chapter 3.)

The case of "How Deep is Your Love?"

"Substantially similarity" by itself is not enough to prove infringement. A fellow named Ronald Selle sued Barry Gibb and the other Bee Gee brothers for an alleged infringement by the song "How Deep is Your Love." The songs were so similar that when Barry played the plaintiff's song on a piano in the courtroom he thought it was his own. But the court ruled that since the plaintiff's song had not been published or performed publicly anywhere that the Gibb brothers could have heard it, there was no reasonable possibility of access so there could be no infringement. One the other hand, if the two works are identical, access can be presumed.

The case of "My Sweet Lord"

The infringing songwriter does not have to have done the dirty work intentionally. George Harrison apparently fell victim to being familiar with the hit song "He's So Fine" as performed by the Chiffons. He wrote his song, "My Sweet Lord," that was similar in structure, much of the melody, and some of the lyrics. Similarities even existed down to accidental grace notes in the two songs. Harrison testified that he did not deliberately copy "He's So Fine." Said the judge:

> [Harrison], in seeking musical materials to clothe his thoughts, was working with various possibilities. As he tried this possibility and that, there came to the surface of his mind a particular combination that pleased him as being

one he felt would be appealing to a prospective listener; in other words, that this combination of sounds would work. Why? Because his subconscious knew it already had worked in a song his conscious mind did not remember.[3]

Even though convinced that Harrison did not deliberately copy "He's So Fine," the judge ordered him to pay $1.6 million in damages. Through rather protracted litigation and a complex settlement, the rights to "He's So Fine" in the US, UK, and Canada ultimately ended up with Harrison for the sum of $270,020.

But the principle of subconscious infringement, every songwriter's nightmare, had ended up a permanent part of copyright law.

DIY Activities

- Visit the CCLI website (www.ccli.com). What kinds of licenses do they give? To whom? For what purpose? Could you submit a song of your own through CCLI?
- Visit a song lyrics site. Can you put lyrics for one of your own songs up on the site? What benefits would you get?
- What if your band wants to do a cover recording of "Roll with it" by Steve Miller. Can you get a mechanical license to do this from the Harry Fox Agency? How much would it cost the band to do this and make 100 CD copies? At the Harry Fox Agency website, use the Songfile search and Limited Quantity Licenses tabs to get where you are going.

New Directions for Copyright?

Much has been written about whether the existing copyright system can serve effectively into the twenty-first century. New media, new methods of creating works, and new delivery systems are certain to stretch the existing notions of copyright, authorship, and fair use. Copyright law has always been changing in response to new technology. It was a new technology, the invention of moveable type by Johannes Gutenberg in 1456,[4] which made possible the mass reproduction of copies of a work. Controlling the right to reproduce copies of works began as a method of censorship in England in the late 1400s and 1500s. The Crown wished to control who could print books and other materials in order to control the content of those books. Only certain printers were granted licenses or "patents" to print. And only those printers who produced publications to the king or queen's liking were likely to get a license.

By the early 1700s it was not political turmoil that resulted in the passage of the first copyright act, the Statute of Anne of 1710, but rather the needs of commerce. By then there were enough competing printing presses in England so that when any printer began to publish a book, it was soon pirated by the competition there, and in the colonies. To get some protection from piracy the printers went to Parliament and requested a statutory privilege in the name of themselves and the authors of the works. Parliament noted:

> Printers, Booksellers, and other Persons have of late frequently taken the Liberty of Printing, Reprinting, and Publishing, or causing to be Printed, Reprinted, and Published Books, and other Writings, without the Consent of the Authors or Proprietors of such Books and Writings, to their very great Detriment, and too often to the Ruin of them and their families.

The right to make copies (copy, right?) was extended to authors and those who took their rights from those authors for the purposes of preventing piracy and "for the Encouragement of Learned Men to Compose and Write useful Books." These twofold purposes, protecting commercial interests and protecting authors so that they will be encouraged to create more works, have been the significant driving forces for copyright law ever since. (Recall the discussion from Chapter 3 about the "Three Cs of Copyright.")

Copyright laws continue to evolve in the face of changing technology. Even considering only changes to copyright law that directly affected the recording industry as listed in Table 4.3, it is clear that many changes have been effected in reaction to new technologies, new media, and new methods of utilizing works.

Table 4.3 Copyright law changes and the music business

1790	First US copyright law protects books, charts, and maps
1831	Musical works first protected
1856	Dramatic works first protected, including public performance rights
1897	Public performance rights for musical works protected
1909	Mechanical rights for musical works added, unpublished musical works could be protected by registration
1912	Motion pictures first protected
1972	Sound recordings first protected
1978	All works created, whether published or not, are protected. Jukebox performance rights protected. Compulsory mechanical license rate subject to change by the Copyright Royalty Tribunal (later the Librarian of Congress)
1982	Piracy of recordings and motion pictures made a felony with increased fines and jail terms
1984	Record rental prohibited
1992	Audio Home Recording Act exempts home copying and places a royalty on digital recorders and blank digital media
1994	Anti-bootlegging rights for performers of live musical events
1995	Digital public performance rights for sound recordings, digital delivery rights for sound recordings, and the musical works embodied in the phonorecords
1998	Digital Millennium Copyright Act, Fairness in Musical Licensing Act, and Copyright Term Extension Act.

Sources: Various statutory provisions, Title 17 US Code; and R. Gorman & J. Ginsburg, *Copyright Cases and Materials*, 7th edition (Egan, MN: Foundation Press/West Academic, 2006).

Everyone is a manufacturer

It is no longer necessary to have a printing press to reproduce a book, a film studio to copy a motion picture, or a record-pressing plant to make a copy of a phonorecord. The photocopiers, computers, and CD and DVD "burners" that are in the homes of many have moved manufacturing out of the hands of the capitalists and into the hands of the consumers.

Mass production allowed copyright owners to control their works at the point of production or distribution. One license issued to one producer was sufficient. Where there are thousands of users and thousands of copyright owners and users, as is the case in musical performance rights, an intermediate agency is needed to keep track of all of the users and to distribute appropriate royalties to all of the many copyright owners. When the number of users and manufacturers reaches into the millions, as is the case with photocopiers and CD burners, the copyright owners are faced with a dilemma. They must either prohibit the users from making copies or using the works in unauthorized ways, find another control and licensing point in the distribution or manufacture or some part of the process, or allow the uses and hope to make their profits through more easily controlled uses. Motion picture copyright owners require that digital video disc systems have a system in the playback hardware that prohibits copying—either single or serial copies—which is moderately effective.

The recording industry tried the approach of allowing analog and digital home taping by placing a royalty on the devices which allows digital recording, thus finding a different point in the manufacturing process where the control is easier to accomplish. Instead of attempting to license the manufacture of the copy of the recording, which occurs in the private homes of millions of consumers, the industry licenses the manufacture of the recorders and blank media which still requires mass production technology and only has a few producers to contend with. For the individual consumer, the barrier to entry into the market of being a manufacturer of high quality copies of recordings is low—the cost of a CD burner (part of most computers), a CD player, and a blank disc. The consumer is not concerned with being able to make thousands of copies per hour or per day. One or two copies are probably all the consumer wants. That system, the Audio Home Recording Act, ultimately did not prove very effective because computers and their "burners" were exempt. (See Chapter 5 for extended discussion of the Audio Home Recording Act.)

The other method is to control delivery of the work itself—that is what the digital delivery of phonorecords provision passed in 1995 does. The provider of the soft copy (which the consumer converts into a hard copy) purchases the license and keeps track of how many digital deliveries have been made so that the copyright owners can be appropriately compensated. Whatever approach is used, the trick is to find a point in the manufacturing or distribution chain where the copyright owner can exert some control (licensing) over the process that ultimately leads to the consumers making their own copies. The trials and tribulations of the recording industry as it attempted to cope with rampant Internet theft of recordings, Internet distribution of hard and digital copies, and Internet promotion and marketing are explored throughout this book.

Everyone is an author

With a computer and a laser printer, anyone can produce copies that would have made Gutenberg proud. With a computer and MIDI set-up anyone can produce high quality orchestral recordings that would have made Beethoven proud. Of course, these people can also author new works. They may not possess the creative writing or composing talent to produce great works, but they can easily produce copyrightable works. They can even distribute copies of these works electronically without the need to secure the services of a production plant. Mass media professor John Pavlik has a framework for media analysis, which concentrates on the way media content is "gathered, processed and produced; transmitted; stored; and retrieved and displayed."[5] But with the proliferation of cell phone video and audio recorders, other consumer audio and video recorders, and simple to use computer software for almost every creative use, we should add consideration of how the content was created. It is that phenomenon that led to the explosive popularity of YouTube.

Where is the editor?

There is one problem with a world where "everyone" is an author or composer and self-distributor via the Internet. With the publisher, who had access to the means of mass production through investment of the necessary capital, serving as a filter or gatekeeper, only those works that the publishers thought worthy would reach the public. The merits and benefits of having a filter or censor in the information stream are debatable. On the one hand, some voices and meritorious works may never be heard or seen. On the other hand, we did not have to open millions of oysters in order to find one pearl.

With so many avenues of free expression open to the public at large we might like to have an editor or publisher do some filtering for us—to select which oysters are likely to contain pearls before we begin opening, or even to present us with a nicely strung set of pearls. Of course, we do have to compensate the publisher or record company for all of the work of opening all of those non-pearl-bearing oysters and for nurturing those oysters that later *do* produce some pearls. If everyone with a computer can produce a book and everyone with a fairly simple MIDI set-up can produce a sound recording, and then make it available for the rest of the public (distribute it) through the Internet, we are still going to need music publishers, record companies, and patrons of the arts to help us decide which works are deserving of our attention because of their artistic merit or even simply because of their mass appeal.

Summary

Copyrights in musical compositions provide important revenues for music publishers and songwriters and protection from unauthorized use of their songs. The right to reproduce a musical composition in phonorecords for distribution to the public is the "mechanical" right. That applies to physical copies and to digital phonorecord deliveries. Licenses to record songs are usually issued through the Harry Fox Agency (see discussion in Chapter 6). The statutory rate, set by the Copyright Royalty Board, is 9.1 cents per copy until 2013. Many record companies negotiate a rate lower than that, often three-fourths of the statutory rate. The statutory rate must be paid if the record company uses the compulsory mechanical license provisions of the Copyright Act. Those provisions mean a song copyright owner must permit others to record and release a song once the first recording of that song is released.

Public performance rights for songs apply to most situations when a song is played live, from a recording, or broadcast to/at a place open to the public or at a place where a substantial number of people outside the family and normal circle of social acquaintances is gathered. That covers most places and although there are many exemptions, there is no broad "non-profit" exemption. Public performance rights are licensed through the performing rights organizations (see Chapter 6).

Infringement of musical composition copyrights comes about through piracy, unauthorized downloading, and plagiarism. In proving an infringement case, the plaintiff must show that the infringer had access to the protected work, either directly or indirectly, through widespread dissemination of the original, and that the two works are substantially similar. It does not matter whether the infringer intentionally copied the protected work.

As the means to manufacture, copy, and distribute works have become more widespread through the diffusion of CD burners, Internet sites, downloads, mobile phones, and copiers, it has become increasingly difficult for copyright owners to protect their works and to profit from the use of their works in ways otherwise protected by the copyright laws.

Case Study: Music Copyrights

The *real* case of *BTE v. Bonnecaze*, 43 F. Supp 2d 619 (E.D. La. 1999).

Better Than Ezra (BTE) is a rock band that was formed by four Louisiana State University Students in 1988. Their first major release was the album "Deluxe" on Elektra records in 1995. (It had previously been released on an indie label.) After that release, the drummer, Cary Bonnecaze, left the group in 1996. After leaving, Bonnecaze sued the other members of the band to claim a share in the copyrights in the songs created by the band. Kevin Griffin, the lead vocalist and guitarist, claimed that he wrote all of the songs. He says he would introduce the basic songs to the band and then they would "refine the material." Bonnecaze claimed he contributed "ideas and insights" in "working up" the songs.

Unfortunately for Bonnecaze, the court held that he had not presented any evidence that he actually contributed anything to the actual songs (as opposed to the recordings of the songs). To have copyright claim as a joint author of the songs, the court said he would have to have some copyrightable contribution and then have some evidence that that contribution was fixed in a tangible medium of expression *separate* from the main recording. Said the court, "If Bonnecaze had wished to share in the fruits of Griffin's 'rough drafts,' then Bonnecaze had either to satisfy the requirements of joint authorship (which he failed to do) or to contract with Griffin for a portion of the royalties." No one disputed that Bonnecaze participated in the creation of the sound recording copyrights on which he had played drums.

Want to learn more? Find the full court opinion in the library or online using the citation at the top of the page. BTE still exists and had a web page, betterthanezra.com. They now tour as a trio.

QUESTIONS FOR REVIEW

- What would it take for members of a band to own copyrights in the musical compositions written by some of the members? Which members would own copyrights in those songs (compositions)?
- What is a compulsory mechanical license? How does it work? What are the royalty rates?
- What are the circumstances under which a songwriter should be paid when their song is played in public? How about a broadcast or Internet transmission?
- Copyright laws generally change with the times. What are some of the problems now with the way copyright laws handle the creation of works, the making of copies, the distribution of copies, and of performances of works in the digital age, especially on the Internet?
- A band performs a cover version of a popular song in a club one night. Who is liable for the public performance of the song? Who usually obtains a performance license? (You may need to look ahead at Chapter 6 on performance licensing.)

5 Sound Recording Copyrights Ⓟ

Introduction–A Sound Recording is Not a Song

Copyrights in sound recordings, as distinguished from the song that is recorded, typically belong to the record company, less frequently to the recording artist or producer. Although rights in musical compositions have existed since 1831, rights in recordings have only existed since 1972. The recording rights are much more limited than the rights in compositions, particularly in the area of public performance. Record companies and artists want to expand their public performance right, now restricted to digital performances via the Internet and satellite, to include regular broadcasts. The history in the US suggests that recording copyright owners have been able to gradually expand their rights but face substantial opposition in the areas of home recording and broadcast performance. Two areas of special interest with sound recording copyrights include the protection of "beats" and the sampling of recordings. Widespread use of both has lead to litigation between the owners of recordings and those using the beats or sampling the earlier recordings.

KEY CONCEPTS

1. A sound recording is not a song.
2. Copyright in sound recordings did not exist in the US until 1972.
3. Rights in sound recordings, particularly the public performance right, are generally narrower than in musical compositions.
4. Infringement of recordings occurs in piracy, unauthorized downloading, and sampling, but not in plagiarism of recordings.
5. Sampling usually takes part of both the song and the sound recording copyrights.

Pre-1972—A Recording is Not a Song

Even after the creation of the compulsory mechanical license in 1909, the labels and the songwriters and publishers continued to be at odds over the creation of a copyright in sound recordings. A series of bills introduced in 1912, 1925, 1926,

1928, and 1930 all contained provisions for copyright for sound recordings. All were met with opposition on the grounds it was not fair to require a compulsory license from the writers and publishers for their songs and give the labels an unfettered right in their recordings. None of the proposals were met with much enthusiasm by Congress.

In 1932, a new player, the broadcast industry, emerged as an important force in the discussions. For the first time the National Association of Broadcasters came forward to oppose the creation of copyrights in sound recordings, contending that small broadcasters would be hurt if record companies were given a public performance right. Better, said the broadcasters, to limit the sound recording rights to "dubbing" or duplication. With record companies, music publishers, and broadcasters all at odds over a copyright for sound recordings, no further progress was made through the 1950s.

Enter—the pirates

8-track tape
An audio tape with room to record eight separate "tracks" of information. Consumer eight track tapes were endless loop tape cartridges, similar to those used in broadcasting, which contained four separate stereo programs.

Piracy Unauthorized duplications of sound recordings where the person or organization literally dubs a copy of the recording and sells a copy with identical sounds on it. Piracy is usually distinguished from *counterfeiting*, although the latter is a form of piracy.

The introduction of the **8-track tape** cartridge player in the early 1960s meant that there was a convenient way for people to take and play prerecorded music virtually anywhere. Recordings could now be played in automobiles or at a picnic with simple equipment that could reproduce reasonable sound quality. The tape cartridge caught on rapidly and by 1974 there were 6.7 million 8-track tape players (including auto and home) shipped in the United States by the hardware manufacturers. The volume of tape sales had risen to 112 million units that same year. At the same time the volume of sales of vinyl records had risen to 480 million units (including singles and albums).

The popularity of tape players enticed others into the market. Tape duplicating equipment was much less costly than record pressing equipment, easier to use, and the product much easier to handle. Without the technological barriers to entry into the market, **piracy** blossomed. By 1971, the volume of unauthorized tape sales had risen to an estimated 100 million per year—about one third the sales volume of legitimate tape recordings.

The record companies were nearly powerless to stop it. A 1955 case had determined that recordings were not directly copyrightable under the 1909 copyright law. Although music publishers had rights in the songs being copied on the pirate recordings, they did not have an effectual remedy for several reasons. The mechanical royalties for music publishing rights on any one album amounted to only about 20 cents (10 songs at the then 2 cents per copy "statutory" mechanical royalty rate). Furthermore, those royalties were often divided between different publishers because the copyrights in the songs recorded did not always belong to the same publisher. So, the publishers' interest per copy was not as high as that of the labels, who were losing about $1.80 gross margin per copy. Additionally, some of the pirates claimed that they could make the copies legitimately under the provisions of the compulsory mechanical license.

Once the copyright owner of the song had allowed a recording of the song to be made and distributed, anyone else was allowed to make a "similar use" of the song if they paid the two cents per copy royalty. The federal courts were divided as to whether a "similar use" meant that a new recording had to be made with new musicians, etc., or whether that phrase meant that a total duplication could be made. So, even if the publishers might desire to stop the piracy they could sometimes be prevented from any remedies if the pirates paid for a compulsory mechanical license. Many pirates included labels on their recordings with statements such as "All royalties required by law have been paid." Sometimes that was true, more often it was not. Finally, the penalties available for criminal copyright infringement were only at the misdemeanor level—a small fine and up to one year in prison. Some pirates simply considered these "inconveniences" part of the cost of doing their business.

There was a push for legislative relief at both the state and federal level. For their part, the labels had been actively lobbying the individual states to pass anti-piracy legislation. However, by 1971 only eight states had done so. Congress had been considering a total revision of the copyright law since 1962 but appeared unable to reconcile all competing interests. A provision protecting sound recordings was included in the 1966 version of the new law passed by the House of Representatives, but that bill failed to pass the Senate before a new House was elected so Congress had to start over the following year.

1972–1977—A Sound Recording is Still Not a Song

In late 1970 the labels got Congress to consider an amendment that would separate the issue of sound recording copyrights from the rest of the revision process. After some compromises on the extent of rights afforded to the owners of the new sound recording copyrights, the legislation passed in 1971, and became effective February 15, 1972. The primary compromise was that there would be no right of public performance associated with the sound recording.

The broadcasters, particularly radio broadcasters, whose programming consisted primarily of playing recordings on the air, objected to the possible requirement that they pay a royalty to the record companies. Their main arguments were that they already paid the music publishers through the performing rights organizations of ASCAP, BMI, and SESAC, and that their airplay of the recordings was the primary vehicle by which the labels gained the promotional exposure necessary to get consumers interested in buying the records. If the broadcasters had to pay, it would be unfair, said the broadcasters, to allow the labels to profit twice from the airplay, once from the sale of the records that the airplay promoted, and once from the payment of a performance royalty by the broadcasters to the labels. Congress also specifically noted in the legislative history, but not in the language of the statute itself, that the new copyrights were not meant to stop private non-commercial home recording from broadcasts or from copying other recordings. The state anti-piracy laws, which ultimately got passed in 48 of the 50 states, would be allowed to remain in effect until 2067.

The legislative history of the 1971 law also noted that the new rights in recordings were specifically subject to the **"First Sale Doctrine,"** which states that once the copyright owner has unconditionally parted with a legitimately manufactured copy of the work, the disposition of that particular copy can no

First Sale Doctrine
The lawful owner of a copy of a work may dispose of possession of that *copy* in any way they wish. Copies may be re-sold, rented, leased, or given away. An exception allows the owners of copyrights in sound recordings and computer programs to prohibit rental of those works.

longer be controlled. Future disposition could include resale or rental. Due to the fact that vinyl records were easily damaged and worn out and that there was not a very large installed base of home recording equipment, the record rental business was not a significant threat to the recording industry in the early 1970s. A decade later the situation had changed and Congress passed the Record Rental Amendment of 1984 (see below).

The music publishers joined with the labels to gain protection for sound recordings. Piracy was hurting their royalties from the sale of legitimate copies of the recordings and Congress added that the unauthorized reproduction of a sound recording was also unauthorized reproduction of the recorded work. So the publishers now also had a remedy to fight record piracy, having discovered that both income streams were negatively impacted by the sale of pirate copies.

1978–Present—A Sound Recording is Still Not Song

The current copyright law (which Congress passed in 1976) took effect January 1, 1978. The new law specifies separate rights in sound recordings. Rights in sound recordings are not as broad as rights in other kinds of works.

Exclusive Rights in Sound Recordings

Sound-alike
A recording made to sound as much like the one by the original artists as possible. It is a new recording, but the musicians and singers imitate the sounds on the previous recording.

- The right to reproduce a sound recording is limited to literally duplicating the recording in ways that actually recapture the actual sounds fixed in the original recording. Thus, one could make another recording that imitated or attempted to sound just like the original recording as long as the new one was made by hiring new musicians, singers, engineers, and so on, and making an entirely independent recording. Unless the makers of the "**sound-alike**" recordings failed to secure mechanical licenses to make recordings of the songs or marketed the recordings in some way that misled consumers to think that they were the original recordings by the original artists, in violation of unfair competition laws, the "sound-alike" would be perfectly legitimate.
- The right to prepare a derivative work is rather limited too, to rearranging, remixing, or otherwise altering the sequence or sounds of the original recording.
- The right to distribute copies to the public is somewhat enhanced for sound recordings, as will be discussed below under the Record Rental Amendment.
- There is no right of public display for sound recordings. However, if one displayed the *artwork* for a recording, that would require a license. Look at the encoded side of a CD. It is not very exciting.
- The right to public performance for a sound recording only covers performances by means of digital audio transmission, and there are some major exemptions to that, as will be discussed later.

Internet Activities

- Visit the Copyright Office website. Search the records to find out who owns the copyright in the Sound Recording (SR), "My Sweet Lord." Recall the exercise from the previous chapter. What is unusual about the ownership of the song and recording copyrights for this song and recording?
- Visit SoundExchange's website, www.soundexchange.com. Look under the "About" tab and the "SoundExchange by the Numbers" sub-tab. What were total collections for the most recent year?
- Visit two Internet music sites of any kind. Should these sites have any licenses to use the sound recordings? Sound Recording Performance? Reproduction? Distribution? Combine your list with the rest of the class.
- Should computers and drives have a built-in license that covers the reproduction of recordings for personal use? Do a broad "Google" or other search to find opposing points of view. Try "home copying" or "home recording license." Combine your results with the rest of the class to get a list of "pros and cons."

Record rental

The Record Rental Amendment of 1984 changed the Copyright Act to create an exception to the first sale doctrine by allowing owners of sound recording copyrights to prohibit rental of phonograms. It prohibits "for purposes of direct or indirect commercial advantage . . . the rental, lease, or lending, or . . . any other act or practice in the nature of rental, lease, or lending." There is an exemption, however, for non-profit lending by non-profit libraries or educational institutions.

With the Record Rental Amendment the record labels and music publishers in the United States avoided the significant losses of revenues that had occurred in Japan when record rental became big business there. By the early 1980s cassette decks had become relatively popular in the United States, having been introduced and widely adopted in Japan some years earlier. In 1983, for instance, cassette sales reached 237 million units, surpassing LP sales (210 million) for the first time. Although not as large an enterprise in the United States as it had become in Japan, record rental loomed as a significant threat to the sale of LPs and pre-recorded cassettes by the labels. In 1981, what had been a "mom-and-pop" kind of business took on alarming proportions for the labels when the first major record retail chain did a trial run at record rental. A customer could rent an LP for about $0.99 to $2.50, and purchasing a blank cassette from the same place, take the disc home, tape it and return the rented disc to the store the next day having copied the album on to tape. The only copy sold by the label was the one originally sold to the rental store. Even assuming some wear and tear on the rental disc, it could be taped many times before becoming unrentable, thereby supplanting sales by the label. In 1983 there were an estimated 200 rental shops in the United States.

Although there was a coalition of rental store owners, blank tape manufactures, tape deck manufactures, and some consumers established to lobby against the legislation, Congress ultimately decided that the potential threat to the labels, music publishers, recording artists, and songwriters was great enough to require action. The pending introduction of the compact disc, a more readily rentable and recordable format, into the US market brought added urgency to the situation. In Japan, sales of pre-recorded albums had dropped precipitously as the rental business mushroomed.

At the present time the practice of record rental exists in only two developed nations, Japan and Switzerland. It is forbidden in nations that are members of the WTO, unless there was already in existence in 1994 a system of remuneration for the labels, publishers, artists, and writers in the particular country. The US labels (and those of other nations) and Japan agreed to a payment of $6.24 million to compensate for rentals occurring in 1992 through 1994. A per copy royalty of about $3.10 is to be paid for each copy delivered to rental outlets. Similar agreements paid royalty artists and background vocalists and musicians. Rental royalties in Japan declined in the late 1990s, with recording artists receiving $2.3 million in royalties for 1996 and 1997, compared to nearly $18 million for the previous year. The amount received by individual artists ranged from a few dollars to as much as $31,000. Foreign recordings can be rented in Japan, but only after they have been released for one year. The Recording Industry Association of Japan reports that the number of record rental outlets declined from a high of about 6,000 stores in the 1980s to about 3,700 stores in 2009.

Home recording

The growth of the cassette hardware market also brought another problem for the recording industry—consumers copying commercial recordings at home for their own use (aka "home taping"). The issue had been raised in Congress during the hearings surrounding the creation of sound recording copyrights in 1971. But the legislative history of that law indicated that the new copyrights in the sound recordings were not intended to prohibit home taping for non-commercial purposes. There was no similar language in the legislative history of the 1976 Copyright Revision Act on the same sound recording provision so it became unclear to some whether Congress had meant to prohibit home taping.

In 1977, a survey commissioned by Warner Communications found that 21 percent of the US population over the age of 10 taped recordings either off the air from radio broadcasts or from pre-recorded albums and tapes. What concerned the industry most at that time was the fact that those who taped were also those who spent the most money on pre-recorded music. The survey concluded,

> It is abundantly clear that people who use tape recorders for recording music are more likely to be buyers of prerecorded music, and on average, spend more money for prerecorded music than people who don't have access to a tape recorder, or have the recorders but don't use them to tape music. This,

however, does not imply that "home tapers" would not spend even more money on prerecorded music if tape recorders did not exist.[1]

By 1980 the International Federation of the Phonographic Industry (IFPI) added its voice, stating that home taping was becoming as big a concern as piracy, estimating losses due to the combination as "in the millions." The IFPI urged a legislative fix to the problem, but saw that as a "long and tortuous path." In 1982, home taping losses were set at $2.85 billion per year, with $1.13 billion coming from taping of recordings already owned by the taper and the rest coming from taping recordings borrowed from others, from broadcasts, or from live events. Forty-five percent of the tapers said they taped to avoid buying the product. And, although the lower quality of pre-recorded tapes was thought to be an incentive to make home tapes, only 10 percent of tapers said they taped to get a better quality recording. The reasons most often cited for taping were convenience (40 percent) and to use in car or office (35 percent). Tape recorder penetration had increased almost 25 percent in the 3 years from 1977 to 1980 with almost half of the population over the age of 10 having recorders in their homes.

The path to the legislative fix sought by the industry was long and tortuous indeed. Formidable opposition from the tape recorder manufacturers, the blank tape manufacturers, and a "right to tape" citizens' group repeatedly fought the labels to a standstill. In a decision not directly on audio home taping, the US Supreme Court held that taping broadcast television programs off the air for private, non-commercial, time-shifting purposes was "fair use" in *Sony Corp. v. Universal City Studios, Inc.* This decision weakened the labels' arguments on the applicability of the existing law to prevent home taping.

In the meantime, digital recordings on compact discs had become extremely popular. By 1987 sales of CDs reached about 100 million units, nearly equaling those of vinyl albums. That same year digital audio tape recorders (DAT recorders) were introduced in Japan and in professional markets and the prospect loomed of generation after generation of near-perfect tape copies of CDs. The tape manufacturers wanted to introduce their machines into the US consumer market. The labels threatened potentially long and costly litigation against the manufacturers of the machines as **"contributory" copyright infringers**. By June 1991 the parties had come to an agreement that they took to Congress. The proposal became the Audio Home Recording Act 1992 (AHRA), as passed September 22 that year.

Contributory copyright infringer
One whose actions make an infringement possible, and who knows that the infringement is occurring. Contributory infringers are also liable for the infringing actions of the direct infringers.

Audio Home Recording Act 1992

The Act represents a compromise between the record companies and music publishers, and the audio hardware manufacturers and blank media manufacturers. It provides that:

1. Analog and digital home copying of music recordings for non-commercial purposes are exempt from liability for copyright infringement.
2. The manufacture and sale of analog and digital home recording devices are exempt from liability for infringement, but the manufacture and distribution

of digital recording devices and blank digital recording media are subject to a compulsory license issued by the Copyright Office.

3. All home-type digital recorders must contain some sort of anti-copying system that prohibits the user from making more than single generation copies.

4. A compulsory license is used to generate royalties for the owners of the sound recording copyrights and the musical composition copyrights. The royalties are collected from the distributors of recorders and blank media, based on wholesale prices and the number of units sold. For recorders the royalty is 2 percent of the wholesale price. For blank media it is 3 percent of the wholesale price. The royalties are collected by the Copyright Office quarterly and distributed according to a specific statutory scheme by the Librarian of Congress.

5. Royalty Distribution is shown in Figure 5.1. The "artists" share includes both featured artists and background musicians and vocalists. When all is said and done, the shares of the *total* fund are indicated in Table 5.1.

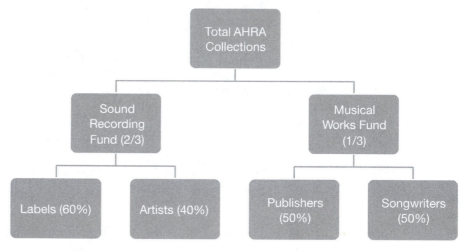

Figure 5.1 AHRA distribution

Table 5.1 Distribution of audio home recording act royalties as a percentage of the total royalty collected (percentages slightly rounded)

- Labels . . . 38.4%
- Featured artists . . . 25.6%
- AF of M members . . . 1.75%
- AFTRA members . . . 0.9%
- Music publishers . . . 16.7%
- Songwriters . . . 16.7%

Source: 17 USC § 1006

Collections of royalties under the Audio Home Recording Act, called Digital Audio Recording Technology (**DART**) royalties by the Copyright Office, were slow to develop. Figure 5.2 indicates a peak of nearly $5.5 million in 2000, then a drop-off. This was due largely to three factors: (1) most home copying is done on computers and there are no royalties collected from computer sales; (2) the rapidly falling prices of audio CD recorders and blank CD-Rs; and (3) the prevalence of unauthorized recording. Theoretically, the royalties should keep pace with the amount of recording.

One proposed solution is for the royalty rates to be adjustable by a Copyright Royalty Board instead of being set "in stone" in the statute itself. That way the royalty rate could be adjusted so that the royalty income bears a closer relationship to the amount of home copying that is actually going on. Or, a small royalty could be collected from computer media sales because such a significant amount of copying is done on computers. In 2010, in Germany, a royalty to compensate record producers, labels, and artists was placed on CD and DVD "burners" in computers and even on computers that did not have the "burner" drives. The Alliance of Artists and Recording Companies (**AARC**) handles distribution of these royalties to the artists and labels. The AARC also handles distribution of rental royalties from Japan.

DART Royalties due to copyright owners under the Audio Home Recording Act from the sale of stand-alone digital audio recorders such as mini-disc and the blank media used to make recordings such as "music" CD-Rs and mini-discs.

AARC A non-profit organization formed to distribute royalties collected by the Copyright Office under the Audio Home Recording Act.

Digital Audio Performance Rights

As noted above, record labels had been attempting to get a performance right for their recordings since the 1909 law. They did not succeed until they got the regular broadcasters, television, and radio to drop opposition to the legislation by exempting traditional broadcast performances, even if the broadcasters later developed digital broadcast systems. Congress ultimately passed the Digital

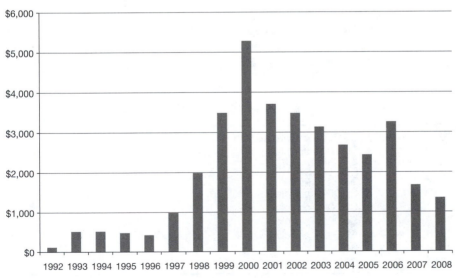

Figure 5.2 AHRA collections (thousands of dollars)

Performance Right in Sound Recordings Act of 1995. It was later amended in 1998 as part of the Digital Millennium Copyright Act to clarify the application to **webcasting**.

Webcasting
Transmitting a performance of songs, recordings, or videos by streaming the performance over the Internet/World Wide Web. Known originally as "Netcasting."

The new public performance right in sound recordings applies *only* to digital transmissions that are not aired by over-the-air broadcasters. The right applies to digital transmissions by subscription services, interactive services, and non-interactive series, including Internet simulcasts of regular broadcast transmissions. Streaming by webcasters, interactive music services, and background music services are subject to licensing. Non-interactive services, such as most webcasters, may use a compulsory license but interactive services must negotiate directly with the record companies for licenses.

The RIAA created an organization, SoundExchange, to collect royalties and negotiate licenses. (SoundExchange is now fully independent from the RIAA.) SoundExchange calls itself, "a modern performance rights organization (PRO) created to collect and distribute performance royalties for sound recording copyright owners, featured and non-featured artists." So, we now have PROs for the music publishers and songwriters and a *different* one for the labels and artists.

The webcasters and other users fought a decade-long battle with the labels over the licensing rates. To get the rates set took a decision by the Copyright Royalty Board in 2007 that initially set rates, then two acts of Congress in 2008 and 2009, and finally a negotiation between the labels (represented by SoundExchange) and webcasters.

- Table 5.2 shows the basic webcaster performance rates through 2015.
- Webcasters with large revenues, like Pandora that had revenues of $19 million in 2008, may pay the rates in the table, or 25 percent of revenues.
- Small webcasters (less than $1.25 million revenues per year) pay 12–14 percent of revenues with a minimum license fee of $25,000 per year.
- Satellite transmitters, like Sirius/XM, pay according to Table 5.3.

Whether the licenses are negotiated or compulsory, the division of the sound recording performance royalties between the labels and performers is dictated by the statute as indicated in Figure 5.3.

Table 5.2 Royalty rates for webcasters for public performance of sound recordings

2006	$0.0008 per play (0.08 cents per play)
2007	$0.0011 per play
2008	$0.0014 per play
2009	$0.0015 per play
2010	$0.0016 per play
2011	$0.0017 per play
2012	$0.0020 per play
2013	$0.0022 per play
2014	$0.0023 per play
2015	$0.0025 per play

Source: 74 FR 34796, July 17, 2009

Table 5.3 Royalty rates for public performances of sound recordings via satellite

2007	6 percent of total revenue
2008	6 percent of total revenue
2009	6.5 percent of total revenue
2010	7 percent of total revenue
2011	7.5 percent of total revenue
2012	8 percent of total revenue

Source: 74 FR 34796, July 17, 2009

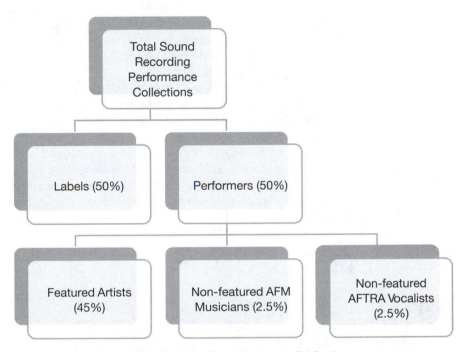

Figure 5.3 Sound recording digital audio performance distributions

In 2008 and 2009 the record companies gained impetus in Congress to broaden the performance right in sound recordings by removing the exemption for terrestrial broadcasters. There was, of course, much opposition from broadcasters, but the labels found two new arguments to make. First, they and the webcasters could argue that some people should not be able to use the recordings for free while others had to pay for a very similar use. Second, in most other countries, broadcasters *do* have to pay for public performances of sound recordings as well as for the songs. Because most international copyright law is based on reciprocity, if the US does not have a public performance right for broadcasting sound recordings, foreign countries that do have such a right do not have to pay royalties to the US recording copyright owners. So, it is not advisable for the US to give less copyright protection than is available elsewhere in the world. At the time of writing, Congressional action was still pending.

Can I Copyright My "Beats"?

"Beats" are the basic rhythmic tracks often used in the production of hip-hop or other popular music. These beats are often looped to form the bed of the song and the lyrics or other melody then superimposed over them. There is a definite business in selling "beats" to producers and artists. But there are two questions that are not without difficulty: are these tracks copyrightable as compositions, or as sound recordings? Certainly they are copyrightable sound recordings, because they are a fixation of some sounds. One case turned on the fact that the producer had made a new recording of the beat, or a sound-alike, and this could not be an infringement of the sound recording. There has not been a case deciding whether beats are copyrightable compositions or not. Generally a rhythm would probably not be deemed copyrightable as a musical composition. (No offense to the beat producers.)

So far, the cases have all turned on a situation where the person creating the beats offered them to some artist or producer without any contractual arrangement specifying what was to be done or how the use was to be paid. When the artist or producer did use the beats and the person who created the beats later sued for infringement, the courts have uniformly held that the use was a non-exclusive license because the beats clearly had been offered for use and used. The courts thereby avoided having to decide whether the beats were copyrightable.

It is pretty much impossible to plagiarize a sound recording. The statute specifically allows imitation of sounds. So, "sound-alike" recordings are not infringements. The most common copyright infringement action for sound recordings is for sampling, discussed below.

DIY Activities

- Go to the SoundExchange website. Look at the "Unregistered List." These are artists that SoundExchange has tracked performances for, but who are not registered with SoundExchange and therefore they cannot collect their royalties. Think of the name of a favorite "indie" artist, local or otherwise. Are they on the list?
- On the SoundExchange website, it is possible for artists and labels to register online. Get with someone in the class, or someone you know who has released their own recording through their website or other means. Check to be sure they are registered with SoundExchange. If not, work with them to do the "click through" registration. Note that they may be both the artist and the sound recording copyright owners if they are truly "self released."
- Know a person who creates beats? Are they licensed through beatswagger. com, or worldwidebeats.net? How do these and other beat sellers work? How much do they pay the beat producer? How much does it cost to buy a beat? What can you do with it once you have bought it?

Sampling—"Thou Shalt Not Steal"

Sampling, sometimes also called "digital sampling," is the process whereby a recording artist or producer takes a small piece from a previous recording, digitizes it (the actual sampling process) so that it can be manipulated by computer sequencers and MIDI instruments, and puts it back into a new recording or song. Sampling is commonplace in most genres of music, particularly in hip-hop and dance music. Everything from James Brown's famous yells, to the rare congas as heard on the "Miami Vice" theme, have been sampled and used by other musicians and producers to make new recordings, not that imitate the original, but that build the actual originally recorded sounds into what is often a new and very different work. There is no question that the use of samples in the creation of new works can be, and often is, quite creative. The problem is that unless the sampling and new use is done with the permission of the owners of the copyrights in the sampled works, copyright infringement is the likely result.

The Case of "Alone Again, Naturally"

The very first sampling case to go all the way through to a court decision was in 1991. It set the tone for future sampling discussions and set into motion a flurry of label, artist, producer, and publisher sampling agreements and clauses. Rap artist Marcel Hall (pka Biz Markie) used three words and their melody from a Gilbert O'Sullivan recording and song, "Alone Again (Naturally)." Hall, his attorneys, and Warner Brothers Records (the distributing label for Hall's Cold Chillin' Records) knew that they should obtain a sampling "clearance" (license) for the use of the three words and their accompanying music, but for reasons not clear from the court record, they released the Biz Markie recording anyway, even though Gilbert O'Sullivan's publishing company, Grand Upright Music Ltd, had refused the license. Federal District Court Judge Duffy's curt opinion quoted the *Bible's* commandment, "Thou shalt not steal," and chided the defendants for their "callous disregard for the law and for the rights of others." The settlement required Warner Brothers Records to physically remove all of the offending recordings from the marketplace and to pay heavy damages, and brought a rather abrupt end to Hall's career.

Sample Once—Infringe Twice

Sampling exposes the labels to copyright infringement charges on two possible fronts—the sound recording copyright owners and, in addition, the song copyright owners. First, whenever *any* sound is taken from a recording made after February 15, 1972, the likelihood is that there is a violation of the sound recording copyright. Whether the sound is an artist's moan or yell, a drummer's kick drum sound, or a hot guitar lick, there is no doubt that the previously fixed sounds are taken. Copyrights in the recordings of those sounds usually belong to the label that did the original release. So, one label will have to ask another label for permission to use the sample. Permission can usually be had unless there is some problem with the artist not wanting to allow sampling. Permission, however, comes at a price. A typical sampling license from a label would cost anywhere from a one-time flat fee of $1,000–$5,000 (typically) up to more than $25,000, to a share of up to 50 percent of the new sound recording copyrights. This depends greatly on the significance of the sample taken and the extent to which it is used in the new recording. If the sample also takes any of the words or melody of the song a second sampling license must be obtained from the copyright owner (usually the music publisher) of the original song. The price there is about the same as for the sound recording sample.

These days, labels and music publishers not only have departments dedicated to tracking down copyright owners and obtaining sampling licenses for their artists who do lots of sampling, but also to chasing down other labels who may have used a sample of one of their recordings or songs. The cost of the sampling licenses is usually deducted from the artist's royalties. The licenses can add up to large sums of money or losses of significant percentages of copyright ownership. Artists who do heavy sampling are frequently quite creative, but they end up costing themselves considerable sums of money. The potential high costs of sampling and loss of ownership of rights have made some labels a bit gun-shy of artists who use lots of sampling. But, judging from the number of recordings that use sampling, the necessity for licenses did not stop uses of samples, creative and otherwise.

The Case of "Get Off Your Ass and Jam!"

Those who use samples in making recordings often say that they should not have to pay for the uses because they often do not use much of the previous recording and because it is often manipulated in such a way that the original sound is not even recognizable. Until 2004 there had not been a case decided where the defendant had made that argument. In one of the many cases involving sampling from the songs and recordings of the popular funk group Parliament, and their leader/songwriter George Clinton, the recording of "Get off Your Ass and Jam!" owned by Westbound Records was sampled and used in a recording of the song "100 Miles and Runnin'." What was taken was a three note arpeggiated chord which played about two seconds in the original recording. This was slowed down, looped, and used several times in the new recording for a total of about 40 seconds.

In a ground-breaking decision, the US Sixth Circuit Court of Appeals held that such a use was **not** *de minimis*, i.e. so small as not to be protected by copyright. Even when the new use altered the original to the extent that one familiar with the works of George Clinton (the author of "Get Off") would not recognize the source of the sample, the court still said this should be an infringement. The rights of the sound recording copyright owner include the right to prepare derivative works in which the sounds are "rearranged, remixed, or otherwise altered in sequence or quality." That is exactly what a sampling use does. The court felt that a simple test for sampling infringement of a sound recording was best, simply saying, "Get a license or do not sample."

The Case of "Pass the Mic"

On the other hand, a US Court of Appeals on the West coast held that a very small, much manipulated sample of three notes from a musical composition was *de minimis*. The Beastie Boys used three notes from jazz flutist James Newton's recording of his composition, "Choir." The suit was not for infringement of the recording, but for infringement of the song. Because the use was a sample, it was clear that the Beastie Boys had used Newton's composition. However, the court said the six second use of the three notes from Newton's composition was a *de minimis* use because it was so short and unrecognizable that it was not "substantially similar." A use is *de minimis*, said the court, "only if it is so meager and fragmentary that the average audience would not recognize the appropriation."

That leaves us with one rule for sampling sound recordings and a different rule for sampling songs. For the sound recording, any use, no matter how small or how altered, is an infringement (at least in the Sixth Circuit). For the song, a use that is very small and not recognizable is not an infringement. The problem is that sampling always takes part of the recording and more often than not takes part of the song, too. So, depending upon who is suing for what the user may or may not be liable. The only safe solution is to do as the court said in the "Get Off Your Ass and Jam" case—get a license.

The "Manufacturing Clause" and Parallel Imports

The music business is a particular beneficiary of a provision of the copyright laws that is little known outside of the music publishing and recording industries. It goes by the name of the **"manufacturing clause"** because it originally required that English language books or periodicals had to be manufactured in the United States in order to achieve full copyright protection. From its birth in 1891 it was quite simply a trade barrier designed to protect US publishers and bookbinders from foreign competition. The clause requiring manufacture in the US to enjoy full copyright protection was abolished when the US joined the Berne Convention in 1989, but the part of the clause pertaining to the music business continues to this day.

The surviving language prohibits the importation of copies of works manufactured outside the US where the US copyright owner has not given permission to import. This applies even if the copies are lawfully made outside of the US. Such an unauthorized importation is an infringement of the distribution right. The clause is particularly effective in stopping the importation of "gray market" goods—those that have been legally manufactured outside of the US for distribution *outside* of the US. Although the copyright law says nothing about goods themselves, it does speak to copyrightable materials that may be part of the goods (such as labels) or boxed with the goods (such as instruction manuals). In some respects the manufacturing clause is a better deterrent to gray market goods than trademark law. For the recording and music

Manufacturing clause A part of the copyright law that prohibits copies of recordings made outside of the US for sale outside of the US from being sold in the US unless the US copyright owner has given specific permission to import.

Parallel imports
Copies of works
lawfully made
outside of a country
for distribution
outside of that
country but then
imported back into
the country of
origin and sold
along side of copies
manufactured in the
country of origin.

industry it prevents the distribution of what are referred to as "**parallel imports**." The clause also prohibits the exporting or importing of copies that would have been infringing when manufactured, wherever they are manufactured.

Domestic Problems

Parallel imports are a problem for the US industry for several reasons. These goods, which are lawfully manufactured outside of the US for sale outside of the US, return a lower profit per copy than copies made in the US and sold in the US by the US label. Often in foreign record manufacturing arrangements the US label gets only a royalty similar to that of a recording artist, based on the retail or wholesale price in the foreign country. This is far less profit than the label would make if the records were made and sold in the United States. Some products are on different labels outside of the United States. And, when the dollar is particularly strong relative to the foreign currency, a retailer or distributor can purchase these imports at a substantially lower price than the domestic product. If they can be sold alongside the US product at the same or slightly lower price, then the distributor and/or retailer can make more money selling the import than they can by selling the domestic product.

Not only does the US record company lose money when copies of parallel imports are sold instead of domestic copies, so does the recording artist who is often paid at a one-half royalty rate for copies made outside of the United States. So also do the music publisher and songwriter because they, too, are usually paid at one half or other reduced royalty for copies made outside of the United States.

Summary

Copyrights in sound recordings are not the same thing as copyrights in musical compositions. There are typically two different owners of the rights with artists, producers, and record companies creating recordings and owning sound recording copyrights, and the songwriters and music publishers creating and owning rights in the songs. Sound recording copyrights were initially created in the US to help record companies stop piracy of their recordings in the early 1970s. Later amendments to the laws helped protect the labels from unauthorized rental of recordings and gave them some limited revenues from home digital recording.

The public performance right for sound recordings is very limited, applying only to public performances of sound recordings by means of digital audio transmission (DAPSR). This means that only Internet, satellite, and some background music service transmissions pay a performance royalty to the copyright owners. Over-the-air broadcasts are exempt. The Copyright Royalty Board sets the rates for DAPSR and SoundExchange collects the royalties for distribution to artists, musicians, and labels.

"Beats" are generally regarded as sound recordings and not musical compositions. As such, someone using a beat in a new composition would have to get permission from the owners of the recording copyrights in those beats. Usually the beat owners want the beats to be used so they will be paid for those uses.

The more difficult question comes about when an artist or producer samples some sounds from a previously made recording. Significant uses of either the song or recording, both of which are typically used in a sample, are generally regarded as an infringement. However, in at least one Federal Court of Appeals case the court held that *any* sampling use of a previous recording, no matter how small or how unrecognizable, is an infringement unless a license is obtained. On the other hand, a different court has held that a small and generally unrecognizable use of the musical composition in a sample may not be an infringement. No wonder there is confusion over whether sampling creates an infringement. It may depend upon which copyright owner is the plaintiff.

Case Study: Maverick Recording Company v. Harper[2]

In 2003, as part of its campaign to curtail unauthorized downloading of recordings, the RIAA began to bring infringement actions on behalf of record companies against individual downloaders. These suits continued until the end of 2008 and were filed against over 35,000 individuals. Although the vast majority of these suits were settled out of court for a few thousand dollars, a few actually went to trial.[3]

In one 2004 investigation, it was found that Whitney Harper, then a teenager, had downloaded as many as 544 recordings from illegal peer-to-peer networks. Media Sentry, a company that worked for the record companies to help identify unauthorized downloaders, identified Harper by her IP (Internet Protocol) address. It captured screen shots of the shared files on her computer, extracted the metadata in the files that identified the titles, artists, and such, and actually downloaded several files from Harper's computer. Harper refused to settle. She testified that she had not copied them from any discs that she owned, but had downloaded them from file-sharing sites without paying for them. She maintained that, "I knew I was listening to music. I didn't have an understanding of file sharing."[4]

The lower court ultimately found that she had infringed the copyrights in 37 recordings and in 2008 awarded the record companies $7,400 in statutory damages because she was an "innocent infringer." In the case of an innocent infringer, who "was not aware and had no reason to believe that his or her acts constituted an infringement of copyright, the court in its discretion may reduce the award of statutory damages to a sum of not less than $200."

On appeal, however, the Fifth Circuit Court of Appeals agreed with the RIAA and record companies that the "innocent infringer" defense did not apply in this case. Another part of the Copyright Act, that deals with the copyright notice, states,

> If a notice of copyright in the form and position specified by this section appears on the published copy or copies to which a defendant in a copyright infringement suit had access, then no weight shall be given to such a defendant's interposition of a defense based on innocent infringement.

Continued

The lower court held that even if Harper had access to copies with the copyright notice, that did not have any influence on whether she knew the copyright notice had any bearing on downloading recordings. But the Appeals Court said, the fact was that the labels had proper copyright notices on their recordings. She had access to those recordings.

It would make no sense for a copyright defendant's subjective intent to erode the working [of the statute] which gives publishers the option to trade the extra burden of providing copyright notice for absolute protection against the innocent infringer defense. Harper cannot rely on her purported legal naivety to defeat the . . . bar to her innocent infringer defense.

The Court then raised the minimum statutory damages per track to $750 making the total award of damages $27,750.

At the time of writing Harper was reportedly considering whether to appeal to the US Supreme Court.

QUESTIONS FOR REVIEW

- What would it take for members of a band to own copyrights in their sound recordings?
- How are sound recording copyrights different from those in musical compositions?
- How does the public performance right for sound recordings differ from that in musical compositions?
- How are Audio Home Recording Act (DART) royalties collected and distributed?
- What is SoundExchange? What does it do? How are royalties paid out?
- How can sampling use of sound recordings and musical compositions have different results when it comes to an infringement suit? When should a sampler get a license? From whom?
- What are "parallel imports"? Why are they a problem for the music business?

6 Music Publishing: The First Stream

"It All Begins With a Song"[1]

Introduction

Without a song, there would be nothing to perform or record, so it is logical to begin a closer examination of the three income streams here, with songwriting and music publishing. This income stream is referred to as the music publishing stream and not the songwriting stream because very few people ever made any money from simply writing a song. The money was made from the publication (uses) of that song. Even when songwriters "own their own" songs, the songs are almost always actually owned, in the copyright sense, by a music publisher, even if that publishing company is owned by the writer. Therefore the primary focus of this chapter is music publishing instead of songwriting. However, there are so many aspiring songwriters in bands and as "just plain" songwriters that the development of writers deserves some attention as well. The same has been done for aspiring recording artists later in the book.

The business of music publishing these days primarily involves two tasks: acquiring rights in songs and licensing the use of those rights to generate royalties for the publisher and songwriter. The business has evolved from one that sold products (sheet music) to one that issues licenses and administers rights. The music publishing stream has also evolved into a market dominated by four major companies, much like the recording stream. Yet, there are thousands of independent and writer-owned publishing companies as well.

Music publishing revenues do not yet equal those from the sale of recordings but music publishing has grown in significance because publishing revenues have fundamentally enjoyed a steady growth for the past decade while the revenue from sales of recordings has been in a steady decline. Worldwide recording sales dropped from nearly $40 billion in the late 1990s to about $18.4 billion in 2008. During that same period, music publishing revenues declined also, but only from about $6.9 billion to about $4 billion. Also, music publishing is more profitable because it does not require an investment in physical product or major recording artists' advances and risks. For example, at Universal Music Group (UMG), music publishing accounted for 14 percent of total revenue in 2008, but 28 percent of profits (EBITDA, i.e. earnings before interest, taxes, depreciation, and amortization). Finally, some publishers have continued to expand their roles into the A&R side of the business, even opening their own labels to develop songwriter/artists who do not have a major label recording contract.

KEY CONCEPTS

1. The primary music publishing income sources are performance royalties, mechanical royalties, and synchronization royalties.
2. The big four music business firms are also the big four music publishing companies, accounting for about 65 percent of the market.
3. Music publishers have two primary functions: acquiring and exploiting copyrights.
4. Songwriters and publishers basically agree to split the income 50/50.
5. The three main performing rights organizations in the US are ASCAP, BMI, and SESAC.
6. Most mechanical licenses in the US are issued through the Harry Fox Agency.

The Music Business Three Income Stream Model—Revisited

The three income streams in the music business discussed in Chapter 2, music publishing, live performances, and recordings, are interrelated. The common gene in the relationship is recordings. There would be very little music publishing revenue without popular recordings. The sale of the recordings provides mechanical royalties for the publishers of the songs in those recordings—about 30 percent of music publishing income (see Figure 6.1). Another 16 percent of publishing revenues are derived from radio airplay of recordings. The majority of print music sales are of piano-vocal editions of popular singles and "**folios**" of popular albums or recording artists. Based on the amount of popular music in motion pictures and television, it is reasonable to estimate that one half (or more) of television performance and TV and film synchronization royalties are the result of songs and recordings by popular recording artists. Finally, the vast majority of live and recorded performances (7 percent of publishing revenues) are of songs made popular by recordings. Totaling these up, over 75 percent of music publishing royalties are the result of popular recordings.

Folios Songbooks containing multiple songs usually either on a common theme or by the same artist or writer, as opposed to sheet music of single songs.

Music Publishing: Then and Now

"Copyrights Don't Talk Back."[2]

The music publishing business is not what it used to be. In the 1890s music publishers sold millions of copies of sheet music. In 1893 "After the Ball" became the first song to sell 1 million copies of sheet music. Hit songs sold as many as 2 million copies in print by 1909. Even though sound recordings were catching on in 1920 and accounted for about 3 million dollars of publishing revenue, sheet music sales still accounted for over 16 million dollars, about 88 percent, of publishing income. Sheet music sales plummeted during the depression to a low of about 2 million dollars in 1933.

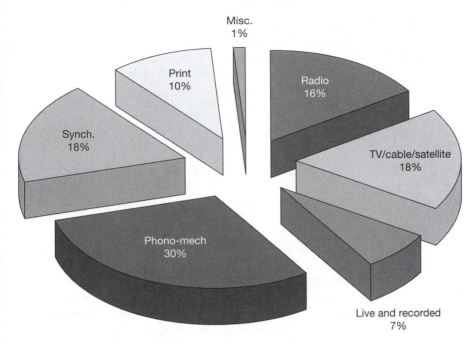

Figure 6.1 Music publishing revenues

During that same time performance revenues, largely from radio, grew and sustained the music publishing industry through World War II. Print sales failed to make a significant recovery after the war. *Billboard* reported in 1955 that publishers faced finding new income, since sales of even the most popular songs in sheet music were usually less than 300,000 units. The "reliable" source of income was performance royalties. That, however, was before rock and roll jolted record sales into ever higher gears and pushed mechanical royalties into a close second place behind performance royalties. Even though revenue from print music recovered and accounted for about 38 percent of the publishers' estimated $283 million share of revenues, by 1978 the "music business" had been forever changed.

By the twenty-first century the recording industry dwarfed music publishing. In 2000, domestic revenue from the sale of recordings in the United States was $14.3 billion—nearly 10 times the $1.98 billion reported by the National Music Publishers' Association (NMPA) for that same year. But sales of recordings declined overall for the next decade. By 2009, domestic revenues from the sale of recordings had shrunk to about $8.5 billion and publishing revenues had risen to over $2 billion to account for more than 20 percent of the revenues of the four major recording companies. But because music publishing is more profitable, the share of music business income attributed to publishing was about 28 percent to 30 percent for the major firms.

Revenues from the sale of recordings and from performances accounted for 77 percent of music publishing income while distribution of print music was reduced to a share of less than 10 percent. A century of technological innovation and evolution and the concomitant change in copyright laws (see Chapters 3, 4, and 5) turned an industry that once created and marketed products into a copyright industry that primarily licenses others to utilize its properties. Much the same thing was happening to the recording companies as sales of digital copies through licensees such as iTunes, Amazon.com, and Wal-Mart replaced sales of hard copies.

Overall Structure

The music publishing business and recording business intersect at nearly every turn. Every major label owns publishing interests. Many smaller labels, independent producers, and recording artists own publishing interests. Some publishers now own their own record labels. Despite the existence of literally thousands of small music publishers, most of the rights are administered through a handful of publishing giants. The small songwriter, artist, and producer-owned publishing companies simply do not have the expertise or personnel to deal with the complexities of music publishing. They usually enter into agreements with large publishers to co-publish or to administer their catalogs.

The large publishing companies are getting larger by acquisition of smaller companies or by entering administration or co-publishing agreements that allow the "Goliaths" to share in the revenues generated by the "Davids." The willingness of the larger companies to use this approach makes it possible for smaller companies to exist and be profitable. It also removes one of the gatekeepers between the songwriters and their audiences. No longer is the publisher trying to second guess what an artist or producer will want to record and therefore accepting only "safe" songs. "Safe" songs in the twenty-first century are songs that are written by songwriters who are also artists or producers who are already under contract or who have good possibilities of obtaining recording contracts.

The four largest music publishers in the world, UMP, EMI Music Publishing, Warner/Chappell Music, and Sony/ATV Music Publishing, are owned by the four largest recording conglomerates in the world. Together they account for about 65 percent of the music publishing business. A group of about a half-dozen others account for another 5 percent of publishing revenues. These include Bug/Windswept, Kobalt, Famous Music, Peer, Chrysalis, and Cherry Lane. The remaining 30 percent is accounted for by over a thousand specialty and as many as 20,000 individually owned publishing companies. From the late 1980s and into the twenty-first century, record conglomerates actively built their music publishing interests. All of them have engaged in major publishing acquisitions. In the stories of the four major music publishers that follow, **catalog** acquisition and merger are the dominant themes.

Catalog Generally refers to all of the songs (actually the copyrights in those songs) owned by a music publisher. May also refer to all of a label's master recordings and to recordings that are not current hits, but which are still available from the distributor and "in print."

The Big Four

UMP began as two different firms, PolyGram International Music Publishing and MCA Music Publishing. PolyGram had rebuilt its publishing interests after the sale of Chappell Music to Warner Brothers in 1984. MCA, which later became Universal, also built its interests through catalog acquisition. When PolyGram and Universal merged in 1998, the new company, UMP, became the third largest music publisher. Universal made a major addition to its status in 2000 with the acquisition of Rondor Music for a reported $400 million. Finally, Universal became the largest music publisher with the acquisition of BMG Music Publishing for a reported $2.1 billion in 2007. BMG had been a major competitor as parent organization Bertelsmann Music Group built its music publishing interests in 1987 after the acquisition of RCA's labels and music interests, buying 73 catalogs in a 5-year period from 1988 to 1993. BMG acquired the entirety of Zomba Music Group in 2002 for $2.7 billion.

EMI Music Publishing began modestly in 1974 after EMI had merged its Ardmoor, Beechwood, Keith Prowse, and Central Songs catalogs into one. It added film music with the acquisition of Screen Gems and Colgems from Columbia Pictures in 1976. The biggest leap came with the reported $335 million paid to acquire the SBK catalog. SBK was formed to purchase the music publishing wing of CBS, CBS Songs, in 1987. At that time CBS Songs was one of the five largest music publishers in the world. SBK also owned the MGM United Artists catalog at the time of the EMI purchase. EMI Music Publishing continued to acquire song copyrights with the 1990 purchase of the Filmtrax catalog and half of the Jobette catalog—the songs from Berry Gordy's Motown Records. In 2003 and 2004 EMI acquired the rest of the share of the Jobette catalog.

Warner/Chappell began in 1929 when Warner Brothers Pictures acquired Chappell-Harms and a number of other music publishing companies in an effort to acquire and promote music for its films. Warner Brothers later sold the music publishing business only to buy it back again as Warner Communications purchased Chappell and Company in 1987 to merge Warner Brothers Music and Chappell to create Warner/Chappell Music. A failed merger of Warner Music Group and EMI in 2000 would have created the world's largest music publishing company, but that merger was blocked by European Union anti-trust regulators. A proposed merger of Warner Music Group and BMG in 2003 had WMG reportedly considering selling off its publishing arm if that would convince regulators to allow the merger, but that never materialized and BMG Music Publishing later went to UMP.

Sony Music had no music publishing when it started in 1989 with the acquisition of the CBS, Inc. record labels. CBS had earlier divested itself of its music publishing with the sale of CBS Songs to SBK Entertainment in 1986. By 1993 Sony Music had emerged as a top ten music publisher in the US through acquisitions such as the Tree catalog (Tree was the most successful country music publisher at that time) in 1989. In 1994 Sony Music entered a "co-venture" deal with Michael Jackson, who owned many Beatles tunes in his ATV Music catalog. Sony reportedly paid Jackson $100 million for that deal. When Jackson got in financial trouble before his death in 2009 he sold Sony the right to purchase half of his share, leaving him with a 25 percent interest and Sony in control. However, when Sony bought out the 50 percent share of the Sony/BMG group in 2008, it was not allowed to buy BMG music publishing. That plum went to UMP.

The competitiveness of the conglomerate-owned publishing companies is evident in their success at having their songs on hit recordings. As Tables 6.1, 6.2, and 6.3 indicate, the top two popular music publishers in terms of chart share across all three most popular genres, pop, R&B, and country, are EMI and Universal. Warner/Chappell was a clear third, with Sony/ATV probably fourth. At the end of 2008 there were no major independent music publishers capable of challenging the power of the "big four" music/media conglomerates in the music publishing income stream.

Table 6.1 Top pop publishers, 2004–2008 (by number of singles in top 100)

Publisher	Average Rank	Years in Top 5	Ave. No. of Singles
EMI Music	1	5	195
Universal Music	3	5	149
Warner/Chappell	3.2	5	117
Sony/ATV Music	4	5	93
BMG*	3	3	81
Bug Music	5	1	33
Kobalt Music	5	1	20

Source: *Billboard*, Year End Issues, 2004–2008

*BMG was acquired by Universal Music

Table 6.2 Top R&B publishers, 2004–2008 (by number of singles in top 100)

Publisher	Average Rank	Years in Top 5	Ave. No. of Singles
EMI Music	1	5	213
Universal Music	2.2	5	158
Warner/Chappell	3.2	5	128
BMG*	3.3	3	89
Sony/ATV Music	5.4	4	51
Windswept**	5	1	26
R. Kelly	5	1	22
Peer Music	5	1	12

Source: *Billboard*, Year End Issues, 2004–2008

*BMG was acquired by Universal Music
**Windswept was acquired by Bug Music

Table 6.3 Top country publishers, 2004–2008 (by number of singles in top 100)

Publisher	Average Rank	Years in Top 5	Ave. No. of Singles
Sony/ATV Music	1	5	69.4
EMI Music	2.2	5	56.6
Universal Music	3.4	5	50.4
Warner/Chappell	3.4	5	50.4
BMG Music*	5	3	27
Windswept**	5	2	19.3

Source: *Billboard*, Year End Issues, 2004–2008

*BMG was acquired by Universal Music
**Windswept was acquired by Bug Music

Why did the recording conglomerates pay so much attention to music publishing? For one thing, the mechanical royalties paid by record companies to music publishers for the right to make recordings of songs are expenses to the labels. If labels owned publishing in the songs their artists recorded, they could take their mechanical royalty expenses out of their record company pockets and put them as revenues into their music publishing company pockets. Most recording artists in the twenty-first century are entirely self contained—they write and perform their own compositions. (There are notable exceptions, particularly in country and pop music.) It is usually no longer necessary to obtain songs from a music publisher who had songwriters creating songs for other people to record.

The record companies market the recordings that create the hit songs. Why, reasoned the labels, should some other party get all the benefit from the label's promotion of the recordings? Finally, the income stream from music publishing is more stable and longer term than the income stream from the hit recording that produced the hit song. A label will probably get only three or four shots at earning income on a hit record: the original recording, a greatest hits collection, perhaps a boxed set if the artist really has a long career, and later reissues as historical or collector's items. Every one of these also makes money for the publisher. In addition, the publisher gets royalties every time the original record gets played on the radio as an "oldie," whenever the artist may perform it on television, when it is turned into background music for use in hotels, restaurants and other businesses or organizations (sometimes referred to in tongue-in-cheek manner as "elevator music"), when sheet music is sold, and, most importantly, when someone else records it. The potential to earn royalties even without recordings is limited but clearly illustrated by the song "Happy Birthday." Very few recordings are made of "Happy Birthday" any more, but the asking price for the copyright of that song, which is *not* public domain, was $12 million in 1988. "Happy Birthday" reportedly earns 1 million dollars every year in royalties.

Cover versions, recordings made by an artist different from the one who originally recorded the song, can generate publishing profits for years. For example, the song "Who's Sorry Now?," originally written in 1923 and a number two hit for Connie Francis in 1958, had been recorded over four hundred times by artists all over the world ranging from the Glenn Miller Orchestra, to Willie Nelson, to Nat "King" Cole by 1985. That is what publishers call an "**evergreen**," a song that keeps on earning royalties long after the popularity of the original recording has faded. Country songwriter/artist Dolly Parton wrote her song, "I Will Always Love You," for her 1974 "Jolene" album. It was a number one country single that year. Then in 1982 it was included in the film version of "The Best Little Whorehouse in Texas" and again hit the top of the country charts. But the greatest success came from the smash hit performance by R&B/pop artist Whitney Houston in the soundtrack for the movie "The Bodyguard" over a decade later.

Even songs written and originally recorded by rock artists may turn into hits by other artists years later. In 1977 the rock group Aerosmith had a number two hit with "Walk This Way." Nine years later, Run-D.M.C. had a number one hit with a version of it in a genre, Rap, which did not even exist when Aerosmith's first version was recorded. In 1984 George Michael had a rock/pop hit with

Cover (band or versions) Recordings or performances of a song by artists and performers other than the artist who originally recorded the song.

Evergreen In music publishing, a song that is recorded by many artists and performed on a continuing basis for many years.

"Careless Whisper." Twenty-five years later, Seether had a major hard rock hit version of the same song.

Copyrights generally last for the life of the songwriter plus 70 years (or for 95 years for works first published between 1923 and 1978; see Chapter 3 for details), long after most people have lost any interest in purchasing the original recording of a song. The value of the copyrights in the master recording is likely to have a much shorter life. The record company can therefore extend the earning potential of the hit recording they originally created by having an interest in the song which that recording made popular as well as in the original recording. All of the above are also reasons why the record companies want to expand the sound recording performance right (see Chapter 5).

Music Publishing Functions

Basic functions

Song plugging A person who works for a music publishing company whose job it is to get the song recorded, performed, and used in other ways.

Professional managers The person at a music publishing company who is in charge of finding new songs and songwriters. They may also negotiate special uses of songs, such as commercials or motion pictures.

A&R In a record company, the department in charge of finding new artists and songs to record. "A&R person" refers to persons who fulfill A&R functions by scouting new talent or listening to demos of artists and songs to decide who and what to record.

Music publishers perform much the same functions with songs that labels perform with recordings. The main difference is that the publisher deals primarily with an intangible property right, the copyright, and the label, although it will acquire copyrights in the sound recordings (masters), has traditionally been much more concerned about selling copies of those masters in the forms of CDs and downloads. The primary functions of a music publisher are (1) the acquisition of copyrights and (2) the exploitation (in a positive, business sense) of those copyrights.

Publishing company structure

The typical music publishing company internal structure and functioning very much mirror the two primary functions of acquisition and exploitation of copyrights. Those functions are usually split between creative and administrative divisions. The creative division is in charge of signing songs and songwriters to contracts with the company, promoting the company's catalog of songs to prospective users ("**song plugging**"), and possibly developing potential songwriter/artists in a role not unlike that of A&R people at record labels. Usually the people undertaking these roles are known as "**professional managers.**" (Do not confuse *professional* managers at music publishing companies with *personal* managers for artists discussed in Chapter 7.) The professional manager is frequently a song doctor, working with songwriters to help them create the most marketable songs. Professional managers must know producers, artists, artist and repertoire (**A&R**) people, movie music supervisors, and as many other potential users of their songs as they can in order to fulfill the role of song plugger. Since they become familiar with what makes the best recording for a song and often produce the demos used to promote the song to producers and the like, it is not uncommon for professional managers to become record producers as well.

For independent songwriters and even for writers under exclusive agreements who want more promotion for their songs, there are independent song pluggers. These people are often former music publishing executives or producers who have the contacts and know how to find hit songs. That is important because they say, almost to a person, that the independent plugger should not take on clients and songs that they do not believe in. Independent pluggers are typically paid a monthly fee ("retainer") based on the number of songs represented. Fees range from a few hundred dollars a month to a thousand dollars or more. They also usually get a bonus when a song is recorded, released, or reaches certain sales or airplay plateaus. A few pluggers simply charge a flat fee for a certain number of **pitches**. The use of independent pluggers has become particularly popular in country music.

Pitch To promote a song to a music publisher or producer, or an artist to a label.

The administrative side of the music publishing company is the paperwork side of the business. It will usually include copyright administration, licensing, accounting, and perhaps business/legal affairs units. The copyright administration unit takes care of registration of the publisher's songs with the Copyright Office, recordation of other information with the Copyright Office, such as notices of death or transfers of ownership, and renewal of copyrights for songs published prior to 1978. The licensing unit works with the Harry Fox Agency (**HFA**) (the primary agency that deals with mechanical licensing in the US; though about 30 percent of mechanicals collections are through other agencies), the publisher's performing rights organization (PRO) affiliate for the clearance of new compositions and recordings, and directly issues other licenses, including print licensing, advertising uses, film, TV, video game, and others.

HFA An agency that issues mechanical licenses on behalf of its member publishing companies, collects licensing fees from the record companies and other users, and distributes those collections to the appropriate publishers. It was created and run by the National Music Publishers Association.

Since the music publishing business is one of pennies earned from royalties from the various uses of the songs, the accounting unit is very important. With thousands of uses for thousands of songs by hundreds of different songwriters it is a major task to insure that everyone receives their proper payments for their songs. If there is a separate business/legal affairs department it will be in charge of contract negotiation with songwriters, complex license negotiations, and catalog acquisitions.

Copyright Acquisition

The traditional way

The classic model for copyright acquisition goes like this. Songwriters, either on their own or under contract to music publishers, are moved to write songs about something. Melody and lyrics are created and woven together. The songs are presented in some manner ("pitched"), perhaps by a live performance, perhaps by a demonstration recording ("**demo**") sent to publishers.

Demo A *demonstration* recording made to promote an artist, songwriter, or song to an agent, manager, music publisher, or record company.

The publisher tries to assess the potential that the song has for being recorded by other people. If the publisher believes a song is likely to be recorded the publisher signs a contract with the songwriter in which the songwriter assigns the copyright to the publisher in exchange for roughly half of any royalties which may be generated by the exploitation of the song. The publisher and songwriter enter into a kind of partnership, with the songwriter creating a product that the publisher will then attempt to market. The publisher will probably have a high quality demo made of the song to present the song to people likely to record it. The publisher will then "pitch" the song to recording artists, producers, and A&R people at record labels with the hope of attracting someone to record it. Once it is recorded and released the publisher will then (perhaps) help promote it to radio stations.

If the song is successful enough, the publisher might cause sheet music to be printed and sold. The publisher will also try to get other artists to cover the song. The publisher may try to get it used in motion pictures or television as well. Meanwhile, the publisher will sit back and collect royalties from the sale of copies of the recording and from the performances of the song on radio and television.

For a long time, even before the invention of phonograph recordings, that is the way it worked. In the late 1800s and early 1900s songwriters wrote tunes and publishers' employees called "song pluggers" pitched them to minstrel show performers and vaudeville performers. The song pluggers got their name from the fact that a performance before an audience was called a "plug" for the song. People would not buy sheet music for the songs until they had heard the song in performance. The more plugs a song got, the more exposure it got. The more exposure it got, the more sheet music it sold. In those days it was common for a songwriter to receive a flat fee for a song instead of a royalty. Songwriters wrote tunes that went into their own or others' theatrical productions.

With the advent and increasing popularity of recordings in the early 1900s the song pluggers pitched tunes to recording artists and A&R people at record companies to get them recorded. In the 1920s, 1930s, and 1940s song pluggers pitched tunes to bandleaders to get them performed on network or local radio. For many of these plugs the publisher would often pay a "gratuity" to the performer. This widespread practice later turned into "**payola**" in the record industry (see Chapter 12).

Payola The practice of paying someone to perform a particular song or recording. Historically, music publishers paid performers to sing their songs. More recently it refers to attempts by labels to make undisclosed payments to radio stations or disc jockeys to play their recordings. The latter practice is illegal.

The "modern" model

> "There are fewer and fewer artists who are just singers. I mean, Bing Crosby's gone.[3]

The emergence of rock and roll transformed the music publishing business just as it transformed radio and the recording industry in general. In rock it was much more common for the songwriter who wrote the song and the artist who recorded the song to be the same person. Some say it was this "genuineness" of message from the songwriters interpreting their own compositions that created much of the appeal of rock music. For performers who understood the business, it may have been an attempt to gain some economic rewards from their performance of a song in addition to its sales in recordings. Since there was no performance right in a recording, the only way to share in the income generated by radio and television performances was to be a songwriter or copyright owner of the musical composition. While there were great pop songwriters who did not record their own material in the 1960s and 1970s—Bert Bacharach, Carole King and Gerry Goffin, Brian Holland and Lamont Dozier and Eddie Holland (the Holland-Dozier-Holland team who wrote many of Motown's great hits—to name just a few), the trend was, and still is, towards the artist/writer dominating the popular music field, particularly rock.

Even in country music, the last bastion of the "traditional" songwriter–publisher relationships, the artist/writer (or artist as co-writer) has become the dominant model. Many of the songwriters whose names appear in *Billboard*'s top ten songwriter lists defy categorization. How about label executives/songwriters/producers/recording artists like Shawn "Jay-Z" Carter or Terius "The Dream" Nash? Consider also writer/artist/producers Ryan Tedder or "Timbaland" Mosley. Then there are songwriter/producer teams like "Stargate" writers Tor Erik Hermansen and Mikkel Eriksen. These songwriter/artists not only write for themselves, but for other artists as well. It is extremely rare to find a songwriter in the pop top ten list who is a songwriter only. The other trend is co-writing. Two-thirds or more of the songwriters in the top ten lists write songs with other songwriters, producers, or artists.

How does a publisher proceed to acquire copyrights under the new model? Many publishers have taken on an A&R function. They actively seek songwriters who are, or have the potential to become, recording artists as well. They attempt to sign these songwriters to publishing deals before they are signed to record companies. The publisher may pay the songwriter/artists an advance in a form that allows them to develop their writing, arranging, and performing talents without having to keep a "day job." The publisher also helps the songwriter/artist seek recording and management contracts, or may even go so far as to use the publishing company's studios to create a master that can be released on an independent label in the hopes of selling even 20,000 to 30,000 copies. Songwriters/producers are also a target for this kind of development by publishers, particularly in the R&B and urban field. In exchange for that developmental advance and the possibility of future royalties the songwriter/artists pledge their output of songs for several years to the publisher.

A great example from the 1990s is Alanis Morissette, whose "Jagged Little Pill" album became the best selling debut album by a female artist when it passed the 8 million copies mark in 1996. She had been signed to a publishing deal with MCA Music Publishing in Canada for 7 years before her 1995 album debut. Twenty-first-century phenoms Coldplay were first discovered by BMG Music (now Universal) but they record for Capitol/EMI. James Blunt initially signed with EMI Music Publishing and later landed his recording contract with Atlantic, a WMG label.

Even in such **developmental deals**, the publishers often have to content themselves with a smaller share of the total publishing income by entering co-publishing deals with the songwriter/artist's publishing company. In 2009, EMI Music Publishing and mega producer Antonio "L.A." Reid launched a joint venture publishing company, L.A. Reid Music Publishing Company, to find new songwriters. Presumably, Reid would end up producing these new talents.

Publishers also bid for the publishing rights to the songs of new songwriter/artists who have just signed with labels. If the songwriter/artist does not sign with the label's affiliated publishing company at the same time they sign a

Development deals Usually a recording contract where a label gives an artist a small sum or perhaps annual amount to remain obligated to sign a full recording agreement with the label. Music publishers may also offer similar deals to songwriters.

recording agreement, then the publishing is particularly attractive since there is a high probability that the songs will be earning royalties as soon as the songwriter/artist and label complete and market their first album. Going one step further, in 2007 Sony/ATV Music Publishing started its own label, Hickory Records, to promote its own songwriters. It simply outsourced all label functions except A&R to others (see Recordings, Chapter 8).

Finally, publishers still sign individual songwriters to agreements even when the songwriter is not likely to develop into a recording artist. In such instances the song material has to be particularly strong since the publisher will have to find a market for it instead of having a ready-made market with a songwriter/ artist's own recordings. It is also still possible for songwriters to have individual songs accepted by a music publisher even though the songwriter is not under any long-term agreement with the publisher. This is, however, becoming much less common in all genres.

Songwriter Agreements

Single song contracts

The most basic agreement between a publisher and songwriter is the single song agreement. It is signed whenever a publisher acquires the copyrights to a song, whether it is from an unsigned songwriter for only one song, or from a songwriter under a long-term **exclusive songwriter** agreement (see below). Most of the terms in a single song agreement, like most of those in an exclusive agreement, are negotiable. What appear below are the terms likely to be in a typical agreement. If the songwriter is of sufficient stature, has their own publishing company already set up, or already has a recording agreement, then they may increase their share of the publishing revenues by negotiating a different kind of deal, such as co-publishing or administration. One observer commented, "Fading into distant memory is the era when, by and large, a publisher took a song and held 100 percent of the publishing."[4]

Typical single song agreement terms:

> **Exclusive songwriter** A songwriter under agreement to write songs only for one publishing company.

- Grant of rights—The songwriter assigns (transfers) all of the copyrights in the song to the publisher for the life of the copyrights, throughout the world. International rights are somewhat negotiable, especially if the publisher is not large enough to have the ability to market the song on a worldwide basis.

> **Reversion** A term usually seen in songwriter–publisher agreements referring to the writer's right to recapture the copyrights in the songs. There is a statutory reversion right called the *Termination Right* in the Copyright Act. The reversion may also be strictly contractual.

- **Reversion**—Any grant of copyright is subject to the Copyright Act's termination right. The songwriter has the statutory right to end a transfer of ownership or non-exclusive license after a period of 35 to 40 years (see Chapter 3 for details). A songwriter with some leverage may also be able to negotiate a contractual right to have the publisher transfer the copyrights back to the songwriter if the publisher fails to have the songs recorded or "published" within some set period of time, usually 1 to 2 years, with 5 years as a maximum. The publisher may be willing to do this if there are no unrecouped advances outstanding at the time.

- Advances—**Advances** are pre-payments of royalties that the publisher will seek to recoup out of royalties earned in the future. In a single song agreement the advance is usually a small lump sum ranging from nothing to several hundred dollars. Several hundred dollars is typical. Publishers usually will not pay advances unless the songwriter has some track record of success or the near assurance that the song will be recorded by some popular artist or by the songwriter/artists themselves. Major advances occur only in exclusive songwriter agreements as discussed below.

- Royalties—
  1. Mechanical royalties are usually divided 50/50 after any collection fee from the HFA or other mechanical collection organization is deducted.
  2. Performance royalties are usually split by the collecting performing rights organization (ASCAP, BMI, SESAC, and a few smaller agencies) and paid separately to the publisher and songwriter. Therefore, the songwriter does not usually get any percentage of what the publisher collects.
  3. Print royalties may simply be split 50/50 out of the publisher's net receipts. More often, the publisher pays a percentage royalty based on the wholesale or retail price of the music being sold, or a "penny" rate (a flat rate of so many cents per copy sold). If a percentage of a price is used, the songwriter typically gets 10–15 percent of wholesale for folios (song books), 10 percent of the wholesale price for other print (not including sheet music). For sheet music (also known as piano-vocal editions) publishers often pay a penny rate of 7 to 10 cents per copy. This approach to sheet music does not come close to a 50/50 split since the publisher is paid a percentage of the retail price approximating 70 to 80 cents per copy. The per copy sheet music rate is not often negotiable. One songwriter refers to it as a "sacred cow."[5]
  4. "Other" royalties and receipts covering a wide range of uses and unspecified uses are usually split 50/50 of the publisher's net receipts. However, there must be a clause in the contract to this effect. Otherwise the writer may not get any royalties from an unspecified use that later arises.

- **Cross-collateralization**—The publisher will usually ask that any advances be recouped out of any royalties due to the songwriter under "this or any other agreement" between the two parties. For example, royalties earned in 1 year can be used to recoup advances paid in an earlier year. Royalties earned from one song can be used to recoup advances paid for a different song. The worst scenario is that publishing advances can be recouped from any recording royalties or advances. Although, it would be more common for recording advances to be recouped out of publishing royalties if the songwriter/artist had signed recording and publishing agreements with the same company. A songwriter can usually at least limit the cross-collateralization in a publishing agreement to recoupment out of publishing royalties. On the other hand, a publisher would have no right to cross-collateralize against a songwriter/artist's income earned from a concert performance, since that agreement would not be between the songwriter/

Advance A pre-payment of royalties or other earnings. Advances are generally not returnable and not the same as a "debt" that must be repaid.

Cross-collateralization The practice (common in the recording industry) of using income from one source to recover advances made for a different source between the same two parties. For example, if an artist records an album that does not sell well, the recording advances for that album may be recovered out of royalties earned by a later album that does sell well, or from earnings under other income streams if the artist and label have a "360 deal."

artist and the publisher, but rather between the songwriter/artist and a concert promoter.

● Demo costs—Publishers try to recoup demo costs by deeming them to be "advances" in their agreements with the songwriters. A new songwriter could expect 50 percent of demo costs to be recoupable, with as little as none recoupable for a songwriter with a good track record. Other publisher expenses are generally not recoupable at all.

Exclusive songwriter agreements

Exclusive contract
Any arrangement where one party promises not to provide services or goods to any third party.

Royalties Payments to writers or performers due from the sale of copies, performances, or other uses of their works.

Under **exclusive contracts** the songwriter agrees to deliver all of the songs written for a certain period of time to the publisher in exchange for a usually substantial advance against royalties. Previously written songs may also be covered if their copyrights have not already been transferred to some other publisher.

Typical exclusive songwriter agreement terms:

● **Royalties**—The base rates and splits are typically structured as in the single song agreement above.

● Exclusivity—These contracts are "exclusive," that is the songwriter agrees that no other publisher can have claim to the songs written or co-written during the agreement. To put it another way, the publisher says, "Thou shall have no other publisher before me."

● Duration—The term of the agreement is usually for 1 year with up to four 1-year options to extend the agreement for another year. These options are the publisher's. If the publisher wants to keep the songwriter under the contract, and keep paying the advances, then the publisher may elect to do so after the end of each year. If not, the contract simply ends. Another variation is for the term of the exclusive songwriter agreement to run co-terminously with the recording contract if the songwriter is also a recording artist. If the recording contract ended, then the publisher would have the option of ending the songwriting contract. Of course, the publisher usually is able to keep all copyrights in all songs written during the term of the agreement. The obligation to pay royalties on those songs would also continue after the end of the agreement since each individual song is transferred for the life of the copyright under a single song agreement as outlined above.

● Advances—The primary reason for a songwriter to enter an exclusive agreement is the promise of the publisher to pay a substantial advance against royalties. These advances (sometimes known as a "draw") usually range from several hundred dollars a week for a new songwriter to thousands of dollars a week for an established songwriter, or a songwriter/artist who is successful. Even songwriter/artists without a recording agreement may get substantial advances if the publisher believes enough in the material and the ability of the songwriter/artist to get a recording contract. Publishing advances for writer/artists tend to be in the neighborhood of $100,000— perhaps up to $500,000 per year if there is a bidding war going on between publishers. Publishing advances may even go so far as to purchase substantial amounts of recording equipment for songwriter/artists to perfect their craft.

- Output requirements—The publisher may require the songwriter to complete a certain minimum number of songs per year, typically 12 to 20. The songs will usually have to be "accepted" by the publisher. Meaning, the publisher gets to say whether the individual song is "good enough" (in a commercial sense) to get recorded and performed. The minimum may even be stated in terms of commercially recorded songs, especially if the songwriter is also an artist.
- Collaboration—Writing with other songwriters is especially important to a songwriter's creative processes and to getting material recorded. Some songwriters take half-finished songs to recording artists and suggest that they finish them together. The result is that the songwriter now is a half writer of the song with the artist. Half a loaf is better than none, but it is important to make sure that the half loaf counts towards the minimum number of songs commitment if there is one. It is also important to the songwriter that other "collaborators," such as producers or artists who did not really create any of the composition, cannot be added to the song as songwriters without the original songwriter's permission. Writers should be sure to get a percentage of income equal to their share of the copyright, no matter how small it is. Especially in hip-hop it is common to have as many as four or five writers on a cut.

Songwriter royalty example

Assume an artist has a number one hit. How much money would the songwriter of that song make? As with many such questions in the recording industry, the answer is, "It depends." Several assumptions have to be made before one can even begin to calculate.

First, it is likely that this song is licensed for mechanical royalties at three-fourths of the statutory mechanical royalty rate, even if the songwriter is not the artist, because of restrictions on total mechanical royalties in many recording artist agreements (see Chapter 9 for details). At the 2009–2012 statutory mechanical rate of 9.1 cents per copy that would equal 6.825 cents per copy. Also assume that the mechanicals are collected through the HFA. In this day of digital downloads it is common for a hit single to sell "**gold**" (500,000 units).

- Let us also assume that the album containing the song has sold 300,000 units and is also licensed at a three-fourths rate.
- Assume that performance royalties are collected and divided by the Performing Rights Organization (PRO) and paid 50 percent to the publisher and 50 percent to the songwriter separately. Performance royalties for 1 year vary greatly depending upon the genre of the music, how long it is a hit, and whether it receives television airplay. Performance royalties for a country hit may vary by as much as $100,000 or more depending upon how much airplay even a "number one" song receives and on what stations. An "average" figure that is close for all three PROs would be about $250,000 for 1 year

Gold award
A recording or music video that has wholesale sales certified by the RIAA to be 500,000 units for an album or single or 50,000 for a music video. There are other "gold" standards for other kinds of video. See also **platinum** and **diamond**.

for either the publisher or songwriter share for a top ten hit. Another estimate placed royalties for a "major across-the-board chart song" at as much as $1 million for a pop song with significant television airplay.

● Assume a 10 cent per copy rate for sheet music and that the song has sold 20,000 pieces. This assumption may be a bit rash since many singles do not have sheet music printed.

● Finally, assume the songwriter is under an exclusive agreement and has been receiving an advance for the past year of $1,000 per week, a total of $52,000 (see Table 6.4).

The advance is added back in to show that it is money that the songwriter actually had received during the year and probably used to live on. Note also, were it not for the songwriter's share of performance royalties, that the writer is "**unrecouped**," showing a negative balance in net due from the publisher. This is not a debt that the writer owes, but the publisher would not be able to use the writer's share of performance royalties to recoup the advance because that is paid directly to the songwriter. Our example, however, is based on an Exclusive Songwriter Agreement where the writer has directed the PRO to pay the writer's share of royalties through the publisher. In that case, the publisher can use those royalties to recoup advances still outstanding. The total earnings look like a respectable sum, but most songs are not top ten hits. In fact, estimates are that only about 2 to 5 percent of songwriters make more than $10,000 per year. Also, if the song was co-written with just one other person then our songwriter would only receive half of the above amount from the various royalties.

Unrecouped A term meaning that an artist, writer, or performer has not earned enough royalties to cover the amount of advance which they have already received. The unrecouped portion of the advance is *not* a "debt."

Table 6.4 Songwriter royalties example

Mechanical royalties:	
Single sales: 500,000 units @ 6.825 cents	$34,125.00
Album sales: 300,000 units @ 6.825 cents	$20,475.00
Total:	$54,600.00
Less: HFA collection fee 5.75%	$3,139.50
Net Mechanicals collections	$51,460.50
Writer's share @ 50%	$25,730.25
Print sales: 20,000 copies @ 0.10 per copy	$2,000.00
Gross earnings from publisher	$27,730.25
Less: recoupable advance 52 weeks @ $1,000	$52,000.00
Net due from publisher	($24,269.53)
Performance royalties (Writer's share paid through publisher since this is a staff/contract writer)	$250,000.00
Net writer's earnings through publisher	$225,730.47
Plus advance	$52,000.00
Writer's net earnings	$277,730.47

Other Copyright Acquisition Methods

Since so many songwriters, producers, and recording artists have their own publishing companies there are lots of small "catalogs" of songs (all the songs owned by a publisher are its "catalog") available for possible purchase. Larger publishers often buy these small publishers' catalogs. For example, Sheryl Crow sold her self-owned music publishing catalog for a reported $10 million to an Irish publishing investment group, First State Media Group, in 2009. She retained her writer's share of income. Larger catalogs of independent publishers are also purchased, typically by the major publishers. The publisher buying the catalog usually obtains copyrights to all of the songs in the catalog as well as demos of those songs. The amount paid for the catalog varies greatly and depends on the number and value of the songs included.

Sharing the publishing

Songwriters or songwriter/artists with better bargaining position may be able to keep part of the publishing in their own publishing company and agree to split the ownership of the copyrights with a larger publisher. This is called **co-publishing**. Songwriters may be able to do co-publishing deals because they are already signed to a label deal or have some record of success with earlier songs. In a "co-pub" deal the songwriters still get their 50 percent share, and the two publishers split the remaining 50 percent in a negotiated share, often 50/50. The net result of such a deal is that the songwriter gets the usual writer's share of 50 percent of the revenues, the songwriter's publishing company gets half of the publisher's share (25 percent of the revenues), and the co-publisher gets the other 25 percent of the revenues. So, the songwriter ends up with a total of 75 percent of the total revenue.

At a minimum, the co-publisher then takes care of administrative duties associated with the songs, such as collection of royalties, licensing, and **copyright administration**. In addition, the co-publisher may actively engage in plugging the song.

Instead of owning a share of the copyright, the larger publisher may be content to make a deal just for a percentage share of the revenues earned in exchange for providing the administrative support for the catalog. These "copyright administration" deals usually involve catalogs from successful artists and producers and from smaller independent publishing companies. Administration fees charged by the administrative publisher are typically 10 percent to 25 percent of gross publishing revenues. Gross publishing revenues would include the share of songwriter income that flows through the publisher, as well as the publisher share. Administrative deals usually do not last for the duration of the copyrights, but rather for a total of 3 to 5 years.

Co-publishing An arrangement where two or more music publishers own the copyrights in a given song. It is frequently seen where an artist's publishing company shares the copyright with a "regular" music publisher, or where two or more writers on a song are affiliated with different publishing companies.

Copyright administration A music publishing function concerning the registration of songs for copyright, the recordation of other documents pertaining to those songs with the Copyright Office, and the licensing of those songs for various uses. A small publishing company owned by a writer, artist, or producer may outsource this function to another publisher in exchange for a percentage fee.

Internet Activities

- Visit the National Music Publishers' Association (NMPA) website at www.nmpa.org.
- Click the "about" link to find out who NMPA is and what they do.
- Read "Music Publishing 101" under the "Legal/Business" tab.
- Check out "Washington Update" to find what legislation or other efforts NMPA is working on in the nation's capitol.
- Visit the three PRO websites: www.ascap.org, www.bmi.com, and www. sesac.com. Get a feel for what these three organizations say about themselves and what they do. Which site interests you the most? Which seems to be the most informative?
- Visit the Harry Fox Agency website, www.harryfox.com. Read the "Licensee Services" page to find out what they do.
- Visit Nashville Songwriters Association International (NSAI) website, www. nashvillesongwriters.com. What does NSAI do? Check out the link on "How Songwriters Get Paid."
- Visit the Songwriters Guild of America website, www.songwritersguild.com. What are the activities that this organization sponsors that would be of interest to a writer?

Exploiting Copyrights

Income sources

Most publishers make all of their revenue from licensing others to use their copyrights. Unlike record companies, which make most of their money from the sale of copies of their masters, music publishers (with a few notable exceptions) do not directly sell copies of anything. They license other people to do that. To develop an understanding of the various income sources for music publishers it is necessary to understand the various licensing arrangements that lead to these income sources. Revenue sources have shifted in import-ance since the heyday of CD sales in the 1990s when mechanical royalties typically accounted for as much as 60 percent of publishing revenues. The dramatic decline in CD sales, the increase in performance and synchronization royalties, and the advent of new royalties like ring tones and ring-backs have painted a new picture. As Figure 6.1 (page 113) indicates, major music publishers now earn most of their revenues from three sources: public performances, sale of recordings (mechanical license fees), and synchronization fees (licensing songs for use in motion pictures, television, and home video). Other significant sources of revenue for some publishers are digital (such as ring tunes and ring-backs) and print music publishing. So, how does one get permission to use a song in any of these fashions? As any publisher would probably say, "No problem, just bring money."

Performance licensing

Copyrights in songs include the right of public performance. Note that this is not limited to "for profit" performances because many non-profit performances are not exempted by the Copyright Act (see Chapter 4 for more details). There are tens of thousands of nightclubs, retail stores, radio stations, television stations, and other places where music is performed publicly. The practical difficulties inherent in any single publisher attempting to license all of these outlets led to the creation of PROs which act as clearing houses for the publishers to license large numbers of performance places and for the performance places to access the thousands of songs of thousands of publishers.

There are three major PROs in the United States; American Society of Composers, Authors and Publishers (**ASCAP**), Broadcast Music, Inc. (**BMI**), and **SESAC**, Inc. A comparison of the three organizations on various points follows the description of basic performance licensing. Figure 6.2 below shows the breakdown of performance license revenues in the US.

How performance licensing works

The three PROs function in very similar manners. They all acquire non-exclusive rights to license public performances from the songwriters and music publishers

ASCAP An organization that licenses music performance rights for songwriters and music publishers. It was the first performing rights organization in the US, started in 1914.

BMI A performing rights organization started in 1940 and owned by broadcasters. It and ASCAP are the two largest performing rights organizations in the United States.

SESAC The smallest of the three main PROs in the US. SESAC used to stand for Society of European Stage Authors and Composers, but now does not have any particular meaning beyond its letters as the name of the organization.

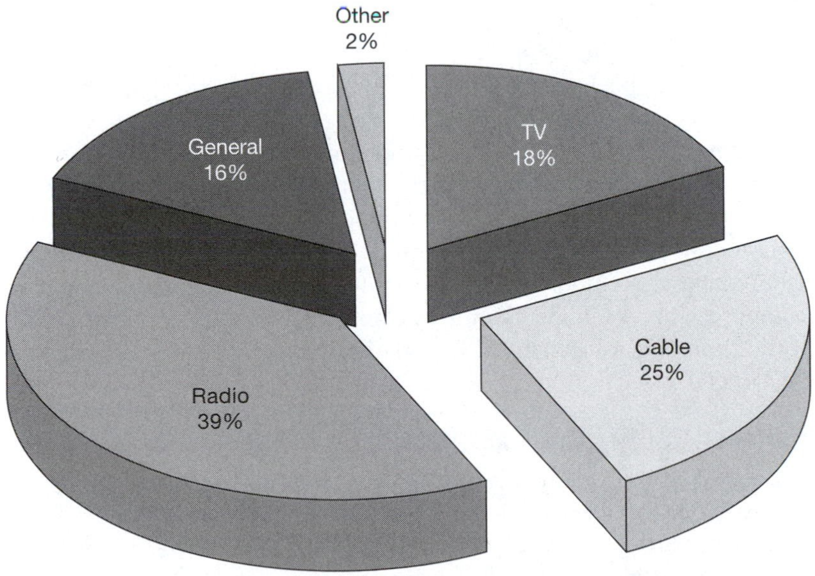

Figure 6.2 Music performance revenue sources

Non-dramatic performance rights
Performance of a single song in such a way that it does not tell any particular story; usually any performance of a single song that is not part of an opera or musical is non-dramatic unless it tells a story accompanied by action or visuals.

Dramatic performance
A performance of a work that tells a story. Usually associated with musical theater or opera and multiple songs, but a single song may be a dramatic performance if accompanied by other action or visuals.

Blanket license
A term used mainly in performance rights licensing where a performing rights organization gives a licensee such as a radio station, nightclub, or web service the right to perform all of the songs or recordings in the PRO's repertoire as many times as the licensee wants.

Per-program use (or license)
Permission to use a single recording or song on a one-time basis, as compared to a blanket license.

that belong to their organizations. The rights are non-exclusive because the publishers retain the right to license the works directly themselves. The PROs obtain only ***non-dramatic performance rights.*** **Dramatic performances**, those which involve the performance of more than one composition from an opera or musical theatrical production or which involve the use of the composition to tell a story in some dramatic manner (as on stage or screen), are licensed directly by the publisher or by a theatrical licensing agency which represents the publisher. Dramatic performance rights are known as "grand rights" and non-dramatic performing rights are known as "small rights." Both the publisher and the songwriter of the composition must belong to the same performing rights organization. Most music publishers of any size operate at least two separate companies, affiliated with different PROs, so that any songwriter whom the publisher may sign can be accommodated, whichever PRO the songwriter prefers.

The PROs then issue licenses to anyone and anywhere their music might be performed publicly. (See Chapter 4 for a definition of public performance under the Copyright Act.) Figure 6.3 indicates the flow of licenses from the initial copyright owners to the licensees, and of the royalties/license fees collected from licensees back to the songwriters and publishers. For most places where music is performed the most economical way to obtain permission to use a vast number of songs is to obtain a "**blanket license.**" The blanket license from a PRO allows the licensee to perform, or have performed under its roof, any of the compositions that the PRO represents, as many times as desired. Such a license is particularly valuable to radio stations and night clubs where thousands of different songs may be performed, some of them hundreds of times. Keeping track of individual performances would be a real nightmare. The Supreme Court of the United States has even recognized the value of the blanket license. In an anti-trust suit brought against BMI by Columbia Broadcasting System, the Court upheld the validity of the blanket license, saying,

> [T]he blanket license developed . . . out of the practical situation in the marketplace: thousands of users, thousands of copyright owners, and millions of compositions. Most users want unplanned, rapid, and indemnified access to any and all of the repertory of the compositions, and the owners want a reliable method of collecting for the use of their copyrights. Individual sales transactions in this industry are quite expensive, as would be individual monitoring and enforcement, especially in light of the resources of single composers. . . . A middleman with a blanket license was an obvious necessity if the thousands of individual negotiations, a virtual impossibility, were to be avoided"[6]

The PROs must also offer a **per-program use or license** to those users who wish to take advantage of it. Per-use or per-program licenses are more costly on a per-song basis, but may be less expensive overall than a blanket license if a broadcaster, particularly a television broadcaster, only needs access to a very limited number of clearly identified compositions on a regular basis.

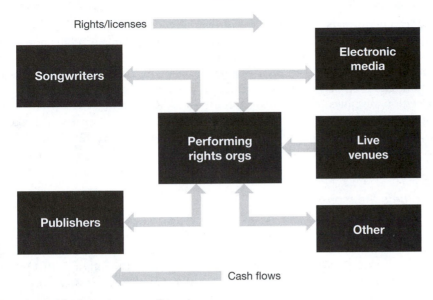

Figure 6.3 Music performance licensing

Who obtains the license?

Although technically speaking the actual musician performing a song live in a club would be liable for the public performance, it is the operator/owner of the venue who is obtaining the benefit of the performances that is also liable for copyright infringement if there is an unlicensed performance. As a practical matter it is much easier to license the premises than to license a bunch of traveling musicians. Therefore, owners of nightclubs, owners of radio and television stations, owners of retail outlets where background music is being played, and owners of concert venues (or the concert promoter if the venue does not have much music performed during a typical year) all must have performance licenses to cover the compositions performed in their establishments. An exception to the public performance right allows many retail stores and food and beverage establishments to play radio programs over speakers in their establishments without having to obtain a license. (See Chapter 4 for more detail on the Fairness in Musical Licensing Act.)

How much is the license?

The cost of the license depends upon a number of factors. Background music licenses cost less than live entertainment licenses. Live entertainment licenses cost less than broadcast performance licenses. The bigger the operation in terms of physical size, number of seats, amount of music being performed, power of transmitter and other factors, the more the license costs. A small retail store playing recorded music might obtain background licenses for a total of about $500 per year. A television network spends millions of dollars per year for broadcast performance licenses. A major concert with a million dollar gross would pay about $10,000 for the license for the single show. A major nightspot, such as a casino in Las Vegas, spends even more on an annual basis. Radio broadcasters negotiate with ASCAP and BMI as a group through the Radio Music License Committee. License fees are now set as flat rates per station and do not depend on station revenues as they had in the past. ASCAP and BMI deduct their operating expenses from the available pot of money. Those expenses ran at about 11 percent to 12 per cent of collections per year in 2009. SESAC does that as well as taking a profit for their owners.

Who gets the money?

The PRO collects the license fees from all of the various users, then determines how much money each song in the PRO's repertoire is entitled to receive. This daunting task is accomplished somewhat differently by the different PROs (see below). Suffice it to say, however, that the best any of the PROs can do is get an exact count of performances from some licensees, such as the television networks, get a sample, or actual "**spin count**" of a larger group such as local radio stations, and use those as an estimate of what songs were performed live in clubs, discotheques, and as background music.

Spin count (also called simply spins) The number of times a particular recording has been played over the radio, as recorded by BDS.

The various methodologies are the subject of great debate among the three organizations as to who does the best job of accurately paying their publishers and songwriters. Their methodologies all have their merits and shortcomings and no one is, or will ever be, perfect because of the virtual impossibility of monitoring all songs played live in clubs. Nightclubs and other live performances account for about 16 percent of performance license fee collections.

Once the amount to pay for each song is determined, the PRO divides the payment in half and sends half to the songwriter and half to the publisher. If there are multiple songwriters or multiple publishers then the PRO divides the money according to the directions supplied by the songwriters and publishers. If a song-writer specifically instructs the PRO to pay the songwriter's share to the publisher, perhaps because the songwriter is a staff songwriter who has a significant advance to be recouped, the PRO will do so (see previous royalty example).

Comparing ASCAP, BMI, and SESAC

- Organization—ASCAP is a non-profit organization run by its "members"— the publishers and songwriters. BMI is a corporation owned by broadcasters but which operates on a non-profit basis. SESAC is a privately held corporation that operates on a profit-making basis for its owners (who are not the songwriter or publisher affiliates). Because SESAC is privately held and does not report revenues and other information publicly it is sometimes difficult to compare it to the other two organizations.
- Size—ASCAP and BMI are about the same size in terms of members/ affiliates and collections. For example, in 2009 BMI represented 400,000 songwriters, composers, arrangers, and publishers and ASCAP 350,000

members of the same kind. SESAC, though clearly the smaller organization with an estimated 3,000–4,000 affiliates, became much more aggressive in acquisition of songwriter catalog in recent years, notably with the acquisition of licensing rights to Bob Dylan and Neil Diamond's catalogs in the mid-1990s. ASCAP reported receipts of $933 million in for the 2008–2009 fiscal year and distributed $817 million to its songwriter and publisher members. BMI stated its 2008–2009 collections as $905 million and distributions as $788 million. (See Figure 6.4 for trends.) SESAC does not publicly report its annual receipts.

- Kinds of music licensed—Initially SESAC had a stronger hold in Latin and Gospel music, ASCAP in "standards" since they were the oldest organization, and BMI in country, R&B, and rock. Now all three organizations compete well in all genres.

- Online clearances and licensing—All three organizations have online listings of their repertoire. All three have many performance licenses available online —some are click-through, some are simply downloadable. They also allow online clearance of songs by users and listing of new songs by their affiliates using their pages on the World Wide Web.

- "**Logging**" methodology—That becomes the basis for how royalties are then split up among publishers and writers. A detailed discussion is beyond the scope of this text, but important recent changes in methodology for all three PROs indicate that more music from more diverse sources and voices is being logged, and paid royalties. None of the organizations can count every performance of every song. So what they do is create a sample that has actual airplay reports from electronic tracking and logs of TV networks and radio stations, and some concerts. These then comprise the basis of the estimate of how much performance a particular song receives. The pot of money available, which includes some money from licensees where exactly which songs are performed is not reported, is then divided according to the estimate.

Logging The practice of keeping track of how many times individual songs or recordings played or performed, usually referring to the performing rights organizations.

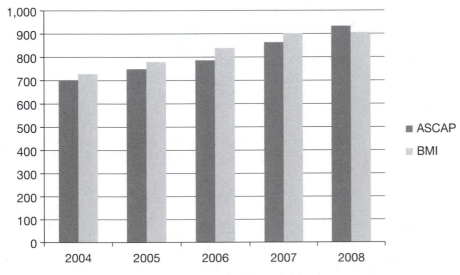

Figure 6.4 Performance rights collections (millions of dollars)

All three organizations have been expanding the scope of their sample and improving its accuracy in recent years. All use electronic monitoring of radio and some other broadcasts. SESAC uses BDS (Nielsen Broadcast Data Systems) "watermarking" system to identify radio airplay. ASCAP uses Mediaguide (a company it co-owns) to monitor radio, TV, satellite, and Internet transmissions through "fingerprinting" technology. BMI uses Landmark Digital Services, a wholly-owned subsidiary, to gather actual airplay data. But none of these systems tracks *every* radio station or transmitter. For example, BDS monitored over 2,000 stations in the US and Canada in 2009, including some in nearly every format. However, there were over 13,000 licensed radio stations in the US.

In addition to the electronic monitoring, ASCAP began actual monitoring of live performance venues and getting song logs from the top 100 touring acts. BMI added college radio stations to its list of stations completing logs. SESAC increased the number of radio formats for which it receives actual airplay information from BDS. All of these changes meant that more songs were being logged and paid for their performances. This means that not only mainstream hits will be logged, but also songs by artists who either do not receive much airplay or who receive airplay on small stations, or less popular formats. This in turn increases the prospect for non-mainstream songwriter/artists to collect performance royalties for their songs and increases the possibility that they can sustain a career.

- Age—ASCAP was founded in 1914 to begin to develop a way for US composers to collect for live performances of their songs. SESAC was founded in 1930 primarily to license European composers' music in the US BMI was founded in 1940 to provide broadcasters with music to play when they refused to agree to pay the fees demanded by ASCAP in the 1940 license negotiations. If the stations refused the ASCAP license they could not play any songs licensed through ASCAP. That sent the broadcasters scrambling to get performance rights for country, blues, and anything else that they could play to fill their programming.
- Payments—The three organizations debate long and hard about which will pay the most money. There are situations in which either might pay more for a given song than the other two, depending on where and how often it was performed. A comparison of average payments on hit songs revealed that the three were within about a $7,000 range of each other out of an average songwriter share of about $140,000. However the PROs reported a range from a low of $114,000 to a high of $194,000 for recent country hits. The three organizations competed to sign songwriters and publishers and aggressively pursued licensing previously unlicensed users into the twenty-first century.

Mechanical Licensing

Although the Copyright Act allows a record company to procure a statutory (compulsory) license to record a musical composition (see discussion in Chapter 4), most labels prefer to obtain negotiated licenses from the publishers. The

National Music Publishers' Association (NMPA) (then the Music Publisher's Protective Association) established the Harry Fox Agency (HFA) in 1927 to provide a clearinghouse for mechanical rights for the rapidly growing sales of recordings and piano rolls in the 1920s. Now the HFA issues and collects for about three fourths of the mechanical licenses in the United States. By 2009 the HFA represented the catalogs of over 37,000 music publishers and had annual collections of over $300 million. Mechanical license collections fell in the 2000s due to the decline in the sales of CDs (see Figure 6.5). The Agency charges the member publishers collection fees of 5.75 percent of mechanical royalties collected. The HFA quit its general service in issuing and collecting for synchronization licenses in 2002.

In addition to collecting fees from the record labels and distributing them to the appropriate publishers, the agency conducts audits of its licensees on behalf of the members. The HFA reported audit recoveries of over $20 million for 2008. As indicated by Figure 6.6, these collections are distributed to the publishers, who then divide them with the songwriters according to their contractual agreement, usually 50/50. The HFA allows potential licensees to obtain licenses electronically via their World Wide Web site, "Songfile," for productions of fewer than 2,500 copies.

Mechanical rates

Although most mechanical licensing is not through the statutory compulsory license, the rates tend to follow the compulsory rate. Because a large amount of the compositions licensed are by songwriter/artists and because these people tend to have controlled composition clauses in their recording agreements (see discussion in Chapter 9), most licenses are for less than the full "statutory" rate.

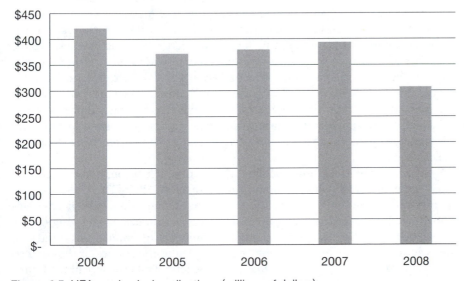

Figure 6.5 HFA mechanicals collections (millions of dollars)

Figure 6.6 Mechanical rights licensing

The negotiated rates range from three-fourths of the statutory rate up to the full rate. The HFA states that it will not issue mechanical licenses at a rate below the statutory rate without instructions from the publisher, but publishers are often willing to do so, especially when songwriter/artists are involved. The net result is that typical mechanical license rates in 2009 ranged from about 6.8 cents per side to the full statutory rate of 9.1 cents per side. Historically, the statutory rate remained at 2 cents from 1909 to 1978. It was then increased in increments from 2.75 cents in 1978 to 9.1 cents in 2008. That 9.1 cent rate will remain in effect until 2013 (see details in Chapter 4).

Synchronization Rights

As sales of hard copies of CDs have declined and other uses of music in movies, advertisements, television, and more have increased, synchronization royalties have moved up to the third most important source of music publishing income. Synchronization (usually referred to as "synch") rights refer to the right to use music, as the contracts often put it, "in timed relation to visual images." In the early days of attempts to accompany motion pictures with sound, recordings were played while the motion picture was being played and elaborate devices attempted to keep the sound synchronized with the screen action. When the sound became integrated on the film on a separate track, it still had to be synchronized because the sound had to precede the image with which it was associated in order for the viewer to perceive the sound as originating at the correct time from the screen.

Synchronization rights must be obtained for film, television, home video, and video game uses (can you say "Guitar Hero" or "Rock Band"?). These uses are licensed on a per song basis directly from the music publisher. Film licenses are highly individualized depending upon the nature of the use of the song (Is it a theme, or featured as in a performance, or simply background?), the amount of the song that is used (a few seconds or entirely), and the stature of the song (is it a recognizable hit or a new song that might benefit from exposure in the film?). For example, synch license fees for a song in a major studio film would be anywhere from $5,000 for a brief incidental use, to $50,000 for a significant use in the movie, and up to $250,000 or more if the song is the main title song for the film. Uses in commercials may run anywhere from $75,000 to $500,000 for a 1-year use. Television program synch licenses will run from $1,500 to $10,000 per episode, all depending upon the nature of the use and the popularity of the song. Video game licenses tend to be a flat fee in the range of $1,000 to $6,000 but can go higher for major song titles. As mentioned earlier, the publisher typically splits synch license fees on a 50/50 basis with the songwriter, after deduction of any collection expenses.

Print Publishing

Structure

Total print music publishing sales in the US amounted to about $600 million in 2008. Music publishers, even the largest, do not manufacture and distribute print editions of their own songs. Some do not even license print editions of their songs at all. Nearly 25 percent of the top 100 hits do not even appear in print editions. Economies of scale in manufacturing and distribution have collapsed print music publishing into a highly concentrated industry with only two major players. Both are independent of the "Big Four." The Hal Leonard Corporation is the largest. In 2005 Alfred Music Publishing purchased Warner Brothers Publications (the print division of Warner/Chappell Music) from Warner Music Group, making it the second largest print publisher. Two former print competitors, Cherry Lane Music and Music Sales Group (the largest European print music publisher), now license distribution in the US through Hal Leonard. EMI Music, arguably the world's largest music publisher, has its print publishing done through Hal Leonard, as do Paramount's Famous Music, Disney, Universal, and Sony/ATV. Warner Brothers Music still licenses print distribution for a large catalog, it just does not do any printing or physical distribution. Hal Leonard and Warner Brothers Music (individually and in some cases jointly) control roughly equal shares of the print licensing for hit songs. It is unusual to see any other print publisher with sheet music rights to more than one or two songs in the top 100.

Print licensing

Print publishing income amounts to less than 10 percent of total publishing income (Figure 6.1, page 113) but the United States has a significantly higher percentage of worldwide print income (estimated at over 40 percent). The print publisher typically agrees to pay the music publisher as follows: 50 to 80 cents per copy for sheet music (piano/vocal) if a penny rate, or 20 percent of the suggested retail list price (SRLP) if a percentage royalty, and 10–15 percent SRLP for folios (pro-rated based on the number of songs the particular music publisher has in the folio). The print publisher may have to pay an additional 2.5 to 5

Personality folio
A songbook featuring songs as recorded by a particular artist or writer.

percent for the right to use the recording artist's name on a **"personality folio"** that is keyed to a particular artist or album. Print rights are usually granted on a non-exclusive basis to the print publisher with the duration of the license being 3 to 5 years.

DIY Activities

Suppose you are in a band that wants to make a CD of the band performing a cover version of the Bob Dylan song, "Blowin' in the Wind."

● Search the three PROs to find out who has the performing rights, who the publisher is, and what the publisher's address is.
● Go to the HFA website. Get into the public search area for Songfile. Search that title to find out if HFA represents that song. Find out if you could use the click through license to make 500 copies of your recording of that song. How much would you have to pay?

Now suppose that you also want to record one of your own songs (or one that you know a friend has written).

● Investigate how to join one of the PRO. Which one did you select? Why?
● What would you have to do to become a Publishing Affiliate of that PRO?
● What would you have to do to become an HFA member publishing affiliate?

Songwriting

> "Great songs are about people's hopes, dreams, and aspirations."[7]

Because, as some people say, "It all begins with a song," why consider songwriters last in this chapter? Because all of the things discussed above have implications for people who want to write songs. With rare exception, the songwriters of pop, rock, and R&B hits tend to be the people who perform them or produce them. Even in country music, being a "just plain songwriter" is becoming increasingly difficult. A connection with an artist or producer is extremely important. A connection with a music publisher is extremely important. Most publishers will not accept unsolicited demos of songs. To get that contact at the publisher, songwriters can perform in showcases, perform in clubs, work through a PRO, or just plain knock on doors. A songwriter will have to do these things someplace where a publisher is likely to hear them. Writing with a songwriter who already has songs placed with a publisher is also a quick track to the inside. Two important organizations for developing and professional songwriters are the Songwriters Guild of America, and the NSAI.

As to song content, we have all heard songs on the radio that we think are not very good. Perhaps they just do not communicate with us personally. Perhaps they really are not very good in that they do not communicate very well with anybody. Those songs may not be well crafted in terms of lyrics and structure. The craft of songwriting can be learned. There are numerous books on the "how to" of songwriting. The songwriters' organizations in major cities often have songwriters' workshops. The PROs often have songwriters' workshops and seminars. The important thing is to write often and to get feedback from somebody who has some background or experience that qualifies them to judge songs.

It is difficult for many songwriters to accept even constructive criticism because the very nature of the early stages of songwriting is that the songs become highly personal statements. There is not much point to complain, "Well, they are *my* songs and I don't care if anybody else will understand them." If that is the songwriter's real perspective then they need not be trying to get a publisher or label interested in the songs. If, however, the songwriter would like to use the songs to communicate or share ideas or feelings with a broader audience then the use of popular music as a communication medium is appropriate. If a songwriter or artist asks others to invest time and money in their message, then the investors need some reasonable assurance that the song or recording stands a chance of recouping the initial investment—i.e. that it is reasonably commercial.

Songwriting is both art and craft. While it is easy to write a song, it is difficult to come up with a song that is well crafted and has enough appeal to get an artist to feel that it could be a hit. Country songwriter, Will Rambeaux, put it this way:

> It takes years to develop that craft to the point where you're writing songs that are good enough for the radio. I know that sounds simple and shallow, but it's not easy to do that, to write songs that have universal appeal.[8]

Few songwriters have ever managed to accomplish that in modern times as well as Diane Warren. She is not a recording artist, nor a producer, yet she has songs recorded by artists in nearly every genre, in motion pictures, and television. She says a good song is, "Something that touches you, makes you feel something."[9]

Summary

Music publishing is one of the three basic revenue streams in the music and recording business. Music publishers make money through licensing the uses of the songs, whose copyrights they own or administer, for uses in recordings, public performances, and motion pictures and television, video games, and sheet music. To do this, the publishers must first acquire, then exploit (market) the songs. The four major music companies each own affiliated music publishing companies and account for a total of about 65 percent of all publishing revenues.

The publisher usually acquires the rights from a songwriter or producer, who may also be a recording artist, by agreeing to market the uses of the song in exchange for paying the writer half of the revenue received from the various uses. This may be done on a single song basis, or by having the writer under contract to write a certain number of songs per year for a period of time. More recently, publishers have taken up an A&R function by trying to find potentially marketable recording artists who write their own material, signing them to exclusive writer agreements, then helping the writers develop to the point where they can get a recording agreement with a significant record label.

The exploitation (licensing) of the songs is primarily through public performances and recordings. Public performances are usually licensed through ASCAP, BMI, or SESAC (the PROs) in this country. ASCAP and BMI are the largest PROs and both work on a non-profit basis. SESAC is a smaller and for-profit organization. All three issue "blanket" licenses to broadcasters, night clubs, performance halls, DJs, and others for performing the music in their catalogs. The PROs then split the money they collect and pay half to the copyright owners (publishers) and the other half to the songwriters. Mechanical licenses for making recordings of the songs are typically issued through the HFA, which was created by the NMPA for that purpose. The HFA issues the licenses, which are negotiated and not compulsory (see discussion of compulsory licenses in Chapter 4), and pays all collections to the publisher, who in turn splits the revenues with the writers, usually on a 50/50 basis. Other significant uses of the music include synchronization (the use in movies or television), print, and game use. The publishers are typically paid a royalty from the uses in print or games, but are usually paid a one-time flat amount for synchronization and sometimes that way for game uses.

Case Study: Bug Music

Bug Music is one of the most successful independent (not owned by the four majors) music publishing companies. In 1975 Dan Bourgoise, who worked for United Artists, decided to administer the music copyrights of and become the personal manager of his friend, performer and writer Del Shannon. In 1977 Dan's brother Fred came over from Tower Records to join him.

Bug Music then slowly built its business not on traditional music publishing but on copyright administration for artists and producers who had their own publishing companies but who needed assistance with the nitty-gritty business side of publishing.

By 1999 they represented a stable of artist/writers as diverse as Stevie Ray Vaughan, Iggy pop, Townes Van Zandt, Johnny Cash, Richard Thompson, and Muddy Waters.

Bug typically charged a standard 10–15 percent fee for administration (like most administrative music publishers) but raised that to 25 percent if they succeeded in getting new uses for the songs they represent. The fee is ordinarily a percentage of the gross publishing income, which includes the writer and publisher share. Bug does not enter co-publishing deals but does administrative deals with "creative clauses."

Bug opened a Nashville office in the mid-1980s and a New York office in 1997. Bug added international offices in London and Munich. As the company grew its revenues, it moved more into copyright acquisition instead of just administration. It scored a major coup with the signing of British folk/rock guitarist/songwriting sensation Richard Thompson's large catalog in 1997.

In 2006 the "Bug Brothers" made a major move to acquire additional capital and change their role in the business. They partnered with private equity firm, Crossroads Media. That move brought additional music publishing expertise into the firm with new CEO John Rudolph, who was a CFO with Windswept Music and a music publishing consultant. The brothers then left day-to-day management of the company, but the infusion of capital set the stage for Bug's next move into the ranks of a major independent publisher.

In 2007 Bug acquired the Windswept catalog from Japanese firms Fujipacific Music and Fuji Television Network. That acquisition included the Lieber and Stoller catalog of Motown hits, and a co-interest in Antonio Reid's Hitco Music. The Leiber and Stolller songs included "Fever," "Happy Together," and "Splish Splash." The Hitco catalog included songs from Beyonce Knowles and Sean Garrett. Later that year, Bug/Windswept entered a joint venture deal with online indie music resource Music Nation and its label, Original Signal Recordings, to find and develop new talent to sign publishing deals with Bug/Windswept.

But the new Bug/Windswept clearly had its eyes on additional acquisitions. It acquired a $200 million line of credit in September, 2008. In October that same year Bug entered a joint venture with rock band Kings of Leon to sign and develop new artists. Additionally, the group signed its publishing over to Bug/Windswept.

So, Bug Music, the former music publishing administration company, moved broadly into the music business in publishing, talent acquisition, and talent development.

QUESTIONS FOR REVIEW

1. What are the four major sources of music publishing income? Which two are the biggest?
2. What are the four biggest music publishing companies? Name two more.
3. What does a music publisher do? What are the two main functions of a music publisher?
4. What are the differences between a full publishing agreement with a songwriter, a co-publishing agreement, and a publishing administration agreement?
5. How do songwriters and publishers split their royalties?
6. How does mechanical licensing work? What is the Harry Fox Agency?
7. How does performance licensing work? What are the three major PROs in the US?
8. How does synchronization licensing work?
9. How do most songwriters get their songs recorded?
10. Name two organizations that help songwriters.

7 Live Entertainment: The Second Stream

Introduction

The Big Picture

The power of popular music and recordings is overwhelmingly evident in the live entertainment business. Popular artists performing the songs they have recorded create the vast majority of the income generated in the live performance stream. *Pollstar* estimated that ticket sale revenues for major concerts in North America amounted to $4.2 billion in 2008 and their top 100 tours only included five non-musical acts (comediennes Jeff Dunham, Chris Rock, George Lopez, and Ron White, and magic act David Copperfield), which accounted for less than 2 percent of ticket sale revenues. As with recording sales, the majority of the revenues are generated by a small number of the artists. The top 20 tours accounted for nearly 25 percent of ticket sale revenues.

For sake of comparison, the Recording Industry Association of America (RIAA) estimates that the value of all digital and physical sales of recordings in 2008 was $8.4 billion. So, the revenue in the live entertainment stream was about half that of the recorded music stream. However, for many artists, live performance generated more income for them than did the sales of their recordings. That is because the artists do not get to keep as much of the money from the sale of the recordings as they do from the sale of a ticket to a live show. Chapter 9 will explain why. And live performance can generate income for artists long after sale of recordings has faded. *Only one* of the top 10 touring acts of 2008 had a top 10 album or digital track that same year. Madonna and Justin Timberlake had the number 10 best selling *digital* track that year.

How big is a big tour? In 2008, top grossing Madonna brought in an estimated $105.3 million by doing 30 shows and selling nearly 700,000 tickets. The Kenny Chesney tour reached the most fans, selling over a million tickets at 41 shows. Very few hard-working musical acts played over 70 shows, and only two, The Trans Siberian Orchestra and Carrie Underwood, did over 100 shows. (There were actually two different touring "Trans Siberian Orchestras" that year.) Fifteen of the top 100 tours had average ticket prices in excess of 100 dollars, including the top three tours by Madonna, Celine Dion, and the Eagles.

The live performance ticket sales generated by major acts nearly doubled from 1998 to 2002, then doubled again from 2002 to 2008 (Figure 7.1). Although some of the increase can be accounted for by increases in average ticket prices (Figure 7.2), ticket prices went up about 160 percent over the same period while

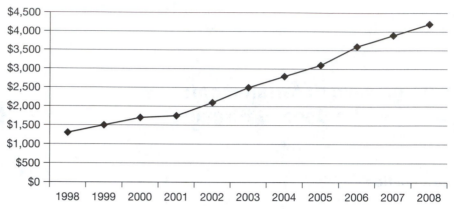

Figure 7.1 Touring grosses, 1998–2008 (millions of US dollars)
Source: *Pollstar*, year end issues

Venue The place
where a live
performance
happens. It could
be a club, a theater,
an auditorium,
a stadium, or an
open field.

revenues increased 300 percent. Over that same 12-year period, inflation (consumer price index) only went up 37 percent. Although not all live entertainment is before large audiences, the big tours in big **venues** account for the lion's share of the live performance revenues. Of the top 40 concert grosses in 2008, only one was at a venue with capacity significantly less than 10,000. Elton John did 13 shows at Caesar's Palace (capacity just over 4,000) to gross $7.6 million. But the "tail" of the venue list is long. There are many, many small venues. Even the largest venue operators SMG, Global Spectrum, and Live Nation operate less than 10 percent of the venues each. *Pollstar* listed over 1,700 venues in its 2009/2010 Venue Directory. Even those 1,700 do not account for the thousands of small bars and clubs where aspiring musicians play for the

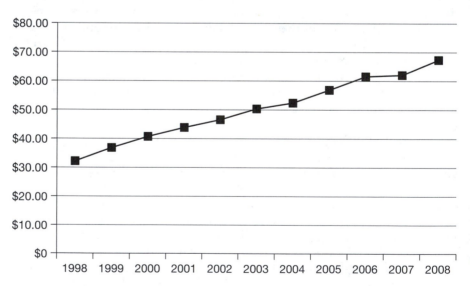

Figure 7.2 Average ticket prices
Source: *Pollstar*, year end issues

"door," for tips, for their supper, or even for free, just for the experience and exposure.

The decade of 1998–2008 saw major changes in the live entertainment business. Ticket prices increased dramatically. Tour grosses increased dramatically. Consolidation of promoters, venue owners, agencies, and management firms into national level organizations impacted every aspect of the business. But the bottom line was still the same—putting on live entertainment for fans of the artists and their music.

The Major Players

There are five roles that must be filled in the live entertainment stream: performer, **personal manager**, **talent agent**, **promoter**, and venue operator (see Figure 7.3.). The role of the label is discussed later in this chapter, but it is not a *must* role. In an idealized situation the performer decides, usually in conjunction with the personal manager, that it is time to do a tour, perhaps in conjunction with the release of a new album. Other details such as what parts of the country to play, what cities, what size venues, and how many dates are roughed out. The manager then contacts the talent agent (aka booking agent) who has contracted to arrange performances for the artist. The manager gives the agent the details that have been worked out to date and the agent and manager, in consultation with the artist, arrive at a minimum price for the show and some basic terms of a performance agreement.

The agent then begins contacting promoters to line up potential dates. The promoters contact venues to see what dates are open for what prices and probably put "**holds**" on dates that would fit the tour. The promoters then call the agent

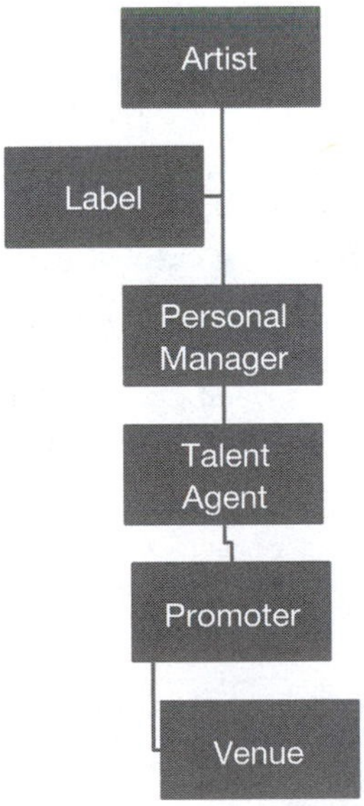

Personal manager An artist's representative who works closely with the artist at all stages and usually for all purposes to develop the artist's career.

Talent agent (aka booking agent) A person who secures employment for performers.

Promoter The person or organization in charge of arranging all aspects of a live performance.

Holds In concert promotion, a verbal agreement between a promoter and a venue to keep a certain date open for that promoter and not to license the venue to another event for that date until the first promoter decides whether or not to use it.

Figure 7.3 Live entertainment players

back and say what dates and venues are available and present the agent with the basics of a deal. As the agent begins putting together pieces of the tour the promoters are notified of any definite dates or at least which holds from the venue operators can be released for some other artist.

Finally, when a tour itinerary is fairly firm, the agent approaches the manager (and perhaps artist) for approval. If the artist and manager approve, then the agent begins to issue contracts to the promoters. The promoters then sign contracts with the venue operators. Then the promoters develop plans for advertising and promoting the shows and begin arranging whatever details are called for by the performer's agreement. With luck the performer shows up for the show, the tickets have all been sold, the performance happens without a hitch, and the promoter and artist's representative divide the receipts according to their agreement. That is the ideal world. In the real world things seldom go precisely that way or that smoothly. A closer examination of the roles of the major players will help explain why.

KEY CONCEPTS

- Live entertainment in North America accounted for about $4.2 billion of ticket sales in 2008.
- Key players in this stream are the Personal Manager, the Talent Agent, the Concert Promoter, and the Venue.
- Personal Managers deal with all aspects of an artist's career and may receive a 15–20 percent commission on all (or most of) the artist's income.
- Talent agents are solely responsible for booking engagements for the artist. They receive a commission of about 10 percent of the artist's bookings that they contracted.
- Concert promoters make money from ticket sales of concerts, but must often pay the artists large sums for their performances. This makes promotion a very risky business.
- Venues make money by renting their space to the promoters, and by selling concessions including food, drinks, and parking.
- A successful artist must have a team of persons helping them with their business, including (at a minimum) a personal manager, a talent agent, an attorney, and an accountant.
- Consolidation has created several giants in live entertainment: Live Nation, AEG Live, and Ticketmaster. Live Nation and Ticketmaster merged in 2010.

Personal Managers

"An artist's career represents a lot of investment in terms not just of money but of time, energy, sweat and disappointment." Ed Bicknell, former personal manager for Dire Straits.[1]

Structure of the personal management business

The business of personal management is run by a large number of firms and managers, who generally manage only five or six acts—very few manage more than a dozen. There is no concentration of market share in the management business. There are probably as many as 2,000 or more personal managers in the United States alone. *Pollstar's* 2009 Artist Management Directory lists about 1,700 personal managers. Some manage major artists—some are just beginners who hope to build their favorite local band into international superstars. That being said, in 2008 one of the largest and most powerful management companies, Irving Azoff's Front Line Management Group, which managed over 200 artists including the Eagles, Christina Aguilera, Neil Diamond, and many more, merged with the largest seller of concert tickets, Ticketmaster. Whatever the stature of their artists, their roles are surprisingly similar.

What does a personal manager do?

It is difficult, if not impossible, to be a recording artist who performs live without someone at least performing the functions of a personal manager. Personal managers are in charge of developing all aspects of a performer's career. To that end they must possess good "people skills" to be able to work closely with the artist and others in all of the income streams. They must also possess significant knowledge of the industry and have contacts within the industry to be able to create the kinds of opportunities that the artist needs to develop a significant career. In the early stages the personal manager will work with the artist to develop a good live act and performance, giving the performer feedback and constructive criticism. Based on the manager's assessment of the artist's talent and potential, the manager will probably develop a career plan that will at least take the artist through the first recording contract.

The career plan will undoubtedly be altered later if the artist achieves substantial success and as other opportunities present themselves. The manager will help the performer become a better songwriter (if they are) by providing feedback on songs or finding or hiring people who can. The manager will attempt to secure the artist a publishing agreement if that is a good possibility. The manager will find an appropriate talent agent for the artist at the early stages of the artist's career if the artist does not already have an agent. Managers do not generally procure personal appearances for the artist, except as ancillary to their job. That is the agent's job. In fact, in California, it is illegal for managers to procure employment beyond a recording contract unless they are licensed talent agents. Most managers are not. The manager's most important task in the early stages is to get the artist to the point where they are ready to sign a recording contract, then help them get such a contract.

Once the artist has a recording contract, the manager works to see that the recording is released and is successful. The task probably begins by encouraging the artist to successfully complete their first master recording. Usually the manager will watch closely the development of the label's marketing and promotion plans and may even assist by hiring independent promotion services or making sure the artist performs the necessary promotional engagements. The manager will work with the label and the music video director to be sure that the marketing and promotion plans of the label and the video fit the artist's image and music. If the artist got the label deal without a publishing agreement or without an agency agreement, the manager will actively seek those deals for the artist as well. Once touring begins the manager will work to assure that everything goes as smoothly for the artist as possible. If the recording and tour are successful enough the manager does it all over again for a second album and tour.

As the artist's career progresses, the manager must begin to expose the artist to an ever-widening audience. The manager will probably attempt to get talk show appearances for the artist, variety show appearances, and, perhaps, if the artist has any acting talent, motion picture and dramatic television appearances. Career growth will require more work from the manager, so the manager will probably expand by outsourcing some functions that the manager had performed at the early stages of the artist's career. Somewhere in this development the manager will probably need to engage the services of a public relations specialist unless the management company is large enough to provide that service itself. In addition, the manager will probably need to engage the services of a business manager to handle the artist's monetary matters to assure that the income from the artist's peak earning years can be spread out and invested in ways to provide for future stable income.

Finally, the manager will attempt to sustain the artist's career for as long as possible, if the artist is willing. Long after most artists have stopped having hit records, they are still able to have a successful performing career. The popular 1990s and 2000s thing to do was the revival or reunion tour and the farewell (maybe) tour. Major artists from the 1960s, 1970s, and 1980s such as the Eagles, Jimmy Page and Robert Plant (Led Zeppelin), the Allman Brothers Band, and the Beach Boys (to name just a few) had top 50 tours in 1995. In 2002 the list included Cher, Paul McCartney, Neil Diamond, Bob Dylan, Santana, and John Mellancamp. In 2008 it was Bon Jovi, the Eagles (again), Van Halen, the Police, and Rush to name a few.

The "personal" side of the manager's role is that of caretaker, confidant, and surrogate mother. Says Bill Curbishley, at one time the personal manager of Jimmy Page, Robert Plant, The Who, and Judas Priest (and others), "To be a personal manager, you're involved in their marriages, divorces, births, deaths, traumas, dramas, happiness, sadness—all of it."[2]

In order to do these things the manager must believe in the artist's abilities and desire to succeed. The artist must trust the manager implicitly with the details of the artist's career and the manager must be deserving of that trust. When the trust breaks down the relationship rapidly deteriorates. For many artists at a lower echelon of success the break-up simply results in frustration for the manager and a "What have you ever done for me?" from the artist. When the artist has achieved substantial levels of success, the break-up can cost the manager literally millions of dollars, especially if the legal and moral trust that the manager holds has been breached. Writer/artist Billy Joel was awarded sums totaling over $2.6 million in separate suits against his former business manager for conversion of Joel's investments in a real estate partnership.

Sometimes the relationship between manager and artist can produce a series of strange events once that relationship is severed. Former Beatle George Harrison won an $11.6 million recovery of half of the debt of his film company of which his business manager had promised to pay half, but never did. Harrison also won a suit against his former personal manager, Alan Klein, whom Harrison had fired in 1973. Klein later purchased Brite Tunes Music catalog that contained the song, "He's So Fine." Brite Tunes then sued Harrison, claiming that Harrison's "My Sweet Lord" was a copyright infringement of "He's So Fine." A court ruled against Harrison on the infringement issue. Later, Harrison won a judgment against Klein that held that a personal manager could not buy the song in order to sue his former client. Harrison wound up owning both songs.

Management Agreements

Some attorneys refer to a personal management agreement as "air," because the manager usually just promises to exercise "best efforts" to promote the artist's career, so these agreements are notoriously difficult to enforce. There are, however, some "typical" terms. As with most entertainment industry agreements, these tend to be highly negotiated, especially if the artist has much stature. While some managers may be willing to work on an oral "handshake" agreement, most attorneys cringe at the thought of their client, either the artist or the manager, working under such nebulous terms.

Compensation—Typically, managers are personally compensated on a **commission** basis with a percentage of the artist's gross earnings. That percentage ranges from 10 percent to as high as 25 percent in some instances. The norm is 15 to 20 percent. Allegedly, Colonel Tom Parker, who managed Elvis Presley, received a 50 percent commission. That commission is usually on the artist's gross earnings, but may be restricted to entertainment earnings, further restricted to live appearances, or restricted to earnings from appearances and agreements that the manager helped obtain. Advances for which the artist does not receive actual cash in hand, such as recording costs, video production costs, and tour support, should not be commissionable. Some attorney's recommend fewer restrictions in order to keep the manager more motivated.

Duration—Most agreements are for an initial term of 1 or 2 years with **option** years adding up to 3 to 5 years. The options are usually the manager's but the artist may be able to limit the manager's right to exercise the options unless the artist has reached some plateau of earnings, for example, $100,000 in year one, $200,000 in year two. If the artist is in the active recording phase of their career the duration may be stated in terms of album cycles—the time between new album releases (which is typically longer than 1 year). An album cycle agreement would normally run two or three cycles.

Key person (a term slowly evolving from the former sexist moniker "key man")—Personal managers are usually *very* personal to the artist. Even if the artist signs an agreement with a management company, it is usually a particular person who is handling the affairs of the artist and in whom the artist has placed his or her trust. For that reason artists often ask that if the "key person" leaves the firm then the agreement is ended.

Commission The percentage of the artist's income taken by the agent for arranging the performance or by the personal manager for being the artist's manager.

Option Usually refers to a label's right to extend the recording agreement for an additional album. May refer to a personal manager's right to extend the management agreement with the artist, too. But this term generally refers to the company's right to keep the writer or artist under contract for some additional period of time.

Key person (aka key man) In contracts, most often personal management, recording, or publishing, a specified person that the artist is counting on being a member of the contracting firm. If that person leaves, then the contract is terminated.

Power of attorney
A contractual right to act on someone's behalf in a way that legally binds that person to obligations entered into by the "attorney" on behalf of the person represented.

Power of attorney—The manager will usually ask for power to enter into agreements on behalf of the artist. While it may be easier for the manager to be able to sign anything for the artist it is usually advisable for the artist to attempt to limit the power of attorney to routine matters such as short engagements. The manager should seek the artist's approval on all but very routine matters, and the artist and manager should have agreed on the parameters of those routine matters. Whether such detail is necessary in the agreement is a matter of trust.

Talent Agents

The agent's role

The primary function of a talent agent is to find employment opportunities for the artist in live entertainment. The agent is the ultimate middle person between the artist and the venue operator or promoter. So the agent's job is simply to sell, sell, sell the talent to the talent buyer. Although the agent strictly speaking represents the artist and must place the artist's interest paramount, there is also pressure to please the promoter or venue operator. If an agent arranges many deals that displease one or the other, agents will find that they either have no artists to book, or nowhere to book them. The agent should have knowledge of the kinds of performers booked in what venues by what promoters or venue operators. Putting the wrong act in the wrong venue is a double disaster. Agents often know promoters and venue operators "personally," at least over the phone "personally." Most of an agent's work is done over the telephone. Agents usually represent a substantial number of artists, although there may be a particular individual at an agency who is in charge of bookings for a particular artist.

The structure of the agency business

Talent agents tend to exist in three varieties, depending upon the size of the geographic area in which they book talent. Local agents work just in a particular city or small group of cities. They tend to book acts into smaller clubs, parties, and local events. Since the acts they book do not command large talent fees, local agents have to work fast to keep lots of acts working lots of weeks per year in order to survive. It is most likely that an aspiring artist or group will encounter a local agency first on their rise to stardom. That agent will probably be one of the first people to pass judgment on the performer and to have concluded that they have enough talent to perform in local venues without embarrassing the venue operator, the agent, or themselves. All a local agent needs to be in business is a telephone, an act to represent, a list of clubs to start calling, and perhaps a license (see below for a discussion of agency licensing requirements).

Regional agents can book artists in several, usually adjoining, states. They book some larger clubs and shows and may have the ability to get an act on as an opening act for a larger artist if they have good connections with the promoter.

The dream of the regional agent is to hook up with some rising artist who becomes a star and who will take the agent along. Regional agents can book an act into a small tour. The number of artists represented by regional agents may be just as many as by local agents, but they are usually of higher caliber and more experience. Regional agencies tend to have several agents in the office.

Finally, national agencies are those that can book an act anywhere in the country, and perhaps abroad. They usually will not represent an artist unless that artist already has a recording contract, or perhaps a substantial development agreement with a publisher. They may represent over a hundred artists and have a substantial number of actual agents working at the agency. These national agencies are the ones that work out tours for established recording artists.

The talent agency business continues to slowly expand, at least in terms of the number of agents. In 1996 *Pollstar's* Agency Roster listed nearly 600 talent agencies in the United States. By 2003 that listing had grown to about 620 agents. The 2009 Agency Directory had about 670 agency listings. Agencies are not owned by media conglomerates but are independent businesses. That is not to say that they are not dependent upon artists who have recording contracts, and other artists who dream of having recording contracts, for their talent. Just like other aspects of the industry, the big money is concentrated in the hands of a few players. There are three major agencies representing over 700 artists each: Agency Group Limited, William Morris Agency, and Universal Attractions. Creative Artists Agency and Paradigm each represent about 500 acts. On a plateau below that are several agencies representing 200 or more artists each, including Columbia Artists Management and International Creative Management. Another dozen or so represent one to two hundred acts.

But the number of artists an agency represents is not the only measure of their success. The gross bookings of the agency in terms of dollars is another good measure. The agency business is somewhat concentrated, because the top five agencies typically account for about half of the live performance income. The industry could almost be characterized as a "tight oligopoly" (top four firms control 60 percent of the market), but it is not quite that tight, and the top four firms vary from year to year depending upon whose artists happen to be making a major tour (see Table 7.1). *Pollstar* listed the top ten agencies of 2008 as booking $2.2 billion worth of shows. That is about half of the estimated $4.2 billion in major concert ticket sales in 2008. The top five agencies generated about 45 percent of the concert gross. There are some quirks in any computing of the major agencies, though. For instance, Live Nation Global had two huge North American tours in 2009. Madonna topped all tours with a $105 million gross, and the Police had a top ten tour with $48 million gross. United Talent Agency represented only one top 100 tour, but it was Celine Dion's $94 million tour. So a single agency with a major tour can generate a lot of revenue for themselves, and for their artist.

Unlike personal managers who sometimes do business on a handshake, talent agents almost never do business on a handshake, either with the artists they represent or with the venues and talent buyers to whom they sell. That is partially because they are usually dealing at a distance, over the telephone, by fax, or by email, with their clients. It is also because they are often subject to specific licensing requirements from the states and/or the unions.

Table 7.1 Top ten talent agencies (based on share of top 100 tours)

Agency	2002 No. of Tours	2008 No. of Tours
1. Creative Artists Agency	28	40
2. William Morris Agency	17	20
3. Monterey Peninsula Artists/Paradigm	10	8
4. Artist Group International	4	6
5. Evolution Talent (2002)	6	
5. Int'l Creative Management (2009)		6
6. United Talent Agency	3	
7–10 numerous agencies had only two shows	2	

Source: *Pollstar*, 13 January, 2003; 19 January, 2009

Agency licensing

Talent agencies, since they are employment agencies, are usually regulated as such by state laws. Some states, among them California, Florida, New York, Minnesota, Texas, and Illinois, require agents to have *specific* licenses to be a talent agent. Most do not. California and New York laws are particularly important because many agencies have their main offices there. Talent agents are known as "theatrical employment agencies" in these laws.

AFM The musicians union. Some locals also allow audio engineers to join.

AFTRA The union for singers and voice announcers.

The two main labor unions concerned with recording artists, the American Federation of Musicians (**AFM**) and the American Federation of Television and Radio Artists (**AFTRA**), also regulate agents in their dealings with the union's members. Generally speaking, a talent agent must be licensed by both the state in which the agency is located, and by the union that represents the musicians or vocalists booked by the agent.

Agency agreements

The licensing requirements mean that agency agreements with performers are somewhat limited in their terms:

- Commissions and fees—These are usually 10 to 20 percent of the gross payable to the performer. The AFM limits the amount according to the duration of the performance, with 20 percent the limit for one-nighters. Most agencies will agree to limit their commissions to a "standard" 10 percent. Major artists with significant live performance income may be able to limit the commission to 5 percent. The commissions should only be applicable to engagements procured by the agency. If the artist has a "360 deal" (see Chapter 9) then the monies deducted from live appearances by the label should probably not be commissionable by the agency.
- Duration—The AFM limits talent agents to 3-year agreements. If the agent is a "general agent" (one who also books film, television, theater, literary, etc.) the duration is limited to 7 years. As a general rule, the lower the level of agency the shorter the term of the agreement should be, so that when/if an artist gets a recording agreement they can switch to an agency that is

capable of booking them nationwide. Even at the national level, artists would want a 1- to 2-year deal instead of 3-year deal. If an agency wants a longer term, they should be willing to promise that certain booking guarantees will be achieved, or the artist has the option to get out of the deal.

● Exclusivity—Agents often ask for exclusive rights, i.e. no other agent can book the artist during the term of the agreement. While this is certainly understandable and "usual" when an artist has reached the national level of agency, it is more questionable at the regional level, and quite undesirable for an artist at the local level.

Promoters

> "This is a business for manic depressives."[3]

The role of the concert promoter

Promoters present live entertainment events. To do that the promoter must obtain some talent to present, presumably from an agency, and must have some place to present it, a club or other venue. Like the agent, the promoter is a middle person in between the artist and the audience. But unlike the agent, the promoter takes on a substantial managerial role and risk in the ultimate presentation of the event. Promoters used to be members of a highly independent entrepreneurial group, working only in one or a few cities, willing to risk substantial losses in order to make substantial profits. They would hear about the availability of an artist from an agent, publication, or the grapevine, contact the agent and the venues for available dates, make a match, then try to sell tickets. A good show that sold out could reap substantial profits for the promoter and the performer. A show that did poorly in terms of ticket sales could spell disaster, especially for the promoter. Pressure was on all parties involved to reduce their risk of loss but still to share in the high profits that were available for successful shows. The person least able to reduce risk was the local or regional promoter who did not have the resources to spread the risk over a larger number of shows. This has led to an ongoing restructuring of the promotion business.

Structure of the promotion business

During the 1960s it was common for a local or regional promoter to have a virtual lock on any significant shows happening in "their" towns. They did this by getting **"buy-back"** agreements with agents and managers. The buy-back allowed the promoter to be the first to bid on a date for an act's next tour date when they had just finished promoting the current date. The promoters could therefore assure themselves of being able to promote the shows most likely to be successful in the future. If they had a profitable show with an artist they would pick up the date for the next tour. If not, they could pass and let someone else

Buy-back In concert promotion, a deal between the promoter and the artist's agent to give the promoter the "right" to promote that artist the next time the artist plays in that promoter's area, city, or venue.

do the show. The promoters also worked closely with the venues by securing large numbers of "holds" (a non-binding agreement to tentatively keep a date open for the promoter and not let someone else book the venue), which effectively kept other promoters from booking that venue.

Beginning in the late 1960s the grip of local and regional promoters on cities began to slip as national promoters, particularly Concerts West, came on the scene. The national promoter could book a large number of dates for a particular tour and spread the risk of a loss on any one or two shows through a larger number of shows. By spreading the risk and being efficient in their operations the national promoters could offer the artists and venues higher percentages and fees and still make profits themselves. Even when the national promoters would use a local or regional promoter to work out the details for a particular show, the local promoter might find themselves getting only a flat fee instead of any percentage of potential profits. Promoters expanded their use of holds to the point where they had exclusive agreements with some venues so that no show could be promoted in the venue unless it was by that promoter.

The other pressure on local and regional promoters' profits came from the artists. Major artists and their managers became aware of the high profitability of promoting a successful act. A sell-out became a given with some big artists. They reasoned that they should get a higher percentage of the profits from such sell-outs. The promoters, however, needed the high profits from the sell-outs to cover high losses from the flops. At the same time the major artists began to put on larger and larger shows. The acts went from requiring the promoter to supply staging, sound, and lights to carrying a self-contained show that only need a place to play. The artists' expenses skyrocketed. Instead of a van-sized truck for the show and a bus for the artist, fleets of tractor-trailers and several buses were necessary to move a show from one venue to the next.

Guarantee In concert promotion, the fixed amount that the artist will be paid, regardless of how many tickets are sold.

Shed Another term for an outdoor amphitheater.

The higher cost to the artist of all this personnel and equipment meant that artists had to demand a larger **guarantee** for each show in order to meet their daily operating expenses and payroll. By asking for a higher guarantee and a higher percentage of the profits the artists reduced the profitability for the promoters on successful shows and increased the risk of loss on shows that did not do well. Guarantees for a "**shed**" or arena show were typically $100,000 to $500,000 by 2009, having increased steadily as ticket prices increased (see Figure 7.2).

Higher costs, higher guarantees, and bigger shows meant that the shows had to have larger audiences. Shows went from local gymnasiums to basketball arenas to football and baseball stadiums. With larger audiences and the party-like atmosphere that often accompanied the concerts came other headaches for the promoters—potential liability for injury to the fans or the artists or the facilities. Law suits for injuries or deaths occurring at concerts became more common with the heavy metal acts of the 1980s. Injuries at rap concerts of the late 1980s and 1990s caused some promoters to cancel shows instead of facing the liability. By the mid-1990s the violent behavior of fans in "mosh" pits and "stage diving" by fans (and even artists on some occasions) raised the specter of even greater liability. The promoter's cost of liability insurance went from pennies per ticket to dollars per ticket over the course of about 5 years. Increased security measures became necessary. Those factors raised the price of tickets even higher and decreased the profitability of the shows even further.

The net result of all of these pressures was the concentration of the promotion business into large regional, national, and international promotion companies that could put on shows in a large number of cities in venues that they owned. In 1995 the top ten grossing promoters accounted for about 44 percent of concert sales. By 2002 Clear Channel Entertainment (now Live Nation) sold 59 percent of all tickets sold by the top 50 promoters. By 2008 the top two promoters, Live Nation and AEG Live, took home 77 percent of the gross sales of the entire top 25 promoters.

Which promoters are the most successful in a given year varies somewhat, just as it does with the most successful agents, depending on who was on tour and which promoter has the major tours of a given year. However, the growth of major international promoters that also own and operate venues has led to some stability among the top promoters. Two major promoters, Live Nation (US) and AEG Live (US), held the number one and two spots respectively in the top ten for 5 years running from 2004 through 2008. Only three other promoters, Jam Productions (US), 3A Entertainment (UK), Gillette Entertainment Group (Canada), and Michael Coppel Presents (Australia), appeared in *Billboard*'s top ten list more than twice in that same time period. Note the internationalization of the business as indicated by the home country of each. Mexican/Latin promoter CIE (Interamerican Entertainment Corp.) is close on the heels of the other six (Table 7.2).

Promoter–artist agreements

Performance agreements for concerts and club appearances typically comprise two parts. The first part simply sets the fee structure, date and time of appearance, and a few other "basics." The other part is the "**rider**." This contains the requirements that the artist must have in order to put on the show. From the artist's point of view, compliance with the requirements in the rider is critical to the artist's being able to put on a good show for the audience. With a major act the rider will contain details of how much parking must be available for the artist's trucks and buses; how much weight the venue rafters must be able to support so the sound and lights can be "**flown**;" how much and what kind of food needs to be provided for the traveling crew and artist; how much power

Rider An attachment to an agreement. In concert promotion, the rider is where the artist spells out specific requirements for the performance, such as sound, lights, size of stage, power requirements, kind and amount of food, and other considerations.

Flown Sound reinforcement, stage lighting, or other effects that are suspended from the rafters of a venue instead of being supported on the floor.

Table 7.2 Top promoters, 2004–2008

Promoter	Ranking	Years in Top 10	Points*
1. Live Nation/Clear Channel	1	5	50
2. AEG Live	2	5	45
3. Jam Productions	3	5	23
4. Gillette Entertainment Group	5	4	17
5. Michael Coppel Presents	6	3	14
6. 3A Entertainment	4	3	19

Source: *Billboard*, year end issues.

* Points are the inverse of ranking. For example, a number 1 rank is worth 10 points and a number 5 rank is worth 6 points.

(A/C) needs to be available and where it needs to be; what local personnel such as musicians, security, follow spot operators, electricians, plumbers, and so on must be provided; how backstage security is to be handled; and more. The larger the show the more details the rider is likely to contain. The promoter needs to have the rider far enough in advance to be sure there are no problems that the promoter and venue cannot overcome. For example, if a show has a large piece of stage set that cannot be disassembled and must have doors of a certain size to be able to get it into the building, the venue may have to enlarge an entrance, or cancel the show. If the roof cannot support the load of the sound and lights, it may have to be reinforced, or the show canceled.

The payment part of the contract typically calls for the artist to get a guarantee of some amount of money and often a percentage of the "**gate**" (ticket sales revenues). There are several ways of structuring the deal. Artists playing small clubs or opening for other major acts usually just get a flat fee for the show. Typically half of the guarantee or flat fee is paid in advance. It is out of this payment that the talent agency takes its commission. The amount of the guarantee can go from a few thousand dollars for an opening act to as much as a million dollars for a superstar act on a major tour. The amount is determined by the artist and manager to be enough to cover their expenses plus make what they consider to be a fair profit, no matter how many people actually buy tickets. In theory, the artist will get this guarantee even if no tickets are sold. In practice, if sales are going very badly, the artist and promoter will try to work out a compromise. It is not good for the artist's reputation to require the promoters to take huge losses if the artist is not able to attract a good-sized audience to the show. Major acts also get a percentage of the profits, which usually kicks in after the promoter reaches a "**break-even point**" (where ticket sales revenues equal the promoter's expenses, including the artist's guarantee).

The percentage is highly negotiable, ranging from 50 percent to as high as 90 percent. With middle level acts the promoter may be able to give away tickets if sales have not reached a certain point by a week or two before the show. This enables the promoter, who is probably also the venue owner/operator, to make money on things such as parking and concession sales, even if the artist makes no money from the ticket sales.

The Venue

The venue business

Entertainment venues come in all shapes and sizes, from football or baseball sized stadiums with capacity of 50,000 or more, to amphitheaters in the 15,000–20,000 range, to theaters for fewer than 5,000, to clubs with capacity for only a few hundred patrons. The promoter, or venue if they are self promoting, must match their size with the potential draw of the artists and the cost of having that artist perform. What is interesting about the top ten venues in any size range is that they all generate 10 percent (usually less) of the total concert business. This might indicate that the venue business is not very concentrated except for

Gate The admission revenues from a concert. Same as "door" but the latter is usually a club term.

Break-even point In concert promotion, the point at which the promoter's gross revenues equal the fixed expenses, including artist guarantees, but not such things as any percentages for the artist or venue. In economics, the point at which total revenues have equaled total costs so the firm is showing neither a profit nor a loss.

the fact that a few operators like AEG and Live Nation own substantial numbers of venues in some size ranges. Although the largest indoor venues like Madison Square Garden in New York City and the O2 in London are usually the largest revenue generators (because they can be open year round), even small clubs can do well if their location is good and their promotion is good (see Table 7.3).

Venue agreements

The promoter must also enter into an agreement with the venue. The details of that agreement include the venue's rental fee and what other services are to be provided by the venue to the promoter. Arrangements run from the venue providing the facility and nothing more, called a **"four walls"** deal, to the venue providing significant services in terms of clean-up, ushers, ticket takers, electricians, stagehands, and so forth. Halls may also want either a flat fee, a flat fee against a percentage of the gate (meaning the venue will get whichever is greater, the guarantee or the percentage of the gate), or a guarantee plus a percentage of profits after the promoter's break-even point. Services provided by the venue are usually billed separately but may be included in the flat fee.

In addition to rental fees, the venues can also make money from other things. Venues often charge the artist a percentage of sales from artist merchandise such as T-shirts, hats, and so forth that the artist has sold at the shows. These percentages can range from nothing to as high as 50 percent. The promoter or artist usually does not receive a percentage of any **"ancillary income"** for the venue from such things as food and drink sales—unless of course the promoter owns or operates the venue.

The example that follows (Table 7.4) shows the basic flow of dollars from a concert to the venue, promoter, agent, manager, and artist. The figures are based on a number of different specific examples to create a generic kind of concert that does not reflect any particular artist, promoter, venue, or concert. Assume a 12,000-seat arena with potential sales of 10,000 tickets (the show production and stage take up 2,000 seats worth of space). Sales are 89 percent of the available seats. The venue fee is a flat fee and includes the venue rental plus ushers, security, technicians, and other services provided by the venue. The ticket price is an

Four walls In concert promotion, a deal to rent a venue that includes only the right to use the facility with the venue providing nothing more than the "four walls," i.e. no box office, no ticket takers, no ushers, no clean up, or other such service.

Ancillary income In concert promotion, the term for revenues for the venue from parking or food sales that are not part of the gate and are not commissionable by the promoter or artist.

Table 7.3 Venue size and share of reported global performance revenues

Share of 2008 ticket sales by top 10 venues in each size range

Venue Size	Top 10 Venues' Sales ($ millions)	Percent of Reported Sales
Stadiums	$149	2.4
Amphitheaters	$163	2.6
Indoor, 15,001 or more	$625	10
Indoor, 10,001–15,000	$159	2.6
Indoor, 5,001–10,000	$339	5.5
Indoor, 5,000 or less	$224	3.6
Total	$1,659	26.7

Source: "Touring Charts," *Billboard*, 20 December, 2008

Table 7.4 Example of live appearance income

Ticket sales	8,900 @ $75.00	$667,500
Less: venue rental and services $ 50,000		
Promoter's gross receipts		$617,500
Less: opening act	$ 10,000	
Less: artist guarantee	$ 250,000	
Less: promotion expenses	$ 100,000	
Available after break-even		$ 257,500
Less: artist's 90 percent		$ 231,750
Promoter's net profit		$ 25,750
Artist's income		
Guarantee	$ 250,000	
Plus % after break-even	$ 231,750	
Artist gross		$ 481,750
Less: 10% agency commission	$ 48,175	
Less: 20% manager's commission	$ 96,350	
Less: tour expenses	$ 100,000	
Artist's net		$ 237,225

average. Some seats sell for more than $75, some for less. The artist has a guarantee of $250,000 plus 90 percent after the promoter breaks even. The agent has a 10 percent commission. The artist's personal manager has a 20 percent commission. An opening act gets a $10,000 flat fee.

Table 7.4 illustrates a successful show. On the other hand, it is not uncommon for shows to sell less than 60 percent of the available seats. If the promoter only planned to sell 60 percent, perhaps because the only available venue did not really match the demand for the artist in that market, then all would be well. But the likelihood is that at 60 percent somebody is losing money. That somebody is undoubtedly the promoter.

In-house promotion
A performance promoted by the venue itself, without any outside promoter.

Papering the house
A practice in the live entertainment business of giving away tickets so that the audience will be large enough to please the performer.

In-house promotion

The existence of national promotion of tours and the possibility of ancillary income led many venues to promote concerts "**in-house**."

If the venue knows it is going to make a significant amount of money from the ancillary revenues then it can afford to give the artist a higher percentage above the break-even. The venue may even provide that if ticket sales have not hit a certain plateau by a week or two before the show, then the venue may give away the rest of the tickets (known as "**papering the house**"). Attendees with the papered tickets pay nothing to see the artist, but do pay for parking and concessions so the venue can make money even if the artist does not, or only makes the minimum guarantee.

Internet Activities

- Visit www.billboard.biz, Industry News, Touring. What are some of the latest developments?
- Visit www.pollstar.com. What are average ticket prices for some of your favorite acts?
- Live Nation is a publicly traded company. Visit www.livenation.com and look at "investor relations." What are two interesting facts you can learn about the company?
- Ticketmaster is a publicly traded company. Look at www.ticketmaster.com, investor relations, and find out how the merger with Live Nation worked out. What portion of Ticketmaster's income is derived from its management ("artist services") activities and what percentage from ticket sales?
- Visit ticketnews.com. Who is selling the most tickets? How are the ticket resellers doing?
- Visit www.afm.org. Find a local chapter in your town or state. What are the local's initiation fees and dues? Exactly where are they located?

Venue owners also sell advertising and naming rights. These changes mean that the venue is no longer really in the concert promotion business, but in the "attract-a-large-crowd business." Major artist tours are so self-contained that there is little that a local promoter has to provide that is not usually provided by the venue. Venues also sell Ticketmaster (or other ticketing companies) exclusive ticketing rights. These rights generate "facility fees" or "house fees" that are added back on to the ticket price by the ticket seller and then paid to the venue. Chain ownership of venues, especially of outdoor amphitheaters, makes it possible for the venue owner to book several dates at large venues in significant markets. Live Nation, for example, could promote a major tour, playing in 26 of the top 30 markets in the country, and never leave Live Nation facilities.

Again, the local or regional promoter is left out. The majority of club shows are also promoted "in house." This practice, coupled with the increasing use of national promoters has led to fewer shows available for local or regional promoters. Sometimes, though, a club will simply rent the facility for a new promoter wanting to break in with a small show.

Ticket Selling

Economic pressures on promoters and venues and the technology of online sales in the 1980s and 1990s changed the way tickets are sold to events. It used to be that if someone wanted tickets to a show they had to go to or call the box office or go to some other physical ticket outlet, such as a record store, that had "**hard tickets**." The selling agent for the tickets printed them, and distributed them, and perhaps ran the box office to sell them, for a small commission. Beginning

Hard tickets
Admission tickets pre-printed and distributed for sale, as compared to **soft tickets**, which are only printed at the time of sale, or on the buyer's computer.

in about 1982, the firm Ticketmaster started selling "soft tickets"—tickets that did not exist at all until printed out by the selling agent's computer when a customer ordered them and paid for them by charge card over a telephone line. The service was much more convenient for the customers than having to go to a location to purchase tickets. Efficiencies in the telephone operations meant that Ticketmaster could sell tickets to many shows at the same time from many locations using networked computers. By the early 1990s Ticketmaster's primary competition, Ticketron, had been bought by Ticketmaster.

In addition to efficient operations, Ticketmaster began to use exclusive selling agreements with venues and some promoters as a means to secure business. The venues and promoters sometimes received a percentage of the service charge added on to the ticket price in exchange for the exclusive arrangements. Since the service charge was not part of the gross ticket sales on which the promoter had to pay the artist it was not subject to the artist's percentage requirements. It was, therefore, a revenue source that did not have to be shared. Independent promoters, in-house promoters, and venues all moved to take advantage of the arrangements. It soon became virtually impossible to play a concert tour without having tickets sold by Ticketmaster. Ticketmaster's service charges increased from $2.50 to as much as $15 per ticket in 2008, averaging $7.84 per ticket in 2008.

Some consumers and artists began to complain. In 1994 the popular group "Pearl Jam" announced that it wanted ticket service charges held to $1.80 on an $18 ticket. Promoters and venue operators complained that their exclusive agreements with Ticketmaster would not allow them to use alternative ticket sellers and Ticketmaster would continue to charge its higher fees. Pearl Jam canceled their summer 1994 tour and complained to the Justice Department that Ticketmaster had a monopoly. At least one legal writer concluded that Ticketmaster's practices did violate federal and California anti-trust laws. The Justice Department began an investigation and members of Pearl Jam testified before a Congressional committee. By the summer of 1995, however, the Justice Department had dropped its probe of Ticketmaster's practices without further comment. Ticketmaster reported ticket sales revenues of $1.6 billion for 1995. For its part, Ticketmaster had expanded its operations into promotional partnerships with credit card companies and even a record label. Capitol records began a promotion to give away sampler albums to people who used the Ticketmaster or Capitol World Wide Web sites.

Ticket resellers
Organizations that acquire concert tickets from original purchasers who can no longer attend the event, or on their own, or other scalpers, and then sell them to the public, often at inflated prices.

Ticket resellers

As Internet sales of tickets increased, so did Internet *resale* of tickets. Resellers would buy up significant blocks of concert tickets to the hottest concerts as soon as they went on sale, then begin to offer them through alternative sources for much higher prices. In fact, Ticketmaster Entertainment owns one of the largest resellers, TicketsNow, which it acquired in 2008. How big is the resale market? The second largest ticket seller behind Ticketmaster is StubHub, a reseller. Not only is the market large, so are the profits. The Madonna tour prompted the biggest resale ticket in 2008. Regular ticket prices for her shows went from about

$60 to $350 per seat in most places. The average *resale* ticket was $378. Ticket reselling sites either charge a commission of 15 percent or more, or simply pay the ticket holder an agreed price and retain the rest for themselves.

Meantime, two other trends in the ticketing business were discouraging resale. The first is paperless ticketing. There the buyer gets an I.D. number and prints a receipt on their computer. When they show up with the I.D. number and present identification at the gate, then they are admitted. Because the I.D. is specific to the purchaser, it is difficult to resell the "ticket." The other trend is preselling the show, particularly from artist websites. The presales allow true fans the first shot at tickets. They are the ones more likely to attend and to buy the higher priced seats that the resellers like to get if they can.

In 2009 Ticketmaster and Live Nation announced plans to merge. Live Nation had earlier threatened to begin its own ticket selling operations. Live Nation was Ticketmaster's largest client, representing about 13 percent of Ticketmaster's business. There were loud complaints about the proposed merger from citizens and promoters, but the merger was approved in 2010 by the Department of Justice. The shareholders of the two companies owned about equal shares of the combined entity.

Labels in the Concert Business

Live appearances by a recording artist help sell albums and downloads. The shows themselves may even be the outlet where the albums are sold. In addition to tee-shirts and hats, many artists are now offering their albums for sale at their concerts. One survey reported that 65 percent of the consumers who attended a concert saw the artist's album for sale at the show. Ten percent said they bought the album at the show and another 25 percent bought the album prior to the show. About a fourth of those who did not see the album at the show said they would probably have bought it if they had seen it.

As sales of CDs continued to decline in the first decade of the twenty-first century, the labels looked for more ways to participate in revenue streams of the artists other than just the sale of recordings. Because it was often the presence and airplay of a recording that prompted an artist's touring success, the labels reasoned that they should receive some of the live appearance income. This is discussed in detail under "**The 360 deal**" in Chapter 9.

In the past, especially for new artists who needed to build an audience through performance, or for an artist who was just beginning to break, the labels would provide **tour support** in the form of extra advertising and promotional dollars when an artist played a market or in the form of "**shortfall**." In those days the label was not attempting to make money in the concert business, but was hoping that the exposure of the artist through live performances would enhance sales of recordings. Tour support dollars spent by the label were usually treated as an advance and were recoupable out of artist royalties earned from the sale of recordings. But with fewer artist royalties available as a source of recoupment, the labels turned to tour income itself not only as a recoupment source, but also as a revenue stream in itself.

360 deal A deal between a label and artist that involves the label receiving revenues from more than just the recordings aspect of an artist's career, but also probably live appearances, music publishing, and merchandising.

Tour support Usually monetary support for new recording artists to help them make personal appearance performances. Tour support is often given when the label believes that live appearances will help sell recordings. It is usually a **recoupable advance** (see shortfall).

Shortfall A kind of **tour support** with the label making up any difference between an agreed-upon amount per performance and the amount the artist actually makes per performance.

Sponsored Tours

Sponsored tour
A live appearance tour where part of the costs and probably some advertising is underwritten by a third party who uses the appearances of the artist to promote and sell non artist-related merchandise, such as soft drinks or clothing.

Other businesses with products to sell to people likely to attend concerts have entered the concert business by **sponsoring tours** for major or even relatively new artists. The sponsor usually provides some underwriting for the entire tour in the form of lump sum or per show payments for the artist and significant promotional money to be spent on radio and television advertising nationally and in markets where the artist is appearing. In return, the artist allows the association with the tour, the use of the artist's name and likeness use in advertising, probably agrees to some time for making ads for the sponsor, probably agrees to allow the sponsor to have a presence at concerts in terms of signs or other product placement, and may agree to "meet and greets" backstage where local employees of the sponsor and local buyers of the sponsor's products can meet the artist personally.

Companies that sponsor musical events and other shows report sales increases of from 50 percent to 1,000 percent in markets where the sponsored show appears. Although sport takes the largest share of sponsorship dollars, entertainment tours accounted for about 10 percent of the over $40 billion global sponsorship expenditures in 2009. North American sponsorship expenditures were about $17 billion that same year. Sponsors are anything from Bacardi, to Miller Brewing, to Honda Motor Company, to Kingsford Charcoal.

Simulcast Theater and Internet Concerts

Artists had been using streaming video of concerts or appearances to promote themselves since 1993. In the mid-2000s live simulcasts of concerts became popular with artists such as the Rolling Stones, Phish, Jimmy Buffet, Prince, and Green Day, putting live shows into theaters, typically at $10–20 per ticket. In 2009 Mariah Carey became the first artist to sell "virtual tickets" for streaming of a previously recorded concert to Internet and Internet enabled mobile devices. "Tickets" were $9.99.

DIY Activities

- Find local or regional talent agencies in your town or nearest city. Contact one and find out where it books acts and what commission it charges. Could it help your act?
- Go to www.afm.org and find the nearest AFM local. What are its dues and initiation fee? What advantages and disadvantages are there to joining the union? Read the union's web pages on this.
- Make a list of local clubs that hire musical acts. Find out the size of each venue and how they pay their performers. Do they use talent agencies to get their acts?
- Performers need a quality demo for just about any purpose. If you do not already have one, find a local studio where it could be recorded. If you do have one, is it time to do another? Does your act sound different or better than it did when the first one was recorded?

The Unions

There is substantial involvement of labor unions in the presentation of live entertainment. The performers themselves are likely to be members of either AFM or **AGVA** (American Guild of Variety Artists). In addition, **IATSE** (International Association of Theatrical and Stage Employees) members will undoubtedly be involved in lighting, sound, and stage crews. Finally, the electricians, plumbers, and other craft unions are likely to be involved with the venue as support personnel, particularly in states such as New York and California, where unions are quite strong.

American Federation of Musicians

The American Federation of Musicians of the United States and Canada is the official name of the AFM. It represents musicians, conductors, arrangers, orchestrators, copyists, and others involved in the preparation and presentation of live music (but not composers). The union has a national organization, which is primarily responsible for the negotiation of national agreements with the major labels (see Chapter 9) and national television and radio networks, and local chapters. The performing musician will be a member of both the national and a particular local. The locals set **wage scales** for live performances in their areas.

The live performance scales vary considerably from local to local depending upon the strength of the union in a particular city. The strongest locals are in cities and states where it is legal to have a "union shop," a venue that has agreed with the union to allow only union members to perform there. Because these are primarily the northeastern and north central states and because most musicians will ultimately want to perform there, they will ultimately have to join the union. Even in "**right to work**" states, where state laws prohibit establishments from agreeing to hire only union members, non-union musicians may have difficulty playing at significant concerts because union musicians have agreed not to perform with non-union musicians.

The locals and national finance their activities through **initiation fees** and **work dues**. When someone first becomes a member they pay a national and local initiation fee. The national fee was $65 in 2009 and the local fees vary from local to local, from as little as $10 to near $200, but tend to be in the $50 to $100 range. Most of that one-time fee goes to the national. Locals may have annual dues as well, from as little as $50 at a small local to over $200 in New York City. Members also pay "work dues" based on the wages they earn as musicians. The amount varies from local to local but ranges from about 1 percent to 5 percent of scale wages. This may be paid by the employer directly to the union or may be paid by the musician.

In addition to setting scale wages the union provides other benefits for its members. Because musicians are independent contractors they usually have no corporate health insurance, life insurance, or retirement benefits unless they arrange for them on their own. The union is able to provide group insurance and retirement plans for its members through its own health and welfare fund, and a retirement pension fund to which the members as well as the record labels contribute (see Chapter 9). The union also protects members from employers

AGVA The union for live entertainers who are not AFM or AFTRA members.

IATSE A union for stagehands, lighting technicians, and other "behind the scenes" people who put on theatrical and concert events.

Scale wages Payments to musicians or vocalists for live or recorded performances at the amount (scale) required by the union.

Right to work Provision of the laws of some states, particularly in the South, that prohibits unions from requiring that all employees of a particular firm belong to that union.

Initiation fees A one-time fee to join a union. Not to be confused with dues which are paid on an ongoing basis.

Work dues Dues paid to the union by performers based on their earnings from live appearances.

Defaulters A union term for people who do not pay musicians or vocalists for their performances in clubs or on recordings. Union musicians will not perform for persons on a defaulters list made by the applicable union.

who do not pay on time. A "**defaulters**" list names conductors, promoters, and record producers who do not pay.

American Guild of Variety Artists

The American Guild of Variety Artists (AGVA) represents singers, dancers, comediennes, and others who perform live. It is one of the "4 As" unions, a group of unions also including the Actors' Equity Association (AEA), the American Guild of Musical Artists (AGMA), the Screen Actors Guild (SAG), the Screen Extras Guild, and AFTRA. The "4 As" nickname comes from the name of the parent union, the Associated Actors and Artists of America. AFTRA is not as important a force in the live performance area, but its impact in record production is discussed in Chapter 9.

International Alliance of Theatrical Stage Employees

The International Alliance of Theatrical Stage Employees (IATSE) represents non-performers in theater, television, and film. Its members include stagehands, camera operators, gaffers, lighting technicians, wardrobe people, and others. Most major performance venues have agreements with IATSE to employ union members. Artist performance contract riders often specify the employment of IATSE members.

The Management Team

It is usually necessary for an artist to have more than one person "taking care of business" for them. That is partly because there is need of expertise that is often not available in a single person and partly because it may not be wise to engage a single person, even if they did have all the expertise. Certainly an artist who has enjoyed, or who is to enjoy, much success must have a personal manager. They will have to have an agent representing them, securing employment and performances. From the artist's perspective, the recording industry is a business providing their personal services to everyone from record companies to concert promoters. Most of the arrangements under which the artist will be performing will be under contract. As has been noted in previous chapters and as will be discussed further in Chapter 9, these contractual relationships are often complex and require the services of an attorney familiar with entertainment industry contracts. Finally, the artist will invariably want/need to audit the accounts of various people with whom the artist has financial dealings, such as record labels, music publishers, agents, and personal managers, so the services of an accountant should be retained. These four people, the personal manager, the agent, the attorney, and the accountant, make up the basis of a management team (see Figure 7.4).

It is important for the members of the management team to be independent of each other. For one thing, four independent opinions, each founded on the

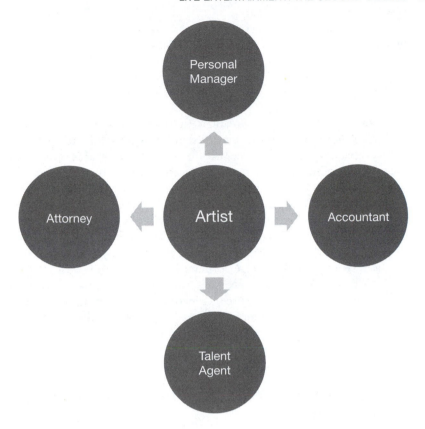

Figure 7.4 The artist's management team

best interests of the artist, are more likely to generate the course of action most appropriate for the artist to take. This is not to say that all four team members would be consulted on every decision. Attorneys and accountants are legally and ethically bound to represent their client's best interests. Managers also have duties to their clients but they are not as clear cut and well enforced as those of accountants and attorneys. Managers generally cannot be talent agents by law in some states and by union agreements generally.

Conflicts of Interest

Suppose the manager is negotiating the recording contract for the artist. That manager may get a 20 percent commission on all of the artist's income. Suppose that manager needs cash now for the management company. Do you suppose that manager would rather go for a large advance for the artist or for higher royalty percentages? The higher percentages may be in the better long-term interest of the artist but the manager finds a conflict between the manager's interest and the artist's interest. The best way to avoid such conflicts is simply to not be in a position where they are likely to arise. The manager should let the attorney negotiate the agreement, within some agreed-upon parameters.

Certainly the manager and accountant have to be different people if the accountant may be called upon to audit the manager's books.

Summary

The live entertainment income stream is the least consolidated of the three streams. That is not to say that there is not significant consolidation, particularly in the concert promotion business, or that the trend is not towards consolidation. The roughly four billion dollars in annual revenues from concert ticket sales in North America in 2008 approached half the size of the just over eight billion dollars in recording shipments (RIAA estimates). Generally, it is the stars of the recording industry who are the stars of the live performance stage. Furthermore, the four billion dollars annual sales does not account for the thousands of lounges, bars, restaurants, and clubs that have live entertainment and pay their bands without selling tickets. Live performance is an important part of the career of most recording artists in that it provides more stable, long term income than recordings and is an important source of income while waiting for the sale of recordings to reach the point where advances have been recouped (see Chapter 9) and after recording sales have dwindled to minimal levels.

Case Study: Live Nation–The Concert Promotion Company Turned Music Company

Live Nation grew out of the consolidation in the music and broadcast industries in the 1990s and 2000s. It did not even exist as a concert promotion entity in 1995. It began in 1996 when SFX Broadcasting, Inc. (SFX) decided to get into the concert promotion business with the acquisition of concert promoter Delsener/Slater Enterprises. At that time SFX was the nation's seventh largest broadcast chain, owning 79 radio stations, and Delsener/Slater was probably the second largest concert promoter behind national promoter MCA Concerts. SFX had earlier been on a buying binge of other radio stations. Delsener/Slater's main area of operations was in the metropolitan northeastern part of the country. The expected synergy of the broadcast and promotion merger was obvious. SFX Chairman Robert Sillerman said "This will guarantee a stream of events for a certain number of our radio stations. Acts will be guaranteed to be accessible to our stations."[4]

In 1997 SFX expanded its promotion ventures into the midwest with the acquisition of Sunshine Promotions which owned venues in Indiana and Ohio. Later that same year SFX got out of broadcasting by selling its radio stations to Capstar (Capstar later became a piece of Clear Channel). With that infusion of capital, SFX acquired other national and regional promoters, PACE Concerts, Bill Graham Presents, Contemporary Group and Concert/Southern Promotions, Cellar Door, and others, easily becoming the largest national promoter. Then, in 2000, SFX merged with its former broadcast competitor, Clear Channel Communications, to bring together the largest concert promotion company with the largest radio conglomerate in the United States. Clear Channel purchased SFX for $3.3 billion.

All the implications of the Clear Channel/SFX merger/purchase were still unclear by the end of 2000. Clear Channel owned radio and outdoor advertising in nearly every market where SFX owned venues. In all, SFX owned or operated 120 live entertainment venues in the top 50 markets, including 16 amphitheaters in the top 10 markets. Clear Channel owned 867 radios stations and 19 television stations in the United States. Various commentators speculated as to whether Clear Channel stations would be interested in promoting concerts from other promoters. The nearest competitor, House of Blues, was a distant second. A House of Blues officer commented, "This business that used to be a bunch of wildcatters has been turned into a big business."[5]

The impact of the Clear Channel purchase on the promotion business was abundantly clear by 2003. The degree of concentration in the promotion business had changed markedly. Clear Channel Entertainment sold over 50 percent of the tickets sold by the top 50 promoters in 2002. Although far behind in ticket sales, the rest of the top five combined with Clear Channel to sell 70 percent of the tickets of the top 50 promoters. Clear Channel continued to expand their share of the promotion business with the purchase of Metropolitan Entertainment Group for an estimated $10–$12 million in 2002.

Clear Channel's hold over the promotion business was largely because of their ownership of over 1,200 radio stations and over 100 of the top venues in the nation. In 2001, a Denver, Colorado promoter, Nobody In Particular Presents (NIPP), sued Clear Channel, claiming violation of anti-trust laws. The suit claimed that Clear Channel Entertainment unfairly competed by threatening musical acts with limited air time for their recordings on Clear Channel radio stations if they didn't promote their concerts with Clear Channel Entertainment. Clear Channel also allegedly used its size to force smaller promoters out of business. For example, House of Blues promoter Barry Fey reported that Clear Channel offered Neil Diamond *all* of the net profits from a show and half of their concession money to prevent House of Blues from getting the show. Clear Channel denied any strong-arm or anti-competitive practices. The suit was settled for undisclosed terms in 2004, but only after the US District Court Judge Edward Nottingham had set a trial date and stated that NIPP had sufficient evidence to show that "Clear Channel intends its manipulation of airplay to interfere with NIPP and other promoters' prospective business relations with artists."[6]

Live Nation itself was created in 2005 when it was spun off from Clear Channel Entertainment to become a separate publicly traded entity. Several commentators said that the expected synergy between promoter and radio simply did not materialize (perhaps it ran into a legal roadblock). Live Nation acquired House of Blues in 2006.

Live Nation became a total music business entity in 2007 with its first "360 deal" with Madonna. That deal tied touring, merchandising, recordings, and more into one package. Later, Jay-Z, Shakira, and Nickleback signed similar deals with Live Nation. (See Chapter 9 for a more in-depth discussion of 360 deals.) How big had Live Nation become? In 2008 Live Nation's reported $2.3 billion worldwide gross was nearly three times the gross of the entire North American concert business in 1998, four times the number of tickets sold, and twice the number of shows.

Finally, in 2010, Live Nation merged with TicketMaster to complete an almost perfect vertical integration for a live entertainment company. Live Nation controlled everything from the performer to the venue, ticket seller, agency, promoter, all the way down to beer sales at the venue.

QUESTIONS FOR REVIEW

- Compare the size of revenues in live entertainment stream with those in the recordings and music publishing streams.
- Describe the roles of artist, personal manager, promoter, agent, and venue in the concert promotion business.
- How do personal managers, promoters, agents, and venues make money from live appearances?
- How has consolidation impacted the live entertainment business in the areas of promotion, talent agencies, management companies, and venue ownership?
- How are Live Nation and AEG Entertainment competing with each other and smaller promoters?
- Which labor unions are involved in live entertainment? What do they do?

8 Recordings: The Main Stream

Introduction

Basic Functions

In order to produce income in this stream, a record company, usually referred to as a "label," gains control over a master recording of a performance by an artist and then sells copies to consumers, or licenses others such as movie companies, games companies, or mobile phone service providers to use the master. Usually this takes the form of getting the artist to sign an exclusive recording agreement with the label, producing a recording, then marketing copies of that recording for ultimate purchase by consumers through downloads or physical copies. The label therefore has two basic functions that it must perform: acquire masters and market those masters. The acquisition of **masters** is discussed in detail in Chapter 9 (on production and A&R functions). The marketing functions are discussed in detail in Chapters 11 and 12. This chapter examines the overall market structure of the recordings stream and the structure of a typical individual label within that stream.

Masters
The recordings from which other recordings are later going to be made or duplicated. May refer to a multitrack master, a stereo master, or a duplicating master.

Evolution

There is no doubt that digital technologies have revolutionized the recording industry, from the creation of the recording to the distribution and use of that recording in a multitude of formats. From the earliest days through the 1990s the record labels built their business on the recording, manufacture, and distribution of physical copies of their masters. Unauthorized downloading and authorized digital distribution through iTunes, Amazon.com, and others began to force the labels to reconsider their reliance on the sale and distribution of physical copies. They began to aggressively seek out other revenue streams from performances of the recordings (see Chapter 5), new uses of recordings in games and mobile services, and new ways to participate in the revenues that the recordings generated indirectly for the artists—the "360 deals" (see Chapter 9 for a detailed discussion). In many ways the recording industry was evolving to look much more like the music publishing business—a business that made very little of its money through the sale of physical copies and most of its money through licensing the use of its intellectual property (copyrights).

KEY CONCEPTS

● Record companies (labels) have two basic functions: acquiring master recordings and marketing those masters to a variety of users.

● The labels are having to rely less and less on the sale of physical copies and more and more on the licensing of their masters to others.

● Four major companies (the "majors" or the "big four"), Universal Music Group, Warner Music Group, Sony Entertainment, and EMI Music Group control the lion's share of the market for recordings.

● All labels must do the same basic tasks to acquire and market masters, whether they do it all "in house" or whether they outsource it to other organizations.

● The "indies" (labels independent of the big four) are not as significant a force as most romantics would like to believe.

Historical development of the recording industry

To understand why the recording industry is in its current state and to even attempt to predict where it might be going it is necessary to know something of its historical development. For most of its history the industry has been controlled by a handful of major firms—and it still is today.

Oligopoly

Oligopoly A market condition in which there are only a few firms competing in the market. A "few" is typically between 2 and 20.

From almost every perspective the recording industry is in an oligopolistic state. **Oligopoly** is usually defined as a "few" sellers occupying the market, with "few" being anywhere between one firm (monopoly) and many firms (pure competition). A more useful definition, which takes into account the concentration of the market in the number of sellers, defines three levels of oligopoly. In a *dominant firm* oligopoly, one firm holds 50 to 90 percent of the market. In a *tight oligopoly*, a concentration of four firms holds more than 60 percent of the market. If it takes more than four firms to reach 60 percent of the market, but less than "many," that is still an oligopoly but would be deemed "*effective competition.*"

Effective competition A market condition in which it takes more than four firms to control 60 percent of the market.

It should be noted that oligopoly is not a "four letter word"—either literally or figuratively. There is nothing inherently bad about an oligopoly existing in any given market. Oligopoly is simply a word that describes a market in which there are certain kinds of conditions. Generally, markets are described by four significant factors—the number of firms, the seller concentration, the product differentiation, and the barriers to entry. The number of firms involved in the distribution of recordings is relatively small as discussed below, but the number of individual labels involved in the acquisition and creation of masters is large.

Looking at the market share of the individual labels (Table 8.1), one can see a market that is fairly well spread. Even the top 15 labels do not control more than 40 percent of the top 200 market. If one considers label ownership, on the theory that the individual labels do not operate autonomously within their corporate organizations, then there is a much higher concentration of sellers. Although all labels sell the same basic products, recordings, there is usually very high differentiation among those recordings. That is why some recordings find favor with consumers and are "hits" and others are not. That is why some recordings are the toast of the critics and others are panned. That is why consumers have favorite artists and favorite recordings.

On the label side, the barriers to entry are not as great as they once used to be. There are many artists wanting to record, the costs of recording are lower than they used to be, and the label does not have to manufacture its own recordings (most of these factors are discussed in more detail in Chapter 9). From the perspective of the distribution of hard copies of recordings, there are high barriers to entry. Setting up a nationwide distribution system entails warehouses, inventory, and personnel, all creating high barriers to entry. On the other hand, if recordings are distributed through cyberspace on the Internet then barriers to entry are very low, even for physical copies.

Oligopoly from Birth to the 1950s

For most of its existence the recording industry has been in a state of "tight oligopoly." Thomas Edison's patent monopoly lasted only 9 years from the invention of the "talking machine" in 1877. The founding of his Edison Speaking Phonograph Company in 1878 led Alexander Graham Bell's associates, Chichester Bell and Charles Tainter, to create a better cylinder and player, and form the American Graphophone Company in 1887. Edison first started offering cylinders for sale to the public in 1889. Shortly thereafter Columbia was formed and started offering cylinders for sale for coin-operated players. By 1901 the Victor Talking Machine Company was formed and began offering disc players and recordings using Emile Berliner's lateral groove disc technology. (On those

Table 8.1 Top 200 album labels and distributors (by number of albums in *Billboard*'s Top 200 Albums Chart)

	1998		2000		2002		2008	
	No.	%	No.	%	No.	%	No.	%
Controlled by top 15 labels	220	26.9	268	25	364	36.5	520	40.5
Controlled by major distributors	732	89.4	960	89.5	882	88	903	70.3
Controlled by independents	87	10.6	113	10.5	120	12	382	29.7
Total albums in Top 200	819	100	1073	100	1002	100	1285	100

Source: *Billboard* Year End Issues, December 30, 2002; December 26, 2000; December 26, 1998; December, 2008.

discs the stylus moved back and forth in the groove to reproduce the sound wave. In earlier cylinder players the stylus moved up and down in the groove to reproduce the sound wave.)

Columbia began to market both cylinders and discs under patent licenses. By 1909 the three companies with patent monopolies (or licenses) controlled the market: Edison, Columbia, and Victor. All three companies had to offer recordings in order to make consumers interested in buying their players. They even entered the record retail business for the same reason. The modern parallel is iTunes offering downloads so consumers will buy Apple's iPod players, which are a much higher profit item than downloads.

A three-firm tight oligopoly continued until the 1950s, although the firms comprising the top three changed over time. Edison folded in the market crash of 1929, but Decca emerged in the 1930s. By 1950 RCA Victor and Decca claimed 67 percent of *Billboard*'s Top Pop Records chart. Mercury and Capitol were emerging as significant labels with a 10 percent share each and Columbia had dropped to a less than 4 percent share. The popularity charts of *Billboard* magazine were a convenient and reasonably accurate way to measure a record or label's success before the days of SoundScan, the company that gathers data from the laser scanners at checkouts to count the *actual* number of physical copies sold. Although the methodologies used in compiling the charts have changed somewhat over time, they have always included a significant sales component.

During the early 1950s more labels and artists began to emerge but the tight oligopoly remained. Phonograph players became more plentiful in the home market, and jukeboxes spread in commercial establishments such as bars and restaurants. As late as 1953 the top four firms, Columbia (re-energized by Broadway cast albums, **MOR** (Middle-of-the-Road) hits, and Mitch Miller recordings), Capitol, Mercury, and RCA Victor, controlled 78 percent of the charted records. Only seven labels had any chart action at all. As R&B, country, and folk became more popular, more labels appeared in the year-end chart summary. In 1954 14 labels reported top 30 chart activity but there was still a tight oligopoly with RCA Victor, Capitol, Mercury, and Columbia controlling 62 percent of chart activity.

MOR Pop music aimed at older audiences. May specifically refer to recording artists popular in the 1940s and 1950s who were not rock, R&B, or country, or a radio format playing recordings by those performers.

Mom and Pop, and Rock 'n' Roll

The birth of rock and roll in 1955 ended the tight oligopoly and brought effective competition with the emergence of many independent labels, especially R&B, into the top charts. In 1955 it took the top six labels to garner a 60 percent share of the charts. In 1956 the top six labels controlled only 53 percent of the top chart share. *Billboard* reported 25 R&B hits on the charts and 20 rock hits (many of them cover versions of R&B songs by pop artists such as Perry Como). The public's demand for the new music drove sales of recordings up with a 44 percent increase in sales volume from 1955 to 1956. The new artists came from everywhere, on dozens of new labels, and the chart share of the independents skyrocketed to 76 percent in 1958. Even as albums began to replace singles as the dominant selling product in the early 1960s it was clear that the oligopoly was broken. The 1962 *Billboard* album chart summary showed

42 labels with at least one charted album and the top six firms controlled fewer than 50 percent of those records.

Back to Oligopoly

Over the next 20 years the major corporations began to assert more control through branch distribution (see Chapter 12) and mergers. By 1972 the top five labels controlled only 31.4 percent of the album charts, but the top five *corporations* controlled 58.2 percent of those charts. The industry was returning to a tight oligopoly (four firms controlling more than 60 percent), with the top four corporations controlling 52.6 percent of the album chart (WEA 26.2 percent, CBS 13.1 percent, A&M 7.7 percent, Capitol and RCA tied at 5.6 percent). As the 1970s wore on into the 1980s, the oligopoly became more pronounced. The most significant independent labels abandoned independent distribution and agreed to become distributed through the majors' **branch distribution** systems. In 1979 A&M joined RCA distribution, followed by Arista and Ariola in 1983. United Artists merged with Capitol in 1979. In 1983 Chrysalis went to CBS distribution and Motown went to MCA. In the flurry of consolidation and merger of the late 1980s and 1990s *ownership* became the key factor. Large labels bought out smaller labels. The identity of the smaller labels may have been retained but ownership was usually in the hands of a large entertainment conglomerate.

Branch distributor A term still applied to a regional distributorship owned and maintained by one of the big four conglomerates.

Into the Twenty-first Century

By 2009 the structure of the industry had returned to a tight oligopoly. For the first half of the 1990s, the top four distributing firms controlled about 62 percent of the market in the United States. WEA averaged about 21.5 percent, Sony about 15.5 percent, and PolyGram (PGD) and BMG about 12.8 percent each. Independent labels had been increasing their share of the market, from 14.6 percent in 1993 to 21.2 percent in 1996. Following the merger of PolyGram and Universal in 1998, the top four firms, Universal, Warner, BMG, and Sony, controlled almost 75 percent of the total album market in the United States (Chapters 11 and 12 provide details). By 2009 Universal alone controlled over 30 percent of the total market, Sony/BMG (which became just Sony in 2009) had about a 25 percent share, and Warner Music Group had about a 21 percent share. That was over 75 percent controlled by only three companies. EMI had less than 10 percent and the share of independents had shrunk to about 14 percent—despite predictions that digital distribution would be a boon for the independents. The likelihood is that the tight oligopoly will continue. EMI appears likely to be purchased by one of the other majors. Even if the share of independent labels increased to 20 percent, the remaining 80 percent would then be divided among three major companies. As history indicates, once an independent label begins to show significant market share and profitability, it is subject to being purchased by one of the majors. (See the LaFace Records case study at the end of this chapter.) Unlike the situation in the late 1950s, the large companies do not ignore new musical genres or trends.

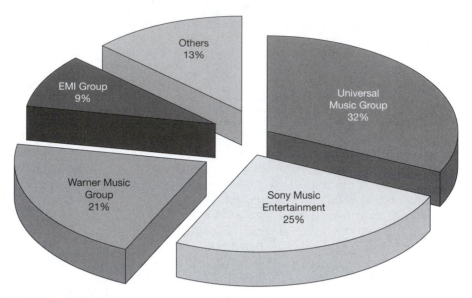

Figure 8.1 Market share of the big four (2008)

The Big Four

Four large international companies own and control the bulk of the recording industry in the world—not just the United States. In case there is any doubt that the recording industry operates on an international level, one only has to look at the ownership of these four largest record companies: Warner Music Group is a publicly held US company; Sony Music Entertainment is owned by the publicly held Japanese Sony Corp.; Universal Music Group is owned by Vivendi Universal S.A. of France (a publicly held company); EMI Music Group is owned privately by a UK investing firm, Maltby Capital Ltd, which is managed by the Terra Firma investing firm. Not every one of the large entertainment conglomerates breaks out the earnings or sales of their music/recording divisions. Where that information is available it is given in the discussion of the "big four" that follows. Financial data from 2008 is used for the sake of establishing a benchmark.

Universal Music Group

Universal Music Group (UMG) is the world's largest record/music company. It was created in 1998 by the merger of Universal Music Group (formerly MCA) and PolyGram. In 2001 UMG was merged with the French company Vivendi S.A. to create Vivendi Universal S.A. Vivendi Universal was the third-largest media group in the world prior to the sale of its film, cable TV, and theme park unit to NBC/General Electric in 2003. UMG's 2008 revenues were $6.975 billion (converted to US dollars). The recorded music division accounted for about 73 percent of its 2008 earnings. UMG's three main components are recorded music, music publishing, and artist services and merchandising.

PolyGram N.V. was a Dutch (Netherlands) entertainment holding company which in turn was 75 percent owned by Philips Electronics N.V. Philips purchased Polydor (a German label) in the early 1950s, Mercury Records in 1961, and MGM Records in 1972. PolyGram was formed in 1972 when parent Philips merged Polydor with Phonogram International. PolyGram continued growth in the 1990s with acquisition of the Island Records Group, A&M Records, Motown, and Def Jam Records.

Prior to 1998, Universal Music Group was composed primarily of the assets of the former MCA Records. The early history of MCA is particularly interesting. It began in New York 1924 as a talent agency and moved to California in 1937 to add film talent to its operations. Television talent booking was added in 1949. The company moved into the production business in 1959 with the purchase of Universal Studios film facilities. MCA added recordings in 1962 when it purchased US Decca and shortly thereafter with the Coral and Kapp labels. The ABC-Dunhill labels were added in 1979.

Ownership of MCA moved to Japan in 1990 when the electronics giant, Matsushita Electric Industrial Co., purchased it for $6.13 billion. MCA added Geffen Records to the label roster in 1991 and the company changed the name of its branch distribution system to Uni Distribution. Another important acquisition was 50 percent of the rock and rap label Interscope in 1996. The Seagram Co. Ltd of Canada (the beverage company) purchased 80 percent of Matsushita's ownership of MCA in 1995 for $5.7 billion. The new parent, Seagram, earned about 63 percent of its revenues from the sales of beverages, spirits and wines, and 37 percent from its holdings in MCA.

UMG operates so many separate labels that they have been assembled into subgroups. These now include MCA/Geffen/A&M (comprised of those three labels); Island/Def Jam; Universal Motown and Universal Republic; UMG Nashville with the MCA Nashville, Mercury Nashville, and Lost Highway labels; the Verve jazz group including the Verve, GRP, and Impulse labels; the Decca Group with its Universal Classical and Decca labels; and separate labels Universal Records South, Universal Music Latin Entertainment, and A&M/Octone. Also under the UMG umbrella is the record and video distribution system, UMGD, the distribution entity for recordings, video, mobile, and digital, and its "indie" distribution organization, Fontana. In 2001 Universal announced the purchase of Internet Music distributors MP3.com and Emusic.com. Universal has positioned itself to be in the "360 deal" business with the acquisition of a merchandising company (Bravado), a management company (Twenty-First Artists), and a talent agency (Helter Skelter). As further evidence that corporations evolve, Vivendi started as a water and waste management company.

Warner Music Group

Warner Music Group (WMG) became the largest stand-alone music company when it was purchased from Time Warner in 2004 by a private investing group. The group took it public in 2005. In 2008 revenues were about $3.5 billion. Income from the recorded music division accounted for about 72 percent of income (before corporate expenses and write-offs) in 2008—a number very similar to Universal's. WMG's two main divisions are recorded music and music publishing.

Warner Brothers records began as the music division of Warner Brothers film company to control music interests for its film productions in the 1920s. In the depression of the 1930s Warner sold off its music publishing interests. In 1958 it reformed its music publishing and record labels, primarily to promote and sell its film and television related music. Warner Brothers had early 1960s success with the Everly Brothers and Bill Cosby comedy recordings and bought Frank Sinatra's MOR label, Reprise, in 1963 and1965 (they purchased the label in halves). In 1967 Warner Brothers purchased Atlantic Records and was in turn purchased by 7 Arts. In 1969 the Kinney Corporation (not the shoe company, but a building services, construction, and parking company) purchased 7 Arts and changed its name to Warner Communications, Inc. With the addition of the Elektra Records label purchased in 1970, Warner/Elektra/Atlantic Distribution (later just WEA Distribution) was formed. In 1987 Warner/Chappell Music was acquired and the parent company merged with print publishing giant, Time, Inc., to create Time Warner. The company continued to grow with the acquisition of Rhino Records in 1998 and Word Entertainment (the Christian music group) in 2001. In 2000 Time Warner merged with America On Line. But the expected synergy of a total multi-media company did not materialize. WMG was spun off Time Warner in 2003 and AOL was spun off in 2009.

WMG consists of the labels Warner/Chappell Music Publishing, an Artist Services division, and WEA Inc., the branch distribution system. In 2003 WEA sold its manufacturing division to a Canadian hardware manufacturing company, Cinram, for $1.05 billion. Like Universal, WMG has organized its labels into subgroups. The Atlantic Group includes the labels Atlantic Records, Atlantic Nashville, Elektra Records, and Roadrunner Records. The Independent Label Group (ILG) includes East West Records, Rykodisc, and Cordless Recordings. Warner Brothers includes Warner Brothers Records, Asylum Records, Nonesuch Records, Reprise Records, Sire Records, Warner Brothers Records Nashville, and Word Record Group. WMG labels are: Warner Brothers, Elektra/Asylum, Atlantic, Atco, Reprise, Rhino, and joint ventures with Maverick, Tommy Boy, and Giant records.

Sony Music Entertainment

Sony Corporation, the Japanese electronics manufacturing company, saw the importance of developing software industries to complement its hardware manufacturing when it entered into an agreement with CBS Records to create the Digital Audio Disc Corporation, the first manufacturer of compact discs in the United States. The cornerstones of Sony Music are Sony Music Publishing and the venerable labels Columbia Records and RCA Records. Columbia, originally the Columbia Graphophone Company of pre-1900, existed as a separate entity until the depression saw the merger of Columbia Graphophone, Gramophone Company, and Parlophone to create Electric and Musical Industries Ltd (EMI) in England. EMI sold its American stock to the American Record Corporation (ARC). Columbia Broadcasting System (CBS) purchased

ARC in 1938 and revitalized the Columbia label. Columbia seceded from EMI in England in 1952. Sony built its music interests primarily through the acquisition of CBS Records group for $2 billion in 1988 from CBS, Inc.

In 2004 Sony and BMG (part of the German owned Bertelsmann, A.G.) formed a joint venture that became Sony BMG (what a clever name). This created a rival equal in size to Universal. In fact the combined Sony BMG controlled about 30 percent of the market compared to Universal's 27 percent at the time of the merger. The merger was approved by the European Commission, and in the US by the Federal Trade Commission. However, E.U. approval was annuled in 2006 after a suit by a group of **indie** labels, then re-approved in 2007. The rocky merger ended in 2008 with further consolidation when Sony bought out BMG's half of the merged company. By 2009 what was then Sony's US market share had shrunk to about 26 percent and Universal's had grown to over 30 percent. The purchase of BMG's half brought all of BMG's former labels under the new Sony Music Entertainment.

> **Indie** A term usually referring to an independent label or an independent record store.

BMG's record business took off in the United States in 1979 when it acquired Arista Records from its founder Clive Davis. In 1986 BMG purchased all the RCA Victor interests from General Electric (which had earlier that year acquired RCA Corporation's recording interests for $6.4 billion). Victor was one of the earliest record labels, going all the way back to 1901 in its founding as the Victor Talking Machine Company. It was the first company to make Emile Berliner's lateral cut disc recordings and players. Before the Sony merger, BMG owned or operated more than 200 labels. BMG had sold its music publishing division to Universal in 2006 and it looked as if BMG was getting out of the music business entirely. But by 2009 it reentered the music business, thanks to a major investment ($300 million plus) by a private investment firm, and created BMG Rights Management to license uses of masters and rebuild a music publishing company. Some remarks by BMG management fueled speculation that it was going to enter the business of licensing master rights for major artists who left the major labels and owned their own masters, like Garth Brooks, or perhaps others who might win copyright termination suits with their former labels (see Chapter 3). Whether it would or could return to the status of a major label remained to be seen.

As the new Sony Music Entertainment entered 2009 it looked as if revenues from the Music division would be 6 to 7 percent of total Sony Corp. revenues. However, the music, film, and financial services divisions were reporting profits while the others were reporting losses in the tough economy of 2008–2009. Sony Corp. also owns film production and distribution interests Columbia Pictures and Tri-Star Pictures, as well as home video production and distribution, television production companies, mobile and networked services and products (Sony Ericsson), financial services, and a large consumer electronics division. Sony Music labels are: Arista Records, Arista Nashville, Bluebird Jazz, BNA Records, Burgundy Records, Columbia Nashville, Columbia, J Records, Jive, LaFace, Legacy, Epic, Epic Associated Labels, Provident, RCA, RCA Nashville, RCA Victor, Masterworks, US Latin, Verity, and Windham Hill. Sony also owns a branch distribution system (Sony Distribution) and CD and DVD manufacturing facilities in the United States.

EMI

EMI began with the merger of three labels in the United Kingdom in 1930. Columbia Graphophone, Gramophone Company (the folks who originated the famous logo of the dog listening to the gramophone player, "His Masters Voice"), and Parlophone joined to create Electric and Musical Industries Ltd (later just EMI Ltd). EMI remained a primarily European operation until 1956 when it acquired Capitol Records in the US Capitol had been formed in the United States in 1942 by Johnny Mercer, Buddy DeSylva, and Glenn Wallichs. In the United States, Capitol-EMI Industries grew into a major label with a branch distribution system. In 1974 EMI acquired the rights to the substantial Decca UK catalog. (There were two Decca record companies until 1974. Decca UK was formed in 1929 and US Decca in 1934.) Thorn EMI PLC was formed in 1979 when electrical/electronics company Thorn merged with EMI. The new company began expansion with the acquisition of Chrysalis Records in 1989, SBK Entertainment World in 1990, Filmtrax and Thames Television in 1990, the Virgin Music Group in 1992, Sparrow Corp. (a gospel label) in 1992, and Toshiba-EMI Music Publishing Co. and Star Song publishing in 1994. In 1996 Thorn and EMI demerged.

The resulting EMI Group contained two divisions: EMI Music Group operated the 65 labels and 23 music publishing companies, including Capitol, EMI Records, EMI Music Publishing, Virgin Records Ltd, and Capitol-EMI Music. The Music Group also includes EMD (EMI Music Distribution, formerly Cema Distribution) distribution, and manufacturing facilities. The HMV group operated a retail division consisting of 240 record stores, 144 of which were outside of the UK. In 1998 EMI spun off the retail division to HMV media group, which operates the HVM music and the Waterstone bookstore chains. The demerger spin-off fueled speculation that EMI would be purchased by some other music or entertainment conglomerate at a speculated price of $9 billion plus. Indeed, both Time Warner and Bertelsmann expressed interest in EMI. The Time Warner deal fell through in late 2000 as the European Union's Merger Task Force was reportedly ready to block the merger. Later that year and continuing into 2001, EMI and Bertelsmann were reportedly in merger talks. By mid-2003, the merger talks had shifted to BMG and Warner, then back to Warner as it became separated from AOL-Time Warner and Sony bought out BMG's share of the Sony/BMG merged organization in 2008.

In 2007 EMI Music was purchased by the UK private investing firm, Terra Firma. It reported increases in earnings in both EMI Music (the recordings division) and EMI Music Publishing for the 2008/2009 fiscal year, with revenues of $1.8 billion and earnings of $163 million from the recorded music division. Totals for the entire group, including music publishing, were $2.6 billion in revenues and $498 million in earnings. Recordings accounted for about 55 percent of earnings. Investment groups such as Terra Firma often buy ailing firms, try to turn them around financially in a few years, then try to sell them to some other firm. So, speculation about when EMI will be for sale again and to whom was still alive and well in 2009.

The success of the big four at producing hits is illustrated in Table 8.1. The success of the various individual labels tends to vary from year to year. But in the years near the end of the twentieth century, the top 15 labels only controlled anywhere from 25 percent of 37 percent of *Billboard*'s Top 200 Album Chart. This would indicate effective competition between labels, but not between distribution companies. Independent labels only accounted for about 10–12 percent of the chart action in each year. But by 2009 the majors' chart share had dropped to about 70 percent. Compare that to the Indie share of *sales* in Figure 8.1 (page 174) and you should conclude that a lot of indie labels got products into the lower levels of the album charts, but they did not sell much.

An important point about this table is that it shows significant diversity and lack of concentration when looking at the individual labels and much more concentration when looking at the distributors. The major distributors controlled nearly 90 percent of the Album Chart action for most of those years. That represents significant concentration. However, if the individual labels function autonomously in terms of A&R and marketing in finding, developing, and promoting new talent, then there is much less concentration of *label* power and there should be much more diversity of music to be heard, regardless of who the corporate owner or distributor of any individual label might be.

Internet Activities

- Visit the corporate websites for the majors. Get their latest financial information by looking under "Investor Relations" for annual reports: www.emigroup.com, www.sony.net, www.vivendi.com, and www.wmg.com.
- Visit A2IM website www.a2im.org for information on their artists and labels.
- Pick an independent label (or one that you think is independent). Find its website. Find out who distributes its recordings.

The Structure of Record Companies

Corporate Structure

The upper-level structure of the two true conglomerates, Sony Corp. and Vivendi-Universal, is basically the same. As shown in Figure 8.2, each corporate owner usually holds several different businesses in addition to its recording companies. These other businesses range from other entertainment enterprises such as film, television, mobile communications, and cable TV, to consumer electronics. The music group, which is all that exists at WMG and EMI, usually includes at least music publishing and record companies. The record group then usually includes various labels, which tend to operate as free-standing units for purposes of A&R and marketing, the record distribution system that distributes all labels owned by the company plus others under a variety of agreements; perhaps a manufacturing division that makes all of the owned labels' CDs and DVDs; and usually also special orders from outside labels and others. As the labels have begun to move more into total music companies with "360 deals" for their artists, they have taken on other functions such as artist management, merchandising, and concert promotion, perhaps while shedding some of the more traditional functions such as manufacturing. These "360 deal" components are more likely to appear at the corporate level. Compare Figures 8.2 and 8.3.

The conglomerates have significant **vertical integration**. That means they seek to own and control all aspects in the production of their products, from the raw ingredients of recording artists and songs almost to retail sale to consumers. Most of these corporations own labels that control the creative inputs from recording artists. They own music publishing companies, controlling the creative inputs from songwriters. They own manufacturing facilities to make the CDs and tapes that will be ultimately sold to the public. They own distribution companies to get the recordings to the retailers. But none own brick and mortar retail stores since EMI sold its HMV stores in 1998. They also appear

> **Vertical integration** A market condition in which a firm owns more than one portion of the total distribution chain from manufacturer to consumer. A record label that owns a pressing plant is an example of vertical integration, as is a distributor that owns record stores.

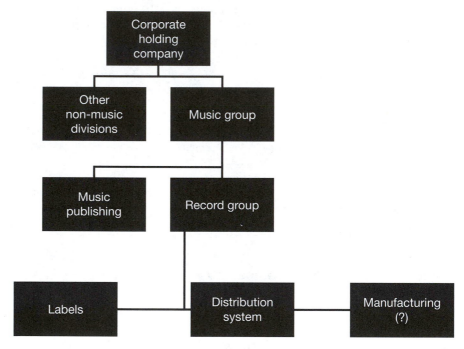

Figure 8.2 Typical corporate structure of the majors

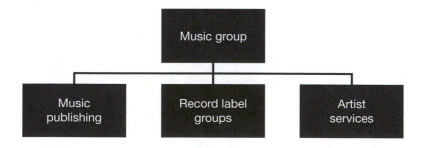

Figure 8.3 Typical "360 deal" music group organization

to be content to let other entities such as iTunes, WalMart, and Amazon.com sell downloads. They also seek **horizontal integration**, when they buy up competing labels in order to insure a larger total share of the recording market.

Structure at the Label Level

The two basic functions of any label are A&R and marketing. But any given label may perform those functions in depth, spread across a number of departments and personnel, or simply either not do them or hire an outside organization to provide the service (**outsourcing**). Figure 8.4 illustrates the divisions likely to be present in a large label. While there is not a great deal of commonality in what a given label may call a particular department, the divisions are typical.

The basic responsibilities of each department are as follows:

- Label president—This person is usually someone who has experience in A&R, though not necessarily. Sometimes the presidents come from the business affairs departments and are attorneys; less often they are from the marketing departments. The president oversees all operations, but depending upon the depth of their personal involvement in A&R, either as producers or "talent scouts," the other divisions may have additional independence. (Note that the business affairs and accounting divisions are "staff" divisions not directly involved in the production and marketing of the recordings.)
- Business affairs—This is usually the legal department of the label. It is in charge of negotiating artist and producer agreements, and other licensing arrangements, including sampling and film use. This department typically

Horizontal integration
An economic term describing the actions of a firm to buy out competing companies at the same level, such as one record store chain acquiring another record store chain.

Outsourcing
A situation where a business hires another firm to perform some function that had previously been performed "in house."

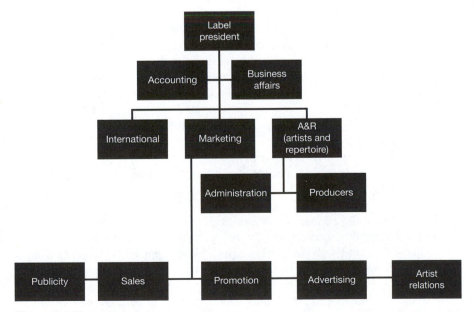

Figure 8.4 Typical label structure

finalizes foreign licensing deals, distribution deals with other labels, and soundtrack album deals. An advantage of this split of the negotiating function from the president or A&R people is that it enables the creative people and the marketing people to be at peace with the artist, while any hard-nosed bargaining goes on with individuals who are not as likely to have to deal with the artist in later production or marketing of the recordings.

- Accounting—Accounting is critical to the profitability of the company in any business that depends upon so many sales of so many different individual units where there are so many people with an interest in each unit. The counting of sales, returns, free goods, and promotional albums and the payment of royalties to at least three (artist, producer, and music publisher) but as many as a dozen or more interests (multiple artists, multiple producers, a different publisher for each song) per recording is a complex task. The accounting departments can rest assured that artists, producers, publishers, and the Harry Fox Agency are all likely to audit the account books for any given album or artist once every year or two.

- International division—This unit works out international distribution deals and coordinates marketing plans around the world. It may be responsible for A&R in foreign territories. Some smaller labels hire other labels either outside of the United States or hire a major US label to take care of international marketing and distribution for them.

- Marketing—This is usually the largest division of a label. However, a small independent label may rely on a deal with a major label to supply all of these services while the small label only provides an A&R function. The term "marketing," generally said to include product conception and development, manufacturing, promotion and distribution (see Chapter 11), is significantly more broad than most record companies use the term in their internal structure. The A&R department handles product conception and development, manufacturing may be through a separate subsidiary, or entirely an outside entity, and actual distribution is through a separate distributing company. The responsibility of the marketing department at most record labels is limited to getting the recordings to the consumer through retail, rack, and Internet sales, and to promoting consumer awareness of the records through radio and TV airplay, print publicity, and advertising in any and all media.

- Sales—The sales department is responsible for getting orders for records from **rack jobbers**, major retail chains, and **one-stops**. There may be merchandising specialists working in sales whose job it is to visit stores and help set up displays. Sales people may be organized on a national, regional, local basis, or may be set up by account size or type, then regionalized or localized.

- Promotion—The primary job of promotion is to get exposure through radio and video airplay, and the label's web presence. Some labels separate the radio, video, and web promotion arms. Most large labels have their own **promotion staffs** and hire independent promotion people as well. Promotion people work with radio and TV broadcast outlets, and work with the artist when the artist is on a tour, whether it be a paying tour with concerts, or a promotional tour with showcases for local media people to

Rack jobber A distributor who buys records from branches or independent distributors and services the record departments in mass merchandiser stores or other non-record stores.

One-stop A kind of distributor that sells all records from all labels to retailers.

Promotion staffs Term applied to record label persons or independent contractors whose job it is to get radio stations to play records released by the label.

hear the act. The promotion staff sees to it that the "right" people from the media and record retail get the opportunity to hear their artists whenever their artist is playing in a given locale. Promotion people may even have to take the artists around to visit local radio and television stations or record stores while the artist is on tour.

- Advertising—Advertising personnel create the media plans to go with a given album or single. Because the advertising plan must be careful to promote a unified and consistent image of the artist and album, many labels create the actual advertisements that go to retailers or local radio or television stations. The advertising department will also make national media buys or dispense **co-op advertising money** to retailers and distributors who come up with additional advertising plans for the label's recordings. Co-op advertising money in the recording industry most often means that the label will pay 100 percent of the advertising costs for certain kinds of ads. Sometimes a label will go for a true cooperative advertising plan where the expense is shared by the label and the retailer. As labels cut costs in the 2000s, they began to look for ways to outsource advertising to agencies, or to get advertising *income* through music video sites and product placement and endorsements in music videos, even going so far as to sell advertising in album booklets.

> **Co-op advertising money** Advertising money given to retailers or distributors by the labels to advertise the label's records in local media. More often than not the "co-op" is not really split between the label and retailer, but is entirely paid for by the label.

- Publicity—Publicity consists of non-paid exposure other than radio airplay or music video airplay. This department contains people who write press releases, create press kits including artist bios (biographies) and photos, and try to get the artist appearances as talk show guests or performers on radio or TV. Publicity is probably one of the easiest functions for a label to farm out to independent publicists. In fact, an artist's manager will often have an independent publicity firm working alongside the label's public relations people. The publicity people try to see to it that while an artist is touring there is publicity material flowing to the media in towns where the artist will be performing, but ahead of the artist's actual appearance dates. Publicity people will work with promotion people to set up press conferences or "meet and greet" opportunities for local media. The publicity department is also in charge of trying to get reviews of recordings in local and national media, and on the Internet. (See Chapters 11 and 12 for a more detailed look at marketing.)

- Artist relations—This department may go by a number of other names, including product development and career development. Whatever it is called, it has a primary task of coordinating the work of the other departments to be sure that there is a unified marketing plan for every album. People in this department often work with the personal manager of the artist to insure that a uniform image is projected. They may work with the artist or producer during the recording of an album to get a better idea of what the album is about and to develop a marketing plan that the artist will support. They will make sure that copies of the recordings for sales and promotion, as well as advertising and publicity, follow the artist whenever the artist is on tour. Artist relations is a function that labels began to add during the late 1970s as they became aware that marketing plans had to be more sophisticated and integrated in order to succeed. This department takes on added significance in a "360 deal" label and may end up being part of the "Artist Services" division.

- A&R—The A&R (Artist and Repertoire) department is in charge of finding and recording artists. It may also look for songs for artists who do not write their own compositions. Because the A&R department is in charge of delivery of a completed product, ready to be marketed, it also has to perform the administrative duties associated with the finished master.

- A&R administration—This is where coordination takes place for getting mechanical licenses and clearances for sampling. The administrative staff must make sure that all people who played on an album get proper credits. They may help the producers screen material for an artist if asked. They coordinate delivery of the recording, artwork, and liner notes to make sure that all materials necessary to complete production of the discs are delivered to the manufacturing plants and download sites. They make sure that all musicians, artists, and producers get paid when they are supposed to for the initial production of the album.

- Producers—These people are in charge of the recording process. They may find the talent and record it, record it after others have found it, or screen talent being pitched to the label. They may be **"staff" producers** who work for a salary and royalty, or be entirely independent of the label and just work for a royalty and advances. Most producers are now independent producers. (See Chapter 10 for an in-depth discussion of producers.)

Profitability in the Recording Industry

The growth of Internet use and the creation of new means of digital distribution and entertainment have created new revenue streams for the recording business. The number of new revenue producing uses of masters expanded significantly in the twenty-first century, partially offsetting label losses due to declining physical copy sales. Compare Figures 8.5 and 8.6. Digital revenues grew steadily in the mid-2000s and amounted to about one third of record label revenues by the end of 2008 (see Table 8.2.) Digital revenues for hits may be substantial. For example, **Mastertone ring tone** sales for a top ten ring tone typically run from over 800,000 to over 2 million units. Single sales for a popular track can easily run from 1 to 3 million downloads. On the other hand, in a given year it is likely that fewer than 1 percent of record albums will sell over 250,000 units (see discussion below). To make matters worse (from the label perspective), the profit margin on compact discs shrank as disc prices were lowered, total sales of CDs declined, and sales of less profitable single downloads soared.

The large record labels are fond of saying that fewer than 20 percent of the recordings they release ever recoup their costs. But is everything really as bad as the labels would say? As explained in Chapter 9, recording costs and some marketing costs are generally **recouped** (recovered) out of artist royalties.

Staff producer
A producer who works on a salaried basis for the label (and probably a small royalty, too). Currently such persons are likely to be label executives who also happen to be producers.

Mastertone ring tone A ring tone that is an edit of an actual original master recording of an artist and label. A "ring tune" is a recording of the song, but probably with synthesizers playing the parts.

Recoupable Recoverable out of royalties actually earned or otherwise due. Advances are usually recoupable but **nonreturnable**, meaning that they are *not a debt* that would have to be repaid.

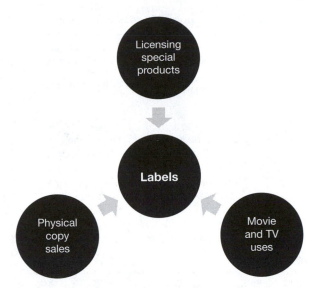

Figure 8.5 Label income sources, pre-1990s

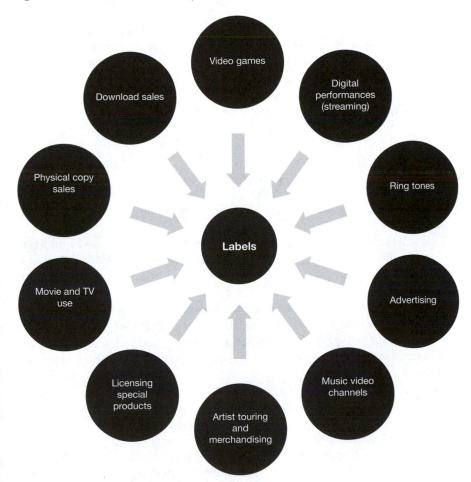

Figure 8.6 New millennium label income sources

Table 8.2 Comparing revenues from physical and digital sources (2008 data)

Physical sales	CDs	368 million units	$5,471 million
	Other "hard" copies	17 million units	$288 million
Total physical revenues		385 million units	$5,759 million
Digital revenues			
	Ring tones and other mobile	405 million units	$977 million
	Subscription services	1.6 million units	$221 million
	Single downloads	1,043 million units	$1,032 million
	Album downloads	64 million units	$635 million
	Music video (sales)	21 million units	$41 million
	Kiosk sales	1.6 million units	$2.6 million
	Digital performance of sound recordings	(not applicable)	$155 million
Total digital revenues		1,536 million	$3,064 million

Sources: RIAA and SoundExchange

Table 8.3 illustrates a typical (and somewhat simplified) situation for pre- and post-recoupment profits. The label does not pay the artists and producers their royalties of $1.30 per copy (about 14 percent of the "wholesale" price; see Chapter 11) until that royalty adds up to the total recoupable amounts. Suppose a major label spends $200,000 in recoupable production and marketing costs. Suppose that total production and marketing costs are $300,000. It will take sales of 153,846 units for artist and producer royalties to equal the "recoupable" amounts ($200,000 recoupable divided by $1.30 royalty per unit). By that time the label's gross profits are nearly $770,000 after deducting the actual costs of mechanical royalties for the music publisher, distribution charges, manufacturing, and the $100,000 marketing expenses that were not recoupable. Even allowing for the label paying for its overhead, that is a substantial figure for a relatively "low selling" album.

To reach the *economic* break-even point, where the total fixed costs (production and marketing) is equal to gross profits, takes sales of only 53,098 units (rounded up). That is calculated by dividing the $300,000 production and marketing costs as "fixed" by the $5.65 gross margin per disc sold. By the time the artist has hit the recoupment point and the label's gross margin drops to $4.35, the label has sold over 100,000 units beyond the break-even point, making a gross profit of $565,000 (okay, $465,000 if you deduct the unrecouped marketing costs, but marketing expenses are not variable costs so would not ordinarily be figured into calculating gross profits).

So, for a lot of artists who never see any royalties on the sale of their albums the record companies *are* making money. Note that the profitability on digital sales is not much different from physical copies in the 2009 marketplace. On the other hand, average wholesale prices dropped nearly three dollars as average retail "list" prices dropped from $17.98 to $13.98. So, although the labels have a much lower profit margin in the contemporary market, they can still make

Table 8.3 Pre- and post-recoupment profitability

Physical Sales	Pre-recoupment	Post-recoupment
Wholesale price	$ 9.10	$ 9.10
Less: Manufacturing costs	$ 1.00	$ 1.00
Artist and producer royalties	$ 0.00	$ 1.30
Mechanical royalties	$ 0.70	$ 0.70
Distributor charges	$ 1.75	$ 1.75
Gross margin	$ 5.65	$ 4.35

Digital Downloads (10 cuts = one album)	Pre-recoupment	Post-recoupment
Wholesale price	$ 6.50	$ 6.50
Less: Manufacturing costs	$ 0.00	$ 0.00
Artist and producer royalties	$ 0.00	$ 0.91
Mechanical royalties	$ 0.91	$ 0.91
Distributor charges	$ 0.00	$ 0.00
Gross margin	$ 5.59	$ 4.68

profits. Therefore, the labels can still afford to try to release more albums, even if sales are relatively low. In effect, artists are subsidizing the labels because recoupment of advances at the artist royalty rate is a lot slower than actual recovery of total fixed costs at the label's gross margin per CD rate. The labels, however, have to be careful to keep their fixed production and marketing costs under control. This high profitability, particularly on CD sales, also fuels the independent labels.

The "Indies"

Independent record companies are usually thought of as those not owned by one of the major labels or conglomerates. Such a definition is rather broad, covering everything from a small label in a large city with a couple of artists which just markets recordings on a local or regional level; to Disney, which is part of a major entertainment company (just not one of the big four *music/recording* companies); to a label with a significant artist roster and national distribution through independent distributors, such as Sugar Hill, TVT, Rap-a-Lot, Koch, or Goner; or a label that has its recordings distributed by one of the big four but is not literally owned by them. Some people would argue that the latter is not a true indie, since it is not distributed through true independent distributors, but in a time of consolidation and vertical integration any label that is not *owned* by a major label is deserving of the title of "indie."

The indies play an important role in the recording industry. They are a development area for record labels. Several of what might now be called major labels began life as indies—Warner Brothers, Def Jam, Arista, and MCA, for example. The indies provide consumers with diversity and specialty music that the larger labels often ignore because the small volume of sales: the 3,000 to 30,000 units range is not enough for a large label to consider. They also provide the larger labels with a source of new talent and new directions in music. The rock and roll explosion began on independent labels. New Age music began as an independent phenomenon. Rap began on small inner-city independents, then entered the mainstream, and then was bought into by the large labels.

Size of the Indie Labels

The digital revolution did not prove to be the boon for independent labels as some had predicted. From a market share of about 21 percent in 1996, the market share of independent labels steadily declined to just over 11 percent by the end of 2009. Several factors account for the drop. First, indies release so much product that there is simply too much competition for consumers who want the cutting edge music that indie labels provide. Second, independent record stores and large record stores with deep inventories steadily disappeared in the late 1990s and 2000s. Even though CD Baby and other indie online sources appeared, that did not stop the bleeding. Worse, the declining market share was of a steadily declining total market in terms of numbers of albums sold. SoundScan and RIAA data indicate that the independent labels account for about 11 percent of the total album sales, yet they release about 66 percent of the titles. The vast majority (85 percent) of current releases (not just new, but catalog as well) sell fewer than 1,000 copies per year. The average sales of a new release from an independent label amount to about 1,500 units, while the average sales of a major label release total about 8,000 units.

How do the independent labels survive? They keep production and marketing costs low. Coupled with high profit margins in CDs and downloads, low cost albums can turn a profit with minimal sales. As Table 8.2 indicates, a low cost CD generates a margin of $5.60 per copy. If that recording can sell 3,000 units it would earn over $16,000 in potential profits. If recording and marketing costs are kept low, $10,000 or less, then there is substantial profit. Even an average selling indie release would generate about $8,400 in revenues before recording and marketing costs. With the growth of project studios and inexpensive CD replication even releases selling at that level could be profitable. There is even profitability in having more low budget, low selling albums than in having fewer. Since these recordings are not so costly to make or market, more titles can be released towards a very small market. Perhaps that is why the indies release so many albums. Or perhaps it is because the indie labels people are really more artist and music fans or aficionados than their major label counterparts. That is the same as it was even back into the 1940s. A *Billboard* article described indie labels in 1949 as having break-even points on singles of 5,000 units, compared to the majors' break-even points of 15,000 units. The American Association of Independent Music (**A2IM**) represents hundreds of small labels, mostly in the specialty music areas of bluegrass, reggae, dance, jazz, classical, and others. That figure does not even count the thousands of custom albums that do not go through independent distribution but are sold by the artists only in their own locales, at their performances, or through such Internet services as CD Baby, TuneCore, Bandcamp, or even iTunes.

A2IM Formerly NAIRD (National Association of Independent Record Distributors) in 1972, A2IM is a trade association for independent record labels, distributors, retailers and those who work with independent labels and artists.

Indie labels and indie distribution

Although some independent labels are distributed by the majors, most indie records find their way to the marketplace through independent distributors. Most independent distributors operate on a regional basis and some even on a national basis. A trend of the 1990s was the growth in size of independent distributors and the consolidation of independent distribution into fewer firms. For example, in 1995 Passport Music Distribution, Inc. was formed out of Encore Distribution and Sound Solutions (USA) Inc. (an import and budget distributor). Passport, in turn, was part of the largest independent distributor, Alliance Entertainment, which also owns Independent National Distributors, Inc. and labels Castle Communications, Concord Jazz, and Red Ant Entertainment. Alliance is the largest independent distributor and claims to control over 8 percent of the CD market—that is probably three-fourths of the indie market. Late in the 1990s the major labels opened up their own competing and wholly owned independent distribution organizations as a way to identify new talent for their major labels (see Chapter 9 on **"upstream" deals**). Sony owns Red Distribution, Universal owns Fontana, Warner owns Alternative Distribution Alliance, and EMI owns Caroline.

Upstream deals
A deal where an artist signs with one of the "independent distribution" companies owned by one of the four majors and the major has the option to sign the artist to one of its wholly owned labels if it wishes to in the future, mainly if the artist becomes successful.

DIY Activities

- Visit ReverbNation's website, www.reverbnation.com, and learn as much as you can from the site, and from other search engines.
- Visit CD Baby's website, www.cdbaby.com, and learn what you can from the site and other search engines.
- Do a search for "CD duplication." Compare two or three places to get CDs made, or CD-R duplication with boxes, inserts, and other packaging. What are the prices? What is included in the service? What does an artist have to provide?

Diversity in spite of itself?

A particularly popular criticism of the recording industry is that it is run by huge conglomerates that for one reason or another are bent upon shoving much "bad" music down the throats of consumers while "good" music and artists languish without access to the system. To be sure, there is much in popular music at any given time that may not measure up well on some critical scale. The majors are large bureaucratic organizations that tend to be conservative in their releases and follow the patterns of previous successes. At the same time a large label must be aware that, because the majority of releases are not likely to produce much profit, the only way to stabilize revenues is to have a sufficiently large number of releases that many of them will make enough profit to support the superstructure. The big four conglomerates must behave like savvy investors. Wall

Street analysts know that the best way to minimize risk in the stock market is through a diversity of holdings. That way the main risk is just that that is inherent in stocks as a kind of investment instead of the risks associated with one particular company.

So the large label will release artists that essentially compete with each other as well as those from other labels instead of risking large sums on a single artist who might not catch the public's fancy. Large numbers of releases make it likely that more consumers will find recordings that they like and will buy. The trend towards larger numbers of releases by the majors and independent labels over the past 5 years does tend to bear that out. The worst problem for the industry would be a market diminished overall because there were fewer releases.

The trend, then, should be towards a greater diversity of music being offered rather than towards homogeneity. That trend has been noticed by some observers as not what would have been predicted by the presence of larger and larger conglomerates controlling more and more of the market. In fact, one observer predicts that levels of high product diversity are most associated with moderately concentrated markets and that less diversity is associated with low and high levels of concentration. Two questions remain. Will the market for music continue to shrink to the point that large numbers of releases simply sell too few copies to be profitable and therefore the number of releases will be cut back? And is the recording industry at such a high level of concentration (now a "tight oligopoly" with almost 80 percent of sales controlled by three firms) that diversity will begin to suffer?

Summary

In any discussion of the basic structure of the recording industry it is important to remember that there are at least three perspectives from which to discuss the labels. First, one can look at the individual names on individual labels. For some purposes that may be the best way because individual labels, even if owned by the same corporate conglomerate, tend to compete with each other for artists and for the consumers' dollars. Labels can also be viewed based upon ownership at the corporate level. From that perspective, the four major conglomerates control about 87 percent of the industry. Finally, one could look at labels from the perspective of distribution. The number of distribution firms is smaller than the number of individual labels, or the number of label firms, due to the high costs associated with distribution. The concentration of distribution in the four multinationals is about the same as the concentration of market share by corporate owner, but there are significantly fewer competing independent distributors and they too appear to be going through a phase of concentration of ownership. The individual label perspective focuses on the A&R function. The distribution perspective focuses on the marketing function. The ownership perspective focuses on the profitability of the "bottom line." All three perspectives can provide valuable insight into the workings of the recording industry. Each is used at different times throughout this book

Case Study: LaFace Records

The story of LaFace Records is the story of a songwriting and production dream team that enjoys great success, gets an infusion of capital from a large label to start their own label, has even more success, and is ultimately bought out for a reported $100 million. The label ultimately becomes part of Sony Entertainment's Zomba group of labels through Sony's acquisition of BMG and Arista Records.

Antonio "L.A." Reid and Kenneth "Babyface" Edmonds first worked together in Indianapolis when Reid was the drummer and Edmonds the guitar player in a group called "Deele." Although the group had some success, Reid and Edmonds left for Los Angeles in 1985 and began songwriting and production. Ultimately they began having success with Whitney Houston, Boyz II Men, Bobby Brown, Paula Abdul, and others. Reid and Edmonds wanted to take their success to the next level and began looking for funding from a major label to start a label of their own. That led them to Clive Davis, then President of Arista Records. Reid later said, "It just clicked; he had a pure appreciation for what we did and what we aspired to do."[1] So, in 1989 Arista created a joint venture with the two that became LaFace (an obvious combination of nicknames) Records and infused the new organization with $10 million. The label located in Atlanta because several of the pairs' artists had moved there and, as Davis noted, Atlanta was easy to get to from anywhere.

The ink was barely dry on the deal when Virgin Records signed a three-group production deal with LaFace. The first production was with the trio "After 7" (which contained two of Edmond's brothers and Reid's cousin) which became a hit single. But the new label really jumped out of the gates in 1992 with major hits from the group TLC and the soundtrack from the film, *Boomerang*. In 1993 the label was propelled further with its first Toni Braxton album which sold more than 9 million copies. Reid took primary control of the label that year and Edmonds returned to production and his own solo career. LaFace entered the rap market in 1994 with a highly successful album from the Atlanta group, OutKast. In 1995 Arista and LaFace renewed their deal for another 5 years, and a reported $15 million for LaFace. Ironically, Sony Music was one of the other labels bidding to get LaFace. Less than 15 years later, Sony would own the label entirely.

The late 1990s were not as kind to LaFace. TLC and Toni Braxton filed bankruptcy in order to get out of their contracts with the label. The suits and countersuits were ultimately settled, the contracts renegotiated, and both released highly successful new albums for LaFace later in the 1990s. In 1999 a lawsuit was filed on behalf of civil rights icon Rosa Parks because the rap group OutKast had used her name as the title to one of their recordings. She claimed that the title misled the public into thinking that she was somehow associated with the group and song or that it was about her and that it used her name for a commercial purpose without her permission. The case was ultimately settled in 2005 for an undisclosed amount of money but not until a federal appellate court had ruled that the group did not have a clear cut First Amendment right to use Ms Parks' name as the title to a song that actually had almost nothing to do with her.

In 2000 BMG (by then Arista's parent company) bought out Edmonds and Reid's share of LaFace for $100 million. Reid was then named CEO of Arista and most of the artists from LaFace moved "up" to Arista to continue their relationship with Reid. But

Continued

LaFace was not finished. When BMG restructured its labels in 2004 as a result of the Sony-BMG merger, it reactivated LaFace and moved most of the former LaFace artists, including Pink, Usher, and OutKast, back to the label. The label had evolved from being an upstart almost independent label fueled by the creative energies of its two founders to being part of one of the three largest recording companies in the world. The lure of big money from the big four has a strong appeal.

QUESTIONS FOR REVIEW

1. What are the four major record companies?
2. What are their market shares and the market shares of the independent labels?
3. How is each of the "majors" owned? Where are they headquartered?
4. What are the two basic functions of any record label?
5. Why is the record industry an "oligopoly"? What kind of oligopoly is it?
6. What functions do most of majors' "Music Groups" include?
7. What does the A&R department do? What does the marketing department do?
8. What are the most important costs in being a label? How can a label make money even though its sales are not platinum?
9. How can the structure of the recording industry drive the labels to release more and more "products"?

9 The A&R Function

Introduction

This part of the book examines in detail the two core record company functions: the acquisition of masters and the marketing of those masters (Figure 9.1). This chapter explores the ways a label can acquire masters, primarily focusing on the label's efforts in finding recording artists, and signing them to contractual obligations to record masters. Chapter 10 explores producers and the production process. Chapters 11 and 12 analyze the ways labels market their recorded products using the "four Ps" approach to focus on product lines, pricing, promotion, and place of sale (including distribution). Although most labels do not sell their recordings directly to consumers, retail, the final phase of marketing, is critical to the industry. The "place" where consumers access and purchase recordings has undergone dramatic changes since the heyday of the record store chains in the mid-1990s. Mass merchants and the Internet drove major record retail chains into bankruptcy. The Internet and mobile networks are full of streaming and download sites.

In order to be a record company a label must acquire rights to market copies of master recordings; this is the A&R (artist and repertoire) function. The labels can either create the masters themselves, or have somebody else do it for them. A&R is about taking and reducing risks—knowing when to take and when not to take risks, and knowing how to reduce the risk of making a poor choice. Like most things in business, higher risks are usually associated with higher rewards if there is success. The label can engage in the higher risk, but greater reward, activity of having new masters created for it by acquiring exclusive recording rights from artists and having those artists make master recordings. To understand how the label tries to reduce risks we examine recording artist and producer agreements with labels.

As an alternative, the label can acquire masters that have already been finished from smaller production companies or labels, thereby reducing risk by knowing what the finished product will sound like, and perhaps by having some marketing track record on a small scale. The label can acquire masters that have already

Figure 9.1 Basic label functions

Remaster Take a previously completed and mastered recording and mix the sounds down to a new master, or take the completed master and tweak the sounds, say for CD or MP3 release.

been successfully marketed in some manner and attempt to repackage, **remaster**, or in some way create a recording that is a new and different assembly of the older masters. There, the initial risk of recording and marketing has already been taken and a market has been established. "Greatest hits," "essentials," boxed sets, repackages, and digital remasterings of older analog recordings are examples of this latter method.

KEY CONCEPTS

- The lifeblood of the recording business is to develop new recording artists who can bring long-term sales success to the label. That is the A&R function.
- Basic recording artist agreements pay artists royalties based on the sale of copies of their recordings, usually in the 13–18 percent range based on the published price to dealers (which is like "wholesale"). Advances for recording costs and other items are paid back out of royalties when, and if, earned. The producer is also paid out of the artist's royalty.
- Labels try to pay artists who also write their own compositions (called "controlled compositions" in the contracts) less for their mechanical royalties, as low as 75 percent of the statutory rate.
- In a "360 deal" the label tries to get involvement and a percentage of the artist's earnings in other income streams of the artist's including touring, merchandising, music publishing, and more.
- The AFM and AFTRA represent musicians and vocalists who perform for recordings. These unions contractually regulate pay scales from the labels for studio work and other record company contributions to the performers and the music business.

Finding and Recording New Talent

New or used?

It is often said that the lifeblood of a record label is new talent. Without infusions of new recordings that excite consumers to purchase them, a label as an entity, or the industry collectively, fails to advance. As noted in Chapter 2, it may even fall into a state of decay moving towards entropy (total disorganization and chaos). Strictly speaking, a label does not have to find talent that has never been recorded before or that has never had a record released on a major (or any other) label. A label can acquire talent by "buying" established talent from other labels when the artist's contract with the former label has expired. That is an expensive proposition for two reasons. First, the artist is already established and will therefore demand a large advance and high royalty per album. When Island Records signed Janet Jackson from Columbia in 1995 she was reportedly given an advance of 5 million dollars per album, plus 25 million dollars just for signing her new contract. When Clive Davis at Columbia signed a 10 album deal with Neil Diamond for 4 million dollars in 1971 it was a major deal. Compare those numbers with Live Nation's "360 deals" with Madonna, JayZ, and Nickelback for $120 million, $150 million, and $50–$70 million respectively. The "360 deal" involves the label getting a cut of touring, merchandising, and other artist revenues in addition to recordings. It is discussed in detail later.

The reward of megadeals is that the label gets an artist who can already sell millions of records without the label having to pour hundreds of thousands of dollars into marketing and a slow development process. The risk is that the label may have acquired the talents of the artist at, or after, their artistic peak—never to be as successful again. In that event, huge advances may never be recovered. Several 1990s megadeals did not bear as much fruit as the labels might have wished, notably Michael Jackson's $60 million deal with Sony Music, Madonna's $60 million deal with Warner Brothers, and ZZ Top's $35 million deal with RCA. Some twenty-first century 360 deals did not bring the label as great a reward either, notably EMI's $80 million Robbie Williams and $25 million Korn deals. One way that labels hedge their bets with such large deals is to make any per album advances contingent on sales performance of the prior albums. In some instances the total package might wind up actually costing only about half or less of its initially reported value.

The reasons to sign and develop *new* artists are that (1) their royalty rates and advances will be much lower since they are an unknown quantity in terms of how many records they can sell; and (2) if successful they will be obligated to the label for a significant number of future albums. New artists do not have sufficiently strong bargaining positions based on track records of sales to negotiate for a high royalty per album and a high advance per album. If such an artist is successful, the label will obtain a much higher profit per copy sold, since their artist royalties will be substantially fewer than those for an established artist. A typical new artist contract usually requires a royalty of 60 to 70 percent of what a superstar can command (see discussion of royalties below). If a new artist nets roughly $1.25 per unit sold, then a superstar probably nets $2.50 or as much as $2.80 per unit sold.

A label would rather sell a million units of the new artist and take home an extra $1,250,000 profit. The problem is that there is much less certainty that the new artist will sell that million units. In fact, there is a likelihood that the artist will sell substantially less than that. Only 22 albums sold a million or more copies in 2009. In fact, the likelihood is that the new artists will probably not sell enough for them to recoup their advances (that does not necessarily mean the label will not have made a profit on the sales; see discussion in Chapter 8).

The other reason for developing a new artist into a major artist is that they will be obligated to make more records for the label than the already developed superstar. A typical new artist deal will call for four to five albums over the life of the agreement. A major artist deal will probably be from three to four albums. So, if a new artist becomes successful, the label will probably have that artist under contract for the most profitable part of their recording career—typically that would last no more than five to seven years.

Finally, because the recording industry runs primarily on popular musical tastes, it is imperative to be seeking and signing the next new sound, the next hit. A label can only rest on its laurels and current acts for so long. After a while, new faces and new sounds catch the public's attention and purchases. The formerly reliable sales from the established acts begin to drop and the label has no new blood under development to take up the slack. It happened to Columbia about the time that Clive Davis took over in the mid-1960s. They were relying on Broadway cast albums and a few middle-of-the-road artists to make up most of their sales—missing the important new wave of rock artists. It happened to RCA in the mid-1970s—relying too much on John Denver and a couple of other artists who were passing their peak. In the 1980s the major labels were late getting into the rap market. No label is immune. There has to be attention paid to what is new, on the streets, in the small clubs, and on the local, regional, or custom labels. That is the job of the A&R department.

Who Has "Good Ears"?

Good ears A music industry term referring to the ability to tell which artists and recordings will be successful. When used by audio engineers, it refers to the ability to distinguish technical and performance nuances in the recording and production process.

Stiff A record that does not sell well at all, or that does not get much radio airplay.

How does an A&R person know whether a particular new artist will be a hit? They don't. Industry people say, "You have to have **good ears**." People with good ears become producers and A&R vice presidents. We know they have good ears because they signed or found the latest hit artist. Of course, that is an after the fact test. If that same artist had "**stiffed**" (done very poorly on their first album sales) the person who found them obviously did not have good ears. Whatever good ears are, they are a product of listening to lots of popular music, not only what is being recorded now, but to what is not being recorded yet. Ear training for A&R people is going to clubs, and listening to demos from bands, personal managers, and publishing companies. It is knowing social trends. It is knowing some history of popular music, for example when a sound or artist that has not been heard in a while might be given a new twist that suddenly fits in. And, by the way, it is a little bit of luck. Hearing the next big act and signing them before some other label does may be simply the result of being in the right place at the right time. The solution to improving the odds is to be in lots of places, lots of times. Knowing the timing of the next sound that will capture the public's fancy and what that sound will be is partially a product of hearing lots of music and talking to lots of people. Those are the reasons why being "on the street" is important to the A&R function.

A good example of someone with "good ears" is Jason Flom, President of Lava Records, part of the Universal Music Group's Universal Republic label. Flom began his career as a merchandiser, creating store displays for the label. While doing that he discovered his first act and got them signed with Atlantic. The success of that act, Zebra, was enough to get Flom moved into the A&R Department at Atlantic. From there he signed national and international successes to the label. In 1995 he was given his own label to preside over. In the next 7 years Lava proceeded to break new artists responsible for sales of over 50 million copies in the US alone. Those acts included Kid Rock, The Corrs, matchbox twenty, Blue Man Group, and more. He moved from Lava to become CEO of Atlantic, then CEO of Virgin USA, then to Capitol. He left Capitol in

2008 following the Capitol and EMI reorganization and reemerged later that same year starting up Lava Records again in a joint venture with Universal Republic Records, and Lava Music Publishing, a joint venture with Cherry Lane Music. It is, indeed, hard to keep a good record man down. (Read about superstar producer Timothy "Timbaland" Mosley in the case study at the end of Chapter 10.)

Money Matters

A label will usually be able to spend only a limited amount of money recording and promoting its artists. Based on the cash flows predicted, on past experience, and on the knowledge that there have to be *some* new artists being signed, most labels set aside a certain amount of money to develop new artists. If they know it will take $150,000 to record an album, and another $150,000 to introduce it to the market, then the number of new artists that can be signed by that label is the number of $300,000 "lumps" the label can afford to spend from its current budget.

The label will want to reduce the risk of spending $300,000 on a new artist whose record turns out to be a stiff. One way to reduce risk is to draw new talent from the pool of artists who have proven themselves in live performances. Live performances sell records. An artist with a great live show that really gets an audience excited will probably be able to sell more records than one with a mediocre live show. That is why A&R people want to hear and see an artist perform before signing them. That is why artists and managers often set up **"showcase"** performances where the artist can play for a select crowd of influential record company, radio, and other people. An artist who can make a good visual appearance will also sell more recordings because of the impact that MTV, YouTube, and other video channels have on record sales. That is why A&R people may even want to see some video on an artist they are thinking about signing.

A&R people do not like to sign artists who do not already have a personal manager—someone else who has already invested time and money, who is an industry insider, and who believes that the artist has the talent and drive to become a success. A&R people *do* like to sign artists who sound like somebody else who has just broken a new sound. The risk there is that the label will be trying to get into a market that is already too crowded. A&R people do like to sign artists who have publishing deals where a music publisher has invested substantial amounts of money in the development of the artist's writing abilities. A&R people do like to hear a high quality demo so that they can get a very good idea of what this artist will sound like on a finished master. All of these are ways for the label to minimize the risk that they will invest several hundred thousand dollars and come up with nothing.

Another way to minimize the risk, but still retain an option to record new artists, is to enter a "development deal" with the artist. These deals are a step short of a full recording contract. A label may feel that the artist has potential but is not quite ready to record, perhaps because they need to work on their songwriting, live performance, or recording techniques. In that case, the label

Showcase
A performance, usually in a small club, designed to promote a performer to radio programmers, label A&R people, music publishing people, or some other industry audience, as opposed to the general public.

may decide to offer the artist an agreement where the artist promises to remain available to enter an exclusive contract with the label in exchange for working on whatever deficiency the label feels exists.

The artist will usually be given an advance to do a demo recording of three or four songs to showcase their abilities. The advances for these recordings are rather small, usually in the $6,000 to $10,000 range. These advances are recoupable from any royalties earned under a recording agreement that may be signed later. (See discussion and example later in this chapter about advances, royalties, and recoupment.) The label substantially reduces its financial risk compared to a full album contract with the new artist, and reduces the risk that someone else may find and sign this potential hit artist first. Labels also can reduce risks by producing just a couple of singles for some new artists instead of entire albums to see if they could get something started in the streaming or download markets, or by releasing an album in digital format several months before a physical release.

Artists' Recording Contracts

At its most basic level, a recording agreement between an artist and a label is a contractual arrangement between the two parties based on an exchange of promises. The artist promises to make recordings for this label, and for no other (an exclusive agreement), in exchange for the label's promise to pay the artist royalties based on the sale and use of those recordings, when and if they occur. What the two parties both want to do with the agreement is to minimize their risks and maximize their profits. To that end recording agreements are highly negotiated. There are a lot more points of concern to both parties, which is why the agreements are likely to be 30 to 60 pages or more in length.[1]

Bargaining Position

The critical factor in deciding who has the upper hand in the negotiations is the relative bargaining power of the two parties. That boils down to a question of size matters—the "size" of the artist and the size of the label. A new artist with no track record of sales has very little bargaining power compared to the superstar whose last album sold 2 million copies. The new artist is all risk to the label —all unknown. From the artist's perspective the size of the label is a factor. A major label has marketing know-how and money to spend on delivery of an album to the public.

A major label also has lots of artists and it is possible to get lost in the shuffle. A smaller, independent label does not have the marketing resources but the artist will be more important to the small label because the label does not have a large artist roster. In order to minimize risks to themselves, artists will want to minimize the length of their recording commitment to the label and maximize profits by getting higher royalties and advances. Labels seek to minimize risk by including as many ways to get out of the recording agreement as they can (i.e. less commitment), and to maximize profits by paying lower royalties and advances. The conflicts are obvious. There is no "standard" agreement, but there are provisions standard to most contracts.

Commitment—A Two-way Street

The labels minimize risk through the artist's recording contracts by trying to build in ways to get out of the deal at every stage.

1. The label will delay signing the contract at all. This gives them more time to make up their minds and to see if anything better comes along.
2. The label may decide not to record the artist once they are signed. The label may want to do this because they have found some other artist who really gets them excited, or because they are running out of money to invest in new recordings, or because the artist in question has committed some major public relations problem, such as the married Christian music artist who was having an affair with a band member, and the label does not want to try to market albums in the face of negative publicity. The label will therefore try to get into the contract a "**play or pay**" clause that lets the label not even hold recording sessions at all, just pay the artist a single session union wage as if the session had been held. That is a lot cheaper than all the costs associated with a production.
3. The label may not accept the finished master or refuse to release it. Even if they have paid recording and studio costs, the label may feel they should cut their losses by ceasing to put money into the project now rather than market what is going to be an obvious (to them) stiff.
4. The label may release the record but only put a minimum amount of marketing money into it, figuring that if the record begins to make waves on its own strength, then they will invest some money in marketing.

The artist wants the label to guarantee everything instead of allowing the label to have options to quit the project. At a minimum, from the artist's point of view, one is not much of a recording artist if there are no recordings available to the public. Even new artists can usually get a label agreement to *record* a minimum number of "**sides**" or perhaps an entire album. If the label fails to record, then the artist is released from the agreement. Similarly, a *guaranteed release* clause, usually only available to a middle-level/established artist or higher, does not mean that the label must release a recording—only that the artist can get out of the agreement if the label fails to release the album within a certain time. It is even harder for the artist to get the label to commit to spending a certain amount of money on marketing. If the artist can get such a guarantee, the label will try to get the artist to underwrite part of the expense by making the marketing guarantees 50 percent to 100 percent recoupable from the artist's royalties. Even if an artist could get all of these guarantees in the contract, there can be no guarantee that the label will do any of this with enthusiasm—just as there is no guarantee that the artist will put heart and soul into the recording.

Play or pay (also, **pay or play**) A clause in a recording artist's contract meaning the label can either have the artist *play* for a recording session, or simply *pay* them scale wages as if a session were held and fulfill their entire obligation to the artist. Not to be confused with **pay-for-play**.

Side A term in recording contracts referring to a recording of a single song. It may also be used in a non-legal sense to refer to all of the songs on one side of an LP, cassette, or single.

Just as the label will seek to minimize its commitment to the artist, it will try to maximize the commitment of the artist to the label. This usually happens in the clause dealing with recording obligation. Typically, a new artist will be obligated to record as many as four or five albums, total. The label has the option to require each successive album, or drop the artist. The label gets to decide which to do, usually on a roughly yearly basis, or within a certain length of time after release of the previous album. The artists can be required to record the total number of albums. What artists would like is being required to record fewer albums, so they could get out of the deal and possibly go to a different label at a much more lucrative arrangement after a few years. (Artists, of course, always assume they will be successful. That is the kind of ego it takes to be a recording artist.) In reality, what most often happens is that the initial deal with the new artist gets restructured (i.e. "**renegotiated**") after (if) the artist has a reasonable amount of success. Then they are "established" artists and less of a risk to the label because they have a track record of sales. This renegotiation process will invariably result in a more lucrative contract for the artist with the same label, but also in a commitment of the artist to deliver more albums to the label.

Renegotiate A term used in the recording industry to refer to the practice of artists who are under recording agreements but who use their substantial success as an opportunity to redefine the terms of the agreement before it would otherwise end.

Why would a label be willing to renegotiate? Why not just say, "Hey, you made this agreement, now stick to it!" The reason is because an artist who is upset with the label over the fairness of their recording agreement is not likely to produce a very enthusiastic recording for the next album. Keeping the artist happy is about the only way the label has of being sure they can get more good albums. They cannot force the artist to record a good album, or even record at all. About all the label can do is come to financial terms with the artist or call it quits, get a "divorce," and maybe prevent the artist from making a new "marriage" with another label until the duration of the original contract is over.

Two excellent examples of the dilemma were the suits between the Dixie Chicks and Sony Music, and the suits between Incubus and Sony Music. After their first album was successful, the Chicks negotiated a new deal with Sony for higher royalties. After the second album's success and total sales for the first two albums were over 20 million copies, the Chicks sued to get out of their remaining recording commitment. Sony countersued for $100 million for the five albums still owed under their second agreement. The Chicks then added another suit, charging Sony with "continual, intentional and wrongful failure to account for and pay royalties it owes." Ultimately the parties were back in business with the Dixie Chicks getting a reported $20 million advance that was only 75 percent recoupable and a 20 percent royalty rate.

In 2003 Incubus sued Sony to get out of the remaining four album commitment in its recording contract. The group had previously sold about 7.5 million albums and claimed the financial reward to Sony was unfair compared to how much the artists had made. Sony again countersued, claiming the band still owed them four albums and potential losses of millions of dollars if the albums were not delivered. As with the Dixie Chicks, money managed to heal the wounds, with Sony and Incubus eventually getting back together. Sony reportedly agreed to pay an $8 million advance for the next album, and $2.5 million for the three after that, and agreed to forego $3 million in unrecouped marketing costs that had been charged against the band's royalties.

Royalty Rates and Deductions

Paying artists royalties for exclusive recording arrangements goes all the way back to Enrico Caruso's arrangement with Victor records in the early 1900s. His 1904 contract called for a royalty of 40 cents per disc (equivalent of more than seven dollars per disc in 2002 prices), and an advance of $4,000. Sales of his recordings totaled into the millions and his total lifetime income from recordings is estimated at $2 million to $5 million. In 2002 dollars, that would be equivalent to total earnings of $36 million to $91 million—earnings as good or better than many of today's superstars.

In the 1950s, typical royalties were 5 percent of retail list, paid on 90 percent of sales. By the 1960s they began to move up, driven by the popularity of rock and roll and the growth of record sales, with *Billboard* reporting nearly a dozen artists with royalties exceeding 5 percent. By the mid-1970s new artist royalties pushed up as high as 8 percent of retail list. If the royalty included the producer's royalty in an "**all-in deal**", new artists could expect to start in the 10 to 12 percent range. By the mid-1990s the all-in deal was the norm. Typical royalty rates for new artists signed with major labels now range from 13 to 16 percent, for established artists from 15 to 17 percent, and for major artists from 18 to 20 percent; superstar artists sometimes exceed 20 percent.

But those royalty rates are not as lucrative for the artist as might first appear. First, they are paid only on records sold. Since most records are sold on a 100 percent return privilege, there is no guarantee that shipment of a million recordings means that a million have been sold. A substantial number may end up being returned to the label by retailers and sub-distributors. Second, most artists are paid on the wholesale price of the recordings (or what most labels call PPD, i.e. "published price to dealers"). That price for a typical new release by an established artist would be around $12. Artists receive no royalties for **promotional copies** and "**free goods**" that are given away to dealers and wholesalers as incentives or discounts. These discounts often reduce the price substantially below the PPD.

An historical practice that has all but disappeared but that goes back to the days when records were made of shellac and broke easily, was for the label to pay on only 90 percent of sales to account for "**breakage**." Those practices are just ways for the label to reduce its royalty costs by paying less to the artist.

Advances

Advances are prepayments of royalties. They are highly negotiable. Some artists get paid an advance upon signing the contract. Most get paid an advance upon delivery and acceptance of the master by the label. As the artist earns royalties these advances are "recouped" (deducted) from earnings. The advances are **nonreturnable**, meaning the artist does not owe them to the label, and if no records sell, or not enough to recover the advance from the artist's royalties, then the label is simply out the difference. That is the label's risk. The labels also include things such as recording costs, producer fees, all or half of the video production costs if a music video is made, and even some marketing expenses

All-in deal A royalty rate designed to include royalties paid to an artist *and* any royalties paid to a producer or others who are paid royalties by the label, such as a remixer or a sampling royalty to another label. All-in rates do not include **mechanical royalties**.

Promotional copies Copies of a recording given away to radio stations for the purpose of airplay or for giveaways to listeners, or given to album reviewers to expose the record to the public.

Free goods In recording artist contracts and record marketing, a term of art meaning recordings given away to a distributor or retailer as a method of discount. These are to be distinguished from promotional copies that are not meant for retail sale.

Breakage allowance A deduction from a recording artist's royalties originally designed to account for the fact that lacquer and shellac recordings were brittle and easily broken.

Nonreturnable A term usually applied to an advance, meaning the advance does not have to be given back to the provider, even if no royalties are ever earned. The advance is therefore not a debt. Advances are usually recoupable, but nonreturnable.

such as independent promotion, or other marketing guarantees demanded by the artist as "advances." Recording and production advances are often included in a lump sum "**recording fund**." If the artist does not spend the entire recording fund advance on actual recording costs then any remainder can be paid to the artist, which in effect will amount to an advance for delivery of the master.

Recording fund
A kind of advance where the record label designates a fixed amount of money available to produce a master recording. Usually the artist and producer are allowed to keep any money that has not been used to create the finished master.

A Gold Record and a Bounced Check

So how much would an artist really make on an album that went "gold" (sold 500,000 copies)? Suppose this is a recording by a new artist with an all-in rate of 13 percent. The producer has a royalty of 3 percent, which is deducted from the artist's all-in rate, making the artist's net rate 10 percent. For the sake of simplicity, suppose that the sales are all CDs with a PPD of $12. The artist is paid 10 percent of $12, or $1.20 per disc. (If the calculation ends with decimal parts of pennies they would generally *not* be rounded in calculating royalties.) That means the artist gets $1.20 for 500,000 discs, or $600,000.

Now, what about those recoupable advances? Recording fund advances for a new artist depend upon the genre of the music and the stature of the artist, and the advances became smaller as CD sales continued to decline into 2010. Suppose this is a new rock/pop artist with a fund of $200,000. A careful artist may have been able to hold on to as much as $50,000 of that fund to actually put into their pockets. Assume the label did two music videos, at a cost of $50,000 apiece. (Typical video production costs for new artists run $15,000 to $50,000 per song.) One half of video production costs are usually recoupable out of record royalties. The label spent $100,000 on promotion and marketing, one half of which also happens to be recoupable. Because this is a new artist, the label will probably withhold payment on 30 to 50 percent of royalties otherwise due (or from the number of records counted as shipped) as a "**reserve against anticipated returns**."

Reserve for returns
An amount of royalties, or the royalties that would be paid for a certain amount of sales, that are not paid to a recording artist because records are shipped to retailers and wholesalers subject to being returned at a later date. Artists are not paid for recordings that are returned. See also **Liquidate reserves**.

The reserve is to protect the label from the possibility of paying out royalties on records that appear to be "sold" but that are later shipped back as returns from retailers and distributors. For the sake of simplicity, assume this artist's 40 percent reserve is out of royalties otherwise earned. Table 9.1 shows the calculations. Now, suppose that $60,000 is for a five-person group. That means

Table 9.1 Sample artist royalty calculation

"Net sales"		500,000
Times base rate per unit		x $1.20
Gross royalties earned		$600,000
Less: reserve (40 percent)		(240,000)
Net earnings after reserve		$360,000
Recoupments:		
Recording fund	$200,000	
Video (50 percent)	$50,000	
Promotion (50 percent)	$50,000	
Total recoupable		($300,000)
Net due artist		$60,000

they have earned $12,000 apiece for the entire time this album has been out, probably more than one year. It is hard to make a living on that.

Unfortunately, the only unrealistic number here is the number of albums sold for a new artist. SoundScan reported that fewer than 160 titles sold more than 250,000 album units in 2009 (out of over 288,000 titles scanned). That was down from over 400 selling 250,000 album units in 2000. The average new release from a major label sold only 8,350 units in 2000, down somewhat from 9,134 in 1995. Had the artist sold only 250,000 units (not really that bad for a new artist) they would have earned only $300,000 gross royalties and still be short of recoupment by $120,000. (Try the math.) The artist would be in an "unrecouped" position. They do not owe the money back to the label but neither have their royalties accumulated yet to the point where they cover all of the advances. Furthermore, those unrecouped advances are "cross-collateralized." They may be recovered from any other income earned by the artist from the label. So, if still not recouped when the next album comes out, they will be deducted from royalties due from sales of the second album, in addition to the other recoupables directly attributable to the second album. If this is a "360 deal," with the label entitled to earnings from live performances, publishing, and merchandising, then it is likely that the unrecouped sum can be cross-collateralized against these revenues, too.

What about the "reserves"? The label cannot keep the reserves indefinitely. When the label **"liquidate the reserves"**, usually over three or four accounting periods (up to two years), the artist will get the $240,000 reserve—minus any unrecouped amounts remaining at the end of the accounting period in which the reserve is paid out (like advances for a new album). Over a 2-year period this artist kept $50,000 from the recording fund advance, plus $300,000 from royalties, a total of $350,000. Is $175,000 per year a lot of income? Again, suppose this "artist" is a five-piece band. Each member gets $35,000 per year *before* taxes. Because recording artists are self-employed they have to pay their regular income taxes plus the additional self-employment tax of over 15 percent (their share of social security and Medicare taxes plus the share normally paid by the employer). This band better hope they make money from their live appearances that have been made more profitable by exposure from the gold album.

Liquidate the reserves
A recording contract term meaning the label must pay out any **reserves for returns** that have not been accounted for with actual returns.

Internet Activities

- Do an Internet search for "A&R." Look at two or three sites such as www.aandronline.com or www.getsigned.com. Are they providing useful information or primarily selling products? Find three pieces of useful information and share them with the class.
- Do an Internet search for "recording contracts." Several sites discuss contracts. Look at one of them. Is the discussion primarily from the point of view of being favorable to the artist, or to the label? What are some of the points made on the site?
- Do a Google or other search for articles about lawsuits between artists and labels. Get creative in your search terms. Try "label lawsuit" or "artist lawsuit."
- Go to the union websites, www.afm.org and www.aftra.org. What are their current recording master scale wages?

Publishing Rights and Controlled Compositions

Many recording artists write or co-write the songs that they record. All labels have affiliated music publishing companies. They would like to have artists who are also songwriters sign publishing agreements with those affiliates. Even if not part of a "360 deal," the label can encourage the artist to sign with the label's music publishing affiliate, and it is possible that an artist who is willing to do so will have more leverage in negotiating the recording or publishing agreement. The label's argument is that the existence of the recording that they paid for and will promote gives the artist/writer the chance to record the songs. Then it is sales of the recordings and airplay of the recordings that generate most of the publishing income. Many established artists who are also writers have their own publishing companies and are able to retain their own publishing rights. In most such cases those artists would pay a regular music publishing company a fee to either co-publish or to administer the writer's company. That fee ranges from 10 to 25 percent of collections through the administrative company. Of course, the administration or co-publishing could be through the label's publishing affiliate (see Chapter 6 for details).

Since the 1909 Copyright Act, record companies have had to pay the music copyright owner, usually a music publisher, a mechanical license fee for the right to make and sell copies of a recording of the song. From 1909 to 1978 that rate was two cents per song, per copy (see Chapter 4 for further discussion). From the label's point of view, mechanical royalties are a per-album or per-download expense, just the same as the manufacturing costs. As would any manufacturer, the label would like to control or reduce these expenses. As early as the mid-1970s the labels, spurred by the probable increase in the "**statutory rate**" to two and three-quarter cents in the 1976 Copyright Act, began to seek ways to limit their **mechanical royalties**. What they came up with is a contractual provision that has caused much controversy but is now the norm—the "**controlled compositions**" clause. Because the recording and music publishing income streams intersect when the artist is a singer/songwriter or a self-contained group, the labels are able to control their costs at the expense of the publishing stream.

A controlled composition is one written, owned, or controlled in whole or part by the artist (or probably the producer as well, especially in a producer–label agreement). The controlled composition clause requires the artist/songwriter to license such compositions to the label at a specified rate, typically three-fourths of the "statutory rate" at the time of release. In addition, the labels often put a limit on the total mechanical royalties payable per album to about 10 times the controlled composition rate. Here is the kicker: any mechanical royalties paid in excess of the limit are recoupable out of controlled composition royalties or out of the artist's recording royalties. It is not unusual for CDs to contain 11 or 12 songs and exceed the limit of total mechanical royalties. So, an artist/writer who puts 12 songs on an album would, in essence, be recording two "for free" in relation to mechanical royalties.

A particular problem arises when the artist co-writes with other songwriters. In such cases the other writers are either forced to take the reduced rate on their shares of the songs, or the artist is forced to allow the label to take any difference

Statutory rate A term usually applied to the compulsory mechanical royalty rate.

Mechanical royalties Payments made from record labels to music publishers for the right to reproduce copies of songs (non-dramatic musical compositions) in the recordings made by the labels.

Controlled compositions Compositions (songs) written or owned, in whole or part, or controlled in whole or part by the recording artist and/or producer.

between the full rate and the controlled composition rate out of his or her own royalties. Those results caused an uproar among artist/writers and co-writers when country artist Randy Travis released an album full of co-written songs and his label refused to pay the co-writers the full statutory rate, even though Travis initially thought they would get the full rate. He ultimately agreed to pay them the full rate with the differences deducted from his own royalties. The NSAI (Nashville Songwriters Association International) formally petitioned (to no avail) most of the major labels to drop the clauses from their contracts, especially as they applied to co-writers.

How would all of this work? Suppose the artist has a controlled composition rate of 75 percent of the statutory rate. That rate is 9.1 cents per song or 1.75 cents per minute of playing time, whichever was greater, until 2013 (see Chapter 4). For the sake of simplicity (and because the contracts usually limit the rate to the per-song rate) assume that the per-song rate applies. That means the label will pay only 6.825 cents per song and a maximum of 68.25 cents for mechanical royalties per album. If the artist records 11 of her or his own songs, the eleventh must be licensed for free, or the record royalties (or mechanical royalties paid for the other songs) will go down by 6.825 cents per copy of the album sold.

If the artist got all of the mechanical royalty, that would not be too bad—a trade-off of songwriter royalties with recording artist royalties. More likely, the artist, as a songwriter, will not get 100 percent of the mechanical royalties. If the songs are owned by a music publishing company that is not the artist's company the writer will usually get 50 percent of mechanical royalties after the publisher/writer split. Even if the writer owned their own publishing company, they would probably be paying someone else to administer the copyrights and still get only 75 percent to 90 percent of mechanicals after the administration fee. If the artist/writer co-wrote with other songwriters, then those other writers would have to be willing to take the reduced rate and limits, or the artist would have to be willing to pay them a full rate, then have the label take the difference out of the artist's record royalties. All of the percentages, amounts, and limits in the controlled composition clause are highly negotiable if the artist has any stature, and are particularly important points for artist/writers.

Mechanical royalties for digital downloads are a different story. The Copyright Act requires that the full statutory rate be paid for "digital phonorecord deliveries" (full downloads) "in lieu of any contrary rates" negotiated between the artist and label. Thus, a track with 4.76 million downloads (e.g. Black Eyed Peas' "Boom Boom Pow" in 2009) would earn $433,160 in mechanical royalties.

Video Rights

The birth of Music Television (MTV) in 1981 caused labels to add yet more pages to their artists' contracts to deal with the creation and ownership of rights to music videos and other video performances of the artist. Initially, many labels paid for all of the video production costs of the music videos. But that increasingly expensive proposition, coupled with the fact that the videos themselves were little more than promotional tools, albeit valuable tools, caused a shift to having the artists pay part or all of the production costs as "advances." By the mid-1990s it was customary to recoup half of the video production costs from recording royalties, with the other half recouped from video royalties. Some labels would allow recoupment of all video production costs from video royalties. But as a practical matter for most artists, video royalties never approached half of the $15,000 to $70,000 production costs for the typical single song music video. However, for concert length videos, usually shot live, the production costs per minute were substantially less and a market existed from the cable services such as HBO, Showtime, Cinemax, and others to show the video as programming, as well as a growing DVD consumer market. It is over the creation and use of such non-promotional music video productions that most of the difficult negotiations occur.

The labels prefer to view the music videos as "recordings" and say that they have exclusive rights to all the artists' "recordings." The artists say those exclusive rights are limited to phonograph recordings, or perhaps promotional music videos, but not to concert length performances. To counter that, the labels often ask a right of first refusal that would allow them to make the same concert video on the same or slightly more favorable (to them) terms if they wish. Royalties earned for the sale of a video tend to be about equal on a per-copy basis to the royalties earned for the sale of a phonorecord. If the videos are sold through licensees then the artist usually gets 50 percent of net label receipts.

As the labels began to realize income from the per-view use of music videos on services like YouTube, another revenue stream and another source of contract tension arose. Agreements evolved from free promotional uses to pay per-stream uses. When the agreement is to pay per-stream it is often as a percentage of advertising revenue for the streaming service. The service must track the number of streams for each label and each video. Armed with that information the label can then pay the artist the usual 50 percent split of revenues from such licensed uses. Of course, those are video royalties and they can be used to recoup 100 percent of video production costs. Big hits generate significant numbers of video or audio only streams. For example the top 10 songs all generated more than 7 million audio streams each in 2009. The top video stream, Beyonce's "Single Ladies," generated 3.3 million streams.

The New "360 Deals"

In these deals the label signs the artist to a contract that goes far beyond the traditional recording agreement. In addition to recordings, the label will typically ask at least to participate in the music publishing, live performance, and merchandising rights revenue streams. The participation may be "active," with the label actually providing services in the stream, or "passive," with the label simply taking a cut of the artist's revenues in the stream. Label use of these deals began as sales of lucrative CD albums began to plummet in the late 1990s.

At first the labels started with megastars such as Korn, Jay-Z, Madonna, and Robbie Williams. But the price tags on those deals, in the multimillion dollar ranges, meant that the label was taking a large risk. The labels bet that the total revenues of the highly successful artists from all the streams would be enough

to recoup the huge advances they were giving and bring them high profits from their participation in multiple revenue streams. The artists bet that, even if total revenues were high, they would still get so much from the large advances and their percentage, it was worth the risk of not being able to keep all their income from all revenue streams outside of recordings. What the labels soon realized was that they could use these deals with new artists more successfully. The new artists could not negotiate high advances for the 360 deals because they did not have much bargaining power. If the artist was successful, the labels got additional revenues. If the artist was not successful, the label had not risked much more than they would have with a new artist anyway.

The typical provisions of a 360 deal (Figure 9.2) call for the label to get a percentage of the artist's net revenues in several income streams, in addition to their basic recording agreement. The percentages vary somewhat, but tend to be in the 25 to 30 percent range. Most often included in the deal are artist earnings from touring and merchandising. Labels may also want to be cut in for a share of earnings from endorsements, fan club websites, movies, and TV. Managers and artists still fight to keep music publishing royalties out of the 360 deal. But since virtually all labels have affiliated publishing companies, this is often difficult. If the label is to actively participate in the revenue stream by providing services, then the artists try to make a separate deal for the merchandising, publishing, or whatever component has active label participation.

Figure 9.2 The "360 deal"

DIY Activities

● Search for "Label-shopping attorneys" in your hometown or a nearby city. How many are there? Where are they?
● Is there a record label in your hometown or nearby? Search to find the nearest and report on who they are and what artists they have.
● Find the story of how one artist got signed to a label deal. Use artist websites, *Rolling Stone*, *Billboard*, or other publications. Share your story with the class.

Union Agreements: AFM and AFTRA

Two labor unions have significant impact on recordings. The American Federation of Musicians of the United States and Canada (AFM) and the American Federation of Television and Radio Artists (AFTRA) have agreements with all major labels (and most independents) that require certain scale payments to non-royalty and royalty performers on all recordings sold by the label. The labels require that all of their artists join the appropriate union. The AFM required payment to a side musician in a standard three-hour recording session in 2009 was $380.02, up from $329.32 in 2003, and from $236.81 in 1995. A maximum of 15 minutes of music could be recorded. The rates, set in the Phonograph Record Labor Agreement, include provisions for overdubs, premium hours, and a wide variety of other issues. The union leader on the session and the record producer make sure that all musicians are credited and proper payments made to the union, including a contribution of 11 percent of total wages to the union pension fund and a $22.50 health and welfare fund payment for each musician.

The AFM has two other agreements with the record labels, the Phonograph Record Trust Agreement (usually called the **Music Performance Trust Fund**) and the Phonograph Record Manufacturers' **Special Payments Fund** Agreement. The total of both payments is less than 1 percent. It is important to the recording artist to not allow the label to deduct these charges from the record royalties payable to the artist. Whereas the union scale wages are recording costs, the per-copy charges are not.

Background singers and other vocal performers are subject to AFTRA agreements with the labels. In 2009 the AFTRA Code of Fair Practice for Phonograph Records required soloists and duos to be paid a scale wage for master sessions of approximately $209 per hour or per song (side) whichever was greater. Group members are paid on a sliding scale depending on how large the group is—the bigger the group, the less each member is paid. AFTRA also requires the labels to make contingent payments of 50 to 75 percent of minimum scale for the master session vocalists when certain sales plateaus are reached. There are 10 steps that go from 157,500 units up to 3,000,000 units, and total up to

Music Performance Trust Fund An agreement between the AFM and labels that requires labels to contribute a small amount per copy of each recording sold (about 0.3 percent) to a fund that is used to pay musicians to put on concerts that are free to the public.

Special Payments Fund A trust fund administered by the AFM composed of payments from record labels based on a small percentage of the price of recordings sold. The fund is distributed to musicians on an annual basis based on the number of master recording sessions on which the musician had played over the previous year.

five times the original scale. Like the per unit AFM payments, these should not be considered recording costs to be charged against the artist's royalties.

Summary

The main functions of a record label are to acquire masters and to market those masters. Acquisition of masters involves deciding what masters to acquire, that's the A&R function and then, if the masters do not already exist, producing those masters. To perform the A&R function, the label must identify talented artists whom the label thinks can sell enough recordings to make it worthwhile to invest in the substantial cost of making new recordings. Alternatively, the label can acquire masters that already exist by purchasing or licensing them from production companies or by licensing their re-release from other labels. The latter is less risky but also has lower potential reward than finding a new artist, recording them, and then marketing those recordings.

Most recording artists are under an exclusive recording contract with a record label. The label pays the artist a royalty based on the sale of copies of anywhere from about 14 to 20 percent of the "wholesale" (PPD) price. That percentage includes the royalty to be paid to the producer, usually 3 to 5 percent, and any others who get royalties from the recording. It does not include the mechanical license paid to the publisher for recording the song. Artists also get advances that cover the costs of recording and other things such as tour support or sometimes marketing costs. Those advances are usually "recouped" from the artist's royalties, when, and if, earned. In exchange for this the artist agrees to make a certain number of recordings for the label over usually an extended period of time, with the label having the option of getting out of the agreement after each album if they are disappointed with the sales or other performance of the recording. An artist may commit to making as many as five or six albums for the label. Other clauses in the agreements may cover video productions, mechanical royalties payable for songs written or owned by the artist (controlled compositions), and more.

A newer form of agreement, the "360 deal," has the label at least participating in the other income streams generated by the artist. This may include the label getting a share of the artist's performance income, merchandising income, publishing income, and more. The labels believe that because it is the recording that promotes the artist's career to a large extent, then they should get some reward from all areas when the artist is successful.

There are two major labor unions in the music business, AFM and AFTRA. Both negotiate labor agreements with the labels that specify how much the performers must be paid at recording sessions and other working conditions. The unions function through locals that the individual performers join. The locals set wages for live performances in their areas and regulate talent agencies through requiring standard union agreements with their members.

Case Study: The A&R Function

On their way to the top most artists enter into a number of contractual relationships with would-be producers, managers, agents, or labels. Most producers start out trying to find talent, produce them, and then get a recording contract for themselves and the artists. But those deals do not always work out well. Sometimes they even come out badly. When those things start to happen, everybody drags out the copies of the contracts to find out what they really said. What follows is the story of one deal between a then unknown artist, Ashanti Douglas, and producer Genard Parker.[2]

When Ashanti Douglas was 16 years old in 1996, she and her mother approached producer Genard Parker (who had earlier produced cuts on SWV's successful 1993 album, "It's About Time") to produce some cuts on the aspiring artist to help her get a record label deal. She signed two production agreements with Parker's T.E.A.M. Entertainment production company. One source indicated that Parker may have done this because he was dating Ashanti's mother, Tina, who later became her manager.[3] The first agreement was short and simply said that Parker had produced three cuts for Ashanti to use to get a deal and the stipulated terms of Parker's compensation if she got a deal. The second 12-page deal, after she had done additional "demos," required Ashanti to provide exclusive services for T.E.A.M. for six months, with extensions, in order to pursue a record distribution agreement. There was an offer from Volcano records, but that was never signed. Ashanti then asked to get out of the deal so she could pursue a deal with Noontime Records. Parker agreed to the release provided that he be paid $25,000 for two masters on any Noontime album and a percentage of any production fund advance and royalties on cuts produced. The Noontime deal was signed in October 1997 but Parker was never paid and never produced any cuts. Noontime, later, entered a distribution agreement with Sony Music Entertainment in 1998 but Sony decided to "shelve" the project.

Then, in August 2000, Ashanti entered an agreement with AJM Records. AJM got a distribution agreement from Universal Music Group to distribute Ashanti's records on the Murder, Inc. label in 2002. Her first album was released in April 2002 and her second in July 2003. Both had platinum level sales. She won a Grammy award in 2003 for Best Contemporary R&B Album and was nominated for several other awards.

In 2003 Parker took steps to sue Ashanti for breach of contract, claiming that the earlier release agreement and second production agreement were still in effect. The jury ultimately awarded Parker $630,000 in July 2005. That was later reduced to $50,000, the amount he was to be paid for producing the two cuts. Meantime, Parker had secured deals to release an album based on her earlier recordings. She sued Parker in early 2006 saying she had never intended for the demo tracks to be released. She also contended that he used her name on the album without her permission, and used a current photograph of her on the cover, despite the fact that it was about 8 years since the project had been recorded. Finally, she contended that she was not the featured singer on some cuts and did not sing at all on one of the cuts. In September that same year, the parties agreed to settle their disputes for undisclosed terms.

The questions to be answered for the Parker–Ashanti contracts were, what efforts were required by Parker to get a deal? If released from her agreement, what actions would still entitle Parker to his compensation for his earlier efforts? Finally, what were the recordings that he and Douglas made? Were they demos and as such only intended for "demonstration" purposes or were they, as some such agreements call them, "demo masters"? If the latter they could be used for either purpose.

As far as Ashanti's countersuit is concerned, artists do have the right to control the use of their names and likenesses. If Parker's agreement did not give him the right to use her name and likeness then he could not have done so. Certainly all major label recording agreements would grant that right to the label as a matter of course. The use of a current picture to sell cuts recorded 8 years earlier raises unfair competition claims, that the public was being misled by the photo, and by the fact that she was not a featured artist on some of the cuts.

All those old contracts and demos do not mean a thing if there is never success and fame. But if there is, you can just about bet that they will both surface—in court.

QUESTIONS FOR REVIEW

- What are the two main functions of a record label?
- What are the two main functions in the acquisition of masters?
- Why does a label need to develop new artists?
- What is A&R? What are the different ways that a label can perform the A&R function?
- What are the basic points of a recording artist's contract with a label, including commitment for recordings, royalties, advances, recoupment, and reserves for returns?
- What are "controlled compositions"? Why are they important? How do artists' contracts usually deal with them?
- What are "360 deals"? What are the basic deal points? What is usually included in them?
- Who do AFM and AFTRA represent? What is union scale for recordings from these two unions?

10 The Production Function

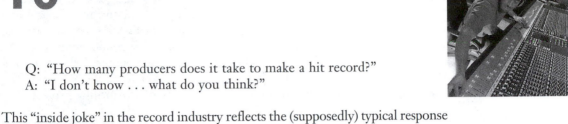

Q: "How many producers does it take to make a hit record?"
A: "I don't know . . . what do you think?"

This "inside joke" in the record industry reflects the (supposedly) typical response by producers to any question about how good a recording, or track, or whatever, is. The primary focus of this chapter is on the role of the producer and the agreements that producers have with labels, but it is not possible to discuss the production process without also addressing the evolution of studios into their present day configuration. Of course, studios are nothing without people to run them, the audio engineers. Finally, this chapter addresses audio and music business education—a process that has evolved from strictly learning on the job into college (and other) classrooms.

KEY CONCEPTS

- Record producers have become increasingly important, especially in hip-hop, and have royalty agreements with the labels, typically getting paid 2 to 6 percent of PPD as well as an often large advance for each master produced. They serve both creative and business functions.
- The studio business has moved increasingly to the "homes" of artists and producers because of digital recording technologies. This has created many smaller studios and forced some larger studios to close for lack of business.
- Audio engineers seldom get rich at their median pay rates of $20–$40 per hour. But being an engineer is one path to becoming a producer.
- Formal education in audio engineering and the music business has become a significant, if not the most important, entry point into those fields.

Producers

Whether it takes an actual individual identifiable as a "producer" to produce a hit record, or any other record, is perhaps debatable. It does require somebody performing the functions that in most instances are relegated to a record producer. The producer may be the artist. The producer may be somebody in the A&R department at the label. The producer may be an independent producer hired by the artist or label to help deliver the finished album to the label. Sociologist Simon Frith argues that the production of popular music is a process "that fuses (and confuses) capital, technical, and musical arguments."[1] It is the recording, not a song or music, that is the final product, and it is the producer who is at the center of the creation of that product.

Producers have one goal, whoever they are—to complete a finished, marketable recording. The producer must bring together the talent, and the physical and monetary resources necessary to create a master recording. The producer must serve two masters to do that—the artist and the label. The producer must possess good ears for hearing hit songs and performances, good people skills for getting the best performances out of artists, engineers, musicians, and label personnel, and good creative instincts to add to the chemistry of a recording project.

Producer Functions

Producers provide input into the process of the creation of recordings on three levels (see Figure 10.1).

1. They perform A&R functions by finding talented artists to record, finding good material to record, and by matching artists and material.

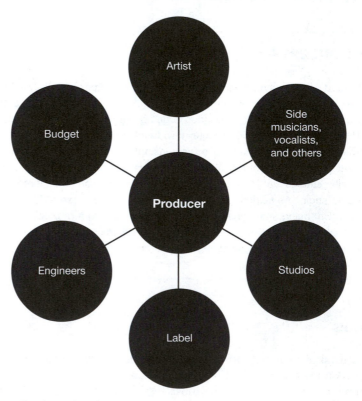

Figure 10.1 Producer functions

2. They are managers of the production process—arranging and supervising recording sessions; hiring studios, musicians, and engineers; getting the best performances out of those people; supervising the creative aspects of the recording and mixing process to get the best sounding recording; supervising and approving the mastering and references—all with the goal of producing a recording that is marketable and at the same time is a good representation of the artist's abilities and any messages that the artist wishes to convey with the recording.

3. Producers perform business functions, budgeting the recording sessions and process, making sure the recording process does not go over budget, and making sure proper tax, withholding, and union forms are completed.

Kinds of Producers

At one time virtually all producers worked directly for record labels. They were "A&R men." They worked on salaries. They found the perfect songs for the recording artists, most of whom did not write their own songs. They set up recording sessions, hired arrangers to create musical parts for trained musicians to perform, then listened as they and the artists plied their crafts for a few "takes" (tries at recording the song), then picked the best one for release. With rock and roll came artists who had great amounts of creativity and energy, but sometimes lacked great musical skills. They needed someone who could nurture their performances in a studio. With multi-track recording came the possibility of taking just a few musicians and turning out a recording that sounded like it had 50 people singing and playing on it, when it really only had four. With computer recording and editing software such as Pro Tools came the possibility of piecing together parts of several takes or even pieces of a performance to "comp" a track.

All of these developments meant that a producer had to take on a much more creative and managerial role. Rock artists did not want producers who were label employees, even though some of those people were quite talented. It was too "**corporate**" for the rock image. The independent producer became the norm. Producers began to be paid a royalty on the sales of albums, just like artists. Reportedly this began with Snuff Garrett, a producer in the late 1950s and 1960s, who was the first to ask his label for a royalty—a penny per copy. Artists began to produce, or co-produce, their own recordings out of ego, out of a desire to be more in control of the creative aspects of their recordings, and out of a desire to keep more of the available money. Some successful producers became label executives, but retained their production deals. In those instances the producer/executive (not to be confused with an executive producer) would typically be paid a royalty on sales of those artists produced, and a salary in their capacity as executives (usually in the A&R department, but sometimes label presidents).

Independent producers work under a variety of contractual arrangements with artists and labels. Sometimes an independent producer will find a potential recording talent, and sign the talent to a deal to make a demo in the hopes that the producer can then succeed in getting a label to sign the artist, and producer,

Corporate Often used as a derogatory term referring to recordings which "sound like" they were produced as products to fill a market niche instead of as inspired performances by writers and recording artists, as in "corporate rock."

to a full-blown recording contract. In such instances the producer may even go so far as to release the recording on the producer's own label, aiming to either start a small record company or create some local sales and excitement to better attract the major labels. In both of these instances the independent producer is performing valuable A&R functions—finding and recording new talent that may later get introduced to the public through a small or even major label. Artists or labels may also hire independent producers to produce recordings or artists under contract to the label. In those instances, the label has done the A&R function of finding the talent, and the producer has the function of bringing a recording to fruition.

Recording artists, particularly after several successful records, may be allowed to produce themselves. In practical terms, that usually means that the artist becomes almost totally in charge of the creative aspects of the production process. But the artist will still need someone, an associate producer, or a co-producer, to be in charge of the business aspects of the process. Artists who successfully produce themselves have usually proven themselves capable of making marketable recordings and making the creative decisions that go into those recordings. It is also possible that artists who have produced themselves can get recording contracts based on the strength of their demos alone, though this is rare. The label still prefers to have an experienced person in charge of the business aspects of the production process. With the advent of project studios owned by the artists and producers themselves, the 1990s saw a movement to artists and producers being even more in charge of their production, with producers taking on a preeminent role in rap and hip-hop, leaving only the marketing to the record companies.

Producer Pay

Through the 1990s advances and royalties for independent producers slowly crept upward, perhaps due to the rising importance of producers in urban and hip-hop. In those genres, the creative role of the producer is extremely important. By 2010 producer royalties were typically 3 percent to as much as 6 percent (the latter for superstar producers, even higher in the urban/hip-hop genres) of PPD and otherwise paid on the same terms as artist royalties. Producers are also paid advances per side (song/cut) or per album, depending on whether they have agreed to produce certain cuts or an artist's entire album. Per cut (aka "per side" or "per master") advances run in the range of $2,500 to $25,000, with the latter figure reserved for superstar producers, even higher for some urban/rap producers. Per album advances begin as low as $25,000 to $30,000 (perhaps zero for some indie labels) per album and run as high as $200,000 per album, even higher for some urban/rap producers. Because producers are not responsible for recording costs or marketing costs to be recouped out of their advances, producers usually actually end up being able to keep and spend their advances. On the other hand, the producer's advance *is* a recording cost to the artist and will be taken out of the recording fund advance that the artist receives.

The size of the producer's advance depends primarily on the experience of the producer, whether the producer has a track record of success in the urban/hip-hop market, and whether that producer also produces other important artists for the same label. Assuming the artist has an all-in royalty, the producer's royalty is paid out of the all-in royalty. This can lead to a variety of complex situations regarding recoupment of artist and producer advances, when the producer gets paid, and possible double recoupment of the producer's advance as a recording cost from artist royalties, and as an advance under the producer's royalties. These complexities are just more reasons why artists and producers are well advised to have music industry attorneys negotiate their arrangements with the labels.

Stages of Production

While much production actually takes place in the recording sessions there is also work to be done in the preproduction phase of the process and in a post-production phase. In preproduction, the songs are selected, studios reserved, arrangers hired, session musicians and singers arranged for, engineers hired, the concept of the song decided upon by the artist and producer, and (for budget-minded producers and artists) rehearsals held. In the production stage, tracks are recorded, overdubs are recorded, and the songs are mixed down to a finished master, ready to be delivered to the label. The postproduction phase is likely to have duties shared between the actual producer and the A&R department for the label. Tasks such as getting correct liner-notes, credits, lyric sheets, and licenses/clearances when needed for samples and for the songs themselves are usually carried out after production is completed. The producer will also oversee or approve creation of masters for manufacturing into CDs, downloads, and other formats. Alternate mixes for clubs or radio or singles are made. Madonna, for example, often had as many as eight or nine versions of commercial singles available and even had multiple albums composed entirely of remixes. The producer may consult with the marketing department or product manager over which cut should be the first single released from an album.

Production Budgeting

One of the producer's responsibilities will be to submit to the label a budget for the production of the recording(s). The sizes of the budgets vary from less than $50,000 to hundreds of thousands of dollars. One of the factors contributing to the variation is the genre: jazz is usually recorded live, with just a few takes, so studio time and musician time is minimal; country can be simple or elaborate with budgets approaching pop or rock in some instances; rap can be very inexpensive, especially if the rappers have their own rhythm tracks already created in a project or **MIDI** (Musical Instrument Digital Interface) studio, or very expensive as hours are spent creating beats, "comping" tracks, mixing and remixing; rock and pop can be very expensive, especially if the artist wants to write the songs in the studio, work out arrangements in the studio, and/or is not really a very good musician/vocalist.

In some respects, the budgets end up being governed by how many recordings the label thinks it can sell of this particular artist. An artist who can sell 200,000

MIDI A computer communications protocol designed to let synthesizers, controllers, and sequencers from different manufacturers communicate with each other. Now also used as a control language for lighting and other equipment as well.

copies on a good album cannot be allowed to spend as much on production as an artist who can sell a million albums. Particularly in rock and pop, album recording fund advances are intended to cover production and leave some money left over for the artist. It is usual for albums after the first to have the per album recording fund advance increase substantially so that the artist has a larger production budget with which to be creative, and so the artist will have more money to take home after all production expenses are paid.

If the production costs exceed the budget, the producer has put the label in a difficult situation. If the project is nearly completed and is worth releasing, the label is just about forced to come up with more money. The label may, however, have a contractual right to demand that any over-budget amount be repaid immediately out of the producer's or artist's album delivery advance, if there is one. It is almost always possible to spend a few more thousand dollars to work just a little more on a track or a mix. One of the producer's jobs is to know when to say "when." Money is not the only factor determining when a production is "finished." The label has deadlines for delivery of the master so that the release date can fit into a certain schedule decided to be best not only for this album and artist, but for all of the label's other upcoming releases.

Creative Controls

The trend in recording contracts and production contracts is to let the artist and producer make most of the creative decisions, especially if they are experienced and have delivered satisfactory masters in the past. So, selection of songs, selection of studios, selection of musicians and vocalists, selection of engineers and assistants, and selection of the producers themselves is usually up to the artist working in concert with the producer. At most, some labels want a right to approve these decisions. In such cases the producers and artists can usually successfully demand that approval cannot be unreasonably withheld.

Master Delivery Requirements

Commercially acceptable A standard by which labels judge masters submitted to them by recording artists. It means the recording must be technically and artistically good enough in the opinion of the label executives to enjoy to public sales and acceptance.

Technically acceptable In recording contracts, this means that a master is of high enough quality to be suitable for release to the public. This is distinguished from *commercially acceptable*, which implies a higher standard.

Both producers and artists are contractually obligated to deliver masters that are satisfactory to the label. The difficult problem is what standard of satisfaction is to be applied. The label would like to insist that the masters be "**commercially acceptable**." After all, the label is in the business of selling records. Artists and producers, on the other hand, do not like the label to be second-guessing their creativity. They would insist that the master merely be "**technically acceptable**." The impasse can often be cured with language that says the label will accept an album that is at least as technically and commercially satisfactory as the previous album or other albums by artists of similar stature on this label. Whatever the language in the contract, it would be unusual for a label to reject an album when the artist and producer have made a serious effort. Acceptability standards most often come into play when artists attempt to throw together an album simply to meet their recording obligations, in the hope of getting out of the contract.

Acquisition through Licensing

Instead of going through all the grief of finding artists, finding producers, and risking the inevitable "stiffs," a label could get all or part of its masters by licensing them from other labels. Rhino Records, for example, sells significant numbers of albums that are repackages, and remasters of older artists. Rhino does careful research on the artists and songs, careful remastering, and produces Grammy-winning albums. The Musical Heritage Society also does this in the art/classical music field.

The label could also acquire masters that already exist by licensing or purchasing them outright from some smaller label or production company. In the 1990s this was a particularly popular approach in rap music. Some labels such as K-Tel sell albums like "The Greatest Hits of 20xx" that are simply collections of masters licensed from the labels that had the original artists and original hits. In those cases the releasing label pays the original label a per-copy royalty per cut, usually 3 to 5 cents. K-Tel even releases their remasters and collections through download services like iTunes.

Probably the greatest licensing success story is the "NOW" records. In 1998 in the United States, 1983 in the United Kingdom, a consortium of labels launched the "NOW That's What I Call Music" series. The collections of pop, urban, and generally teen-oriented singles were the most successful in the history of the recording industry. The consortium of labels sharing the releases of the various NOW albums claimed sales of over 74 million units in the US and 200 million worldwide by 2010. Several of the installments debuted at #1 in *Billboard*'s Album chart. By 2010 there had been over 30 NOW albums released in the US.

Internet Activities

- Do an Internet search for "Record Producers." Several sites discuss contracts. Look at one of them. Is the discussion primarily from the point of view of being favorable to the artist, or to the producer? What are some of the points made on the site?
- Visit www.spars.com, www.aes.org, and www.smpte.org. Compare who they represent and the services offered by each.
- Visit www.mixonline.com and check out their directory for recording and music business schools. Look up two of them and compare their program to the one at the school you are currently attending.

Studios and Recording Engineers

No discussion of production could be complete without at least an overview of the recording process as it involves studios and recording engineers. The recording gear and the people who operate it have become an integral part of the creative process in the production of master recordings. The diffusion of recording technology through lower costs and greater availability to musicians has created a situation where the production process has become more "democratized." More people are able to afford and produce high quality recordings and the "big four" conglomerates are in much less than total control of the production of recordings.

Studios, then and now

Studios have not always been studios. In the late 1800s and early 1900s they were often referred to as "labs." The first professional disc recording studio was set up in Philadelphia in 1897 for recording the Berliner discs. A lot of early recording was done by taking the recording machines to locations that were convenient to the artists and setting up in some hotel or warehouse. In fact, Caruso's first major recordings were done in a hotel in Milan, Italy, in 1902. He cut 10 master cylinders in one day. Prior to 1902, when the making of molds for cylinder mass production was finally a viable procedure, every cylinder was an original or a direct dub of an original. When recording facilities were set up for cylinders they often involved the performers singing into a set of horns, with each attached to a different cylinder cutter. As many as 20 cylinders could be recorded at once. Of course the performer had to repeat the performance many times. Those who could perform steadily and repeatedly found plentiful work. One source called them "durable citizens with lungs of brass."[2] The number of times a performer had to record were referred to as "rounds." The studios were small, often barely able to hold more than a dozen musicians and the recording machines.

Until the advent of electrical recordings in 1925, all recordings were acoustic. The sound pressure energy from the performer had to be transferred into mechanical energy that moved a cutting stylus to make a groove in the master disc or cylinder. This was done by singing or playing into a large horn. Isolation from surrounding background noise was not critical since it would not likely be picked up from the recording horns, much less then reproduced by the consumer's playback machine. But the electrical process, which captured the sounds in a carbon microphone and converted the sounds to electrical energy that could be amplified to run an electromechanical cutting lathe, meant much greater frequency response. Response improved from 200 Hz to 9,000 Hz— almost two and one half octaves greater than the purely mechanical systems. The microphones were also more sensitive than acoustic horns and necessitated more isolation from outside sounds. Studios that were more like modern ones began to develop.

World War II caused the development of more high quality amplifiers, radios, microphones, and, most importantly for the recording industry, the practical development of recording tape. Tape could be easily edited and it became possible to "construct" a recording by splicing together bits and pieces of a performance or of several performances. Bing Crosby was the first to utilize this important ability for the creation of his network radio show in 1948. Later, multitrack recording made it possible to break down the construction of the recording into even more components, one track per instrument. Fewer musicians were needed to produce a complex recording and the importance and size of the control room grew. Popular music researcher Steve Jones points out that the increasing amount of control over time, timbre, and all of the musical and sound elements of the recording became integral to the process. Digital recording and editing software in the twenty-first century made possible the control over virtually every parameter of the performance, even allowing the engineer and producer to correct the pitch of the vocalists and other performers.

The industrial model

Although it had always been possible to do location recordings, the assemblage of a large number of cylinder or disc cutters in the early days, the use of expensive amplifiers and disc cutters not available to the general public, the need for isolation from outside sounds, and the required presence of a significant number of skilled players and vocalists, dictated an industrial model for the recording process. By analogy, the studio was a "factory" where capital and labor were gathered together to complete a product. Not until the 1970s when good quality multitrack recording equipment, known as "semi-professional," became available to consumers was there significant diffusion of the recording process away from the factory/industrial model. By the mid-1990s high quality recording was possible with digital multitrack recorders available for the semi-professional market. The MIDI (Musical Instrument Digital Interface) and sequencing revolution meant that single musicians could create complex sounds and even orchestral arrangements. In the early twenty-first century, laptop and desktop recording with computer software moved the process into virtually every musician's kitchen, bedroom, or closet. The diffusion of recording technology does not necessarily create more high-quality recordings, any more than the diffusion of water color paints creates more great water color paintings, but it does give more creative people ready access to the possibility of creating quality recordings and it has had a significant impact on the studio business and recording processes.

By 1995 70 percent of professional studios reported at least some degree of competition from home-based private production studios. Of all respondents, 28 percent reported "very much" competition from the home studios. In many instances the artists and producers used these home facilities to create basic synthesis tracks or sampled tracks, or to work out arrangements so that when they did go to the higher end professional studio, they spent less time and money. The label practice of paying advances in the form of a "recording fund" where the artist and/or producer keeps what is left after expenses encourages such a reduction of expenditures. Also, the labels often approved the practice of the artist charging recording time and expenses from the artist's own facilities towards the recording costs. The artist is then in a position to set up their own studio and recover the cost through their own recording budgets. After a few albums, the studio is paid for. By 2010 the home studio had become the wave of, not the future, but the now. One commentator noted that a modern studio could be built for about half of what one would have cost in the 1990s.

Project rooms
A recording studio,
usually owned by an
artist or producer,
which is used mainly
to make recordings
for that particular
artist or producer
and is not rented out
to outsiders.

This same practice has led established and superstar artists to build their own top of the line studios to be used in their own productions. These facilities are most commonly known as "**project rooms**." Again, 70 percent of studio owners said in 1995 that they felt at least "some degree" of competition from such rooms, with 24 percent reporting "very much" competition from the project studios owned by producers or artists. The trend continued into the twenty-first century. A fairly typical path of development is for a small private studio to develop into a project studio, which then begins to book commercial clients and then turns into a part-time commercial studio. Even the major artist-owned studios sometimes book outside clients. A problem with project studios is that they are often built in homes in residential neighborhoods. When they become commercial they may run afoul of zoning restrictions and tax laws.

Kinds of studios

While the lines of distinction between professional and semi-professional, and between private, project, and commercial are blurring, the latter classification system still has some usefulness in understanding the studio business. Private studios tend to be small in size and track capability. They are usually owned by aspiring artists, songwriters, or producers and seldom book any outside time. They most often use top of the line semi-professional equipment and desktop recording software with 24-track digital capability and more.

Commercial studios are those which are primarily used by "outside" clients and which are in the studio business for profit. These studios are primarily 24 track and higher. They are virtually all digital recording systems and a few retain analog recording capabilities as well. Smaller "demo" studios usually charge $30 to $40 per hour for demo music recording or for small advertising clients. Larger studios charge higher rates, ranging from $85 to $165. Some "world class" studios charge as high as $300 per hour.

Project studios, to distinguish them from private studios, are most often owned by established artists and producers. They have all the capabilities of commercial studios and some are as well equipped as the best commercial facilities. They tend to be 24-track (or more) digital format rooms. They are used primarily by the owners for producing their own recordings (projects) but may sometimes be rented to outside clients.

Analog recording nearly died completely in 2005 with the filing of bankruptcy of tape manufacturer Quantegy-Ampex's plant in Alabama. Quantegy finally sold off its last inventory of magnetic tape in 2007. Two smaller companies, ATR Magnetics and Recordable Media Group International (RGMI), continue production of analog tape.

Studio business survival

The recording studio business in the US is centered in six geographic locations: New York City, Los Angeles, Nashville, Atlanta, Chicago, and Southeastern Florida (Orlando to the Keys). Any city of over 100,000 population has at least one commercial studio catering primarily to advertising clients. Private studios are as widespread as aspiring artists and writers, but the bulk of the recording for released masters, major client advertising, and film is done in these six areas.

As sales of recordings began to go flat at the beginning of the twenty-first century, studio owners found themselves in difficult times. One analyst laid most of the blame on the decreasing price of digital recording devices and the increasing ease of starting a project studio. Writing in *Pro Sound News*, Chris Steinwand noted that the price of a 24-track hard disc recorder was about one-fiftieth of the price of a 24-track tape machine. "Project studios can now afford truly professional quality equipment and can turn out recordings that are every bit as professional as what the major studios are producing."[3]

Project studios tended to be more focused on lower priced gear and that drove down the impetus for manufacturers to produce top-end gear for the major studios. The number of major studios was also declining due to competition from project studios. That, said Steinwand, contributed to even less demand for expensive gear that only major studios could afford. The difficult times for the studios then landed on the recording hardware manufacturers as well.

By 2003 incomes at nearly all studios, but especially the larger ones, had shrunk. The decline in sales of recordings led to cutbacks in artist rosters and album budgets by the major labels. As one studio owner put it, "The cost of promotion is up, because you've got to buy your way into distribution. The cost of pretty much everything, including talent, has been inflated, whereas the actual studio cost has stayed flat or even gone down a little."[4] By 2010 recording budget cutbacks at the labels had reduced label-financed business at many major studios to only about 50 percent of their income, with the other half being self-financed by the artists or bands themselves.

Profile of the typical recording studio

Most studios have only one control room (67 percent), are about 10 years old, are equipped with MIDI (70 percent), are 24 tracks or more (55 percent), earn most of their income (58 percent) from music recording (advertising and broadcast recording revenues are a distant second at 13 percent), and are booked an average of 180 hours per month. Note that this last figure is an average of about 42 hours per week, just in case one is inclined to think that recording engineers do not work long hours.

By the mid-1990s recording studios as businesses were faced with difficult times. A *Pro Sound News* article summed up the problem, "In a nutshell: traditional studios find that they cannot raise their rates to offset the cost of equipment demanded by an increasingly sophisticated clientele that does more and more of its recording outside of those same studios."[5]

In response, a number of studios started their own record labels or began manufacturing audio gear, in addition to providing other ancillary services, such as duplication/replication or post-production of audio for video. In addition, other places, including churches, clubs, and radio stations, began to develop the capability to create high quality recordings. In fact, the expansion of multimedia in worship services opened up new sources of employment for engineers and acousticians and new markets for equipment manufacturers.

DIY Activities

- Search for recording studios in your hometown or a nearby city. Compare their rates and facilities and services. Report back to the class.
- Research how much money it would take to start recording on a laptop, including costs for computer, interface (such as M-Box or Lexicon), two or three quality microphones, and high quality powered monitors and headphones. Identify three sources for these products.
- Want to record at home? What are some of the acoustic problems associated with recording in a rectangular room that is not isolated from the outside or surrounding rooms? How can those problems be minimized?

Audio Engineers

As the importance of the control room grew, so did the importance of the recording engineer—the person who ran all of the machinery that controlled the sound. At one time, for example, the effect of reverberation (the "echo" effect of sound bouncing around in a room and gradually dying out after the initial sound was made) was only possible to create by actually having a room into which the sound could be fed and allowed to reverberate, or by recording live in such a room with some separate microphone available to pick up the reverberant sound. With digital processors it is possible to simulate many different rooms and echoes and control many different aspects of how that "room" sounds with an electronic "box" no bigger than a ream of paper or with a piece of software as a "plug in" for the recording software. More sophisticated devices meant that a higher level of technological expertise was required from the engineers. Because of their knowledge of and ability to control all of the technology of recording, the engineers began to take on more of a creative role in the process.

The task of the recording engineer is to operate the equipment that captures and, in some instances, creates the sounds that the artist and producer want on the recording. To that end the recording engineer is more of a technician than an "engineer" in the sense that the term is used in other professions. In addition to a thorough understanding of the specific equipment that they operate, most engineers find useful a basic level of knowledge in the areas of electronics, acoustics and sound, and music. Recording engineers must also possess the ability to work with and get along with people, some of whom will have quite large egos and be difficult to work with. Engineers must have "good ears" capable of discerning often subtle differences in sounds and an understanding of how those differences will contribute to or detract from the overall sound which the artist and producer are trying to create. Engineers must also be capable of making creative decisions. The producer or artist may not be at every recording session for a particular project. The engineer may then have to decide what is the "best" sound for the purpose. Even when the producer or artist is present, they will often ask the engineer what they think about a particular track or sound. Sometimes they want real advice, sometimes they only want their egos stroked. For all of those reasons, being an audio engineer is one of the more common paths to becoming a producer.

Recording engineers are often classified based on their knowledge, experience, and skill, into four groups: senior engineers, assistant engineers, freelance engineers, and maintenance engineers. Senior engineers are usually associated with a particular studio. As their name implies they are the most knowledgeable and experienced engineers available at that facility. Even when an artist or producer brings their own favorite independent engineers to a session, the presence of a senior staff engineer from the studio is usually necessary to help with knowledge of the ins and outs and particular quirks of the studio and its equipment. Assistant engineers, also known as second engineers, often work primarily at one studio or primarily with one particular independent engineer.

Freelance engineers tend to be senior level engineers who have a track record of recording successful albums with established artists. They work in studios wherever their artists want to work. They may have worked with the artist in the early days of the artist's career, they may have been doing the live sound reinforcement for the artist, but, in some way, the artist has become convinced that this particular person is helpful in getting the sound which the artist wants on record. Maintenance engineers have the most electronics expertise. They tend to be associated with one particular studio, but some successfully freelance their time among several smaller studios. Engineers are usually paid on an hourly basis. By 2010 median wages for assistant engineers were around $10 per hour with median rates for freelance senior engineers anywhere from $20 to $40 per hour.

Organizations

Three industry professional organizations are of particular interest to studio owners and audio engineers: the Society of Professional Audio Recording Services (SPARS); the Audio Engineering Society (AES); and the Society of Motion Picture and Television Engineers (SMPTE). SMPTE is the oldest of these organizations, having been formed in 1916 as the Society of Motion Picture Engineers. Its membership consists of engineers involved in the creation of "motion pictures, television, computer imaging, telecommunications, and the related arts and sciences." Among other things, it helps set technical standards for those areas and publishes the technical journal, *SMPTE Journal*. Members of the AES are involved in the creation of audio and recording devices and the creation of recordings and live sound reinforcement. AES, like SMPTE, is an international organization, publishes a technical journal, *Journal of the Audio Engineering Society*, and helps set technical standards for its industry. AES was founded in the mid-1940s. The newest of these organizations is SPARS. It was founded in the 1970s to represent professional studio owners as a trade organization. For more information on all of these organizations visit their World Wide Web sites listed in the Internet Activities box in this chapter.

Going to School

Two factors, the complexity of recording and the popularity of recordings in general, have lead to the growth of preparatory programs for recording engineers and the music business. In addition, the continued popularity of recordings and popular music in general has led to an increased interest of young people in careers in recording and the music business. Those two factors prompted a significant number of institutions to offer programs that aim to provide some of the necessary training.

In the 1960s and 1970s, someone who wanted to learn audio would show up at a studio, convince the owners of their desire to work, and be assigned to help keep the studio clean. After a while they could usually convince the engineer to teach them something about some of the equipment. They learned on the job by doing it. However, the equipment has increased in complexity and sophistication to the point where it is very difficult to come in off the street and pick up the necessary knowledge in an apprenticeship situation.

There are well over 200 and perhaps as many as 500 institutions offering some kind of training in audio engineering and/or the music business. The programs range from seminars and short courses, often at studios seeking to sell their downtime, to accredited vocational programs, associate degree programs, 4-year bachelor's degree programs, master's programs, and even a few Ph.D. programs. The providers range from individual studios, to schools of the arts, to major colleges and universities. At all levels, there are some very good programs and some that are not very good. There is no industry certification or accreditation process for these programs and students need to investigate carefully the range of alternatives and compare the relative merits of various programs to the student's particular needs. The two most thorough listings are in the *Mix Master Directory* published by *Mix Magazine*, and the Audio Engineering Society's *Directory of Educational Programs*. Both are available on the Web.

These audio and music business programs began to develop in the early 1970s, and by the mid-1990s a number were quite sophisticated. They, like the studios themselves, have benefited from the diffusion of lower priced high-quality recording equipment and technology. While having a degree or certificate is not a requirement of being a recording engineer or a label promotion person, many of these programs place interns in the slots formerly occupied by apprentice-type learners. They also provide entry-level personnel who do possess the base level knowledge required of assistant engineers and employees. A study for NARM found that over 65 percent of NARM affiliates (including labels, retail, wholesale, and distribution firms) would give preference to graduates of a music business program when hiring new employees.[6]

Some studios and music industry businesses will not hire entry-level employees that have not been through one of the audio or music business programs, in part simply because there are quite a few students from these programs seeking employment and employed in the recording industry. There is a professional organization of college faculty who teach in such programs called the Music and Entertainment Industry Educators Association (MEIEA), which promotes the development of college audio and music business programs. During the late 1980s the Recording Academy (NARAS)[7] launched its "Grammy in the schools" program to pique the interest of high school students in the music industry.

Summary

What does it mean to be a record label or record producer in the twenty-first century? To be a label is still about the acquisition of masters by creating them, or buying or leasing them, then distributing and marketing copies through some process. However, digital technologies make the creation of masters easier and the distribution easier—or at least less expensive. As sales of the high revenue producing CDs declined, the labels cut back on artist signings, big budgets, and big advances to artists. The "360 deal" was born where the label began to participate more broadly in all phases of the artist's career and in all income streams. Independent producers and production companies became more of a force with hip-hop and the advent of project studios.

Technological advances are making it more possible for musicians and bands to record and distribute their music to wider audiences. On one front, the advances in low-cost, high-quality "home recording" equipment mean that many bands and musicians can afford their own recording gear or to go to a low-cost demo studio. The equipment available enables them to make high-quality recordings without having to go through any record company or pay studio rentals of hundreds of dollars per hour. Lower costs in manufacturing of compact discs now mean that these same bands can make CDs in small numbers. By 2010 the prices for custom manufactured CDs had dropped to the point where 1,000 CDs could be made complete with boxes, trays, inserts, and shrink wrap for as low as $1,000. One hundred could be had for $200 to $300. Bands with patience and computers with CD "burners" could make them one at a time and print their own labels and jewel box inserts with inexpensive software for pennies apiece.

The Internet makes possible distribution by individual bands and musicians (or by very small labels) of their recordings to a worldwide audience. This should ultimately mean that more recordings of more music would be available to more people. The difficulty is in sorting through the myriad of available recordings to find those with merit or appeal. That is where the marketing function, discussed in the next two chapters, comes into play.

Case Study: Timothy "Timbaland" Mosley

In 2008 a reviewer for the *New Yorker* magazine called Timbaland, "[The] most important producer of the past decade."[8] Maybe so. Timothy Z. Mosley was born in Virginia in 1972. While in high school, Mosley began creating tracks and beats and called himself "DJ Tiny Tim." He then joined a group S.B.I. (Surrounded by Idiots) that also included Pharrell. Missy Elliot heard some of his work and started working with him. When she went to New York to record with DeVante Swing (producer and Jodeci member), Mosley went

Continued

with her. It was reportedly Swing who gave him the nickname after the "Timberland" boots that had become popular hip-hop attire at the time. By 1995 he was working on Jodeci projects and Elliot projects.

Timbaland's first major production credit was in 1996 on Ginuwine. He later produced tracks on many albums, including for artists Ludacris, Jay-Z, Beck, and Aaliyah. It was the Ginuwine hit "Pony" that first emphasized his new rhythmic style, as he puts it on his website, "[Hip]-hop mixed with an eclectic smorgasbord of effects held together by complex syncopated snare beats."[9] The unique rhythms and sounds became his trademark. *The New Yorker* reviewer noted, "When you hear a rhythm that is being played by an instrument you can't identify but wish you owned, when you hear a song that refuses to make up its mind about its genre but compels you to move, or when you hear noises that you thought couldn't find a comfortable place in a pop song, you are hearing Timbaland, or school thereof."[10]

Timbaland is always experimental. He has used tabla drums, mouth pops and clicks, sampled Bjork cuts, and produced grunge artist Chris Cornell. His Nelly Furtado cut "Promiscuous" was a breakthrough pop/hip-hop success. He followed that with equally successful cuts for Justin Timberlake. He has done his own albums as an artist, *Tims Bio*, *Shock Value*, and *Shock Value II*, and albums in collaboration with other major hip-hop artists and producers. His credits as a producer or writer are too numerous to detail here, so check him out on Wikipedia or his own website.

As Timbaland's success grew, so did controversy surrounding his use of samples in many of his recordings. A 2007 lawsuit alleged that he used an Egyptian song, "Koshana, Koshana," in Jay-Z's hit "Big Pimpin'." Another that same year alleged an unauthorized use of a sample from Indian film and music company Sareguma Film in *The Game*'s "Put You in the Game." Finally, a Finnish label sued over the alleged unauthorized use of a recording of "Acidjazzed Evening" in Nelly Furtado's recording of "Do It" on the *Loose* album.

Timbaland participates broadly in the entertainment industry. He has his own 5,000 square foot studio, Thomas Crown Studio, in Virginia Beach and his own record labels, Beat Club Records in the mid-1990s and later Mosely Music Group (MMG) in 2006. In 2008 he began production on the movie "Vinyl", about five women and their relationships with the members of a rock band. That same year he was inducted in Trinity College, Dublin's Philosophical Society as an Honorary Patron. In 2009 he launched "Beaterator," a music beat portable studio that works with Sony's PlayStationPortable, with Rockstar Games.

Readers should check on the outcomes of the sampling litigation and on Timbaland's continued activities.

QUESTIONS FOR REVIEW

- What business and creative functions does a record producer perform?
- What are the stages of recording production?
- What are the basic points of a producer's contract with a label, including commitment for recordings, royalties, advances, and creative controls?
- What are the current trends in the studio business?
- What are the different types of studios? At what stages of an artist's career would they be likely to use the different kinds of studios?
- How are recording engineers usually paid? How much?
- How can a formal education in the Music Business or Audio Engineering enhance a person's prospects for finding a job in those businesses?

11 The Marketing Function: Product and Price

Introduction: What is Marketing?

"Marketing is simply defined as the performance of business activities involved in the planning and creation of products, the pricing of these products, the promotion of these products, and the flow of these products from the producer to the consumer."[1] Marketing involves satisfying customer needs or desires. To study marketing, one must first understand the notions of *product* and consumer (or *market*). The first questions a marketer should answer are: "What markets are we trying to serve?" and "What are their needs?" Marketers must understand these consumer needs and develop products to satisfy those needs. Then, they must price the products effectively, make the products available in the marketplace, and inform, motivate, and remind the customer. In the music business, this involves supplying consumers with the recorded music they desire, while making a profit for the company.[2]

At record labels, the marketing department may be set up differently than one would expect. Historically, the marketing functions for labels consisted of getting radio airplay and distributing records to retail stores. So labels developed sophisticated departments in sales and radio promotion. Other marketing functions evolved as the record business became more sophisticated, and therefore the "marketing department" may involve **publicity**, advertising, and retail promotion as well. More recent marketing functions may include video promotion, corporate sponsorships, new media marketing, **grassroots marketing**, and tour support.

On a more basic level, marketing functions can be described by the concept of the "four Ps" of marketing: product, price, promotion, and place.

1. Product—goods or services designed to satisfy a customer's need
2. Price—what customers will exchange for the product
3. Promotion—informing and motivating the customer
4. Place—how to deliver and distribute the product

Publicity Getting media exposure for an artist in the mass media that is not in the form of advertising.

Grassroots marketing A marketing approach using nontraditional methods to reach target consumers.

KEY CONCEPTS

1. Marketing involves decisions and actions relating to product development, determining the pricing structure, all the promotional activities, and distribution of the product to the marketplace.

> 2. The recorded music business offers a variety of products, including music from various genres, provided in a variety of formats that includes singles, albums, physical product and digital product, and new as well as older recordings.
> 3. Pricing is much more involved than how much to charge for a product. Decisions also involve pricing incentives for consumers and retailers to maximize sales and income for the label.

This chapter will look at the first two of the four factors involved in a label's attempt to market and sell their recorded music and promote their artists: product and price. The next chapter will cover the final two factors: promotion and place.

Recordings as Product

The marketing mix begins with the product. It would be difficult to create a strategy for the other components without a clear understanding of the product to be marketed. New products are developed by identifying a market that is underserved, meaning there is a demand for products that is not being adequately met. To be successful in the marketplace, any new product must have a market, must appeal to that market, must be unique enough to differ from other offerings in the marketplace, and must be able to be produced at an affordable cost, yet profitable for the company. In the music business, it is the A&R and production functions that are involved in product creation. In other industries, this is referred to as "research and development" or R&D. The marketing department will often have input and may conduct research on the viability of any new product (in our case, the artist or recording), but it is the artist, the A&R department, and the producer who create the product. The word "product" may have a negative association among some artists who hold the notion that creative works of art are not "product." However, when referring to sales volume of mass produced copies of that creative work, the word product is often used by marketers.

Product Life Cycle

All products have a *product life cycle*, meaning there are four (or perhaps five) distinct stages in the life of a product, whether the product is a record release, an artist's career, a popular configuration such as the compact disc, or even a music genre. These stages are: introduction, growth, maturity, and decline. The introduction stage is a period of slow growth as the product is introduced into the marketplace. Profits are nonexistent because of heavy marketing expenses and sales have not yet reached economies of scale, meaning the cost per unit of production is still high. The growth stage is a period of swelling popularity for

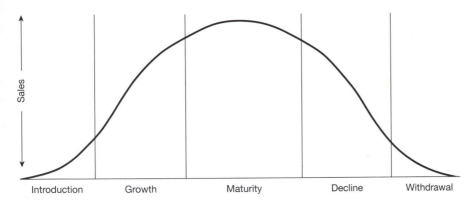

Figure 11.1 The product life cycle

the product in the marketplace and profits tend to increase. Maturity is a period of leveling in sales mainly because the market is saturated, meaning that most consumers have already purchased the product. Marketing at this stage may be more expensive (to the point of diminishing returns) as efforts are made to reach resistant customers and to stave off competition. Decline is the period when sales fall off and profits are reduced. At this point, prices are cut to maintain market share.[3] Eventually, the product ceases to be lucrative and is dropped from the company's portfolio of products.

In the record business, the introduction stage of an album release often depends upon where that artist is in *their* product life cycle (new vs. established artist; see Figure 11.1) and is dependent upon the marketing plans. For example, a new artist may have a slower introduction period as the artist tours and builds a fan base. For an established, popular artist, sales may be intense from the moment of the record's release. At some point, most members of the market who want to own this album, or these recordings, have purchased them, and sales begin to decline.

In the days of physical only sales, there would come a point in each record's life cycle in which it was no longer financially feasible to keep copies of that product in retail stores. Recordings were often discontinued, or rereleased through some subsidiary label that featured older records and served niche markets. Digital distribution has lowered the costs of providing these older recordings and now many of them are once again available for purchase, thus eliminating the withdrawal stage.

Even some music genres exhibit characteristics of "product life cycle" with some lasting longer than others. Often they are referred to as "eras" such as the Big Band Era or the Disco Era.

Music Genres

One unique distinction that separates product in the record business is genre, or music style. Throughout the last half of the twentieth century, the music industry saw a proliferation of music genres, as markets became more fragmented. Earlier in that century, the major music genres included classical, opera, folk and parlor music, country and western, and race music. The list was soon expanded as new genres took hold, including jazz, blues, swing, bluegrass, rock n' roll, rap, punk, new age, heavy metal, and others.

A look at the *Billboard* charts through the years presents evidence of this explosion in genres. In 1961, *Billboard* used only three popular music genre categories to classify and tabulate song popularity. By 1974, *Billboard* was up to five charts, increasing to nine in 1982, and by 1991, utilized 13 musical genre categories in compilation of popular music.[4] A quick glance at the 2010 offerings reveals both singles and album charts for 27 genres in addition to the Top 200 and Hot 100: Heatseekers, Independent, Mainstream Top 40, Adult Contemporary, Rock Albums, Alternative Albums, Hard Rock Albums, Folk Albums, Hip Hop, Rap, Adult R&B, Country, Bluegrass, Latin, Regional Mexican, Tropical Albums, Classical, Christian Albums, Gospel Albums, Jazz, Contemporary Jazz, Smooth Jazz songs, Dance/Electronic Albums, Blues, Comedy, New Age, Reggae, Soundtrack, and World Albums.

There is a handful of genres that tend to dominate the market. First, the category of rock music is a wide and diverse genre, representing everything from classic rock to alternative rock. Rock has dominated the genre category every year for a few decades. The genres of country, rap, R&B, and pop have volleyed back and forth, currently settling at near 10 percent of the market each (see Figure 11.2).

Country music began the 1990s with a surge, sending it into a solid second place for market share, thanks to a freshmen class of performers that included Garth Brooks and Alan Jackson. A steady decline through the 1990s put country at fourth place by the end of the decade. Country had a resurgence in the mid-2000s, before settling back down in a near dead heat with its three market share rivals. Some experts believe the upsurge in country music in the mid-decade (and religious music in 2002–2003) can be traced to the effects of the terrorist attacks of September 11, 2001. In country music, several popular artists took on the themes of patriotism and national defense in their songs.

Religious music, dominated by contemporary Christian music, enjoyed sustained growth throughout the 1990s before hitting a slump in 1999. The terrorist attacks on New York and Washington D.C. on September 11, 2001 are widely credited for stimulating the sales of religious music.

The RIAA reports Christian sales under the more general "Gospel" category. Christian artists began appearing on the *Billboard* Top 200 album chart as soon as **SoundScan** data from Christian bookstores was added to the database because the predominant source of sales is not through mainstream record outlets but through Christian bookstores. The Christian Booksellers Association represents most Christian bookstores.

A handful of major Christian artists appear in the Top 200 Albums chart, and some, such as Switchfoot, Jars of Clay, and Casting Crowns, cross over to sell as many as 50,000 to 80,000 units during their first week of release. In 2009, crossover band The Fray captured the Contemporary Christian music charts with their self-titled album and sold nearly 800,000 units. Their songs have been featured on hit TV shows Grey's Anatomy, One Tree Hill, and Bones.

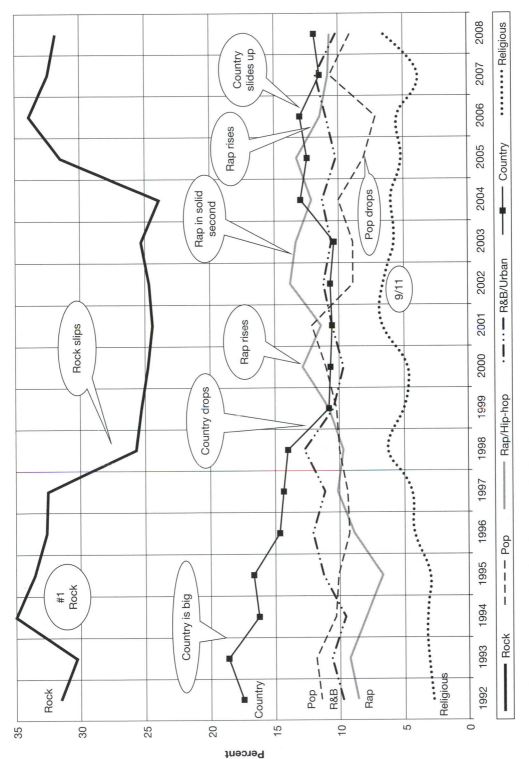

Figure 11.2 Comparison of market share for top music genres

Source: RIAA

Rap music first gained popularity in the late 1980s to early 1990s. Soon, pop-infused hip-hop songs (such as M.C. Hammer's "Can't Touch This") dominated the rap charts and the genre temporarily lost its momentum. However, soon a new generation of rap artists began to dominate the airwaves and rap grew enormously in the mid- and late 1990s. A drop in 2001 was followed by a few years of up-and-down activity before rap eventually slipped into the dead heat with market share rivals pop, R&B, and country.

The genres of *pop*, *R&B*, and *rap* have played an interesting game of ping-pong, with drops in one genre being offset by gains in another. As indicated in Figure 11.3, all three genres were enjoying growth in 1992, and suffered a market share drop in 1993. While rap and pop music continued to lose market share through the mid-decade, R&B turned around a year earlier and began a three-year growth spurt in 1994, pulling ahead of rivals to peak at 12.8 percent in 1998. From that point forward, the three genres engaged in a scenario where one was always gaining market share at the expense of one of the others.

Among genres with smaller market share, categories are listed by the RIAA for jazz, classical, soundtracks, new age, oldies, and children's music. While a breakout hit from one of these genres does not sustain an increased market share, there is some evidence that for the duration of the breakout hit, the genre will show an increase in market share, provided that the hit is counted in the correct genre category and not reported as pop or some other major genre. For example, a blockbuster album from Enya in 2001 finished the year at number four on the *Billboard* 200 year-end chart, selling 4.4 million copies and temporarily buoying the *new age* genre. Another spike was assisted by Mannheim Steamroller in 2004, with one new record going gold and three catalog albums—all selling around Christmas time—achieving the same spike effect.

Movie soundtracks had a strong showing in 1998 and again in 2001, assisted by the top-selling soundtrack to the *Titanic* in 1998 and *O Brother Where Art Thou?* in 2001. Soundtracks had a strong showing again in 2003 despite the fact that there were no soundtrack titles in the top ten albums for the year.[5] However, there were several titles in the top 50, including soundtracks to the movies Chicago, Lizzie McGuire, and Bad Boys II. The category of soundtracks then took a slide through 2008.

Children's music was boosted by the introduction of Radio Disney in 1996 and a series of releases around the live-action remake of the movie *One Hundred and One Dalmatians*. The boost sustain has been sustained and supported by the 2004 successful children's record *Miracle* from pop star Celine Dion, and in the late 2000s by the efforts of Disney to reach younger consumers with recorded music and music-related products such as the Jonas Brothers, *High School Musical*, and Hannah Montana.[6] (See Figure 11.4 for details.)

Genre Preferences and Demographics

Much research has been conducted to identify and compare music genre preferences for particular demographic groups. In 1948, Sociologist Karl Schuessler provided the earliest such study by examining preferences for eight types of music, and subsequently correlated these preferences with age, gender,

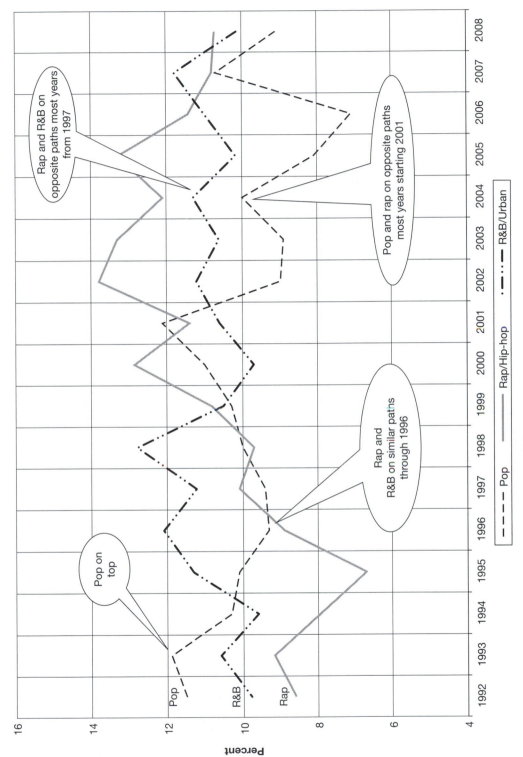

Figure 11.3 Comparison of market share for pop, rap, and R&B music genres

Source: RIAA

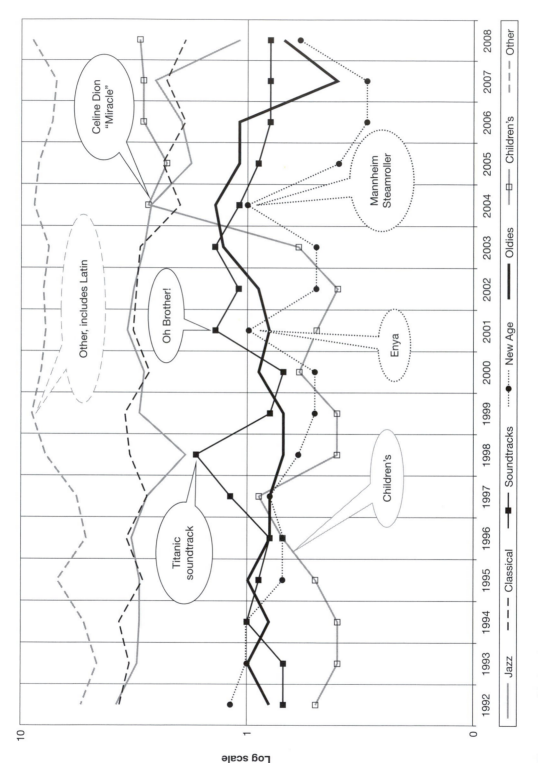

Figure 11.4 Market share comparisons for smaller genres

Source: RIAA

and occupation of the listener.[7] Academic research conducted in the 1970s and 1980s supported the existence of "taste cultures," which are described as "aggregates of similar people making similar choices."[8] Music genre preferences have been well documented for both age and gender. Research suggests that music consumers prefer genres that were popular during their adolescent and early adult years, and that these preferences persist throughout life. For example, consumers who "came of age" during the 1940s retained a preference for swing, big band music.[9] Consequently, it would be expected that the young adults of generation X would prefer heavy metal or rap music.[10]

The radio industry perhaps conducts the most extensive research into demographics and genre preferences as a tool to establish radio formats. **Arbitron**'s quarterly ratings and annual publication *Radio Today* provides a wealth of information (see Table 11.1). The 2009 edition lists Pop/Contemporary Hit radio as the number one FM radio format among teenagers (12–17), with a shift to country as the number one format among adults age 18–44. For the 45 plus demographic, News/Talk/Information holds the number one spot.

Comparing for gender, the 2009 Arbitron report indicates differences in format preference between males and females (see Figure 11.5). Men prefer alternative, classic rock, and news/talk. Mexican regional also draws a heavier male audience than female. Females prefer contemporary Christian radio, adult contemporary, pop/contemporary hit radio, the urban formats, and, to an extent, country.

Arbitron A data collection service of the Nielsen Company that provides ratings to radio stations that show how many listeners the station has at various times of the day and the demographics of those listeners.

Configuration

Configuration of recorded music is another variable to be considered. The term configuration refers to the different formats or storage media for recorded music such as cassette tapes, vinyl records, and compact discs. The actual storage medium for music has evolved from cylinders to vinyl discs, to magnetic tape, digital discs, and now downloads. These various configurations have historically followed the traditional life cycle outlined earlier in the chapter. Each new configuration has an introduction into the marketplace and those that have been successful go on to the growth and maturity stages (there have been several, such as the minidisc, that have flopped).

Table 11.1 Leading radio format by age

| Arbitron 2009: Leading Radio Format by Age Group | | | | | | |
12–17	*18–24*	*25–34*	*35–44*	*45–54*	*55–64*	*65+*
Pop/CHR	Country	Country	Country	News/Talk	News/Talk	News/Talk
Rhythmic CHR	Pop/CHR	Pop/CHR	News/Talk	Country	Country	Country
Country	Rhythmic CHR	Adult contemporary	Adult contemporary	Adult contemporary	Adult contemporary	Adult contemporary

Source: Arbitron Radio Today 2009 edition

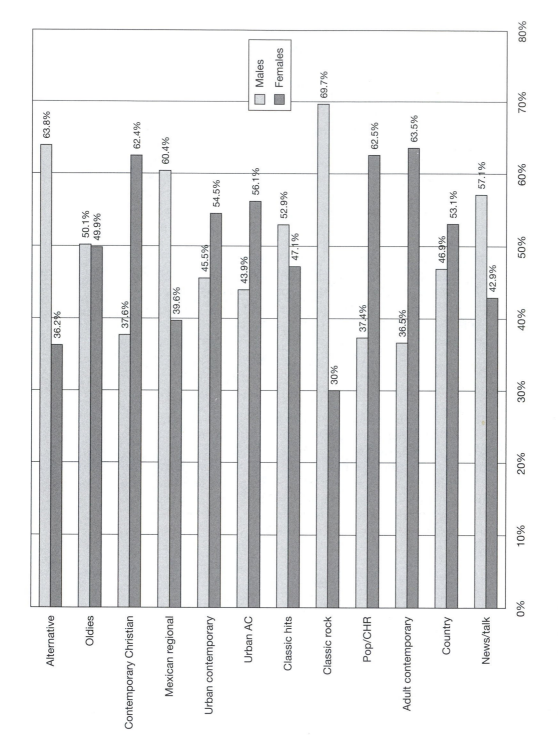

Figure 11.5 Gender comparison for radio formats 2009
Source: Arbitron

Until 1948, all releases were single 78 rpm (revolutions per minute) discs, or a package of single discs packaged in an album format, like a photo album. Then in 1948, two new competing formats were introduced. During the 1940s, CBS Records developed a longer playing (LP) record to give consumers the opportunity to listen to longer pieces of music without the interruption of changing discs.[11] Meanwhile, RCA Records was developing a smaller single 45 rpm disc to replace the 78s. The 7-inch 45s held as much music as the old 12-inch 78s. While the LP record originally catered to older record buyers who wanted longer classical and operatic selections of music that often ran for twenty minutes or more without a break, the 45 format was adopted by the singles-oriented rock n' roll genre. The LP was not intended to hold short songs like the 45 rpm.[12] The two formats coexisted but served different markets. Then in the mid- to late 1960s, the album format of eight to twelve songs became popular among the youth culture with the release of themed albums such as the Beatles concept album *Sgt. Pepper's Lonely Hearts Club Band*.

In the early 1960s, Philips Electronics introduced the magnetic tape cassette. It did not take off as a viable configuration for albums until the mid-1960s—in 1963, Philips, who was reluctant to license the format to other companies, sold only 9,000 copies. The cassette was seen as a poor quality substitute for vinyl recordings[13] even though the music cassette (MC) first appeared in stores in 1965. Improvements, including the inclusion of the **Dolby noise reduction system** helped the cassette eventually overtake its rival, the eight-track tape, as the popular choice for portable recorded music. In 1970, the first Dolby-enhanced cassette machines were introduced into the marketplace.[14]

> **Dolby noise reduction system** A form of dynamic pre-emphasis employed during recording, plus a form of dynamic de-emphasis used during playback, that work in tandem to improve the signal-to-noise ratio.

The cassette dominated the market in the late 1970s and 1980s, but was eventually overshadowed by the compact disc (CD) format by the end of that decade. The introduction of the CD in 1983 was a windfall for the industry, as labels were able to mine catalog product as consumers replaced their vinyl and cassette collections with the more durable and better sounding CD format. The CD had a great run from 1983 through to the end of the century. But by the year 2000, sales were eroding as several factors assaulted the industry: (1) illegal peer-to-peer file sharing cut deeply into CD sales; (2) consumers had completed their replacement cycle of updating their music libraries; (3) competition stiffened for entertainment dollars as mobile phones, video games, and DVD sales encroached on consumers' music budget. The research firm NPD reported in 2009 that there "were 17 million fewer CD buyers in 2008 than in 2007."[15] The introduction of DRM-free (digital rights management systems—a form of copy protection) music in 2008 and 2009 has further cut into CD sales—the DRM-free compact discs lost that sales advantage.

According to SoundScan, in 2009 the CD accounted for almost 79 percent of album sales, with digital making up slightly over 20 percent. That leaves about 1 percent for the combination of vinyl and cassettes (see Figure 11.6).

Digital Sales

The popularity of digital music downloads, both legal and illegal, was fueled by several factors in the late 1990s:

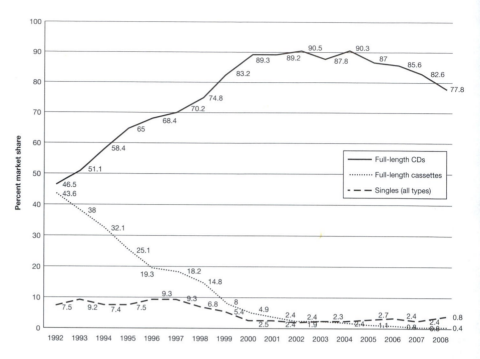

Figure 11.6 Market share for the three major configurations 1992–2008
Source: RIAA

- Internet connections had become faster, with universities and businesses offering high-speed ISDN (Integrated Services Digital Network) connections.

- In 1997, the first viable audio compression format, **MP3**, was being introduced to consumers through several computer audio players such as the popular WinAmp. Consumers were able to take audio files from their CDs or master tapes, compress the files, and e-mail them to other Internet users.

- Also in 1997, the Rio was introduced as the first mass market portable MP3 player.[16]

- There was widespread adoption of unauthorized peer-to-peer file-sharing services, starting with Napster in 1999.

- Consumers were developing a preference for "cherry picking" the best songs rather than purchasing an entire album.

MP3 (full name MPEG-1 Audio Layer 3) A patented digital audio encoding format using a form of data compression. It is the most popular digital audio compression format for the transfer and playback of music on digital audio players.

In the fall of 1999, Napster was in full swing, and MP3 players were popular with college students. The RIAA began contacting universities and targeting college students, who were the most likely copyright violators. Access to high-speed Internet on campuses was fueling massive peer-to-peer music file sharing. The RIAA sent notices to more than 300 universities warning them that students were hosting illegal MP3 files on campus servers. Janelle Brown, writer for

Salon.com, wrote in November 1999 "there are probably millions of illegal MP3 files and music traders online—pity the poor fool whose job it is to track them all down."[17]

After the success of Napster in 1999, the record labels reluctantly took steps to enter the legal digital download market. Concerns were raised over security issues, including how to provide copy protection for the labels while still providing the consumer with a product they could use and legally copy to portable devices. Consumer frustration was growing because the major labels were not providing this legal, commercial alternative to illegal downloading at a time when the consumer was more than ready to convert from CDs to digital tracks stored on a computer system.

By 2000, the debate was on, with companies like Liquid Audio vying for access to music catalogs to sell tracks, and companies like PressPlay requesting licensing for subscription services.[18] Many of the startups were having a difficult time with profitability because the labels were unwilling or unable to license music. The major labels created online distribution services of their own, but they failed to capture the commercial market with their cobbled together group of startups such as MusicNet and Duet. They had yet to hit on a formula for success in making a dent in the illegal P2P file trading, until Steve Jobs of Apple convinced them he had the answer.

iTunes Story

In January of 2001, Apple introduced the iTunes jukebox software at Macworld. Unlike predecessors, such as WinAmp, iTunes was simple with most of the screen dedicated to a browser for finding music. The initial release was only for Mac users, with the promise of a Windows version to follow. iTunes included support for creating mixes, burning CDs, and downloading to popular MP3 players, including the Rio. Unfortunately, the current crop of MP3 players did not offer a Mac user-friendly interface. Steve Jobs ordered the development of an MP3 player that would work seamlessly with the iTunes system. Part two of that plan was to create an online music downloading store. Thomas Hormby wrote "Apple was not the first to create such a store, but it was the first not to fail spectacularly. The most notable pre-Apple music store was Pressplay, which was a joint venture between major record labels."[19]

The early 2003 launch only serviced Apple computers, but by fall of 2003, Apple launched a Windows version, and could boast sales of 13 million songs at that point. Steve Jobs, CEO of Apple, reassured nervous label executives by providing a closed system whereby customers who used the iTunes store for purchases were limited by DRM to burning their own discs and loading only to a limited number of Apple portable devices.[20]

Unlike the other legal downloading services that used a cacophony of policy restrictions (limited number of downloads and streams per month), the iTunes policy was simple: 99 cents per download, up to three copies. It was an instant success, quickly capturing 76 percent of the hardware market and 82 percent of the legal music download market.[21]

The RIAA and SoundScan began tracking digital sales in the US in 2004. From 2005 to 2006, there was a 65 percent increase in digital download sales, with a 45 percent increase by 2007. In the United States, more than 844 million digital tracks were sold (SoundScan) in 2007 compared to 582 million in 2006. In 2008, over one *billion* tracks were sold. Sales of music downloads have continued to grow, although that growth is slowing from the rapid pace of the 2000s. Growth of digital tracks in the US was only 8.3 percent in 2009. Global digital revenues increased 12 percent in 2009. The IFPI claims that in 2009, digital channels accounted for 27 percent of revenue, up from 21 percent in 2008.

US digital *album* sales (without track equivalent albums included—see following section) reached the 50 million mark in 2007, a 53.5 percent increase over 2006. Digital album sales for 2009 were up by 16 percent from the previous year. In terms of market share, digital *album* sales accounted for 5.5 percent of album sales in the US in 2006, jumping to 10 percent in 2007, up to 15 percent by 2008 and 20.4 percent in 2009.

The popularity of CDs vs. digital downloading varies when compared by genres, as indicated in Figure 11.8. According to Nielsen SoundScan, digital album sales for both 2007 and 2008 were as follows: the genres of alternative, rock, soundtracks, and electronic showed an active downloading market, with fans of these genres more likely to select to download an album over the CD than fans of other genres (see Figure 11.8). Fans of country, R&B, rap, and Latin are more likely to choose CDs over download albums.

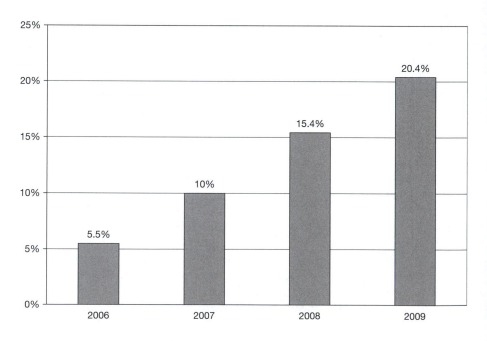

Figure 11.7 Digital album sales as percent of all album sales
Source: SoundScan

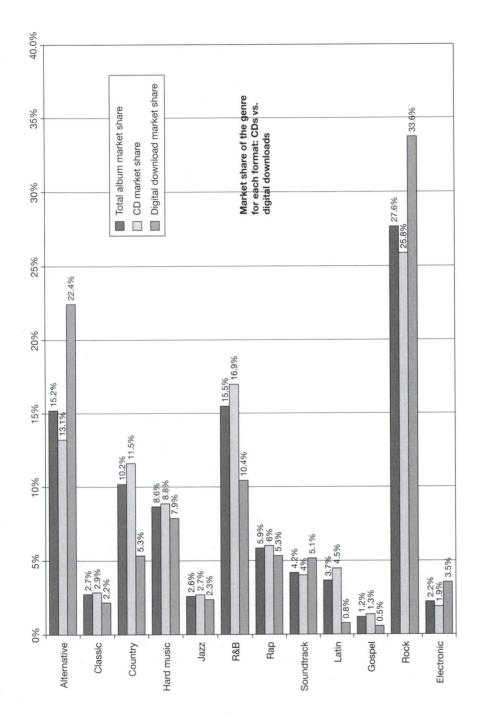

Figure 11.8 Sales by genre for digital vs. physical album units

Source: SoundScan

Tracking Sales with Track Equivalent Album Measurement

In an effort to monitor recorded music sales and determine trends and patterns, SoundScan came up with a way to measure digital album sales and compare them with music sales in previous years. When SoundScan first started tracking digital download sales, the unit of measurement for downloads was the single track, except when the customer purchased the entire album at once. But this did not give an accurate reflection of how music sales volume had changed, because most customers who download buy songs *a-la-carte* instead of in album form. In an attempt to more accurately compare previous years with the current sales trend, SoundScan came up with a unit of measurement called *track equivalent albums* (TEA), which means that 10-track downloads are counted as a single album. Thus, the total of all the downloaded singles is divided by 10 and the resulting figure is added to album downloads and physical album units to give a total picture of "album" sales. Here is an example of how this works, from Billboard.biz.

> "When albums are tallied using the formula of 10 digital track downloads equaling one album, the 582 million digital track downloads last year translates into 58.2 million albums, giving overall albums a total of 646.4 million units. The overall 2006 total of 646.4 million is a drop of 1.2 percent from 2005's overall album sales of 654.1 million."[22]

Having established the TEA as a new unit of measurement, industry trends show the following: US album sales have continued to slide every year from a high in 2000 of 785 million units to 489.8 million units in 2009 (including TEA) (see Figure 11.9). (Without the addition of the TEA, album units in 2009 were 374 million.) The difference between the sales figure with TEA and that without TEA represents the number of TEA units: multiply by 10 and you get the number of tracks that were sold individually, for example (489,800,000 - 373,900,000) x 10 = 1.159 billion tracks.

The Rise and Fall and Rise of Singles

In the 1960s, pop music was singles-driven, with vinyl 45s holding a substantial share of the music market. When albums became more popular in the late 1960s and throughout the 1970s, singles were released at intervals from an album in order to generate airplay and, thus, sales for the album.

The decision whether to release a given cut as a commercial single is one of the more difficult decisions for a label. Until the recent resurgence of singles in the digital realm, the single was primarily a promotional tool—an expense. It is what most radio stations actually play, though some also play cuts off of albums. The release of a single indicates which cut the label thinks will develop popularity on radio and that the label is willing to promote. During the late 1980s and throughout the 1990s, it was secondarily a product to sell. Figure 11.10 indicates that the popularity of singles as an item to purchase declined fairly steadily from 1973 through 2001.

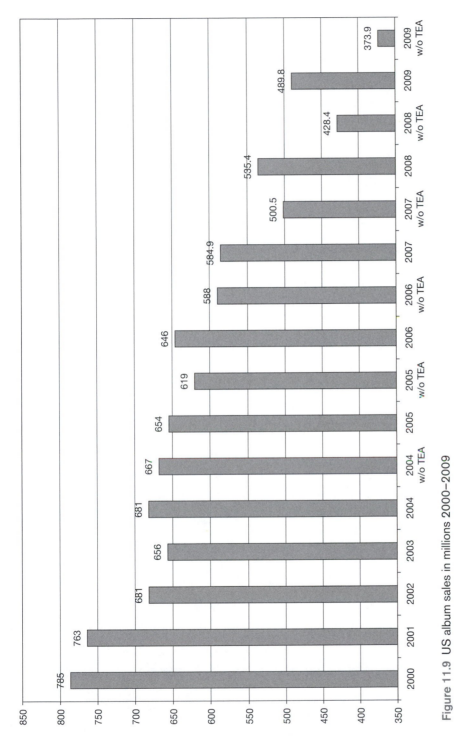

Figure 11.9 US album sales in millions 2000–2009

Source: SoundScan

Vinyl singles had all but disappeared by 1995, declining to 10.2 million units shipped—less than 1 percent of total recordings shipped that year. The cassette single, or "cassingle," had replaced the vinyl sales to some extent, but popularity continued to decline. In 1996, the National Association of Recording Merchandisers (NARM) research indicated that only 16 percent of buyers had purchased a cassette single within a six-month survey period and only 11 percent had purchased a CD single.[23] For both the cassette and CD formats, the cost of manufacturing a single rivaled that of manufacturing costs for an entire album. Singles commonly sold for $2.49, and included remixes and "B-sides" in order to justify the cost, but consumers were not buying. Labels actively pushed the sale of singles in the mid- to late 1990s through deep discounting. This was done in hopes of influencing the Hot 100 *Billboard* chart, which calculated the popularity of singles based upon a combination of airplay and sales.

Other labels complained that the popularity of their songs was miscalculated if they failed to release a commercial version of the single for sale. In response, *Billboard* modified their methodology to reduce the influence of sales of singles from 40 percent of the Hot 100 Chart's points to 25 percent.[24] This gave labels even less incentive to release commercial singles into the marketplace simply to secure chart standing. By 2001 the bottom had fallen out of the singles market, despite the labels' efforts at heavy discounting, price reductions, and including additional bonus tracks on singles. Singles accounted for less than 1 percent of unit volume and less than 0.5 percent of sales dollars in 2002.

The launch of iTunes in 2003 signaled a turnaround in the sale of singles. In 2003 *Billboard* introduced the first download singles chart, using SoundScan data.

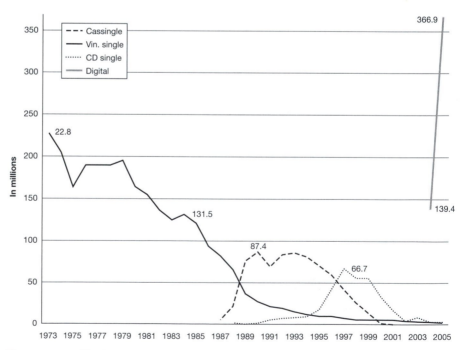

Figure 11.10 The life cycle of the single formats before digital tracks, from 1973–2005

In the first week, Beyonce's "Crazy in Love" generated 1,500 legitimate downloads to be in the top position.[25] By 2010, top selling singles were generating sales of over 200,000 in their first weeks on the chart (see Figure 11.11).

The debate at the time centered on how or whether to include these sales in the premier chart, the Hot 100. In 2003, *Billboard*'s Director of Charts, Geoff Mayfield, commented:

> The consumer's rapid and enthusiastic acceptance of iTunes and other download services gives great meaning to that data. It is obvious that at some point, we will need to factor those transactions into the *Billboard* Hot 100 and some of our other singles charts, as they will restore the voice of the consumer that has been lost since labels have practically abandoned the retail-available single.[26]

Since that time, the digital single has been incorporated into the Hot 100 chart methodology—accounting for the majority of sales points towards chart position. And the sale of singles has been steadily increasing.

But this trend has come at the expense of album sales as consumers choose to "cherry pick" their favorite tracks rather than purchasing a whole album. A 2009 study from Anita Elberse of Harvard Business School found an inverse correlation between album sales and sales of digital tracks. "For every 1 percent increase in the downloading rate, there is a 6 percent decrease in album sales and a 9 percent increase in single track sales per bundle of an artist's music." She concludes that "the unbundling of music online poses a significant risk to

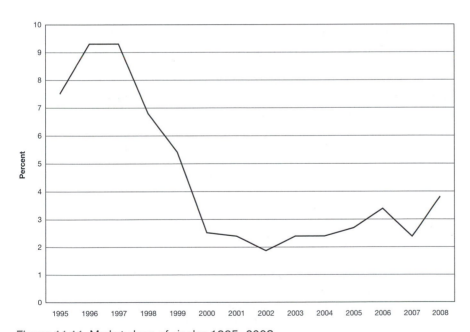

Figure 11.11 Market share of singles 1995–2008

Source: RIAA

record labels which, over time, will probably see a further erosion of revenues."[27] In an effort to boost sales of digital albums, labels have begun bundling some new, popular digital albums, forcing consumers to purchase the entire bundle (album) of tracks rather than cherry picking their favorite tunes. In 2009, iTunes launched the iTunes LP, a premium digital album format for bundled tracks. The new premium items were responsible for 65–70 percent of sales of major digital releases in 2009.[28]

Internet Activities

Log on to the iTunes Store. Pick a familiar album in which songs are sold individually. Look at the relative popularity of each song. Are there some that stand out as extremely popular while others are not at all popular? This is the effect of *a-la-carte* sales.

Add up the prices of all the individual tracks and subtract the total from the album price. How much money does the customer save by purchasing the entire album? Now, how many songs would you actually want to purchase from this album? Would it be cheaper for you to buy them individually, or purchase the entire album?

Catalog Sales

Catalog sales are defined as sales of records that have been in the marketplace for over 18 months. Current catalog titles are those over 18 months old but less than 36 months old. Deep catalog albums are those over 36 months old since the release date.

When the CD was first introduced in the early 1980s, it fueled the sales of older catalog albums as consumers replaced their old vinyl and cassette collections with CDs. This windfall allowed labels to enjoy huge profits and led to the industry expansion of the 1980s and early 1990s. However, catalog sales started to diminish in the mid-1990s as consumers finished replacing their collections. The closure of traditional retail stores also contributed to the decline in catalog sales because the "big box" stores carried fewer catalog titles.

Pricing strategies to sustain catalog sales were introduced as early as 1996. In the late 1990s, labels sought new ways to promote catalog sales through reissues, compilations, and looking at new formats. Michael Omansky, senior VP of strategic marketing at RCA, stated in 1999, "We [now] put out what I think is substantially better product [on Elvis], with substantially more unreleased material."[29] An article in the *LA Times* in 2001 stated, "Companies have watched catalog sales slip from about 50 percent to 38 percent over the last decade."[30]

During the early 2000s, catalog sales declined until the introduction of digital downloads saw a spurt in catalog sales as consumers sought to fill in their collections with catalog singles and albums that had not been available for some time (see Figure 11.12). In 2009, the sales share of catalog albums increased from

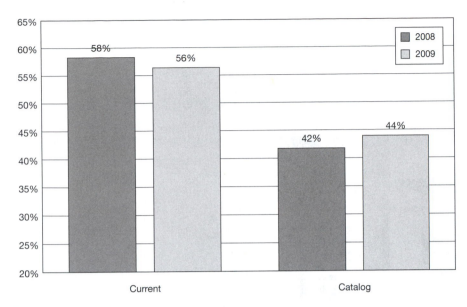

Figure 11.12 Market share of catalog sales
Source: Nielsen SoundScan

42 percent of sales to 44 percent while sales of current albums dropped from 58 percent to 56 percent.

Market Share of the Majors

Label market share (Figure 11.13) is measured for both new releases and for a combination of new releases and recent sales of catalog titles. Measuring by distributor, Universal has dominated market share since acquiring PolyGram Records in 1998 for $10.4 billion. It is impressive that Universal managed to grow additional market share for several years after the purchase of PolyGram. They have grown from about one quarter to nearly one third of the industry market share. The only other segment of the industry showing consistent growth over 10 years is the indie sector.

The 2004 merger of Sony and BMG created a second behemoth in the industry and put the joint venture at number two, just behind Universal. BMG held a strong market share in the late 1990s and early 2000s with their partnership with Jive Records who, at that time, was responsible for the teen hit sensations N'Sync, Britney Spears, and Backstreet Boys. Sony enjoyed success in the late 1990s with Celine Dion, Mariah Carey, and other pop artists but saw their market share slip when the pop movement subsided. The merger of these two companies, with Sony ultimately purchasing the music division from Bertelsmann, originally failed to yield any advantages in market share. The new company, Sony Music Entertainment, shed expenses, eliminated redundant departments and increased its market share in 2009 for the first time in several years.

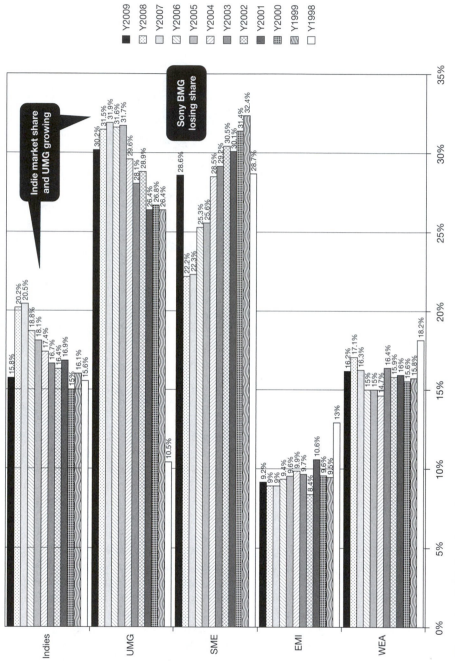

Figure 11.13 Market share of majors from 1998 to 2009: current and catalog

One of the strengths of a record label can be measured by the relative market share for new releases, and this indicates the vitality of its A&R skills. Labels that are increasing market share of the sales of new releases are those with success in finding and developing new acts and releasing successful new recordings from their established acts. The following figure, Figure 11.14, shows that only Universal and the indies have been successfully increasing market share of new releases over the past several years until 2009, again with Sony surging early on, dropping back and then surging again in 2009.

Comparison of all and current albums

In the following charts, a comparison is made for market share of all albums and market share of new releases for each label. So not only is an increase or decrease in current album market share an indicator, but a comparison of all albums and current albums indicates how much a label relies on catalog sales compared to sales from its new releases. Of the major labels, only UMG has a larger market share for current releases than for all album releases, while the indies, Sony, EMI, and WMG are all more dependent on catalog sales than Universal and the indies. Sony (SME) holds a smaller market share for current releases than it does for the combination of catalog and new releases (see Figure 11.15). After several years of turmoil, however, Figures 11.14 and 11.15 indicate Sony Music Entertainment is beginning to gain market share for both new releases and total product.

Price

The second component of the marketing mix is price. But price is about more than just how much to charge for a product such as a CD or digital track. It is about pricing strategy—setting up a fundamental structure that will maximize both sales and profits for the record label. Pricing starts by determining the retail and wholesale price for a product and determining the estimated overall profit per unit. It is a combination of the three pricing strategies outlined below. Once this is established, the process continues by introducing price-based incentives aimed at both consumer and retailer.

There are three methods for deciding the retail price of a product: *cost-based pricing*, *competition-based pricing*, and *consumer-based (value-based) pricing*. Cost-based pricing is achieved by determining the cost of product development and manufacturing, marketing and distribution, and company overhead. Then an amount is added to cover the company's profit goal. The weakness with this method is that it does not take into account competition and consumer demand.

When determining cost-based pricing, consideration must be given to the fixed costs of running a business, the per-unit costs of manufacturing products, and variable costs related to marketing and product development. Fixed costs include items such as the recording and production costs associated with an album or single,[31] label overhead, employee salaries, utilities, mortgages, and other costs that are not related to the quantity of goods produced and sold. Per-unit costs

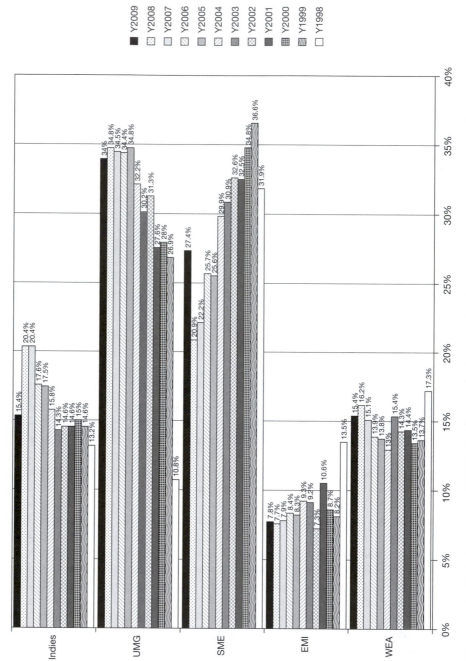

Figure 11.14 Market share from 1998 to 2009: current albums by label

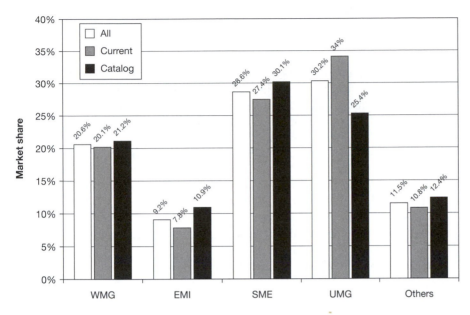

Figure 11.15 Comparison of all and current albums by market share, 2009
Source: Nielsen Soundscan

are usually associated with manufacturing, and vary depending on the number of units produced. For recorded music, that would include discs, CD booklets, jewel cases, and other packaging. Variable costs are those that are not tied to the number of units, but may be based upon decisions made by company executives, such as how much to spend on artwork, imaging, marketing, and production.

Competition-based pricing attempts to set prices based on those charged by the company's competitors—rather than demand or cost considerations. Even this strategy has nuances. The company may charge more, the same, or less than its competitors, depending on its customers, product image, consumer loyalty, and other factors. One such strategy includes *loss leader* pricing (see loss leader subsection later in this chapter). Under loss leader pricing, the retailer actually loses money on one product in an attempt to bring in customers who will purchase other products that are more profitable. CDs are commonly used by retailers as loss leaders because the practice generates traffic to the store and increases sales of other items. One problem with loss leader pricing is that it undermines the perceived value of a product and undermines value-based pricing—a strategy that is important to record labels.

Value- or consumer-based pricing is based upon charging what the consumer perceives to be a fair value for the product. It is not necessarily associated with the actual costs of creating the product, nor based upon the retail value of competitive products. If the music consumer believes a CD is worth $15, then the label is able to enjoy both sales success and sustainable profit if the costs associated with that product are not outlandish.

Compact Disc Pricing

In marketing terms, the perceived value of the CD is significantly higher than that of the previous dominant album formats, the vinyl LP and the cassette. There are many components of that perceived value. CDs do have significantly higher quality of sound. They are more durable, more compact, more convenient, and more visually impressive. The CD technology introduced by Philips and Sony in the early 1980s gave consumers a highly desirable product for which they had been willing to pay a higher price.

Manufacturing costs for early CDs in the mid-1980s topped $4 per unit— partially because each disc included a "long box." The long box was introduced to resolve several problems brought about with the conversion of record stores from LP-dominant format to CD-compatible. The bins that stores used to display LP albums were too deep to showcase the compact disc, so the long box provided elevation. Compact disc jewel boxes are an easier target for shoplifting; the long box made it more difficult for shoplifters to conceal stolen product, and consumers were used to larger packaging, which was provided on most long boxes.

Price and profit

As a result of declining manufacturing costs and increasing wholesale prices the profit margins of the record labels rose during the 1990s. Consider the example below. The calculations operate on several assumptions: SRLP is $18.98 (which would be a front-line product with a PPD of about $12 before any special discounts), manufacturing costs of a completed disc with all graphics and inserts, shrink-wrapped, and ready to sell are about $1; distribution charges amount to about $1.50; artist and producer royalties (all-in) are 20 percent (PPD basis) in the high-cost example and 12 percent in the low-cost example; the CD royalty rate is 100 percent of the base rate in both examples; mechanical royalties are for 12 cuts at full "statutory" rate (9.1 cents per cut for the years 2006 until 2013) in the high-cost example, and at 75 percent rate in the low-cost example. Even in the high-cost example, the label ends up with a gross margin of $5.81 per disc; and over $1.20 more, most of which is accounted for by lower artist and producer royalties, in the low-cost example.

Certainly there is a logic, as far as the label is concerned, in raising prices in order to increase profits. This is especially true given the apparently price inelastic demand (i.e. an increase in price does not bring about an offsetting decrease in demand) for CDs (see Table 11.2). The concern must be that they could price themselves out of the market or create an even greater demand and market for used CDs or free downloads.

Pricing tiers

Front line (aka full line) The label's most recent releases from their top artists.

The record business has a long-standing tradition of three-tiered pricing: **front line** are usually the highest priced "regular" releases pricing for new and high-

Table 11.2 Low-margin and high-margin CD example

	Low Margin (High Cost)	High Margin (Low Cost)
Wholesale price	**$12.00**	**$12.00**
Less: Manufacturing costs	$ 1.00	$ 1.00
Artist and Producer royalties	$ 2.70	$ 1.62
Mechanical royalties	$ 1.09	$ 0.82
Distributor charges	$ 1.70	$ 1.70
Gross margin	**$ 5.51**	**$ 6.86**

demand product; **mid line** pricing for catalog titles; and **budget** pricing for the least popular but still active titles—mostly deep catalog product. This served the industry well until the turn of the century, when a host of factors drove music sales down year after year.

In response to the challenges faced for effective pricing strategies, labels began to experiment with alternative pricing strategies. In 2003, Universal Music Group unveiled a new strategy for setting retail and wholesale pricing, a program they call Jump Start.[32] The premise behind the Jump Start program was that Universal would discontinue their practice of providing rebates to retailers in the form of advertising and promotional subsidies (see section on **co-op advertising** in Chapter 12). Instead, they would offer a lower wholesale price to stores who signed up for the program, which included a new lower retail price in exchange for 33 percent of in-store promotional efforts—which was roughly equal to Universal's market share.[33] This was the first time prices on CDs had dropped since their introduction in the early 1980s.[34] So, for stores who accepted the program, they would benefit from a lower wholesale price designed to stimulate sales, but would be bound by the in-store promotional requirement. By 2004, Universal had revised its JumpStart program (Table 11.3), raising wholesale prices from $9.09 to $9.49 for most titles, and from $10.10 on premium titles to $10.35. List prices were raised from $12.98 to $13.98, and $14.98 for premium titles.

Other labels responded with their own revamped pricing structure.[35] In 2004, Warner Music Group dropped prices on nearly 1,800 titles, moving them from mid-line pricing of $11.98 retail to budget line at $9.98. The company also created a "super midline" tier at $13.98 retail, and gave retailers extra discount and **dating** for catalog product. Sony responded by offering variable pricing strategies including rapid devaluation of some front-line titles and promotional incentives such as discounts and promotional allowances. BMG came up with a pricing initiative in 2004 that offered an additional 15 percent discount on some

Mid line A label's record albums that have a PPD of 66.66 to 75 or 85 percent of the PPD of front line albums.

Budget line or price An album product line of a label that sells at a list price usually less than two-thirds of the price for a current front line (new releases for established artists) album.

Dating The date by which the retailer had to pay for the purchases or lose the early payment discount. An example might be 3 percent discount if paid in 20 days, the net is due within 60 days.

Table 11.3 Universal Music Group Jump Start Program

	MSRP	Card Price	% to Distributor	% to Retailer	Actual Profit for Retailer
Previous pricing	$17.98	$12.02	67%	33%	$5.96
New pricing	$12.98	$ 9.09	70%	30%	$3.98

new releases in addition to the standard 5 percent that had been offered.[36] This meant that titles in the program would carry a list price of $12.04 and a wholesale cost of $9.63. The program also eliminated cooperative advertising funds.

By 2008, the industry again revisited pricing strategy, but this time it was some of the major retailers who took the initiative. Wal-Mart proposed a five-tier pricing scheme to include a promotional retail pricing of $10 for the top 15–20 hottest titles, a $12 price for front-line hits and current titles, $9 for top catalog and $7 for mid-line catalog, with a budget category of $5.[37] The policy also shifted the store's pricing to rounder sales prices, instead of the usual 5 to 22 cent markdown from an even dollar amount. Under the program, they expected the labels to supply product at lower wholesale prices. At the time, three of the four major labels were charging a wholesale price of $12 and Universal was charging $10.30. That same year, Best Buy initiated a test marketing program whereby they dropped the retail price of all CDs in three stores to $9.99 "to prove to the labels that CDs priced at that level would produce enough incremental sales to justify the lower pricing."[38]

In 2009, Transworld, the largest remaining traditional record retailer, persuaded the major labels to participate in a new pricing scheme. The strategy was test marketed in 118 stores and included a retail price point of $9.99 for all CDs, securing a wholesale pricing of $6.50–$7.50 from the labels. In mid-2009, Sony Music Entertainment (which included BMG) proposed a four- or five-tier pricing strategy similar to that of the other labels.[39] It reduced wholesale prices from $11.86 on all front line, to a combination of wholesale price ranging from a low of $5.50 to $7.50 for all but the top 140 titles (see Figure 11.16).

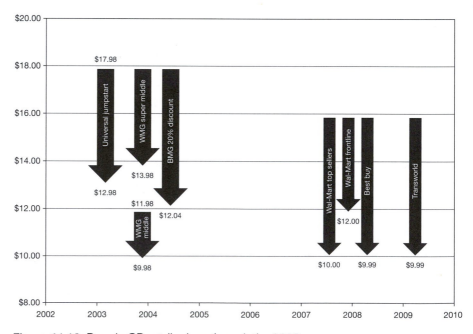

Figure 11.16 Drop in CD retail prices through the 2000s

DIY Activities

- Visit a store that sells current records; perhaps a big box or discount store. Look at the pricing on new releases that are on sale. How many titles from each genre are on sale? Where are they positioned? What is the price difference between the new releases on sale and other recent releases at front-line prices? If you get the chance, visit the next week and see if the same new titles are still on sale, or if they are now at the full retail price.
- Look in the circulars in the Sunday paper for stores with CDs on sale. Compare the various ads. Are they all the same titles? Are they listed for the same price at each store?
- Visit several major chain stores that sell new CD releases. Do any of them have special bonus materials that are not found on versions in other chains?

Loss Leader Pricing

As previously mentioned, the practice of loss-leader pricing undermines the labels' efforts to establish a perceived value for recorded music. (This becomes even more important in the age of removing the physical attributes of music purchases, and merely selling the creative work as a digital download.) In the 1990s, retail market share moved away from traditional retail stores toward the "other store" category that included big box stores Best Buy and Circuit City, and discount stores such as Wal-Mart and Target. These stores began to take advantage of the fact that CDs were an excellent way to drive traffic into their stores through loss leader pricing. They began to offer front-line new releases for less than $10, often below cost, in an effort to increase store traffic and generate sales in other product categories that offered a higher profit margin.

This practice created hardship on traditional record stores, who depended upon CD profits for financial success. Many of the retail chains faced financial crisis and most were forced to file for bankruptcy or reorganization. They appealed to the labels to come to their aid and curb the practice of loss-leader pricing. But despite the fact that loss-leader pricing was eroding the perceived value of their main product, the labels were enjoying the increased sales from their new partners, and only reluctantly implemented policies that would discourage loss-leader pricing.

MAP Policies of the 1990s

Since loss-leader pricing was tied to big box and discount stores, and the traditional stores were looking to labels to help them survive, the labels responded with a program called **MAP** (minimum advertised price) policies. In a move that tied price with promotion, the labels in the 1990s began to threaten retailers— mostly the larger stores—with the loss of co-op advertising money if they advertised product for sale at less than a certain minimum price.

MAP (minimum advertised price) A price established by a label to discourage retailers from selling recordings below cost. The labels attempted to cut off some advertising funds for a retailer that advertised albums below that label's MAP. The FTC found this to be an illegal restraint of trade and the labels entered into a consent decree to stop the practice.

MAP policies varied among the major distribution companies, but each distributor set prices for each category or list price of product. If a retailer advertised the product for sale below that price then the label might go so far as to stop all advertising funds for all product from that distributor for a period of time (WEA's policy), or just cut off funds for that particular record for a period of time (BMG's policy).[40] Theoretically the store could still sell a recording for less than the MAP, just not advertise that price using money that the label had provided.

The labels put the policies in place to help regular record retailers who found themselves in price competition with some non-record retail chains such as Best Buy, Circuit City, Lechmere/Montgomery Ward, and Target, who used the low-balled prices on CDs as loss leaders to entice people into their stores to purchase electronics and other merchandise. As the price wars intensified in the last quarter of 1995 the labels began enforcing or strengthening their policies. By June 1996 *Billboard* reported, "Thanks to the majors' new-found resolve on MAP, prices of hit CDs at discount chains rose by $2 to $11.99 over the last month."[41] Meantime, NARM reported that the average price paid by their SoundData Consumer panel during December 1995 through February 1996 was $13.64, up from $12.71 from the previous survey.[42]

The MAP policies spawned an unwanted side effect—an investigation into price fixing by the Federal Trade Commission (FTC). In 1993 the Commission began investigating advertising price policies of the major labels.[43] By early 2000 it was becoming apparent that the FTC would likely rule against the major distribution companies.[44] They began to consider settlement with the FTC and in May of 2000 the FTC and the five majors entered consent decrees. The majors agreed not to link advertising funds with advertised prices of retail clients for 7 years. For an additional 13 years, the majors could not condition promotional money on the prices contained in advertisements that the majors did not pay for. In its news release on the agreement, the FTC said,

> The Commission has unanimously found reason to believe that the arrangements entered into by the five largest distributors of prerecorded music violate the antitrust laws in two respects. First, when considered together, the arrangements constitute practices that facilitate horizontal collusion among the distributors . . . Second, when viewed individually, each distributor's arrangement constitutes an unreasonable vertical restraint of trade under the rule of reason.[45]

The FTC settlement did not stop the Attorneys General of 42 states from suing all of the major labels and three major retail chains, Tower, Transworld Entertainment, and Musicland in 2000, alleging that the MAP policies were a form of price fixing. In 2002 the defendants settled with the states for $67.4 million in cash and $75.7 million worth of CDs. The cash was awarded at the rate of about $13 to each consumer who registered at the court's website. The recordings were to be distributed to the states on a pro-rata population basis and then distributed to libraries and archives in the states.[46]

The MAP pricing problems were not the first time that the major labels had come under scrutiny for their possibly anti-competitive practices. In 1985 WEA,

Capitol, PolyGram, RCA, MCA, CBS, and ABC settled a decade-long price-fixing suit by independent and other distributors. A settlement fund of over $26 million was approved for distribution to distributors who purchased recordings for resale from January 1971 through December 1982.[47] In the mid-1990s the labels were again the target of suits contending that they had conspired to fix CD prices and a separate suit claiming that they conspired to keep some wholesalers out of the business of selling cutouts.[48] Finally, in 1996 the Justice Department began an investigation against Time Warner, Sony, EMI, BMG, and PolyGram for price fixing of license fees for music videos. The altercation centered on an alleged attempt by the majors to keep "MuchMusic USA" from launching a music video channel.[49]

Even sectors of the industry sometimes claim that a different sector of the industry is violating anti-trust laws. In 2000, NARM, which represents record retailers and distributors, sued Sony Music for anti-trust violations. NARM claimed that bundling of services such as computer links to Sony direct retail sites and other merchandise advertising on Sony CDs and other products was an unlawful "tying" arrangement. The suit was finally dropped in late 2001 as NARM decided a better course of action would be to focus "on educating industry executive and government officials about retail concerns relating to digital distribution, copyright law, and antitrust via other channels."[50]

Three price fixing investigations were instigated in 2005 and 2006 against the majors for allegedly conspiring to fix prices on digital downloads. The New York Attorney General, the Department of Justice, and a separate consumer group all complained of anti-trust violations. In 2010 a Circuit Court of Appeals decision held that the consumer group suit could go forward.[51]

Pricing of Digital Product

In the early 2000s the labels stepped up to the plate to embrace the sale of licensed digital download tracks. Labels were charging a retail price of $2.49 per track and were offering tracks through their bricks and mortar retail partners' websites.[52] Pricing for subscription services was more confusing, with the business model not yet firmly in place.

In 2003, Apple launched its iTunes store, featuring an *a-la-carte* purchase format of 99 cents per song.[53] The original plan called for a wholesale rate of 65 cents, with 10 cents of that going to the artist (assuming the artist gets a normal royalty rate of around 15 percent), and 8 cents (now 9.1) going to the song publisher. That leaves 47 cents as gross income for the label. The service provider (online retailer) grosses about 34 cents.[54]

In 2007, the record labels sought a price restructuring of iTunes but were unable to persuade Apple president Steve Jobs, who believed the current pricing strategy of 99 cents was crucial for the continued success of the service. The labels were asking for a retail price of $1.29 on top selling tracks. When Jobs resisted, "Universal Music Group chief Doug Morris and his fellow music executives realized they had ceded too much control to Jobs".[55] Morris refused to re-sign a multiyear contract with iTunes and instead opted for a month-to-month agreement while nurturing alternative retailing options, including the ill-fated subscription service called Total Music.[56] The existing subscription services had only a few million customers, whereas iTunes had hundreds of millions of users. Then in April 2007, EMI announced an arrangement with iTunes where they would offer the first iTunes **DRM-free** tracks at $1.29, in what was the first tiered pricing strategy for iTunes.[57]

In addition to being free of copy protection, these premium tracks were higher in fidelity. The variable pricing model at iTunes was in full swing by 2009. Apple announced the introduction of a three-tiered pricing model at the MacWorld conference, including the end of DRM. The new retail prices were set at 69 cents for catalog, 99 cents for most current sellers, and $1.29 for top selling tracks.[58] The impact was an 11 percent reduction in sales volume for the more expensive tracks, but the 29 percent increase in price more than offset the decrease in units.[59]

Meanwhile, in 2007 Amazon rolled out the soft launch of their new MP3 retail store, with licensed music from EMI and some indie labels.[60] In 2008, Sony adopted a new business model for selling tracks on Amazon—through the agency or commission model. Under that arrangement, Sony is a "merchant" under the Amazon umbrella and has control over their "store" content, including pricing. The other labels and independents were selling to Amazon under the wholesale model. Amazon allows for tiered pricing.

Sidebar: **DRM-free** Tracks that were free of "digital Rights Management" codes that could prevent them from being repeatedly copied.

Summary

This chapter has examined the first two of the four "P's" of marketing: product and price. We began the product section by covering the concept of the product life cycle so that we could then apply it to specific situations in the recorded music business. Next, we covered music genres, including the more popular genres of rock, pop, rap, R&B, and country. We examined the market share of each and how that has changed over time.

Following that, the various music configurations were discussed, including an historical perspective on the evolution of physical storage media from vinyl records, to magnetic tape, to the compact disc, and finally to digital track download. Within the realm of digital downloads, we analyzed the challenges brought upon by the marketplace moving from an album-based format with the CD, to the singles-based format of digital downloads, and how the industry is responding to this change. Finally, we covered the concept of relative market share for each of the major labels/distributors and looked at current vs. catalog sales.

The second factor, price, began with a look at pricing strategies, including cost-based, competition-based, and consumer-based pricing. The three traditional pricing tiers of compact discs—front line, mid line and budget—were discussed, along with the recent transformation to a more complex multi-tier pricing strategy sought by both labels and retailers to protect CD sales in the face of rising cannibalism from digital downloads, both legal and illegal. The concepts of discount and dating and loss-leader pricing were presented, along with the controversial minimum advertised pricing strategies adopted by the labels to combat loss-leader pricing. Finally, issues surrounding pricing of digital tracks and digital albums were covered, completing the section on pricing. Issues and concepts associated with the last two factors of the marketing mix—promotion and place—are discussed in the next chapter.

QUESTIONS FOR REVIEW

- Define "marketing."
- What are the four Ps of marketing? How do they apply to the music and recording business?
- What are the traditional products of the music business? What are new products of the twenty-first century?
- How does the product life cycle apply to individual recordings? To recording formats? To genres? Is rock dying? Is hip-hop dying?
- How does radio format listenership vary with age?
- How are "track equivalent albums" calculated?
- What does the fact that the download market is primarily a singles market mean for the music business? For individual artists?
- What are the market shares of the Majors?
- How do labels make profit given current album and single prices?
- What are "front line," "mid line," and "budget" price lines?
- What is "loss-leader" pricing? Who would use that with recordings and why?

12 The Marketing Function: Promotion and Place

Introduction

The previous chapter examined the first two of the four Ps of marketing, product and price. This chapter explores the last two Ps, promotion and place. Promotion of a recording involves all the activities of informing and motivating the buyer, including all types of media coverage, personal selling, tour support, promotional incentives for retailers, grassroots marketing, and new media marketing. Place refers to the process of distributing recorded music products to consumers and involves both traditional "bricks and mortar" stores as well as virtual stores and other online (and wireless) methods for providing recorded music to consumers.

> **KEY CONCEPTS**
>
> 1. Promotion of a recording involves all the activities of informing and motivating the buyer, including all types of media coverage, personal selling, tour support, promotional incentives for retailers, grassroots marketing, and new media marketing.
> 2. Recorded music is sold in a variety of locations, both physical and online. The landscape is changing as physical stores yield market share to other sectors, especially online music sales.

Promotion

The third element of the marketing mix is promotion. The Merriam-Webster dictionary defines promotion as "the act of furthering the growth or development of something; especially: the furtherance of the acceptance and sale of merchandise through advertising, publicity, or discounting."[1]

Promoting an artist or any recorded music product involves a marketing plan with several elements; the relative importance of each element is dictated by the resources available for promotion and the particular marketing goals of the project. For instance, marketing for an international star would probably focus on the mass media: television appearances, radio airplay, magazine articles, and so forth, while promotion for a local band with limited resources would probably be more focused on developing a market in the geographic area where the artist performs. The components currently being used to promote recordings include the following:

- publicity;
- advertising;
- radio promotion;
- retail promotion;
- music videos;
- grassroots marketing;
- new media marketing;
- tour support;
- special markets and products.

The primary components, utilizing the majority of label resources, include media coverage (publicity and advertising), radio promotion, and retail promotion. Retail will be covered in the next section on the fourth "P" of the marketing mix. Secondary promotion components include the other items of video, new media, grassroots, tour support, and others.

Street date The date a recording is made available for sale to the public.

The marketing plan for a recording usually kicks in well before the release date or "**street date**" of the recording. Six months in advance of the street date, the publicity department gears up by developing an image for the product and perhaps the artist. This involves the creative services department at the label, which is in charge of photography, graphic design, and other visual elements. After those elements have been created, the next step involves getting media placement—again conducted by the publicity department. The next stage, at about three months before street date, involves releasing a single to radio for airplay. The promotion department works on getting stations to add the song, to build up demand for the album when it is finally released. Then one to two months before street date, retail functions and promotions are set in place. Other aspects of the plan are implemented at appropriate times to maximize marketing synergy for the release of the album into the marketplace. Marketing plans are still geared around the release of albums, but that may change as singles continue to grab market share and labels move beyond the traditional model of releasing all tracks at once.

Publicity

Press release A formal printed announcement by a company about its activities that is written in the form of a news article and given to the media to generate or encourage publicity.

Publicity consists of getting exposure for an artist in the mass media that is not in the form of advertising. In other words, publicists are responsible for getting news and feature coverage for an artist as well as exposure on television. The publicist is the liaison between the artist and the media. The publicist's tasks include, but are not limited to, the following:

- creating and disseminating **press release**s;
- providing information to journalists for news stories (often based on press releases);

- pitching and providing information to journalists for feature stories;
- pitching and providing images for magazine covers;
- managing photo shoots and disseminating photos to the media;
- pitching and making arrangements for television appearances;
- pitching and making arrangements for interviews.

The one media exception is radio airplay. The publicist is not responsible for getting songs played on the radio. That job would fall to the radio promoter (described in a later section of this chapter).

For publicity tools, publicists rely on press releases, biographies (**bios**), "**tear sheets**," a **discography**, publicity photos, and publicity shots. These items are often compiled into a **press kit**, which is the primary tool created and used by the publicist. It is the publicist who writes most of the copy for these items and prepares the press kit, although other branches of a record label may actually use the press kit in their marketing functions. For example, press kits may be sent out to radio stations and retail stores to assist with the efforts of the promotion and sales departments of the label.

More recently, publicists have turned to electronic press kits (EPK) that include the aforementioned items and music videos, video interviews, and other digital media items all stored on digital media such as optical discs or online. The electronic press kit is a more powerful and flexible tool: journalists can lift text, photos, and video clips directly from the electronic files. The inclusion of video offers a more comprehensive view of the artist. The EPK is often less expensive to reproduce and disseminate using the Internet. Several companies, most notably Sonic Bids and Reverb Nation, have begun providing EPK services to artists, giving them a place to store and a means to disseminate electronic press kits.

Publicists are also responsible for media training the artist, for setting up television appearances and press interviews, and holding press conferences. They target a variety of media vehicles, including:

- late night TV shows (Letterman, Leno, Jimmy Kimmel, *Saturday Night Live*, etc.);
- daytime TV shows (Oprah, Regis and Kelly, etc.);
- morning news shows (*Good Morning America*, etc.);
- local newspapers (weeklies and dailies);
- national entertainment and music magazines;
- trade publications such as *Billboard*;
- online e-zines and blogs;
- local TV shows (in support of concert touring);
- cable TV shows (including music television channels, but for news and feature items, not airplay).

Advertising

Advertisers determine where to place their advertising budget based on the likelihood that the advertisements will create enough of a sales increase to justify

Bio Short for biography. The brief description of an artist's life or music history that appears in a press kit.

Tear sheets A page of a publication featuring a particular advertisement or feature and sent to the advertiser or public relations firm for substantiation purposes; or copies of previous articles.

Discography A bibliography of music recordings.

Press kit An assemblage of photos and other information that provides background on an artist.

their expense. Advertisers must be familiar with their market and consumers' media consumption habits in order to reach their customers as effectively as possible.

Consumers are targeted through radio, television, billboards, direct mail, magazines, newspapers, the Internet, and mobile media. **Consumer advertising** is directed towards potential buyers to create a "pull" marketing effect of buyer demand. **Trade advertising** targets decision makers within the industry, such as radio programmers, wholesalers, retailers, and other people, who may be influenced by the advertisements and respond in a way that is favorable for the marketing goals. This creates a "push" marketing effect where the label is more in charge of "creating" the demand.

Advertising is crucial for marketing recorded music, just as it is for other products. The primary advertising vehicle in the recording industry for the major labels is local print publications, done in conjunction with retail stores to promote pricing of new titles, and is referred to as *co-op advertising*. Under co-op advertising, the store places ads in the local media publications promoting sale pricing on new releases. The cost of the ads is passed along to the labels, which will sometimes pay in product, known as free goods, or **cleans**. These are records provided to store that they can sell to customers at retail price. It is a win-win situation because the store ultimately makes more money on the record sale than they would on direct compensation for the cost of the advertisements; and the labels win because they pay out in records (at the wholesale rate) rather than in cash.

In addition to local print media, the record industry relies also on magazine, radio, television, outdoor, and Internet advertising. But the plethora of music and niche music magazines that for decades brought music information to fans has come under financial pressure. As a result of falling revenue and subscriptions, and increased production costs, magazines and newspapers are closing or moving to a web-based service. Several music magazines folded in 2009, including *Blender*, *Vibe*, and *No Depression*.

The impact of advertising is not easy to measure because much of its effect is cumulative or in conjunction with other promotional events such as live performances and radio airplay. *SoundScan* has improved the ability to judge the impact of advertising, but because marketing does not occur in a vacuum, the relative contribution of advertising to sales success remains somewhat of a mystery. The most complex issue facing advertisers involves decisions of where to place advertising. The expansion of media has increased the options and complicated the decision. The chart in Table 12.1 represents a basic understanding of the advantages and disadvantages of the various media options.

Advertising is beginning to shift away from traditional media outlets and towards the Internet for the second time. After initial efforts in the late 1990s by advertisers to reach consumers on the Internet failed to produce the expected results, advertisers pulled back from the Internet, contributing to the burst of the "dot-com" bubble in 2001. Now, advertisers are returning to the Internet as *pay-per-click* (PPC) advertising has offered a new way for advertisers to pay only for those ads that lead to consumer action. Under the old advertising payment method on the Internet, advertisers paid for impressions; in other words, they paid based upon the number of potential customers who saw the ad on a

Consumer advertising Ads directed towards the consumer as compared to trade advertising. Generally, this audience is reached through mass media.

Trade advertising Ads aimed at decision makers in the industry, including people in radio and retail, and booking agents.

Cleans Promotional copies that are not marked as such and may, therefore, be sold at retail. The artists get no royalties for promotional copies.

Table 12.1 Comparison of media for advertising

Medium	Advantages	Disadvantages
Television	Reaches a wide audience but can also target audiences through use of cable channels Benefit of sight and sound Captures viewers' attention Can create an emotional response High information content	Short life span (30–60) seconds High cost Clutter of too many other ads Consumers may avoid exposure May be too broad to be effective
Magazines	High-quality print ads High information content Long life span Can target audience through specialty magazines	Long lead time Position in magazine not always certain No audio for product sampling (unless a CD is included at considerable expense)
Newspapers	Good local coverage Can place quickly (short lead) Can group ads by product class (music in entertainment section) Cost-effective Effective for dissemination of pricing information	Poor quality presentation Short life span Poor attention getting No product sampling
Radio	Is already music-oriented Can sample product Short lead, can place quickly High frequency (repetition) High-quality audio presentation Can segment geographically, demographically, and by musical tastes	Audio only, no visuals Short attention span Avoidance of ads by listeners Consumer may not remember product details
Billboards	High exposure frequency Low cost per exposure Can segment geographically	Message may be ignored Brevity of message Not targeted except geographically Environmental blight
Direct mail	Good targeting Large information content Not competing with other advertising	High cost per contact; must maintain accurate mailing lists Associated with junk mail
Internet	Best targeting; can target based on consumer's interests Potential for audio and video sampling; graphics and photos Can be considered point-of-purchase if product is available online	Slow modem speeds limit quality and speed Effectiveness of this new medium still unknown Does not reach entire market Internet is vast and adequate coverage is elusive
Mobile media	Good targeting Instant exposure to message Potential for viral effect	Limited information Limited "call to action" For only specialty or just-in-time promotions

Source: Adapted from Hutcheson, Tom (2008). *Web Marketing for the Music Business*. Oxford, UK: Elsevier/Focal Press.

website. This is similar to the business model used by magazines and newspapers, where ad prices are set based upon not only the ad size, but also on the circulation—the number of people who read that publication. With the advent of PPC, advertisers pay the website owner only when someone clicks on the ad and is then taken to the advertiser's web page. This provides reduced risk for the advertiser, who only pays when viewers express further interest in their product and respond to the ad.

Radio Promotion

The impact of radio airplay on record sales and artist popularity is still the most powerful singular force for breaking new artists. A 2008 study by Jupiter/Ipsos found that 65 percent of music consumers say radio is their primary means of discovering new music.[2] The reliance on radio to introduce new music to consumers motivates record labels to focus a lot of resources on obtaining airplay. This is done through the promotion department, where radio promotion people engage in personal selling to influence radio programming. A radio program director (**PD**) makes the key decisions as to which music is played on the radio station and which is rejected. As a result, record labels and artists lobby radio program directors to encourage them to play their music. Decisions by radio programmers are the keys to the life of a record and have become the basis for savvy, smart, and creative record promotion people to carry out this lobbying effort.

Here is how songs are typically added to the playlists for those stations that program new music:[3]

1. A record label promotion person, or an independent promoter hired by the label, calls the radio station music director (**MD**) or PD notifying them of an upcoming release. This is typically done several weeks before the release of the song. MDs have specific "call times"—designated times of the week that they will take calls from record promoters. For example, an MD may have call times of Tuesdays and Thursdays, 2 to 4 P.M.
2. Leading up to the **add** date—the day the label is asking that the record be added to the station's playlist, the promoter will call again to tout the positives of the recording and ask that the recording be added to the playlist.
3. The music director or program director considers the promoter's selling points, reviews the trade magazines, **spins** of the recording in other cities, considers current research on the local audience and its preferences, looks at any guidance provided by the station's corporate programmers/consultants, and then decides whether to add the song.
4. The PD will look for reaction or response to adding the song. The "buzz factor" for a song will be apparent in market research and call-in requests as well as through local and national sales figures.
5. The promoter's work is not done with the "add." After the song is added, the promoter works on getting "spins" or "**rotations**" meaning the number of times a song is played during the week. Light rotation is a record with the fewest spins (usually under 15 per week); a medium rotation record will

PD The person at a radio or TV station in overall charge of all programming for the station. May make music programming decisions if there is no separate music director. This person has authority over everything that goes out over the air.

MD The person responsible for a radio station's playlist of songs.

Add A recording added to the playlist at a radio station, webcaster, or video channel.

Rotation Radio programming term referring to a group of records that is played through in a certain period of time. A station may have several rotations, such as a "power rotation" that is played through entirely every couple of hours and an oldies rotation that is played through every few days. Also refers to video programming.

have between 10 and 25 spins; and heavy rotation is one with more than 20 spins.[4]

Radio playlists have gotten shorter as they tend to rotate through fewer songs than in the past. Add to that the fact that they may only replace a handful of songs each week with new songs, and the likelihood of breaking into to that elite club is bleak for most releases. There may be more than 50 new releases in one week all vying for one of those coveted opening slots in a station's playlist. Radio markets are divided into major, medium, and small markets, depending upon the population served by that media hub. The major markets are the top 30, and are most difficult to break into for airplay (from #1 New York to #30 San Antonio, TX). The medium markets are those ranked from 31 to 100 (from San Jose, CA to Johnson City, TN). Small markets are those above 100 in rank.[5] The smaller markets are easier to break into for airplay because the competition is less, but these small market stations reach fewer listeners.

New forms of "radio" broadcasting, including XM/Sirius satellite radio and webcasting, have opened up the possibility of getting airplay for lesser known artists. The addition of several thousand new radio stations, many with unique formats such as indie bands or regional music, has increased the opportunities for emerging artists. Many of these newer formats have less restrictive and longer playlists, so competing for airplay is not as difficult. Airplay through these media also increase income for the record label because sound recording performance royalties are collected for airplay and distributed to labels (see Chapter 5).

Internet Activities

- Visit www.radio-media.com/markets/main.html and see if your town is on the list. Then look for nearby cities. Where do they fall on the list? You can use the right column to look up particular cities alphabetically. Next, find your hometown market on the left column. What other markets are approximately the same in size?
- Now use Arbitron data to learn more about drive time in your market. Find out how long it takes the average person to commute to work in the morning. What percentage of commuters ride in a car (and are more likely to be listening to radio)? Go to www.arbitron.com/home/content.stm. Click on the button "information for radio stations" or follow the link www.arbitron.com/radio_stations/home.htm.
- Click on reference library or use the link www.arbitron.com/radio_stations/reference.htm. Click on the "metro, market and survey info" button. Then click on the "Metro Commuter Profiler" link. Select your market (or a nearby major market) from the drop down menu. The report will open with Adobe Acrobat Reader. Look at the report. How long does it take the average commuter to get to work in the morning? How much has this gone up (or down) in 10

years? What percentage of commuters ride in cars? Is the percentage of people commuting to work by car higher than the national average? Now compare that with the #1 market New York City.

● Log on to www.youtube.com/watch?v=Cw6xesXLIAA and watch a recording of the launch of MTV. What video images preceded the launch of the first music video? What artist performed that first song? What meaning does that song have for "things to come" in the recording industry?

Music videos

On August 1, 1981, the first music video channel, MTV, launched with the appropriately themed song *Video Killed the Radio Star*, and gave record labels a reason to produce more of the new video entertainment format. Other genre-specific channels soon followed, such as Black Entertainment Television (BET), VH-1 for adult contemporary music, and Country Music Television (CMT). It became evident early on that music video exposure was beneficial to developing artists' careers and promoting their music. Stars like Madonna and Michael Jackson owe a lot of their star power to video exposure. **Telegenics** became an important aspect in artists' careers, forcing record labels to concentrate on signing artists with visual appeal.

Telegenic
Presenting a pleasing appearance on television.

The costs of producing a music video are exorbitant, and record labels must examine the potential return on investment (ROI) for each video produced. Additionally, a plethora of music videos were crowding the airwaves by the early 1990s, so that producing a music video did not automatically guarantee airplay on the major video outlets. Then, these video channels began replacing music videos with non-music television shows, further reducing the exposure for music videos. Labels began to question the ROI for making videos. The budgets for music videos often run around $300,000, so labels are producing fewer of them.[6]

The importance of music videos as a promotional tool still exists, if not for consumer promotion, then to showcase the artist to booking agents for TV shows and concerts. The rise of YouTube, Yahoo! Video, VEVO, and other online video outlets has spurred a new kind of less expensive video format that is more edgy and is an alternative to the slick Hollywood-style videos on cable TV. It is called the **viral** video, but virility is but one component. To begin with, many of the successful viral videos were not actually made by hobbyists but are produced to give that appearance—like the movie the *Blair Witch Project*. Then, because the videos seem to come from "the street" but have interesting qualities, they are passed around as consumers get the impression that they "found it first" and want to share this treasure with their friends. If they had the impression it was a corporate-sponsored mass media product, they would probably not bother with grassroots "sharing" because they would assume everyone would be exposed to it soon enough. Some type of video presence is recommended for all artists regardless of the level of their career or promotion budget.

Viral video and viral marketing A video that becomes popular because of Internet file sharing. Viral marketing is using file sharing and social networks to spread the popularity of a product or recording.

WHEN VIDEOS GO VIRAL

The Internet is full of stories about catchy and interesting videos being shared by hundreds of thousands of people within a few weeks of their release. There are even TV shows such as Tosh 2.0 set up to find and share these. One story involves a little-known folk singer from Canada who wrote a song and produced a video about a problem he had with the way United Airlines treated his guitar while on a flight from his hometown to a concert. After getting frustrated with the airline for their lack of response, the protest song and video "United Breaks Guitars" was released on YouTube on July 6, 2009 and generated a lot of interest—7.5 million hits by January 2010. The popularity garnered a response not only from the airlines, who reversed course, but from the well known guitar company who created a response video about their repair services, to a road case company who took on sponsorship, to traditional news outlets who covered the story on television and in newspapers, and to the Harvard School of Business, who decided to create a case study on the effects of social media.

Grassroots Promotion and Viral Marketing

Grassroots promotion, sometimes called guerrilla marketing or street marketing, consists of avoiding the mass media and traditional promotional channels. Instead, grassroots marketing uses less expensive, nontraditional promotional tools in a bottom-up approach to develop a groundswell of interest at the consumer level that spreads through word of mouth (WOM).

Diffusion of innovations theory discusses the role of "opinion leaders" or trendsetters who are instrumental in the diffusion of any new product, trend, or idea. In grassroots promotion, these opinion leaders are targeted, sometimes by hiring them to work for the artist or label, and their influence on their peers is exploited to promote new products and trends.

Groups of trendsetters that become a part of the promotion establishment are called **street teams**. They are hired to "talk up" a product or artist. Sometimes it is enough to have the street team members adopt the new styles or consume the products visibly in the marketplace (such as drinking Sprite or wearing a new outfit). This peer-to-peer promotion is very influential, especially among younger consumers, because of the credibility or "street cred" of peer recommendations. Record labels commonly have grassroots marketing departments who manage street teams in various geographic locations around the country.

The current popular grassroots trend is viral marketing. *Viral marketing* is a new buzzword for the oldest form of marketing in the world: referral or word of mouth, but with promotional messages attached to the viral communication. Viral marketing is any strategy that encourages individuals to pass on a marketing message to others, spreading exponentially as one group of people pass on the message to each of their friends. This creates an ever expanding nexus of Internet users "spreading the word." Viral marketing capitalizes on social networking and the propensity for Internet users to pass along things they find interesting.

Diffusion of innovations theory The process by which the use of an innovation is spread within a market group, over time and over various categories of adopters.

Street teams Local groups of people who use networking on behalf of the artist in order to reach the artist's target market.

Some examples of viral marketing include:

● *E-mail signature files.* The most common form of viral marketing is through e-mail signature attachments. Hotmail.com and Yahoo! have successfully employed this technique by appending their message to the bottom of every e-mail generated by their users. If that message is passed along, the advertising tag goes with it.
● *Sharing.* Legally sharing free goods, such as software, audio files, videos, links, ring tones, etc. Recipients are inspired to share, or pass along these freebies to their friends.
● *Tell-a-friend script.* These are usually found on the artist's website and can encourage visitors to pass along the information to their friends. A visitor to the site may not have a personal interest, but they may know someone who might.
● *Postings.* Marketers may reach out to fans in forums, chat rooms, and *message boards*, leaving behind links to an artist's site. As people respond to a posting, the original message is usually copied, leading to numerous mentions of the product/artist's name and web address.
● *Online articles and blogs with embedded links.* Electronic press releases with embedded links have the potential to be passed along and republished from blog to blog—links intact.

There is another reason marketers like to uses viral strategies: By spreading links to an artist's website all across the Internet, the search engine ranking for that website is improved.

Other Internet Promotion

Internet promotion is the focus lately of much in the way of promotional efforts. It is common these days for every television show, radio station, and print publication to host its own website. Often these sites can be used for interactive promotional campaigns, such as contests. Contestants who appear on American Idol get their weekly affirmation from viewers who log on to the Internet or use their cell phone to cast their votes. The program benefits from the additional commercial messages viewers are exposed to online.

Building a website is not enough. With all the clutter on the Internet, it is necessary to promote the website by reaching out to web surfers and encouraging them to visit the website. It is a commonly held belief among Internet marketers that most of the website traffic will come from viral and traditional marketing techniques, and word of mouth.

Table 12.2 illustrates the relative importance of various Internet activities for finding new music. While email may not seem like an important activity, it may be important in driving traffic to the website in a two-step process to finding new music.

Promotion for artists and record releases often incorporates a web component for each media event, whether to drive traffic to the media vehicle's website or to encourage fans to sign up for information or prizes. A debut of a new video

Table 12.2 How Internet users find out about new music

Method	Ages 18–35	Ages 36–50	Ages 51+
Going to the website of an artist, band, or record label	41%	38%	30%
Listening to free streaming samples of songs online	46%	25%	21%
Visiting an online store that sells music	42%	32%	26%
Downloading music files to your computer	42%	24%	14%
Listening to an Internet radio station	29%	25%	21%
Reading online reviews or blogs about songs and artists	28%	22%	21%
Watching music videos online	34%	21%	16%
Going to a MySpace profile of an artist, band, or record label	31%	13%	8%
Receiving an email from a band, artist, or record company	15%	9%	8%
Median number of online music-seeking activities	3	2	1
Number of cases (Internet users)	133	171	190

Source: Pew Internet Project: The Internet and Consumer Choice, May 2008

on CMT can be coordinated with a promotion on www.CMT.com, where fans enter contests, get free music, purchase priority tickets, or participate in other promotions. In-store autograph signings by an artist can be publicized on the retailer's website. Tour schedules can include links to each of the venues so the concert attendee can learn more about the venue and its location (where to sit, where to park, etc.).

So each aspect of a marketing plan, whether it is coverage in a particular media vehicle, tour support, or supporting an album at retail, should contain an online counterpart to make the experience interactive for consumers and to drive traffic to the media or retailer's site.

Social networking

The use of social networking to promote artists, both major and minor, has exploded in the past several years. Capitalizing on the power and credibility of word-of-mouth promotion, labels have developed new media marketing teams that act like online street teams. These "ambassadors" reach out to potential fans, "befriending" them on sites such as Facebook, Twitter, and MySpace. Then, the artist or their representatives engage their fans with information and entertainment through the networks. These and other efforts can have a viral effect.

Mobile Media

The wireless handset that we used to refer to as a cell phone is now morphing into a multimedia personal communication device, and continues to grow in popularity around the world. Beginning with the third-generation (3G) handsets a few years ago, mobile data networks and increasingly sophisticated handsets have been providing users with a variety of new media offerings. Whereas the

DIY Activities

Making the Most of Web Promotion

To promote yourself as an artist, you need a strong Internet presence. There are several steps to developing a successful web promotional campaign. The most important is having a home base—preferably a website, but alternatively having an artist page on Facebook, MySpace, or some other hosting site. It helps to own a simple, easy-to-remember domain name. Then you can forward it wherever you want: to your website, your Facebook page, and so forth.

The email newsletter is the single most important piece of communication from the artist to her/his fans. You should collect email addresses from fans at live shows and from visitors to the web page. Be sure registrants grant permission for you to send periodic email newsletters. Then, send one *only* when there is news to report, such as an upcoming show or record release.

Make videos and audio samples available to potential customers so they can sample your music, and provide an e-commerce setting so that fans can order online or purchase downloads of your music. But do not neglect to include bricks and mortar stores that support you.

And finally, do not forget to promote your web presence both online and offline. Announce the web address at gigs, include the web address in all press releases and other communication. Develop contests that tie in show attendance with web visitation. Offer occasional freebies, such as a bonus track, ring tone, screensaver, and so forth. Create a buzz around your website.

Internet and desktop computers have dominated the paradigm shift in the past, the future belongs to wireless mobile technology. Already, the growth of cell phone adoption outstrips Internet adoption. In late 2008, it was estimated that there were over 4.4 billion cell phones in operation globally.

The Pew Internet and American Life Project reported in early 2008 that over 75 percent of Americans use either a cell phone or a personal digital assistant (PDA). And 62 percent of all Americans have some experience with mobile access to digital data of some form, whether it is text messaging or music downloading.

Mobile Internet penetration in the US has been slower than in many European and Asian countries where the communication industries have bypassed wired cable connections in many areas. In 2007, M:Metrics Research reported that only 5.7 percent of mobile subscribers in the US listened to music on their mobile phones, compared to 13 percent in France, 15 percent in Germany, and 19 percent in the UK.[7]

The Pew Center for Research reported in mid-2009 that "more than half of Americans—56 percent—have accessed the Internet wirelessly on some device, such as a laptop, cell phone, MP3 player, or game console."[8] By April 2009, nearly one third of Americans had used mobile devices to access the Internet for emailing, instant messaging, or information seeking. The same study found that

45 percent of adults have iPods or MP3 players, but only 5 percent of adults have used such a device to go online.

Mobile Music Sales

Until 2007, the majority of music sales for mobile devices took the form of ring tones, or more specifically, **mastertones**—short excerpts from an original sound recording that play when a phone rings. The market for ring tones and mastertones developed in the mid-2000s but saw a decline in sales for the first time in 2007 as consumers moved away from phone personalization features and began to adopt full track downloads to mobile devices.[9] Ring tones accounted for 62 percent of the mobile music market in 2007. Ringtone sales fell by 33 percent in 2008, to 43.8 million units in the US (SoundScan), with a 25 percent reduction in dollar value, from $714 million in 2007 to $541million in 2008.[10] The drop has been attributed to consumers "*side loading*" their own mastertones, meaning they create and load their own ring tones from a computer rather than purchasing them via their mobile network.

The global mobile music market is expected to rise to more than $17.5 billion by 2012, driven by subscriptions and sale of downloads, according to a Juniper Research study released in early 2008.[11] The mobile music market is expected to be more successful in the area of subscription services, unlike the home-computer-based networks that have seen disappointing numbers for music subscription services. A 2009 study by Juniper Research claimed the global mobile music market would double by 2013 to $5.5 billion.[12] In 2009, Japan was the leader in mobile music purchases, with 140 million mobile singles sold in 2008.

Mobile service providers and handset manufacturers are introducing value-added features to cell phone subscribers that include music subscription services. Nokia introduced the "Comes with Music" program in 2008, offering a one-year music subscription service with the purchase of handsets, and the ability to retain music and purchase additional music at the end of the year. Sony-Ericsson's PlayNow(tm) plus "allows users to download, play, and recommend music wherever they are and whenever they like, directly over the mobile network."[13]

Marketing to Mobile

The emerging area of mobile use creates new challenges for marketing music to mobile devices. The mobile industry continues to test unique marketing ideas to get music consumers more involved with using mobile devices for music discovery and consumption.

- Advertising via cell phones. According to Nielsen in 2008, over 60 percent of mobile subscribers use text messaging on a regular basis and texting is now more prevalent than voice calls. As a result of the popularity of text messaging, cell phone marketers have begun using push messages to consumers' cell phones to market products. SMS (short message service) messages are limited to text only and to 160 characters. Despite its limitations, it has proven to be highly effective in generating high response rates.

In a UK study of teens by Q Research, they found that teens were open to receiving ads on their cell phones as long as the ads were targeted to their interests and especially if they offered coupons.[14] US teens are twice as likely as adults to accept mobile advertisements.[15] Although currently the majority of advertising on cell phones takes place through text messaging, marketers are beginning to look at other options including voice messaging, graphics, and video ads.

- Voice messaging. Some artists are beginning to use voice marketing messages to communicate with fans who have opted to receive such messages on their mobile devices. In 2008, Disney and Wal-Mart launched a campaign where kids could sign up to receive a prerecorded wakeup call from Hannah Montana.[16]
- Tickets and coupons via mobile images. Concert promoters and airlines are beginning to offer ticketing and boarding passes via cell phones. A bar code image is delivered to the phone to be scanned at the gate. Retailers are beginning to accept coupons in the form of phone images. In 2010, Juniper Research predicted that nearly 15 billion coupons would be delivered via mobile devices by 2014.[17] Presently, much of the marketing surrounding mobile phone couponing is still tied to Internet access, but Bluetooth and other proximity transmission systems such as GPS will soon be delivering marketing content to willing consumers directly on their mobile devices, including bar code images that can be scanned at the point of sale. Coupons are delivered based upon the customer's proximity to the item on sale. For example, customers of a particular restaurant chain can sign up to receive a mobile coupon when they reach the parking lot of the restaurant.
- Mobile promotional campaigns. Marketing company Mozes develops mobile marketing campaigns for artists such as Taylor Swift and Racal Flatts. The company boasted having 5 million subscribers by late 2009. Fans can sign up for alerts that may allow for advance ticket purchases, or first access to a new track from their favorite artist.
- Push/Pull and viral marketing via text messaging. A mobile push message is a specially formatted SMS text message that gives the receiver the option of connecting directly to a particular wireless application protocol (WAP) (mobile Internet) site, using their phone's browser. In other words, the text message has a link; by clicking on the link, the user's cell phone is directed to a special mobile friendly website. The majority of mobile campaigns today use (SMS) messaging.

A mobile pull marketing strategy involves using some other form of medium to request that users send a text message in response to the advertiser's call to action. An example of pull marketing would be the American Idol TV show that encourages viewers to "text in" their votes.

Viral marketing campaigns are new to cell phones and incorporate the notion of recipients passing along the message to others. The four factors to successful viral campaigns on cell phones include: (1) offer exclusive content: something that is not available on the Internet but only via cell phones; (2) make it useful and timely: i.e. concert times, directions to venues; (3) make the "call to action" straightforward; (4) make it simple for recipients to pass along the message to others.[18]

Mobile Websites

Marketers are also developing special WAP websites for mobile devices. These sites are pared down versions designed to be manageable on a small mobile screen. The content is also limited to that which is important for consumers on the go, such as show times and directions to venues. Additionally, these sites are being developed to accommodate a wide variety of mobile handsets, often by creating several WAP sites and relying on information from the handset before the correct version is downloaded to the consumer.

Tour Support

Tour support in the broad marketing context (compare "Tour support" as a recording contract term in Chapter 9) involves money and/or services that a record company provides to help promote an artist on the road and ultimately sell more records. This is one aspect of promotion that is crucial for independent artists and those on indie labels. Generally, indie label marketing budgets do not allocate for retail product placement, radio airplay, or advertisements. So the indie artist must rely on touring to build a fan base and generate record sales. Marketing tour support consists of contacting local media and retail in each market where the artist is to appear and providing any promotional materials and support necessary, including appearances. Aspects of tour support may be handled by publicists and the sales department of a label. The publicist is responsible for getting local media coverage and arranging for the artist to appear for interviews and impromptu performances on TV and radio. The sales department is responsible for setting up retail promotions and in-store appearances by the artist for autograph signings.

Major labels may offer tour support in the form of financial compensation for expenses incurred on the road, such as transportation, equipment rental, and accommodations. They may offer these in addition to the support functions mentioned in the previous paragraph (see Chapter 9).

Special Markets and Products

With traditional record sales on the decline, labels and artists are always looking for new ways to make money from selling music, often referred to as special markets and special products. Getting songs included in a movie, on a TV show, or in a commercial are some examples of special markets. Compilations and samplers are special products that the industry has traditionally relied upon to boost CD sales. The *Now That's What I Call Music* compilations of hit singles rode high on the charts in the 2000s. The Christian music counterpart *Wow* also topped the charts. But the rise of digital *a-la-carte* tracks has taken the luster off of hit compilations since consumers can now just purchase the tracks they want.

Digital formats have allowed the special markets options to develop even further, with record companies trying out all sorts of new business models to make money from recorded music. Social networking sites such as MySpace have made agreements with record labels to share advertising revenue in exchange for licensing their music to the site for streaming. MySpace has also launched MySpace Music Videos. Microsoft agreed to pay record labels a small token for each one of its Zune hardware players sold in exchange for offering music tracks for download that are compatible with the hardware.

Labels have begun partnering with ISPs (Internet service providers), starting with TDC's Play service in Denmark in 2009.[19] Subscription services, which accounted for only 5 percent of global digital sales in the late 2000s, may get a second life with mobile subscription services. Nokia's Comes with Music expanded to 11 countries in 2009. Spotify is the fastest growing advertiser-supported streaming music service. The VEVO advertiser-supported music video service was launched by Universal, Sony, and YouTube in 2009. Hula is another service offering music videos and live concerts online.

Place

The fourth and final "P" in the chain is place, meaning where records are sold and how they are made accessible to the consumer. Aspects of the place element include distribution, inventory management, retailing, retail promotions, delivery of goods, and customer service. As with the other three marketing elements, the places in which music is sold have undergone drastic changes in the past 10 years, with many of the traditional retail outlets either abandoning music or folding.

Distribution of Recorded Music

Music distributors are important for getting both physical and digital music in the hands of retailers. Since the advent of the Internet, traditional stores are being referred to as "bricks and mortar" stores, in comparison with online shopping in the virtual retail market. The concept of using a distributor, wholesaler, or other "middleman" in the process of moving any product from manufacturers to retailers can be illustrated by Figures 12.1 and 12.2. Without distributors, the number of contacts between labels and retailers is a function of the number of labels multiplied by the number of retailers (L x R). With the inclusion of a distributor, the number of contacts is reduced to the number of labels plus the number of retailers (L + R).

The Big 4 Distributors

Consolidations in the past 10 years have reduced the number of major labels with their own distribution to four: Warner Music Group's WEA, Universal Music Group's UMVD, Sony Music Entertainment's SME, and EMI's EMD. The major labels also own "indie" distributors that focus on music from indie labels, including RED, Caroline, and ADA.

Under this umbrella, most recorded music is distributed through three primary channels: distributors, rack jobbers, and one-stops. A *one-stop* is a record

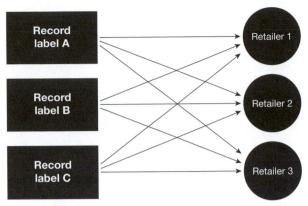

Figure 12.1 Distribution without a middleman

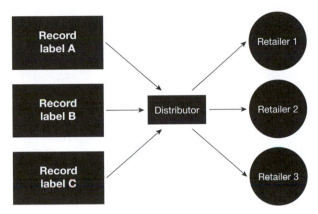

Figure 12.2 Distribution with a middleman

wholesaler that stocks product from many different labels and distributors for resale to retailers, rack jobbers, mass merchants, and juke box operators. Once the provider for juke box operators, they are now prime source of product for small mom & pop retailers. Occasionally, when major chains run short on top-selling titles, they may turn to a one-stop for *fill-in* until the next shipment from their distributor. A *rack jobber* is a company that supplies records, cassettes, and CDs to department stores, discount chains, and other outlets and services ("racks") music and/or video departments with the right music mix. Rack jobbers typically supply the "big Box" stores like Wal-Mart and Target. Since the demise of Handleman in 2008 there are only two major recording rack jobbers: Alliance Entertainment and Anderson Merchandisers.

Bricks and Mortar Store Types

There are several types of stores (Figure 12.3) where records are sold. They are generally categorized as follows and account for about 70 percent of album sales in 2009.

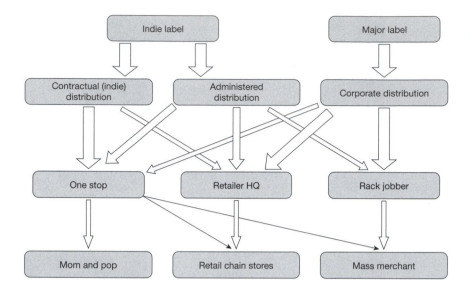

Figure 12.3 Distribution channels for music product

- Independent music stores cater to a specific niche market, and are generally owned and operated by someone with a keen interest in the genre(s) of music featured in the store. They may get product from one-stops as well as focusing on the used CD market. Independent stores (including "mom and pop" stores) accounted for about 6 percent of album sales in 2009.
- **Mom and pop** retailers, also a one-store operation, are generally owner managed with a personal understanding of their customer base. They also often get their inventory from one-stops and may trade in used CDs.
- Alternative music stores are generally life-style oriented, with other product lines that appeal to their market. They may carry collectable items as well as vinyl titles.
- Chain stores have multiple locations under the same ownership usually in multiple cities. SoundScan has moved some multi-location stores out of the "chain" classification for purposes of reporting the place of purchase. Chains attract customers who are looking for more variety and more depth than they can find in other record stores. They often participate in promotional campaigns sponsored by the labels. They receive their music from their central distribution centers—purchased directly from the distributors. As sales of CDs declined, so did the number of operating chains and the number of chain stores. Bankruptcies, mergers, and downsizing took their toll, reducing the number of available traditional record stores to the point where the largest chain, Trans World Entertainment, which operated the FYE, Wherehouse Music, and Secs Music stores, was reduced to fewer than 800 stores by 2010. Trans World had plans to further reduce the number of outlets in 2010. Chain stores accounted for about 29 percent of album sales in 2009.

- Electronic superstores do not make a profit from CD sales, but carry them to create traffic in the store. They are very likely to engage in loss-leader pricing for new titles. They buy their inventory directly from the distributors.
- Mass merchants, such as Wal-Mart and Target, use the sale of music as event marketing for their stores, hoping that the new releases each week will bring customers back to the store. They are most likely to use rack jobbers to supply the music mix to their stores. They and the electronic superstores accounted for about 36 percent of album sales in 2009.

Digital Distribution and Retailing

The digital distribution of music on the Internet, and ultimately mobile devices, has been a two-edged sword. The problems of illegal peer-to-peer file sharing are abundantly obvious: The IFPI reports that 95 percent of all music downloads are illegal copies. The IFPI states that "[T]he growth of illegal file-sharing has been a major factor in the decline in legitimate music sales over the last decade, with global industry revenues down around 30 percent from 2004 to 2009."[20] Efforts by the RIAA to thwart illegal file sharing by arresting offenders have not been successful in discouraging the practice. More recent efforts are aimed at ISPs. These services have the capability to monitor and remove offenders. As these companies move more into the area of content ownership themselves (Comcast purchased Universal/NBC in 2009), they have a vested interest in discouraging the practice, which also tends to hog bandwidth from law-abiding users.

Nonetheless, the digital sector is the only growth area in recorded music sales this century. Global digital revenues grew by an estimated 12 per cent in 2009 totaling US$ 4.2 billion and accounting for 27 per cent of music sales (including tracks and albums), up from 21 per cent in 2008. According to a study by the NPD Group in 2009, physical CDs in the US were accounting for 65 percent of all sales in the first half of 2009, while digital sales were accounting for 35 percent. This is up from 20 percent a year earlier.

One of the advantages of digital distribution is that there is no inventory depletion, meaning that the sale of one unit does not deplete the inventory of available units for sale. This provides drastic cost savings for labels. With physical product, the industry operated with an average return rate of 20 percent. In other words, 20 percent of all units shipped were ultimately returned to the manufacturer unsold. The costs of manufacturing, shipping, handling, return shipping, and processing added to the operating expenses of a label. If return rates were reduced through a reduction in number of units manufactured, there was always the risk of **stockouts**—product unavailable for customers seeking it out in retail stores. Computer-assisted inventory management systems in the 1990s did help reduce inventory management costs, which helped with the industry's bottom line. This was further improved by the implementation of automatic inventory replenishment systems, which would monitor record store sales and automatically reorder new stock for titles whose inventory was reaching critical levels. But as digital distribution begins to dominate market share, the issues associated with physical product management disappear.

Stockout
A situation where the demand or requirement for an item cannot be fulfilled from the current inventory.

Digital distribution has leveled the playing field somewhat for independent artists. Emerging artists used to struggle to get any physical distribution to retail outlets. Now, there is a plethora of online retail outlets catering to both major and developing artists. In 2009, iTunes was the top US digital retailer, with 69 percent of the digital market, while Amazon had 8 percent. Wal-Mart is another major player in the online retail sector. These online retail giants have direct distribution deals with the majors. The one exception is Sony, who have a unique agency deal with Amazon, whereby they maintain control of their online inventory and pricing and Amazon charges a commission. Other online music distribution networks include Tunecore, Ioda, IRIS, Songcast, and The Orchard. Online retailers for indie artists include CD Baby, AmieStreet, and EMusic.

Retail Promotions

Since radio is the most important promotional tool for influencing consumers to buy new music, it would seem that music retailers would use radio as their primary advertising vehicle to promote their stores and products. But that is not the case. Music retailers rely primarily on local print advertising—mainly the Sunday circulars—for sales and featured products on a host of media items, including music, movies, and videogames. Major retailers such as Best Buy and Wal-Mart now use these ads as a way to promote new releases that are being offered on sale the following Tuesday.

Listening stations Reintroduced into record stores in the early 1990s, these offered customers the option to preview tracks on albums they were considering for purchase. Most often, these customers had heard only one track on the radio and wanted to preview the rest of the album before making the final purchase decision.

End cap In retail merchandising, a display rack or shelf at the end of a store aisle; a prime location for stocking product.

Promotional activities inside record stores feature particular releases to motivate consumers to purchase the titles being promoted. It is often said that the last 10 feet before the cash register is the most influential real estate for promotional activities. "Whether it is **listening stations** near a coffee bar outlet or posters hanging in the front window, a brief encounter within the store's walls will quickly identify the music that the store probably sells."[21]

The decision of which titles to feature is often decided by the labels, although some retail chains are beginning to take the initiative to decide upon their own which titles should be offered at sale pricing (see pages 254–255). Labels create promotional campaigns that feature a specific title, coordinated via the retailer through an advertising vehicle called cooperative advertising. Co-op advertising is usually the exchange of money from the label to the retailer, so that a particular release will be featured. The following are examples of co-op as given by Hutchison, Macy, and Allen (2009) *Record Label Marketing* (2nd Edition). Oxford: Focal Press (used by permission).[22]

- Pricing and position. P&P is when a title is sale-priced and placed in a prominent area within the store.
- **End caps**. Usually themed, this area is designated at the end of a row and features titles of a similar genre or idea.
- Listening stations. Depending on the store, some releases are placed in an automatic digital feedback system where consumers can listen to almost any title within the store. Other listening stations may be less sophisticated and may be as simple as using a free-standing CD player in a designated area. But all playback devices are giving consumers a chance to "test drive" the music before they buy it.

- **POP**, or point of purchase materials. Although many stores will say that they can use POP, including posters, flats, stand-ups, etc., some retailers have advertising programs where labels can be guaranteed the use of such materials for a fee
- Print advertising. As a primary advertising vehicle, a label can secure a "mini" spot in a retailer's ad (a small picture of the CD cover art), which usually comes with sale pricing and featured positioning (P&P) in store.
- In-store event. Event marketing is a powerful tool in selling records. Creating an event where a hot artist is in store and signing autographs of his or her newest release guarantees sales while nurturing a strong relationship with the retailer.

> **POP materials** Include posters, flats, stand-ups, window displays, etc. Some retailers have advertising programs where labels can be guaranteed the use of such materials for a specific release.

As a larger percentage of record sales move to the Internet—for physical sales as well as downloads—many well known retailers have been forced to close their doors. Tower Records is one example. Other retailers have simply reduced the amount of floor space dedicated to recorded music and have begun to diversify if they had not already done so. In 2007, the National Association of Recording Merchandisers (NARM) awarded the large retailer of the year award to Amazon.com, the first for an online retailer.

Retailers sometimes create "branded" CDs that are special editions available only through the sponsoring retailer. This concept is popular with all types of retailers, not just record retailers, because it draws traffic into the stores. Hallmark, Williams-Sonoma, and Starbucks are nontraditional retailers who use special products to draw customers to their retail establishments. In 2007, the Eagles decided to release their new album only in Wal-Mart stores. In exchange for the exclusive opportunity to offer the album, Wal-Mart spent a lot of money promoting the album that otherwise would have been spent by the record label— or, in some cases, not spent at all.

All this effort is being spent by retailers and labels to stem the tide of dwindling music sales through bricks and mortar stores. Record stores that have folded or been absorbed into entities offering other products include Blockbuster Music, Circuit City, Media Play, Musicland, National Record Mart, Peaches, Record Bar, Strawberries, Tower Records, The Wall, Wherehouse Music, and Virgin Megastores. By mid-2009, iTunes was the number one music retailer in the US with 25 percent of the market share, followed by Wal-Mart with 14 percent. Rounding out the top five were Best Buy, Amazon, and Target.[23]

Outlook

The record business is undergoing dramatic changes this century, beginning with the challenges caused by rampant piracy of intellectual property. But the advances in technology that have brought on these challenges also offer opportunities to change the way the recorded music business has always operated. In the first one hundred years, the recording industry operated as a product-oriented business—creating and selling physical products. It is now moving towards digital products, but may be headed towards providing music services instead of products. Music ownership is still important to consumers, but as mobile devices begin to replace computers for providing more of our information and entertainment, there is potential for monetizing recorded music in new ways. This drastically alters not only the first "P," product, but also pricing, promotion and, of course, place.

Case Study: Lady Gaga *The Fame* album

On October 28, 2008[24] Interscope Records launched the US release of *The Fame* (or *Fame*), the debut album of artist/songwriter Lady Gaga. The first single,"Just Dance," had been released on April 8, 2008 to set up the album release and create an upfront demand. The single did not enter the *Billboard* Hot 100 Chart until August 19, after spending the summer on the *Billboard* Hot Dance Music–Club Play chart. "Just Dance" took 22 weeks to climb the *Billboard* Hot 100 chart, finally peaking in January 2009. There was no unique sales spike evident since this was just after the holiday sales spike and the single had been out for several months (see Figure 12.4).

But in February, the rise of the second single, "Poker Face," and the momentum of having two singles in the top ten, began to show in sales (Figure 12.5). From a low of 18,000 album sales the week of February 1, the sales climbed each week to a high of 56,000 for the week of April 12. During this time, "Poker Face" was climbing up the top twenty-five, peaking at number one on April 11.

"Poker Face" remained near the top through early June, while the next hit single, "Love Game," was concurrently climbing the Hot 100 chart. On the week of June 7, the two singles captured the fifth and sixth slots on the chart. During this time, sales rose from a lull on April 19 of 36,000 units, to another peak on June 21 of 47,000 units.

From there, the album slid gradually until September 6, where it hit a low of 18,400 units. But one week later, Lady Gaga took home the Best New Artist award from the MTV Video Award show, and was nominated in two other categories. Her single "Paparazzi" entered the Hot 100 chart at the same time. This brought a temporary spike in sales through September 22 with sales of 33,255. In mid-October, "Paparazzi," the next single, peaked at #6, but had little immediate effect on sales. However, the single stayed in the top ten for several weeks after that.

She had a remarkable performance on the American Music Awards on November 22 and a performance the next night on the Jay Leno primetime show. The momentum from this and a feature in the December issue of Vogue magazine carried the album into the Thanksgiving weekend, with reported one-week sales of over 151,000 units. The average album sales spike for Thanksgiving 2009 (week #48) ran about double the fall low point in week #43. For *The Fame*, sales numbers went from 28,600 for the week of November 22 to over 151,000 the week of November 29–a five-fold increase (see Figure 12.6).

The announcement of her Grammy nominations on December 2 contributed to a second holiday spike of over 168,000 units leading up to Christmas (Figure 12.7). Typical for the after Christmas lull, the album slid to just under 62,000 units by January 24, but the Grammy Awards show and her Grammy win contributed to another spike of almost 80,000 units on February 7, 2010.

The overnight sensational rise of Lady Gaga to stardom was anything but overnight. She was signed to Def Jam records in 2005, but was dropped after three months.

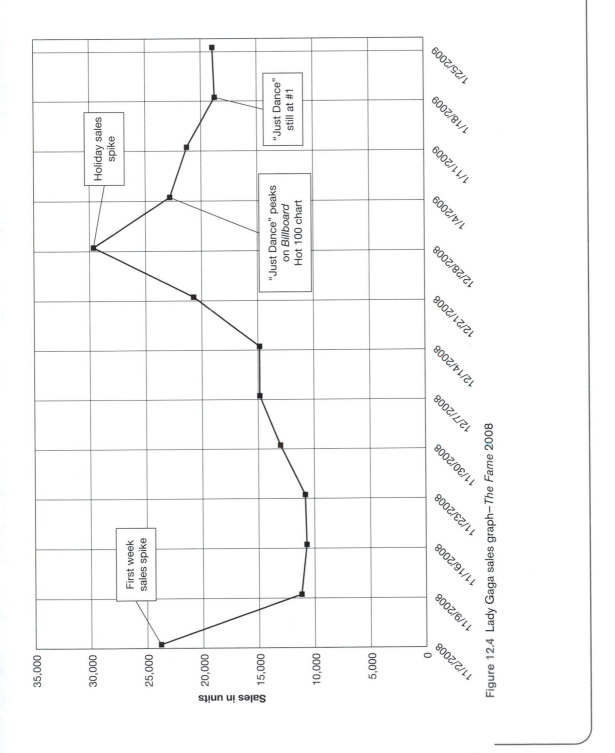

Figure 12.4 Lady Gaga sales graph–*The Fame* 2008

Continued

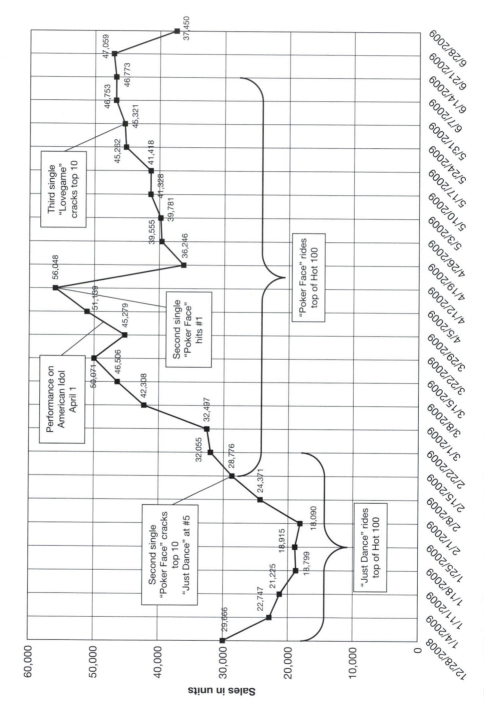

Figure 12.5 Lady Gaga sales graph–*The Fame* early 2009

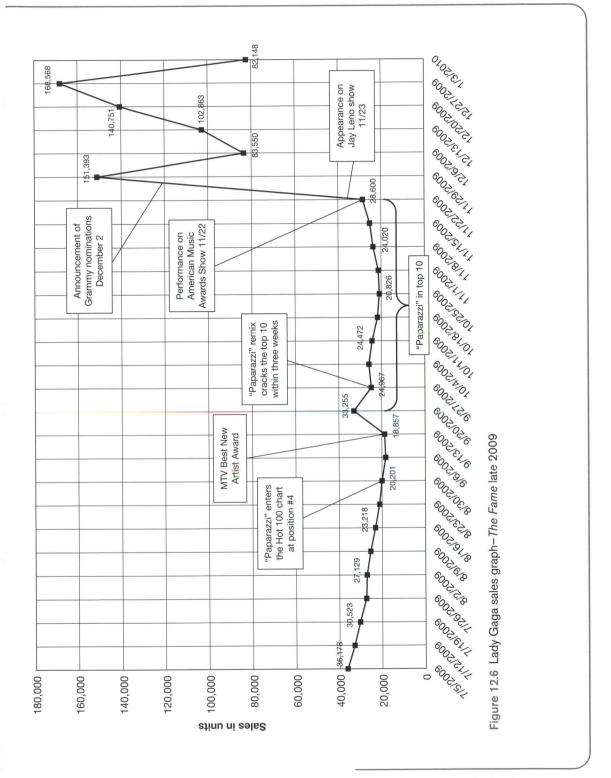

Figure 12.6 Lady Gaga sales graph–*The Fame* late 2009

Continued

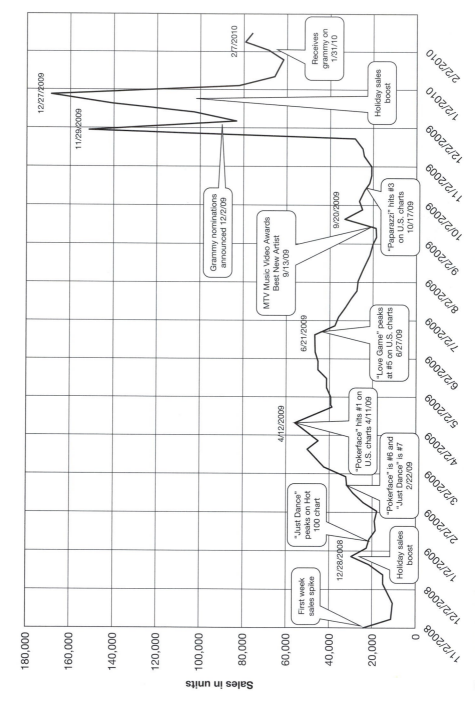

Figure 12.7 Lady Gaga sales graph–*The Fame*

In 2007, she was signed to Interscope Records, after a stint as a professional songwriter. She began work in this album in 2008, and the album *The Fame* was actually released into the marketplace in August 2008, although the US rollout did not really begin until October 28, 2008 after she had already enjoyed international success with the album. For US sales, it got off to a slow start, perhaps because much of the appeal is in her visual media performances. As singles were released to the US charts, one right behind the other, momentum was building. When this momentum began to include video performances in late 2009, she had reached the fame she sings about on *The Fame*.

QUESTIONS FOR REVIEW

- Define promotion. What activities does it involve?
- How do the recording labels engage in promotion with radio, advertising, retail, and tour support?
- Be able to define radio terms: spins, rotation, add, PD, MD.
- What is "viral" promotion?
- How can labels use mobile (cell phone) marketing?
- What are the Majors' distribution arms?
- What do rack jobbers and one-stops do?
- What is the current state of "bricks and mortar" retailing?
- What is the current state of digital retailing?
- What are labels and stores doing to encourage more CD sales in the face of a dwindling market?

13 The Global Music and Recording Business

Introduction

As the first decade of the new millennium comes to an end, traditional international boundaries that have defined countries, economic regions, and the global entertainment industry have irrevocably changed. What has taken their place is a global market that continues to provide companies and individuals the opportunity to sell and purchase goods from far flung corners of the planet. Today the entertainment industry, as well as the music industry, is a global industry with a potential audience of over six billion people. Furthermore, the international music industry has become an important component of economic growth, employment, trade, and innovation for developed and developing countries. For music companies, foreign markets are attractive because of the possibility of additional revenues beyond the company's home market. Exporting music products beyond national boundaries often requires minimal additional costs, as economies of scale increase the potential of products on an international market. Nonetheless, entering the global market requires the interaction between economic, cultural, technological, and social attributes. Even with restrictions, the production, consumption, and trade of music on a global level have become the norm for the music industry and will continue to develop in the near future.

Because the major international music markets differ in so many aspects, there is no single "case study" in this chapter. Rather each region is examined and one country in that region is profiled for sake of comparison.

KEY CONCEPTS

- The music industry operates in a global market.
- Interconnectedness of different markets has led to the globalization of economic systems since the 1950s.
- Cultural sovereignty is a major issue within the globalization of the world.
- Special international organizations monitor and provide a forum for disputes between nations, such as the WTO and WIPO.
- Countries engage in international trade through trading blocs, through a free trade agreement, or through other associations.
- The global music industry is divided into five regions:
  North America; Latin America; Europe; Africa; Asia pacific.

World Music Business

Global market demand for entertainment commodities continues to rise steadily, particularly within the entertainment and media industry. Entertainment and media spending is projected to reach $495 billion in the US by 2013.[1] A report by the United Nations Conference on Trade and Development (UNCTAD) stated that the value of world exports of creative industry goods and services reached $424.4 billion in 2005 as compared with $227.4 billion in 1996.[2] In many respects, technology has played an important role in the dissemination and distribution of music products throughout the globe.

Although the music industry has seen rapid growth of international markets over the past decade, developed countries dominate the global music industry, both in terms of products and market size. The US music market accounts for 44 per cent of global spending on entertainment and media, and is likely to remain the largest market, given current trends. In Europe, Germany dominates the region with a market share of 23 percent followed by the United Kingdom and the Netherlands with about 10 percent each.[3] As with the US market, multinational recording labels and their subsidiaries represent 80 percent of the world market for recorded music.

Globalization

Globalization is a widely used term that has multiple definitions. As a term, globalization often describes the increasing internationalization of business activities by companies on a worldwide level. The term also refers to the trend away from distinct national economic, cultural, legal, and political boundaries towards a single global market. This unified global market has come about through the elimination of trade barriers and the harmonization of intellectual property laws across national boundaries. The "free trade" theory states that goods and services should be produced wherever they can be most efficiently made. As a consequence of open international trade, smaller countries are able to gain access to larger markets in which they can sell their music products. Although there are benefits associated with open markets, companies face greater competition, both from international and regional firms. This requires music companies to restructure in an effort to meet the new demands associated with operation in multiple markets. Music companies use a variety of techniques to engage in the global music market, including:

1. Licensing and rights purchasing. This technique involves the sale of licenses to companies in another country to produce a domestic product. Recording labels may sell a license to a sister or subsidiary company and to others interested in purchasing rights to sell the recording in a specific region.
2. Joint ventures. As a business structure, joint ventures involve two organizations entering into an equitable partnership to produce a recording or other musical product. At the conclusion of the production, each company will obtain the exclusive right to distribute the product in their nation or region.

3. Direct foreign investment. This technique involves a firm purchasing an existing company in another nation or establishing a subsidiary firm in that country (see Figure 13.1). Companies engage in this practice for several reasons, especially when local markets are either mature or saturated. Foreign investment is an opportunity to grow without diversification into other businesses. Finally, companies engage in foreign investment, especially in countries that have national regulations that inhibit expansion due to anti-trust laws.

Globalization and Culture

Business leaders, academics, and politicians have debated the advantages and disadvantages of globalization in recent years. Proponents of free trade state that globalization has opened markets to previously restricted foreign goods. For example, free trade advocates argue that globalization has resulted in the spread of cultural products such as "**Bollywood**" films, world music, ethnic foods, to name a few. In contrast, critics state that globalization has opened the way for large multinational corporations to dominate national cultural markets, thereby destroying local input and creating **cultural hegemony**.

Culture, in the broadest sense, is the collection of images, texts, and ideas through which we make sense and meaning of our world. Our culture helps us frame and shape our identity—both individually and collectively—and how we view the world. Nonetheless, our cultural identity is not something we choose but find ourselves belonging to. As such, culture is never static. It morphs and changes over time as societies grow and come into contact with other cultures. Many scholars believe that there is never an equitable exchange of ideas and business practices between cultures. Established organizations have greater access to capital, knowledge, and technology, thereby giving them an advantage over local cultural organizations. This inevitably leads to three negative outcomes:

1. Cultural corruption. This theory (established by the Frankfurt School, which includes scholars such as Theodore Adorno, Max Horkeimer, and Jurgen

Bollywood Refers to the Indian film production industry centered in Mumbai (formerly Bombay).

Cultural hegemony The theory that a dominant culture or class can assert itself through ways, especially in mass communication messages, that appear "normal." In this way the dominant culture or class can continue to rule while ordinary people are unaware that they are being influenced or dominated.

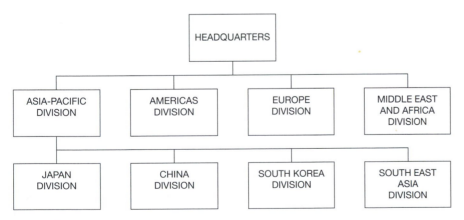

Figure 13.1 International corporate structure

Habermas) states that an introduced culture will manipulate the general population, thereby leading to the moral and societal decay of that culture.
2. Cultural imperialism. This theory states that interaction between various cultures will inevitably lead to conflict. The outcome of such interaction will lead to one society reacting to the introduced culture, either through rejection, violence, or the domination of the alien culture and the eradication of traditional cultures. For example, those who oppose globalization state that of the 25 top selling recording artists of all time (as of March 2010) 17 were American.
3. Cultural homogenization. A theory that states corporate-produced mass entertainment will move individual values towards those associated with mass consumer capitalism. Many see that American companies have such an advantage in economies of scale, organization, efficiency, and superior marketing that they will drive traditional producers out of business. For example, in 1981 MTV was created in the US for a local cable market. In just 10 years after its creation, MTV was available in 201 million households in 77 countries ranging from Australia to Brazil to Hong Kong. MTV Europe grew from 3 million households in 1988 to 14 million in 1991. By 1992 the number of households that had access to MTV Europe had grown to 37 million.

International Music Piracy

Illegal copying and sale of music has been an issue for the music industry for over 100 years. However, with the rapid expansion of national and international markets due to globalization, the potential for massive piracy is now a reality that the international music industry faces. The International Federation of the Phonographic Industry (IFPI) claims that "piracy results in job losses, undermines creativity and deprives governments of tax revenues . . . Adequate intellectual property rights and effective enforcement are the bedrock of a modern economy."[4]

Piracy is a blanket term covering a variety of activities, including counterfeiting, pirating, bootlegging, home recording, and online file sharing. Unlike counterfeiting and pirating, which reproduce recordings already released by labels (and the artwork in the case of counterfeiting), bootlegs are albums that a record label has never officially released. This includes recordings of live concerts or "out-takes" of alternative versions of released songs or songs that did not make it onto the finished album. Despite claims that bootlegging is rampant, the practice has always been a small-scale activity. Nonetheless, the effects of counterfeiting, piracy, and online file sharing have had a significant effect on the music industry, which has resulted in national and international efforts to reduce or stop this practice.

Commonly, when one thinks of piracy, it is imagined that pirated discs are created from factories that run off thousands of CDs and DVDs. The IFPI estimates that "37 percent of all CDs purchased (legally or otherwise) in 2005 were pirate—1.2 billion pirate CDs in total."[5] Most studies indicate that physical piracy rates are higher in developing countries with limited digital infrastructure.

Nonetheless, several developed countries—Italy, Spain, Greece, Taiwan, and Brazil—have recently had police and government officials dismantle and arrest individuals involved in large-scale physical piracy manufacturing.

Although there are organizations selling cheap copies of music to less discriminating members of the public, piracy has evolved from the physical form to the digital. The flow of pirated digital products is more difficult to track by law enforcement agencies. The large number of individuals involved and the absence of monetary transaction present further challenges for effective cooperation among enforcement agencies. In an effort to combat international music piracy, rights holders undertake different actions in various areas including: (1) educational campaigns; (2) cooperation and coordination at the industry level; and (3) cooperation and legal action by government and intergovernmental agencies.

Education programs throughout the world have targeted public opinion and attitudes towards music piracy. Most educational campaigns stress the unethical aspects of digital piracy, while explaining the potentially damaging financial consequences of such actions. For example, in Australia the Australian Federal Police and Music Piracy Investigations (MPI) have created the "Music for Free" campaign to educate people on the consequences of illegal downloading. At the industry level, there are several programs developed by music organizations to curtail music piracy. The British Phonographic Industry (BPI) protects the interests of its members by enforcing copyright law in the United Kingdom. It does this through a variety of techniques including public relations, criminal litigation, and lobbying the UK government to improve copyright laws both in the UK and abroad. The NMPA (US National Music Publishers' Association) engages with government agencies on legislative, litigation, and regulatory issues. At the international level, the IFPI provides information to members on global music industry statistics, legal strategies, litigation, lobbying and representing members at international intergovernmental agencies.

Governments collaborate on reducing international piracy through various means including legislation, membership with intergovernmental organizations, international treaties, and cooperation with specific countries. At the national level, governments combat piracy using a variety of methods. From a legislative perspective, governments have created laws that make piracy a civil or criminal offense. In the UK the Copyright, Designs and Patents Act 1988 (CDPA) increased criminal sanctions against piracy and enforced powers against piracy and secondary infringement (knowingly enabling or assisting in the infringement of copyright). In the US, the National Intellectual Property Law Enforcement Coordination Council (NIPLECC) is "an interagency council responsible for coordinating US domestic and international IP enforcement activities."[6]

Governments also cooperate on combating piracy through international agencies. In an effort to enforce international copyright protection from an enforcement perspective, Interpol (International Criminal Police Organization) has established the Interpol Intellectual Property Crime Action Group (IIPCAG). This group consists of intergovernmental organizations, national law enforcement agencies, customs authorities, and representatives of industry bodies—such as the IFPI—who provide information, tools, and strategies to combat piracy. Governments also curtail piracy through international agreements.

Becoming a member of an international copyright treaty requires a country to adhere to legal obligations required of signatory nations. Both the WIPO Copyright Treaty and the WIPO Performances and Phonogram Treaty require signatory nations to provide legal protection and remedies against the circumvention of technological protection measures. The TRIPS Agreement requires that all WTO members provide effective criminal remedies for commercial scale infringement. Furthermore, the agreement contains minimum standards for civil, administrative, and criminal enforcement of copyright. The provisions on administrative enforcement also mandate special measures for the seizure of goods at national borders.

Conclusion

The music industry operates within a global market. Record labels, music publishers, and artists are aware that the commercialization of music is no longer limited to national boundaries. The debate on the advantages and disadvantages of globalization has been scrutinized heavily in recent years. Proponents of globalization say that it helps developing nations obtain access to developed countries' markets previously closed due to protectionist measures. Critics of globalization say that it weakens national sovereignty and cultural identity, especially when local music companies must compete with large multinational corporations.

The growth of the music industry has not only opened markets for the legitimate transaction of music, but has facilitated the free movement of illegal (pirated) goods. Governments have used a variety of methods to limit piracy including education, cooperation between industry representatives, and international intergovernmental agencies.

Global Institutions

Introduction

As music markets globalize and an increasing proportion of businesses transcend national boundaries, there is a need for institutions to manage, regulate, and police the global marketplace. In an effort to develop a fair business environment, nations have established several multinational treaties and agencies to govern international trade. For the protection of intellectual property on a global level, the music industry has relied on several international treaties for over one hundred years. Treaties such as the Berne Convention have sought to provide an equitable framework for the recognition of intellectual property beyond national boundaries. In 1996, the WIPO treaty and the WIPO Performances and Phonograms Treaty established anti-circumvention laws with regard to digital rights management. In light of the global reach of the Internet, these treaties encourage the protection of intellectual property by restricting the creation, sale, or distribution of devices that circumvent copyright protection. Similarly, nations have entered into trading agreements to standardize international commerce and open markets through the reduction of tariffs and barriers.

GATT and the WTO

In 1947, leaders of 23 nations created the General Agreement on Tariffs and Trade (GATT) treaty to promote free trade by reducing tariffs and non-tariff barriers to international trade. In 1994, treaty revisions clearly defined intellectual property rights, recognizing their importance in trade and giving protection to copyrights, trademarks, and patents. GATT also created a special exemption for cultural products by providing protection for countries that had expressed concern with nations having a competitive advantage in the production of entertainment. For example, Article 4 states that countries can impose quotas on the number of foreign films that can be distributed and exhibited.

During the Uruguay round of GATT that ended in 1994, signatory nations created the General Agreement on Trade in Service (GATS). GATS allowed signatory nations to develop schedules for the integration of their service and telecommunication industries into the global economy. Many European nations, led by France, argued that audiovisual products should be exempt from the free trade rules in the GATS treaty. The consequence of GATS was the strengthening of international copyright laws governing creative works. However, the agreement also made it easier for international corporations to buy and own companies, especially telecommunication companies, around the world.

The 1994 amendment of GATT also established an international organization with the power to enforce the rules of international trade, the WTO. The WTO's principles are set within the concept of free trade which states that trade should be nondiscriminatory. As such, the WTO has three main goals:

1. free flow of trade;
2. negotiation between nations to open markets;
3. establishment of a forum for trade disputes between member states. (See Figure 13.2 for a complete structure of the WTO.)

Although the WTO is a forum for negotiating outcomes to international trade disputes, companies that have issues with international trade must lobby their home country or those with whom they do business to act on their behalf. (See Figure 13.3 for a description of how disputes are settled by WTO.) The US has cited several countries for restricting global trade in music products. In 1993, the European Union ratified the "1989 Broadcast Directive" requiring the majority of broadcast entertainment—movies, television, and popular music— be reserved for European origin programs "where practical" and "by appropriate means."[7] Although the US has not filed a dispute with the WTO in this matter, a report to Senate Committee on Foreign Relations recommended that the US monitor developments.[8]

The WTO also administers the Agreement on Trade Related Aspects of Intellectual Property Rights, commonly known as TRIPS. As with other international agreements, TRIPS provides a minimum standard for the international

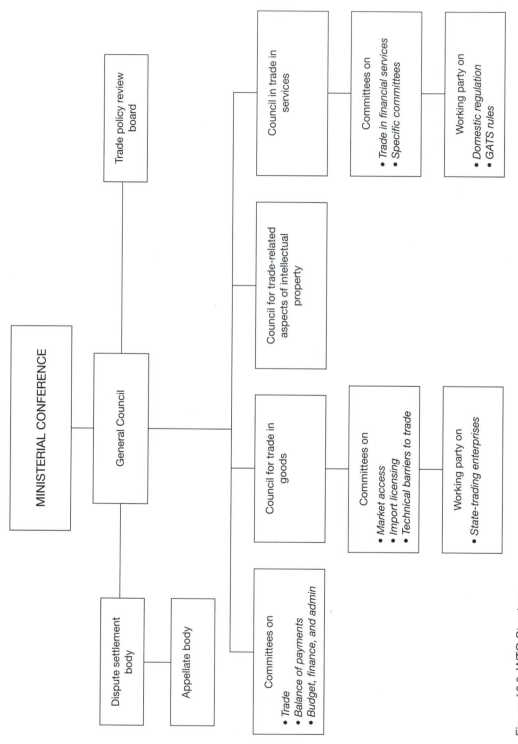

Figure 13.2 WTO Structure

trade of intellectual property, especially with regard to copyright law. In 1999, the EU (represented as the European Communities [EC]) filed a complaint with the WTO against the adoption of the "Fairness in Music Licensing Act" as part of the US Copyright Act. The dispute centered on two exemptions within the Copyright Act that permitted public places (bars, shops, restaurants, and other "establishments") to play radio or television music without royalty payments. The EC considered the statute not consistent with US obligations to the TRIPS agreement. As such, a WTO panel found in favor of the EC. In July 2002, the US Congress decided to create a fund to pay settlement of WTO disputes. Both parties agreed on a temporary arrangement, with the expectation that the US Congress will bring the US Copyright Act into compliance with the TRIPS agreement.

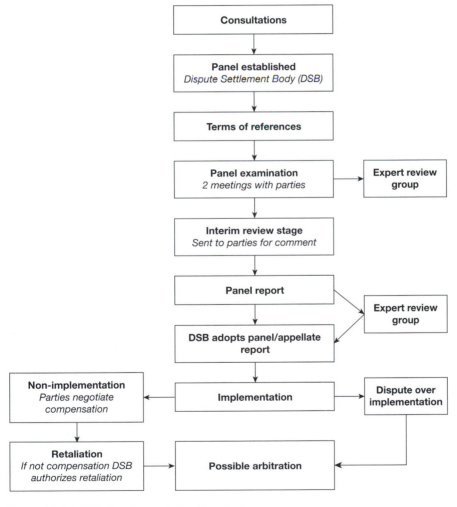

Figure 13.3 WTO dispute resolution flowchart

Trading Blocs

Apart from international treaties dealing with the protection of intellectual property, trading blocs have played an important role in the creation of a global music market. The aim of such treaties is not only the improvement of economic growth, but social progress and cultural exchange among member nations. To achieve these goals, intergovernmental organizations have reduced or eliminated regional barriers to trade. The effect of such legislation for music consumers in participating nations is the availability of foreign music products at lower prices due to the elimination of custom duties. Mansfield and Milner[9] divide trading blocs into five categories based on the level of economic integration among member nations:

1. economic and monetary unions (European Monetary Union);
2. common markets (European Economic Area);
3. customs unions (European Customs Union);
4. preferential trading areas (North America Free Trade Agreement);
5. free trade areas (European Free trade Area); see Table 13.1 for a listing of trade blocs in each category.

Preferential Trading Areas (PTAs) are trading blocs where participating nations—often within a geographic region—have trading agreements. In most cases, countries will agree to reduce tariffs between member states, with the eventual goal of eliminating them entirely. An example of a PTA is the North American Free Trade Agreement (NAFTA). NAFTA came into existence in 1994 covering trade between Mexico, the United States, and Canada. The goal of NAFTA was to eliminate trade barriers between the three member states. The entertainment industries of all the member states were explicit in the adoption of a "national treatment" standard. In other words, each member state must provide nationals of other countries with treatment that is "no less favorable" than that which it accords its own citizens.

However, the three nations had difficulty in reaching agreement in the sale of cultural goods. Canadian officials argued against free trade in entertainment products between the three countries, especially the US, in an effort to protect their own cultural identity and economic viability. Many US entertainment companies pressured the US government to reject protectionist cultural trade clauses in NAFTA for a wide range of entertainment goods including films, TV programs, home videos, books, and sound recordings. Nonetheless, NAFTA allows members, such as Canada, to retain laws regarding copyright, foreign content, and the ability to tax entertainment products differently.

Free Trade Areas, viewed as the second stage of economic unity among countries, exist when countries move towards complete economic integration. Regions achieved this economic unity when member states begin to remove trade barriers among member nations. Most countries adopt this system if there is economic, geographic, or cultural similarity between member states. Examples of free trade areas include AFTZ (African Free Trade Zone), SAARC (South Asia Association for Regional Cooperation), European Free Trade Association (EFTRA), and the TPP (Trans-Pacific Strategic Economic Partnership

Table 13.1 Trading blocs

Trade Bloc	Name	Population	GDP US$ (2007)	Number of Members	Members
FREE TRADE AREAS					
NAFTA	North American Free Trade Agreement	449,227,672	16,189,097,801,318	3	United States, Canada, Mexico
APTA	Asia-Pacific Trade Agreement	2,714,464,027	5,828,692,637,764	6	Bangladesh, China, India, Laos, Sri Lanka, South Korea
SAARC	South Asian Association for Regional Cooperation	1,567,187,373	1,428,392,756,312	8	Afghanistan, Bangladesh, Bhutan, India, Maldives, Nepal, Pakistan, Sri Lanka
CUSTOMS UNIONS					
EAC	East African Community	127,107,838	61,345,180,041	5	Burundi, Kenya, Rwanda, Tanzania, Uganda
EUCU	European Union Customs Union	574,602,745	17,679,376,474,719	33	EU members (30) Andorra, San Marino, Turkey
MERCOSUR	Mercado Común del Sur (Southern Common Market)	55,681,675	305,692,671,540	5	Argentina, Brazil, Paraguay, Uruguay, Venezuela
COMMON MARKETS					
EEA	European Economic Area	499,620,521	17,186,876,431,709	30	EU members (27) Iceland, Liechtenstein, Norway
CACM	Central American Integration System	37,388,063	97,718,800,794	5	Costa Rica, El Salvador, Guatemala, Honduras, Nicaragua
ECONOMIC & MONETARY UNIONS					
EMU	European Monetary Union	324,879,195	12,225,304,229,686	16	Austria, Belgium, Cyprus, Finland, France, Germany, Greece, Ireland, Italy, Luxemburg, Malta, Netherlands, Portugal, Slovakia, Slovenia, Spain
OECS	Organization of East Caribbean States	593,905	3,998,281,731	6	Antigua and Barbuda, Dominica, Grenada, Saint Kitts, Saint Lucia, Saint Vincent
UEMOA	Union économique et monétaire ouest-africaine (West African Economic and Monetary Union)	90,299,945	58,453,871,283	8	Benin, Burkina Faso, Ivory Coast, Guinea Bissau, Mali, Niger, Senegal, Togo

Source: United Nations Statistics Division, "National Accounts Statistics Database"

Agreement). The Central American Free Trade Association (CAFTA) is a free trade agreement between the US, the Dominican Republic, and five Central American nations (El Salvador, Costa Rica, Nicaragua, Honduras, and Guatemala). CAFTA nations must ratify or accede to several international agreements on intellectual property rights as well as adopt US copyright protection for the life of an author plus 70 years. CAFTA provisions also include strict enforcement penalties for piracy and counterfeiting.

Customs Unions are free trade areas where the collective of nations agree to have non-tariff barriers within all member states. This allows for the free flow of goods between the states, while offering protection against goods imported by external nations. For example, Mercosur (*Mercado Común del Sur* or the Southern Common Market) is a Latin America Customs Union that promotes the free trade of goods among four member states: Brazil, Argentina, Uruguay, and Paraguay. Unlike free trade areas, customs unions have a definitive institutional structure that functions as a decision maker and dispute resolver. Like other trading blocs, there are exceptions to the extent of the agreement for certain intellectual properties, especially radio broadcasts and trademarks within Mercosur.

Common markets are economic regions that have a common regulation policy as well as freedom of capital, taxation barriers, and the free movement of human resources across borders. Although there are numerous benefits to nations developing unified markets, companies face difficulties in the initial stages of a common market with the loss of government subsidies and national market protection. Furthermore, the freedom of distribution associated with common markets can create gray markets (also known as parallel imports). Parallel imports are when goods from one country are imported from another member country without the permission of the intellectual property owner. For example, the UK music industry has seen problems associated with parallel imports of CDs from other European Economic Area (EEA) members. Retailers and wholesalers in the European Union (EU) can buy international products from any licensee in the region. At issue is when UK wholesalers' import lower priced CDs from other EEA member states and sell them for a higher price in the UK.

Economic and Monetary Unions are trade blocs with a single currency. A single monetary market has numerous benefits with regard to the production, distribution, and productivity of goods within a trading bloc. These benefits equate to production becoming more efficient and improving productivity. Such structures also affect consumer confidence, corporate infrastructure, retail power, product pricing, and profit margins. The establishment of the EU in 1993 and creation of a single currency (the Euro) within members of the European Monetary Union (EMU) has had an effect on the music industry landscape of Europe. In 1997, Rudi Gassner, then BMG Entertainment Chairman, stated that a single currency within the EMU would lead to the creation of a single price for CDs and

> if we have one price in Europe, you'd better make sure that your returns, discount structures, and so on come into place. We must also make sure we're not going to have a price structure which is keyed to the lowest denominator, but the highest one.[10]

Internet Activities

● The Central Intelligence Agency's (CIA) purpose is to gather information. The agency shares information about foreign countries on its website through *The World Factbook,* www.cia.gov/library/publications/the-world-factbook/. Click on links to the appropriate countries to answer the following questions:

1. What major industries play a role in Australia's economy? How is Australia's economy similar to the western European economies?
2. What current trade issues does China face? How many radio and TV broadcasters are there? How many Internet users are there?
3. How might a music company use the country information in the *World Factbook* when considering its options for global expansion?

Conclusion

In an effort to improve trade between nations, countries have established intergovernmental organizations and trading blocs to facilitate the movement of goods between members. To ensure that international business is conducted in a fair and orderly manner, the countries of the world have created a number of trading agreements. The major trade organizations and agreements that affect the music industry include GATT, WTO, and WIPO. Countries have also removed barriers by establishing trading agreements between member states. These trading blocs have become a significant force in the global market and include organizations such as NAFTA, EU, ASEAN (Association of Southeast Asian Nations), and Mercosur.

Global Music Markets

Introduction

The international music market is similar to geographic, political, economic, and social regions of the world. Geographically, the world is divided into five continents: Africa, Asia, Australasia, Europe, and the Americas (North and South America). Regions can be grouped by cultural, political, and economic definitions. Music organizations have also divided the world based on geographic, economic, and political divisions, notably North America, Latin America, Europe, Asia/Pacific, and Africa. With the growing need for standardization in the international music market, there are several organizations not associated with an intergovernmental agency such as WTO or WIPO. BIEM (*Bureau International des Sociétés Gérant les Droits d'Enregistrement et de Reproduction Mécanique*) is an international organization representing mechanical rights societies coordinating mechanical statutory license agreements among 51 societies in 54 countries.[11]

Not only does BIEM provide a forum for the exchange of mechanical licenses, it also represents member societies in forums such as WIPO, TRIPS, and WCO. BIEM also negotiates standard agreements with representatives of IFPI. The IFPI is a nongovernmental organization that represents the interests of the recording industry throughout the world by promoting the protection of copyright through advocacy and legislation. The organization also campaigns against music piracy and coordinates with other organizations, such as the RIAA, in reducing music piracy through legislation and technological innovation.

North America

Introduction

The United States dominates the North American music market, both in terms of music production and consumption. Countries within this region have developed a music business that relies on the US market for the majority of their sales, while retaining cultural identity. Nonetheless, NAFTA provides each member state a minimum of protection with regard to cultural goods.

Canada (see Table 13.2)

The Canadian music industry has a well developed music infrastructure that not only has produced internationally renowned artists, but continues to represent the diverse range of musical and cultural styles that have shaped the country. Canada is the sixth largest market for recorded music in the world, behind the US, Japan, the UK, and Germany.[12] As with other developed music industry countries, Canada faces issues with piracy and associated legislation that prohibits such actions.

Table 13.2 Canada country profile

Official Name: Canada
Population: 33,259,349 (2008)
Languages: English, French
Monetary Unit: Canadian Dollar
Gross Domestic Product: $1.499 trillion (2008 estimate)
Per Capita Income: $45,085
International Treaties: Berne Convention (1928) UCC (1962) TRIPS (1995) WIPO
   Copyright Treaty (signed)
Performing Rights Organizations: Society of Composers, Authors and Music Publishers
   Of Canada (SOCAN)
International Organizations: WTO (1995), WIPO Convention (1970)

Source: WTO; GDP statistics: World Bank

Canada is a signatory nation to all international intellectual property agreements including the Berne Convention and Universal Copyright Convention and is a member of WIPO and the WTO. Canadian copyright law follows international protocol on copyright duration, which is life of author plus 50 years. However, due to Canada's NAFTA membership, copyright duration is compliant with US law (life plus 70 years). NAFTA membership affects other areas of Canadian copyright law. Like the US, Canada has a mechanism similar to "fair use." "Fair dealing," like fair use, allows users to engage in activities associated with research, news, and criticism. Unlike fair use, Canadian copyright law has limitations on works created for parody. US and Canadian copyright law also differ with regard to mechanical delivery licenses. In the US, a mechanical delivery license covers the right to "reproduce" and "distribute" a composition. Canadian law does not cover the distribution right. Unlike the US, Canada enforces moral rights for works within their country.

As with most countries, copyright is under the jurisdiction of the federal government via the constitution. The Canadian federal government is granted exclusive right to enact laws related to copyright according to the Constitutional Act of 1867. The constitution also allows for the establishment of governing bodies to establish rates and laws that encourage intellectual property development in Canada and protect Canadian authors' rights within the country. An example of this power is the Canadian Copyright Board's royalty rates established in 2007 for 1996 to 2006, which cover only permanent downloads, temporary downloads and on-demand streams provided by services that charge a fee. The board set royalty rates from 1996 to 2006 at 3.4 percent for permanent downloads, minus a 10 percent discount 7.9 percent rate collected on behalf of CMRR.

Music Publishing

Canada has three performing rights societies that collect license fees as set by the Copyright Board of Canada. The Society of Composers, Authors and Music Publishers of Canada (SOCAN) collects license fees on behalf of their members for music performed in Canada as well as works performed overseas. SOCAN also pays royalties to members of affiliated international performing rights organizations for public performances in Canada.

Founded in 1975, the Canadian Musical Reproduction Rights Agency (CMRRA) collects mechanical, online, and synchronized royalties as well as broadcasting mechanical royalties.

Societe du Droit de Reproduction des Auteurs Compositeurs et Editeurs au Canada (SODRAC) was established in 1985 by several Canadian performing rights societies. SODRAC negotiates collective and individual agreements with users of their works, collects royalties, and redistributes them to the rights holders it represents. It therefore controls all reproduction of its members' works on any type of audio, audiovisual, visual, or digital media, as well as the use of recordings in these media. In collective agreements, SODRAC grants users a general use license for which it collects a set amount or a percentage of income that it redistributes to the members whose works were used. In individual agreements, notably in the reproduction of preexisting musical works in certain audiovisual productions, SODRAC generally consults rights holders when a moral right can be invoked. In 2002, SODRAC and CMRRA entered into a joint venture to act as a "one-stop" for the collection of royalties from online licenses and broadcast mechanicals.

Latin America

Introduction

The Latin American market contains one of largest economic regions in the world. At the same time, Latin America has one of the highest rates of piracy in the world. This not only affects the importation of recorded products, but has consequences on internal markets reaching their true potential. Although the region consists of twenty countries, international record labels divide Latin America into seven markets: Brazil, Chile, Colombia, Mexico, Peru, Venezuela, and Central America. Record labels treat the smaller markets (such as Bolivia, Ecuador and Uruguay) as branches of their larger neighbors. However, much of the volatility in this region goes well beyond piracy and market size. Many countries face a higher rate of poverty, economic uncertainty, and political instability. Colombia's music industry is primarily concentrated in the capital Bogotá due to regional violence, while Peru has higher rates of poverty than other countries, thereby reducing the overall size of the music market. Added to these concerns are fluctuations in local currencies which affect both the price of music exports and imports into the region. For many years, the Latin American music industry was protected by tariffs and subsidies. However, as most nations are now members of the WTO, free trade practices have opened music markets to international competition.

Unlike many other international regions, Latin America is practically absent from world markets for recorded music despite the international appeal for their music. This is due partly to Latin America's strong affinity for local musical styles and artists. For example, Brazil is an important music producer, with a large domestic market but with a very timid presence in the world market in terms of exports. This is despite the fact that its famous music is performed worldwide. In 2007, an IFPI report showed that domestic repertoire accounted for 73 percent of total sales, while international artists accounted for 23 percent. According to *Music & Copyright*, if the sales were counted in units instead of "dollars," local repertoire would have accounted for 79 percent of the total in 2000, compared with international at 20.3 percent, and classical at 0.7 percent.[13]

Brazil (see Table 13.3)

Introduction

Brazil is the fifth largest economy in the world with a GDP of US$796 billion in 2007 and a population of 181 million.[14] Its economy outweighs that of all

Table 13.3 Brazil country profile

Official Name: Federal Republic of Brazil
Population: 191,971,506 (2008)
Languages: Portuguese
Monetary Unit: Real (BRL)
Gross Domestic Product: $759.7 billion (2009)
Per Capita Income: $8,587.8 (US$42,129)
International Treaties: Berne Convention (1922) UCC (1960) TRIPS (1995)
International Organizations: WTO (1995) WIPO (1975)
Performing Rights Organizations: Brazilian Society of Authors, Composers, and Music
    Writers (SBACEM)
Mechanical License Organization: União Brasileira de Compositores (UBC)
Other Bodies: MERCOSUR (1991), UCC (1959), UPOV (1999)

Source: WTO; GDP statistics: World Bank

other Latin American countries and is expanding. Added to this has been the relative stability of the Brazilian currency, the Real. According to a PricewaterhouseCoopers study, entertainment represented approximately 3.5 percent of the Brazilian GDP in 2004, i.e. more than US$10 billion (C$ 12.1 billion). This study forecast a 3.8 percent growth for the entertainment market between 2005 and 2008.[15]

Copyright in Brazil is consistent with international law with regard to deposit, duration, and moral rights, and is centered in the Ministry of Culture. Brazil is a signatory to the Paris, Berne, and UCC conventions on intellectual property rights protection. The National Copyright Council (CNDA) provides general policy guidance and coordination on copyright issues but rarely involves itself in the registration process. Normally, copyright registrations are made at one of ten different entities, depending upon the nature of the work.

Music Publishing

Currently, 12 societies collect performing right royalties in Brazil. The major record companies pay mechanical royalties at 8.4 percent of the published price to the dealer, which is one of the highest royalty rates in Latin America, to the publishers' organization ABEM. Six of the country's 12 music rights societies are part of the government-backed umbrella organization, the Escritório Central de Arrecadação e Distribuição (ECAD). Created in 1973 as a type of "association of associations," ECAD collects and distributes public performance royalties for 13 Brazilian societies including UBC, ABRAMUS, AMAR, SOCINPRO, SICAM, and SBACEM. Like many other collection societies across the globe, ECAD is criticized for its lack of transparency, internal democracy, and equity in distributing proceeds to its members. Like most other international music collection agencies it prohibits members from releasing their works under Creative Commons licenses. Furthermore, the double cost structure (costs include each ECAD member as well as ECAD's own) and ECAD's high legal bills increase the organization's administration costs significantly. Cable and satellite television operators have not made any payments for the use of music since the early 1990s. ECAD's activities also include lawsuits against several organizations. About 120 lawsuits filed by ECAD are pending against such operators, led by Net Rio and GloboSat. ECAD also has 74 lawsuits pending against cinema operators.

Associacao Brasileira dos Produtores de Discos (ABPD) [Brazilian Association of Disc Producers] is a representative body of recording labels in Brazil. Music piracy remains a serious problem in Brazil. The International Intellectual Property Alliance (IIPA) estimated that the level of music MC piracy was 98 percent in 2000, with CD piracy at 34 percent. According to the IIPA, these levels of music piracy represented losses to US copyright holders of $300 million in 2000, unchanged on the previous year.

Europe

Introduction

Europe as a region accounts for 30 percent of the global music industry in terms of value. In terms of recorded music sales Europe—if measured as the European Union—is the largest market in the world. If measured on an individual nation basis, countries such as the UK, Germany, France, Italy, Spain, and the Netherlands are within the top 10 recorded music selling countries in the world.[16] Although the establishment of the European Union has had a profound influence on unifying the region's economy and music industry, divisions still exist between mature EU territories, such as the ones previously mentioned, and the developing countries to the east. This is due to the rapid changes by Eastern European nations to adopt a market based economy and to their ability to finance a vibrant music industry in light of high rates of piracy. This is not to say that Western Europe is immune to piracy. High rates of piracy have contributed to declines in recorded music sales in legitimate markets in Germany and France.

The United Kingdom (see Table 13.4)

The UK has had an important role in the history and development of popular music for over 50 years. It is the third largest recorded music market in the world, behind the US and Japan, and accounts for 25 percent of total music sales in the European Union.[17] As a mature market, the UK has a distinct and well structured market that covers all aspects of music creation, distribution, and retail. There is a long history of government regulation with regard to intellectual property and the country is signatory to all international copyright treaties.

A controversial issue for the UK record industry is parallel imports of CDs, especially from other European Union countries. At issue is the strength of the UK pound against the Euro, which has made it profitable for retailers and

Table 13.4 UK country profile

Official Name: United Kingdom of Great Britain and Northern Ireland
Population: 61,230,913 (2008)
Languages: English (de facto official)
Monetary Unit: Pound Sterling
Gross Domestic Product: $2.198 trillion (2009 estimate)
Per Capita Income: $36,000
International Treaties: Berne Convention (1887) UCC (1955) TRIPS (1995) WIPO
    Copyright Treaty (signed)
International Organizations: WTO (1995) WIPO (1999)
Performing Rights Organizations: Performing Right Society

Source: WTO; GDP statistics: World Bank

importers to buy international hit albums from other EU countries and sell them domestically, due to the relative strength of the UK pound. In an effort to reduce this practice, some record labels have responded by adding extra tracks to UK-released albums.

Copyright in the UK is under control of the UK Intellectual Property Office. Copyright protection as a concept in the UK stretches back over two centuries, with the creation of the Statute of Anne in 1709. In 1998, the UK reformulated its copyright law (governed by the Copyright Act of 1956) with the passing of the Copyright, Designs and Patents Act 1988 (CDPA) which brought UK copyright law in line with the Berne Convention. With regard to copyright law, the CDPA had significantly updated copyright law, as to duration, fair dealing, and moral rights. Copyright duration in the CDPA follows international protocol at life of the author plus 50 years.

In 1996, copyright duration was extended via "Duration of Copyright and Rights in Performances Regulations Act" to the life of the author plus 70 years, thereby harmonizing UK copyright duration with countries in the EEA. Under CDPA, the concept of "fair dealing" is limited to the purposes of research and private study (both noncommercial), criticism, review, and news reporting. Provisions of the CDPA do not restrict the copying of literary, dramatic, musical, or artistic works for the purposes of noncommercial research or private study to a "reasonable proportion" of the work or to single copies of the work. Finally, the CDPA included moral rights, with the right to object to false attribution of a work expiring 20 years after a person's death. On February 1, 2006, an amendment extended moral rights to include performers that are broadcast live or a recording played in public.

Music Publishing

Established in 1914, the Performing Right Society (PRS) is the primary performing rights organization in the UK. As with other international PROs, the PRS distributes music licenses and collects royalties on over 10 million pieces of music for 60,000 members.[18] As with many other collection agencies throughout the world, PRS also has affiliations with other international organizations for the collection of royalties. In 1997, the Mechanical Copyright Protection Society (MCPS) and the PRS formed the MCPS-PRS alliance, renaming itself PRS for Music.

Apart from collecting and distributing licenses and royalty collection, PRS has begun to branch out into collecting royalties for social networking sites.

In 2007, PRS was the first organization in Europe to license music on YouTube. However, in 2009 negotiations between YouTube and PRS broke down over royalty payment for videos on the social network site. At issue is the expiration of the original content licensing arrangements between YouTube and the major record labels. Under this agreement, YouTube agreed to pay a minimum per-stream fee. The PRS views YouTube as an on-demand music site, just as Rhapsody, and thus should pay similar licensing fees.[19] In September 2009, both parties announced a new licensing agreement that covered music contained in videos streamed on the online platform.[20]

DIY Activities

- The music industry operates within a global community. It is important that artists not only understand how the music industry operates in their own country, but how they can maximize their presence and earnings in other countries. With over 200 countries, it is often difficult to understand how each state treats music as a business endeavor.
- Visit the IFPI website at www.ifpi.org. This site offers a vast range of information about the international music industry.
- Click on the "links" tab. Here you will find four categories:

  1. digital music retailers (direct links to international online music retailers via pro-music);
  2. local record industry associations (a listing of member record industry associations from around the world);
  3. IFPI member record labels (direct links to member record labels and international independent labels);
  4. other links (links to international agencies and music licensing companies).

- Suppose you want to know more about international recording markets, especially Japan?
- Open the other links tab and click on the RIAJ (Recording Industry Association of Japan) link. In case your Japanese is not flawless, you can open the site in English. In the "related data" tab you can find information on sales figures of digital music, audio recordings as well as recipients of the Japan Gold Disc Awards.

Asia/Pacific

Introduction

The recorded music market in the Asia Pacific region was worth $4.77 billion in 2008, according to the IFPI.[21] This represents a 25 percent share in the total global recording market. Like many other regional music markets, the Asia Pacific market consists of mature music markets and developing markets. Mature markets, such as Japan, the Republic of Korea, Australia, and New Zealand, have well established recording, distribution, and collection agencies. Nonetheless, Japan dominates this market and is second only to the US market in terms of total sales. This is in part due to the population of Japan, but also to the long-standing history of music production in the country.

The Asia Pacific region also has the greatest potential for growth in the global music industry, as three countries—China and India each have populations greater than one billion and Indonesia has the world's fourth largest population, with more than 200 million people[22]—represent almost 40 percent of the world's population. Smaller music markets, such as the Republic of Korea, have a comparative advantage for future development over other countries due to well formed infrastructual systems that are capable of developing technology based music. Nonetheless, the Asia Pacific region, like other music regions, is sensitive to economic and currency fluctuations, especially in music imports.

Both music publishing and the collection of music-related royalties have been slow to develop. The Music Copyright Society of China (MCSC) collects mainly mechanical royalties for its members. However, the society has failed to collect performance royalties from broadcasters, mainly because there is no provision for this in China's copyright law. Despite talk of reform, the legal definition of "performance" remains unclear. Moreover, powerful user groups, such as broadcasters and hotels, want to limit the notion of performance to live performance only. Under such a definition as this, broadcasters and hotels would not have to pay for their use of recorded music.

As a region, there is uneven treatment towards piracy. Some countries, such as Japan, have relatively low rates of piracy in comparison to other nations. China, which at one stage was the largest exporter of pirated music, is now a net importer of pirated music. Music piracy is now located in neighboring countries, including Hong Kong, Macau, Malaysia, Singapore, Thailand, and Vietnam. The International Intellectual Property Alliance (IIPA) estimated the level of music piracy was greater than 85 percent in several Asia Pacific nations, resulting in trade losses to music copyright holders of $791 million in 2008.[23] Since joining the WTO, China has strengthened its legal framework and related laws to comply with TRIPS and combat music piracy.

Japan (see Table 13.5)

The size and maturity of the Japanese music industry contrasts sharply with many music markets within the Asia Pacific region. Nonetheless, the Japanese music market is sensitive to economic fluctuations that affect the country's economy.

Table 13.5 Japan country profile

Official Name: Japan (Nippon-koku)
Population: 127,293,092 (2008)
Languages: Japanese
Monetary Unit: Yen
Gross Domestic Product: $4.910 trillion (2008 estimate)
Per Capita Income: $38,457
International Treaties: Berne Convention (1899) UCC (1955) TRIPS (1995) WIPO
   Copyright Treaty (2002)
International Organizations: WTO (1995) WIPO (1999)
Performing Rights Organizations: Japanese Society for Rights of Authors, Composers
   and Publishers (JASRAC)

Source: WTO; GDP statistics: World Bank

For example, the country has seen a decline in record sales in part due to the poor economy. In addition to internal economic weaknesses, high CD prices and music industry structure have contributed to a decline in the value of the market.

Another significant problem is that the Japanese music market is relatively old in terms of average buyer age. As with mature music markets in the Asia Pacific region and worldwide, the development of online and mobile platforms has contributed to growth of digital music sales in Japan. In 2008, Japanese digital sales accounted for sales of 91 billion yen ($990 million).[24] Yet Japan faces problems with online piracy and peer-to-peer downloading. The IIPA estimates that 150 million tracks are downloaded every year, 10 times more than legitimate music downloads in 2005.[25]

As with the Latin American and parts of the European music market, "geolinguistic" traits affect the export of Japanese music. For example, the Japanese market has been traditionally a local market due to the linguistic limitations within the region. This has resulted in Japan having one of the highest percentages of local repertoire sales in the world. Over the past decade, international repertoire (including classical music) has never accounted for more than 28 percent of sales by value. Moreover, domestic repertoire is more profitable for local record companies. It usually has a higher retail price and Japanese artists' royalties are generally lower than those paid to leading international acts. The only exception to this situation is the growth of Korean music within the Japanese market. Similarly, Japanese labels, such as Avex, have been successful at marketing Japanese and English-language recordings by Korean girl singer, BoA, in Japan and the rest of Asia. Furthermore, the Japanese music market is heavily reliant on TV as a means to promote music.[26]

Established in 1889, Japan copyright laws came into existence the same year that the country acceded to the Berne Convention. In 1970, Japan developed a new copyright law that was in line with developments in international copyright law. The major characteristics of the "new" Japanese copyright law included provisions such as the expansion of copyright duration to life plus 50 years. Prior to this, copyright duration in Japan was life plus 30 years. Second, the new law expressed in detail the fair use of works under exceptional circumstances. Fair use is not included in the Copyright Act. This is due to the Japanese using the civil law legal system. Third, the new copyright laws established neighboring rights (authors' rights) to protect the rights of performers, phonogram producers, and broadcasting organizations in compliance with the Rome Convention.

As a mature market, Japan has been a signatory of most international copyright treaties for over 100 years. Since 1899, Japan has been a member of the Berne Union and has ratified all international treaties including the Universal Copyright Convention (1956); the Rome Convention (1989), and the TRIPS agreement (1994).

In order to keep abreast of changes associated with digitization, Japan acceded to the WIPO Copyright Treaty in 2000 and the WIPO Performances and Phonograms Treaty in 2002. In 2009, Japan passed new laws aimed at deterring the illegal distribution of music over the Internet. The Act clearly stated copyright infringement includes the known sale of pirated works through the Internet and reproduction of music downloaded illegally through the Internet for private use.

Music publishing

Established in 1939, the Japanese Society for Rights of Authors, Composers and Publishers (JASRAC) is the largest copyright administration society in Japan. JASRAC provides one-stop processing of every possible form of copyright use, including performances as in concerts, karaoke, broadcasting, and film and CD rental. Unlike most countries where CD rental is prohibited, the CD rental market in Japan is strong, with 4,000 shops nationwide. Based on the "lending rights" under Japanese copyright law, JASRAC had been collecting royalties from CD rental businesses in cooperation with the Compact Disc and Video Rental Commerce Trade Association of Japan (CDV-Japan). As with other collection agencies, JASRAC royalties are collected on a formula, known as the "Tariffs for Use of Music Works."

JASRAC had enjoyed a monopoly on copyright royalty collection and distribution for over 60 years until 2001 when the Japanese government enacted the "Management Business of Copyright and Neighboring Rights Act," allowing for greater competition. In late 2000, 11 companies formed Japan Rights Clearance (JRC) as a competitor to the JASRAC. Unlike the JASRAC, JRC allows writers greater control over royalty rates and the commissions charged on their collection, particularly in Internet-related fields.

Africa

Africa is a vast continent both from a geographic and cultural perspective. Despite the profusion of talent in Africa and the richness of cultural traditions, there has been limited commercialization of African music in domestic and foreign markets. Consequently, Africa's share in global trade of music products remains marginal at less than 1 percent of world exports.

Much of what hinders the development of the African music industry is lack of infrastructure to support the growth of a vibrant music industry, investment and entrepreneurial skill in the music industry, and limited capital. A consequence of this weak market is the absence of the big conglomerate record labels in most countries. As a result, music production—with the exception of South Africa—is largely independent, informal, and domestically oriented. Problems associated with the recording industry are also present in the intellectual property regulatory environment. For example, a sound legal framework governing the writing and enforcement of contracts is ineffective or not present in many African countries. Without an effective copyright regime, creative producers are unable to receive equitable payment for their output and hence lack the financial incentive to continue in production.

Although many countries in the developing African nations are making progress in establishing workable legislative arrangements for dealing with intellectual property, there is still a long way to go. In Africa, however, because artists expect to receive little or no royalty from record sales, owing partly to piracy and partly to the inadequate collection of copyrights, they negotiate a bigger share of an up-front payment that essentially signs away their rights to the music. Combined with this career-limiting decision is the poor understanding of the music business, which results in there being few professional producers or managers.

The United Nations Education and Scientific Organization (UNESCO) Global Alliance for Cultural Diversity divides the African music market into two sectors: Countries with emerging or previously established music industries and countries where music production and consumption are undertaken on "craft-like scale." The report also states that there are seven countries in Africa that have established performance industries; but only South Africa has an established recording industry and a substantial international profile. Although there is little progress in developing a continental music industry, Africa trading organizations, such as the Organization of African Unity (OAU) and the Southern African Development Community (SADC), have begun to develop a cultural policy.

South Africa (see Table 13.6)

In contrast to the world's largest markets, the US and Japan, South Africa's music industry is relatively small. In 2007, the South African recording industry accounted for $243 million in record sales, representing 0.812 percent of total world record sales. Although South Africa is not a significant global player, it has developed a strong local and regional presence. In 1996, South Africa was the twenty-eighth largest music market in the world. Since 2001, South Africa has expanded and remains one of the top 20 international markets in recorded music sales.

As with other mature music markets, South Africa has a well developed copyright law and is a signatory to most international copyright conventions. In 1928, South Africa acceded to the Berne Convention and has subsequently signed to several other international treaties and organizations, such as the WIPO convention (1975) and TRIPS (1995). South Africa's primary piece of

Table 13.6 South Africa country profile

Official Name: Republic of South Africa
Population: 49,667,628 (2008)
Languages: Afrikaans, English, Southern Ndebele, Zulu, etc (11 official languages)
Monetary Unit: Rand
Gross Domestic Product: $276,764 billion (2008 estimate)
Per Capita Income: $5,684
International Treaties: Berne Convention (1928) TRIPS (1995) WIPO Copyright Treaty
    (signed)
International Organizations: WTO (1995) WIPO (1999)
Performing Rights Organizations: Southern African Music Rights Organization Limited
    (SAMRO)

Source: WTO; GDP statistics: World Bank

copyright legislation is the Copyright Act of 1978. As with other Berne signa-
tories, South African copyright duration measures from the life of the author
plus 50 years. In compliance with the Berne Convention, the Copyright Act
also provides for the protection of moral rights. Finally, South African copyright has provisions for fair dealing. Currently, the South African copyright
Act does not contain any provisions prohibiting the circumvention of technological protection measures. Since the country has not ratified the "WIPO
Internet Treaty" South Africa is not obliged to introduce this provision into its
copyright law.

Music publishing

The enforcement of the Copyright Act is a valuable source of income for
composers and the South African music industry. As in many other international
music markets, South Africa has a number of member societies representing the
mechanical and performance rights of composers. The South African Recording
Rights Association Limited (SARRAL) and the National Organization for
Reproduction Rights in Music in South Africa (NORM) represent the mechanical
rights of authors. The South African Music Rights Organization (SAMRO)
represents the public performance rights of musical composition. Collectively,
these organizations represent approximately 4,000 members.

As with performing rights organizations throughout the world, authors and
publishers must register their works with SARRAL or SAMRO. SARRAL and
NORM collect revenue for members on the basis of the number of mechanical
copies that they make of a particular recording. These organizations also collect
royalties from a variety of other sources including the national broadcaster and
the recording of music programs for "in-house" music. SAMRO collects revenue
arising from the public performance of a composition. Broadcasters submit
playlists and musicians submit cue sheets that detail the songs that they have
played at any given venue. SAMRO also has a "policing" role, bringing over
1,000 cases against organizations for non-payment of music licenses.

Summary

In an age of continuing internationalization, music is truly a global industry. With increasing conglomeration and internationalization, music companies must be able to operate within this market. The global market is an open system with the elimination of trade barriers and the harmonization of intellectual property. Music companies not only must understand the means of disseminating products to multiple markets, they must understand the very markets themselves from a marketing, copyright, and publishing perspective.

Regulating this new market is a host of institutions and treaties that cover trade between nations, administer international agreements, and provide a forum for dispute resolution. Organizations, such as WTO and WIPO, administer several important treaties including the GATT and TRIPs.

Globalization is not only an economic phenomenon, it is a cultural event. Advocates of globalization see it as a means of opening markets and as an opportunity for the dissemination of music in multiple markets. Opponents see a world with Western, vis-à-vis American culture, dominating local production. This view warns of a world in which a dominant "monoculture" obliterates all divergent cultures.

QUESTIONS FOR REVIEW

- Why do countries join trading blocs?
- What actions might a government take to help protect its intellectual property on the global market?
- What are some of the risks a small music company might face by exporting its products directly to another country?
- How can a company use a licensing agreement to enter world markets?
- How do individual country's copyright laws affect the sale of music in foreign markets?

Glossary

If the abbreviated form of a term is most commonly used it is listed first.

360 Deal—A deal between a label and artist that involves the label receiving revenues from more than just the recordings aspect of an artist's career, but also probably live appearances, music publishing, and merchandising.

45—The 45 rpm single with one song recorded on each side.

78—The 78 rpm record, usually with one song recorded on each side, which was the standard record from its introduction until the 1950s, when the 45 and LP formats became dominant.

8-track tape—An audio tape with room to record eight separate "tracks" of information. Consumer eight-track tapes were endless loop tape cartridges, similar to those used in broadcasting, which contained four separate stereo programs. When the loop of tape had played all of two of the tracks (one program) a signal on the tape would cause the player to switch to playing back the next two tracks. On crudely recorded eight-tracks the program change would sometimes occur in the middle of a song.

A2IM (American Association of Independent Music)—Formerly NAIRD (National Association of Independent Record Distributors) in 1972, and AFIM (Association for Independent Music), is a trade association for independent record labels, distributors, retailers, and those who work with independent labels and artists.

A&R (Artist and Repertoire)—In a record company this is the department in charge of finding new artists to record. "A&R persons" refers to persons who fulfill A&R functions by scouting new talent or listening to demos of artists and songs to decide who and what to record. Traditionally A&R people also found songs for their artists to record and still do so where the artist does not record only their own compositions.

AARC (Alliance of Artists and Recording Companies)—A non-profit organization formed to distribute royalties collected by the Copyright Office under the Audio Home Recording Act.

Add—A recording added to the playlist at a radio station, webcaster, or video channel.

Adult Contemporary—A current radio format playing recordings by contemporary artists and primarily targeted at a listening audience that is over 24 years old. The overall sound tends to be softer than CHR or the various rock formats.

Advance—A prepayment of royalties or other earnings. For example, a recording artist may be paid a flat sum upon delivery to the label of a finished master in advance of earning any royalties from the sale of copies of the recordings. Many items such as recording costs or promotion expenses may also be considered "advances" under the definitions in the agreement. Advances are used in many different agreements in the recording industry including label-artist agreements, songwriter agreements, and master licensing agreements. Advances are generally not returnable and not the same as a "debt" that must be repaid.

AES (Audio Engineering Society)—A trade and educational organization for audio engineers. Founded in the 1950s, its members include recording engineers, equipment designers, and other professionals involved in audio engineering. It helps set technical standards and publishes a technical journal for members.

AFM (American Federation of Musicians of the United States and Canada)—The musicians union. Some locals also allow audio engineers to join.

AFTRA (American Federation of Television and Radio Artists)—The union for singers and voice announcers.

Agent (aka talent agent or booking agent)—The person responsible for securing employment for a performing artist.

AGVA (American Guild of Variety Artists)—The union for live entertainers who are not *AFM* or *AFTRA* members.

Airplay—Primarily refers to play of a recording on the radio, but may also refer to play in a record store, online, or play of a music video on a television or video channel, on the Internet, or in a club.

Album—A recording containing usually eight or more individual songs or "cuts," totaling 30 or more minutes of playing time. CDs can contain up to 75 minutes of playing time. Vinyl albums usually contained no more than 45 minutes of playing time. (See also **Track Equivalent Album**.)

All-in royalty or "all-in deal"—A royalty rate designed to include royalties paid to an artist *and* any royalties paid to a producer or others who are paid royalties by the label, such as a remixer or a sampling royalty to another label. An all-in deal provides the label with the services of the recording artist, producer, and others for a single royalty rate. All-in rates do not include **mechanical royalties** (see below).

Alternative—In radio, a format that does not play the mainstream hits in any particular genre, such as "alternative rock" or "alternative country." May also refer to a genre of music that styles itself as "alternative" to the mainstream styles.

AMC (American Music Conference)—A nonprofit organization that promotes music and music education.

Ancillary income—In concert promotion, the term for revenues for the venue from parking or food sales that are not part of the gate and are not commissionable by the promoter or artist.

Anti-trust laws—Laws that attempt to control whether businesses unfairly compete by forming monopolies or fixing prices to the detriment of consumers.

Arbitron—A data collection service of the Nielsen Company that provides ratings to radio stations that show how many listeners the station has at various times of the day and the demographics of those listeners.

Artist concessions—In concert promotion, artist revenues from the sale of merchandise at the concert, such as t-shirts, hats, nightgowns, that bear the artist's name and likeness. The venue may demand a percentage of artist concessions.

ASCAP (American Society of Composers, Authors, and Publishers)—An organization that licenses music performance rights for songwriters and music publishers. It was the first performing rights organization in the US, started in 1914.

Audio engineer (see also recording engineer)—A person who operates or designs equipment for recording and reproduction of sound. The term is broader than recording engineer and includes sound reinforcement and facilities sound.

Author—In copyright law, the person who creates a work, whether a songwriter, recording artist, sculptor, poet, or novelist—all are called "authors."

Bar code—Generally taken to mean the Universal Product Code (UPC) appearing as a series of vertical black and white bars on a product that identifies the specific product and its manufacturer.

BDS (Broadcast Data Systems)—The company (part of Nielsen Retail Entertainment) that monitors radio airplay with computers that identify what records are being played by comparing the broadcast to identifiable "signature" parts of the recording stored in the computer's memory. BDS can deliver the actual count of the number of times a particular record is played.

Beats—The basic rhythm tracks (often just bass and drums) that are often used in the production of hip-hop (and other) recordings. The beats are looped in the production process to form the rhythmic bed of the recording.

Berne Convention—The Berne Convention for the Protection of Literary Property is an international treaty in which over 160 countries have agreed to protect copyrights from each other.

BET Networks (originally Black Entertainment Television)—As its name implies, cable television channel targeted primarily at African Americans, specializing in music videos and other entertainment programming.

Bio—Short for biography. The brief description of an artist's life or music history that appears in a press kit.

Blacklist (see Defaulters)

Blanket license—A term used mainly in performance rights licensing where a performing rights organization gives a licensee such as a radio station, nightclub, or web service the right to perform all of the songs or recordings in the PRO's repertoire as many times as the licensee wants. The "blanket" covers all of the songs as compared to a per-song or per-use license for one song at a time.

BMI (Broadcast Music, Inc.)—A performing rights organization started in 1940 and owned by broadcasters. BMI and ASCAP are the two largest performing rights organizations in the United States. BMI licenses radio and television stations, nightclubs, retail outlets, and others to publicly perform musical compositions.

Bollywood—Refers to the Indian film production industry centered in Mumbai (formerly Bombay).

Boom box—A small portable stereo system with attached speakers.

Bootleg—A recording not authorized by the artist's label, usually of a live performance or studio out-takes, that is manufactured and sold to the public outside of the normal channels of distribution, not to be confused with counterfeit or pirate copies. Beginning in 1995, such recordings violated the performers' rights in the copyright law to be the first to record or transmit their performances.

Boxed set—A special package containing usually three or more individual albums with special notes, photos, and other matter. The sets often contain previously unreleased cuts and alternative versions of recordings.

Branch distributor—A term still applied to a regional distributorship owned and maintained by one of the big four conglomerates.

Break—To "break" an artist or recording is to have sufficient airplay or other national exposure that is beginning to translate into significant sales and additional airplay.

Breakage allowance—A deduction from a recording artist's royalties originally designed to account for the fact that lacquer and shellac recordings were brittle and easily broken. The label would deduct typically 10 percent of sales to account for broken records. The allowance still exists in some contracts even though CDs rarely break and downloads cannot "break."

Break-even point—In concert promotion, the point at which the promoter's gross revenues equal the fixed expenses, including artist guarantees, but not such things as any percentages for the artist or venue. In economics, the point at which total revenues have equaled total costs so the firm is showing neither a profit nor a loss.

Broad inventory—A selection of goods that crosses a number of different product lines, such as exists in department stores and "big box" mass merchandisers. Record stores typically have a narrow inventory.

Budget line or price—An album product line of a label that sells at a list price usually less than two thirds of the price for a current *front line* (new releases for established artists) album.

Burn-out—As used in radio or TV programming, a term indicating that the public is tired of hearing a particular recording.

Business manager—A person hired by an artist or the artist's personal manager to take care of managing the artist's money and business ventures.

Buy-back—In concert promotion, a deal between the promoter and the artist's agent to give the promoter the "right" to promote that artist the next time the artist plays in that promoter's area, city, or venue.

Call-out—Radio research initiated by the station where someone calls random or selected listeners to ask their opinions on certain records or other programming that the station may be doing.

Capital costs—The upfront costs of creating, distributing, and marketing the product.

Catalog—Generally refers to all of the songs (actually the copyrights in those songs) owned by a music publisher. May also refer to all of a label's master recordings. May also refer to recordings that are not current hits, but which are still available from the distributor and "in print."

Census—As used in performing rights, refers to a PRO's logging of every performance of every song by a certain broadcaster or other licensee. It is compared to a *sample*, in which only some licensees or some performances of the licensee are logged.

Chain (retail)—A group of two or more stores that are owned by the same entity. Strictly speaking even if "mom and pop" opened a second store it would be called a chain, but most people would still call it a "mom and pop store" with two locations.

CHR (Contemporary Hit Radio)—The successor to the Top 40 format, usually with fewer (20–25) current hits being played, instead of 40.

Cleans—Promotional copies that are not marked as such and may, therefore, be sold at retail. The artists get no royalties for promotional copies.

Clearance—In rights generally, permission to use a particular song, recording, photo, or other work. In music publishing, the writer or publisher will "clear" a new song for licensing by listing it with the PRO.

Closed system—A business system that does not have to interact with its external environment.

CMT (Country Music Television)—The cable channel devoted to programming country music videos and other programs featuring "country" artists and themes.

Coin-op—An early coin operated "jukebox."

Collective work—A work (in copyright) formed by the assembly of a number of separate independent works into a collective whole, such as an anthology, periodical issue, or (perhaps) a record album.

Commercially acceptable—A standard by which labels judge masters submitted to them by recording artists. It means the recording must be technically and artistically good enough in the opinion of the label executives to enjoy public sales and acceptance.

Commission—The percentage of the artist's income taken by the agent for arranging the performance or by the personal manager for being the artist's manager.

Commissioned work—In copyright, a work that is created at the behest of some party other than the author, usually for pay, and not as part of the author's job (see also **Work made for hire**).

Common law copyright—Originally, the right of authors to be the first to publish their works as protected by common law, and not the federal copyright statute. Since 1978, common law copyright would generally only apply to works not fixed in a tangible medium of expression. But it has been held to protect even published recordings that were made before 1972, when sound recordings were first made copyrightable in the US.

Compulsory license—Refers to a license that is granted by the Copyright Act to use a musical composition, sound recording, or other copyrighted work. It is "compulsory" because the copyright owner must permit the use if the user conforms to the requirements of the statute regarding payment of royalties, and so on. The term is often used in the music industry to refer to the compulsory mechanical license for phonorecords, but the term is really broader than that because there is more than one kind of compulsory license.

Concept video—A music video usually not much longer than a single song, which features visual images *other than* the artist performing the song. Usually these images tell a story or set a certain mood to accompany the song.

Configuration—The type of phonogram in which a recording is fixed, such as LP, cassette, compact disc, or even electronic/digital file.

Conglomerate—A business corporation that is formed by the ownership of a number of other businesses or divisions operating in a wide variety of areas. For example, Sony Corp. owns record companies, music publishing companies, film production and distribution, and consumer electronics hardware manufacturing.

Consolidation—The creation of larger and larger organizations as smaller ones are absorbed, purchased, or merged into larger ones.

Consumer advertising—Ads directed towards the consumer as compared to trade advertising. Generally, this audience is reached through mass media.

Container charge—A deduction from a recording artist's royalties to account for the fact that the label produces the package or container for the recording and claims it should not have to pay royalties on that part of the list price which covers the package. The reduction, typically 20–25 percent for CDs, is usually from the list price (SRLP) of the recording and typically amounts to much more than the actual cost of manufacturing the recording and its container. This deduction is *not* taken when the artist's contract is based on PPD (see below) instead of MSRP (see below).

Contributory infringer—One whose actions make an infringement possible, and who knows that the infringement is occurring.

Controlled compositions—Compositions (songs) written or owned, in whole or part, or controlled in whole or part, by the recording artist and/or producer. The term usually appears in recording agreements between recording artists, producers, and record labels in a clause that attempts to permit the label to use such compositions at a reduced rate.

Co-op advertising—Sometimes referred to as just "co-op money," this is advertising money given to retailers or distributors by the labels to advertise the label's records in local media. Usually this ad must feature the label product with mention of the retail location. More often than not the "co-op" is not really split between the label and retailer, but is entirely paid for by the label.

Co-publishing—An arrangement where two or more music publishers own the copyrights in a given song. It is frequently seen where an artist's publishing company shares the copyright with a "regular" music publisher, or where two or more writers on a song are affiliated with different publishing companies.

Copyright—A property right in a creative work which allows the author, and those who receive rights from the author, to control reproduction and other uses of the work. Copyrights are intangible personal property.

Copyright administration—A music publishing function concerning the registration of songs for copyright, the recordation of other documents pertaining to those songs with the Copyright Office, and the licensing of those songs for various uses. A small publishing company owned by a writer, artist, or producer may outsource this function to another publisher in exchange for a percentage fee.

Copyright Royalty Board—The panel of three administrative judges established by Congress to adjust or set compulsory royalty rates for compulsory mechanical, cable television secondary transmission, non-commercial broadcasts for nondramatic musical works, digital performance of sound recordings, and digital delivery of phonorecords, and to oversee distribution of some of these royalties.

Corporate—Often used as a derogatory term, referring to recordings which "sound like" they were produced as products to fill a market niche instead of as inspired performances by writers and recording artists, as in "corporate rock."

Corporation for Public Broadcasting (CPB)—The private, non-profit organization set up by Congress in 1967 to promote the development of non-commercial broadcasting services and programs (see also **PBS** below.)

Counterfeit recordings—A form of record piracy in which the packaging and graphics as well as the recording is duplicated, so that the counterfeit not only sounds like, but looks like, the original, legitimate recording. Counterfeit copies are sometimes so good that only someone working at the label can tell them from legitimate copies. Sometimes they are so poorly done, with smudged ink, color registration errors, and things such as improperly printed or aligned UPC bar codes, that anyone could recognize them.

Cover (band or versions)—Recordings or performances of a song by artists and performers other than the artist who originally recorded the song. A "cover" band does mostly cover versions of songs originally recorded and performed by other artists. Sometimes the term is also used to refer to artists who do not write the compositions that they record.

Created—A work is "created" under copyright law when it is fixed in a tangible medium of expression for the first time.

Creative controls—Authority to exercise control over the creative aspects of a recording, such as selection of material to be recorded, studios to use, producer, and side musicians. Artists and producers seek more creative controls from the labels.

Cross-collateralization—The practice (common in the recording industry) of using income from one source to recover advances made for a different source between the same two parties. For example, if an artist records an album that does not sell well, the recording advances for that album may be recovered out of royalties earned by a later album that does sell well or from earnings under other income streams if the artist and label have a "360 deal" (see above).

Cultural hegemony—The theory that a dominant culture or class can assert itself through ways, especially in mass communication messages, that appear "normal." In this way, the dominant culture or class can continue to rule while ordinary people are unaware that they are being influenced or dominated.

Cultural theory—A communications theory which states that the meaning of a communication is understood in a variety of ways that are influenced by the culture into which that communication is sent. The focus of this theory is then on the recipient(s) of the communication instead of the senders.

DART (Digital Audio Recording Technologies) royalties—Royalties due to copyright owners under the Audio Home Recording Act from the sale of stand-alone digital audio recorders such as mini-disc and the blank media used to make recordings such as "music" CD-Rs and mini-discs.

Dating—The date by which the retailer has to pay for the purchases or lose the early payment discount. An example might be 3 percent discount if paid in 20 days; the net is due within 60 days.

Deep inventory—A selection of goods covering a lot of different varieties of the same basic good. Record stores typically have fairly deep inventories of recordings.

Defaulters—A union term for people who do not pay musicians or vocalists for their performances in clubs or on recordings. Union musicians will not perform for persons on a defaulters list made by the applicable union.

Demo—A *demonstration* recording made to promote an artist, songwriter, or song to an agent, manager, music publisher, or record company.

Derivative work—In copyright law, a work that is based substantially on a preexisting work or works that edits, recasts, or changes the form of the prior work into a new copyrightable work.

Development deal—Usually a recording contract where a label gives an artist a small sum or perhaps annual amount to remain obligated to sign a full recording agreement with the label. The label may want to keep the option of signing the artist while the artist works on songwriting, performance, or some other aspect that the label feels is not quite ready for master recording. Music publishers may also offer similar deals to songwriters.

Diamond award—A diamond album or single that the RIAA certifies has sold 10 million units at the wholesale level. There are no multiple diamond awards like there are multi-platinum awards.

Diffusion of innovations theory—The process by which the use of an innovation is spread within a market group, over time and over various categories of adopters.

Digital performance of sound recordings—The public performance of a sound recording (as opposed to the song contained in the recording) by means of a digital audio transmission. This includes Internet streaming, satellite transmission, and background music services, but does not include transmission via the airways by regular licensed terrestrial broadcasters such as radio stations and TV stations, even though they may be broadcasting a digital signal.

Digital Phonorecord Delivery—A term in the Copyright Act for a download of a recording. A digital phonorecord delivery (DPD) may be accomplished under the terms of a compulsory mechanical license. The Copyright Royalty Board has also determined a DPD includes full downloads, limited downloads (like from subscription services), ring tones, and interactive (i.e. on-demand) streaming, and some short promotional on-demand uses.

Digital sampling (see also **sampling**)—The electronic process where an audio signal is transformed into a numeric (digital) sequence which represents the level (amplitude) of the signal at various times during its duration. Those digits are then stored in a digital form on some computer-readable device such as a computer disc, audio tape, or compact disc. If the sampling device measures (samples) the level of the signal often enough it can then reproduce the level of the signal with the stored digits which represent the amplitude at very close intervals of time. The closer the intervals of time, i.e. the higher the sampling frequency, the more accurate can be the picture of the complex audio signal. Compact discs, for example, have a sampling rate of 44.1 thousand times per second. The name "sample" comes from the fact that the digital representations are really only a sample of the entire signal. They are just so close together that when reproduced they sound so much like the original that the human ear cannot detect any difference.

Digitization—The turning of some analog work, such as a recording, book, or map into a digital format that can be stored and transmitted via computers.

Disc jockey—The person at a radio station who announces which recordings are being played. In the 1940s and 1950s these persons also tended to select which records were played but those decisions are usually now in the hands of a music director or program director.

Discography—A bibliography of music recordings.

Dolby noise reduction—A form of dynamic pre-emphasis employed during recording, plus a form of dynamic de-emphasis used during playback, that work in tandem to improve the signal-to-noise ratio.

Door—The revenues made from admission fees, usually at a club. (See also **gate**.)

Download—An Internet or other digital transmission of a recording that enables the person receiving the download to retain a file copy of the recording.

Dramatic performance—A performance of a work that tells a story. Usually associated with musical theater or opera and multiple songs, but a single song may be a dramatic performance if accompanied by other action or visuals.

Draw—Another term for an advance, more often heard in relation to exclusive songwriter agreements with music publishers, or in live entertainment where musicians performing in clubs may get a "draw" after performing for a portion of their contracted term, say three days out of a six-day engagement.

DRM-Free—Tracks that were free of "Digital Rights Management" codes that could prevent them from being repeatedly copied.

Dubbing—In copyright law, literal duplication of a prior recording. In audio engineering, taking a recorded sound and editing it into or with a preexisting recording.

Duopoly rule—The Federal Communications Rule that prohibited the same company from owning two radio or TV stations in the same market. This rule was modified to allow ownership of AM and FM stations, then later abandoned completely.

Effective competition—A market condition in which it takes more than four firms to control 60 percent of the market.

Elasticity of demand—The percent change in quantity demanded (sold) that is brought about by a percent change in price. When the percent change in quantity demanded is greater than the percent change in price then the demand is said to be price *elastic*. When a given percentage change in price results in a smaller percentage change in quantity demanded it is said to be price *inelastic*. The demand for current hit records is generally said to be price *inelastic*.

End-caps—The portions of record browsers (or other retail displays) located at the end of the aisles, facing the main aisles of the store.

Entropy—A state of business or physics in which there is total disorganization and chaos.

Established artist—A recording artist who has had at least one (labels would say two) successful album on a label of significant stature.

ET (Electrical Transcription)—A recording distributed to radio stations for the purpose of broadcast, and not for sale to the public. National advertisements, syndicated programs, and musical recordings (into the 1950s) were distributed to radio this way. The ET had higher quality audio than was available on consumer records.

Evergreen—In music publishing, a song that is recorded by many artists and performed on a continuing basis for many years.

Exclusive artist—A recording artist under agreement to make recordings only for one record company.

Exclusive contract—Any arrangement where one party promises not to provide services or goods to any third party.

Exclusive license—Permission to use a song or some other right which is given only to one user and may not be given to any competing user.

Exclusive songwriter—A songwriter under agreement to write songs only for one publishing company.

Fair use—A provision of the copyright law allowing some limited uses of works where the use is particularly beneficial to the public and does not do much harm to the copyright owner.

First sale doctrine—Part of the copyright law that allows the lawful owner of a copy of a work to dispose of possession of that copy in any way they wish. Copies may be resold, rented, leased, or given away. There is an exception to the doctrine which allows the owners of copyrights in sound recordings and computer programs to control rental of those works.

Flown—Sound reinforcement, stage lighting, or other effects that are suspended from the rafters of a venue instead of being supported on the floor.

Folios—Songbooks containing multiple songs usually either on a common theme or by the same artist or writer, as opposed to sheet music of single songs.

Four walls—In concert promotion, a deal to rent a venue that includes only the right to use the facility with the venue providing nothing more than the "four walls," i.e. no box office, no ticket takers, no ushers, no clean-up, or other such service.

Free goods—In recording artist contracts and record marketing, a term of art meaning recordings given away to a distributor or retailer as a method of discount. For example, the retailer may get one free copy for each nine copies that are ordered. These are to be distinguished from promotional copies that are not meant for retail sale.

Front line (aka full line)—The label's most recent releases from their top artists. These are usually the highest priced "regular" releases.

Gate—The admission revenues from a concert. Same as "door" but the latter is usually a club term.

Gatekeeper—In communication theory, a person who decides which messages will be communicated from one channel to another. Thus, radio music directors are gatekeepers, deciding which recordings will be communicated through radio.

GATT (General Agreement on Tariffs and Trade)—An international trade treaty that established the World Trade Organization and that provides for trade sanctions for member nations that do not properly protect copyrights.

Gold award—A recording or music video that has wholesale sales certified by the RIAA to be 500,000 units for an album or single or 50,000 for a music video. There are other "gold" standards for other kinds of video. See also **platinum** and **diamond**.

Good ears—A music industry term referring to the ability to tell which artists and recordings will be successful. When used by audio engineers, it refers to the ability to distinguish technical and performance nuances in the recording and production process.

Grammy Awards (see **Recording Academy**).

Grand rights—Dramatic performance rights (see **Dramatic performance**).

Grassroots marketing—A marketing approach using nontraditional methods to reach target consumers.

GRid (Global Release Identifier)—The IFPI's GRid provides a system for the unique identification of "Releases" of music over electronic networks, so that they can be managed efficiently. A Release is defined precisely in the Standard but can be understood as a collection of recordings or other media that are grouped together for commerce. Products can be made from Releases by, for instance, choosing a technology to encode the recordings (such as MP3 or AAC) or a business model (such as sale or rental). By assigning a unique GRid to a Release, it can be identified without ambiguity in, for instance, reports of sales of products based on the Release (Source, IFPI).

Guarantee—In concert promotion, the fixed amount that the artist will be paid, regardless of how many tickets are sold.

Hard tickets—Admission tickets preprinted and distributed for sale, as compared to soft tickets, which are only printed at the time of sale, or on the buyer's computer.

Harry Fox Agency (HFA)—A collection and licensing agency created and run by the National Music Publishers Association (NMPA). It was designed to serve as a clearing house for mechanical licensing. The agency issues mechanical licenses on behalf of its member publishing companies, collects licensing fees from the record companies and other users, and distributes those collections to the appropriate publishers.

Head arrangement—A musical arrangement where the parts are not written out, but simply made up on the spot by the musicians out of their heads. Such arrangements are usually more simplistic and probably not subject to copyright protection as are derivative works.

Hold—In music publishing, a verbal agreement between a publisher and producer to not pitch the song to other producers until the first producer decides whether to record the song. In concert promotion, a verbal agreement between a promoter and a venue to keep a certain date open for that promoter and not to license the venue to another event for that date until the first promoter decides whether or not to use it.

Horizontal integration—An economic term describing the actions of a firm to buy out competing companies at the same level, such as one record store chain acquiring another record store chain.

Hype—Exaggerated claims as to the worth of a particular product or event. Short for "hyperbole."

IATSE (International Association of Theatrical and Stage Employees)—A union for stagehands, lighting technicians, and other "behind the scenes" people who put on theatrical and concert events.

IFPI (International Federation of the Phonographic Industry)—An international trade organization for record labels, composed of the trade associations from individual countries, such as the RIAA in the US. The offices are in London, UK.

IMRA (Independent Music Retailers Association)—An ad hoc group of record retailers who banded together to fight the labels' policies against stores selling used CDs.

Independent distributor—A record wholesaler who distributes records from independent labels.

Independent label—A record label not owned by one of the four major conglomerates or their subsidiaries. Independent labels may have their recordings distributed by one of the big four and still be referred to as "indies."

Independent producer—A record producer who is not on salary from a record label. Independent producers usually work on a royalty basis similar to recording artists and may also be paid fees for each recording completed. (See also **staff producer**.)

Independent record store—A record store that is not part of a chain. A "mom and pop" store.

Indie—A term usually referring to an independent label or an independent record store.

Information age—Social and economic theories state that society has entered a new stage of development where society and development will be characterized not by the production of products, but by the production of content and the distribution and use of information.

In-house promotion—A performance promoted by the venue itself, without any outside promoter.

Initiation fee—A one-time fee to join a union. Not to be confused with *dues* which are paid on an ongoing basis.

Intellectual property—Copyrights, patents, trademarks, and trade secrets are all intellectual property, which means they are not physical property like land or books, but rather are rights associated with the use of works, inventions, marks, and information.

International Intellectual Property Alliance—A coalition of trade associations representing the various copyright industries in the United States, including recordings, motion pictures, book publishers, and others.

ISRC (International Standard Recording Code)—This is the international identification system for sound recordings and music video recordings, created through the IFPI (see above). Each ISRC is a unique and permanent identifier for a specific recording which can be permanently encoded into a product as its digital fingerprint. Encoded ISRCs provide the means to automatically identify recordings for royalty payments.

Joint work—In copyright law, a work created by two or more people with the intention that their contributions be merged into an integrated whole.

Jukebox—The contemporary name for a coin operated "record" player.

Jukebox Licensing Organization—The organization that issues public performance licenses for musical compositions played on jukeboxes. The jukebox operators pay a fee per box.

Key person (aka key man)—In contracts, most often personal management, recording, or publishing, a specified person that the artist is counting on being a member of the contracting firm. If that person leaves, then the contract is terminated.

Label—An individual record company, identified as a trade name on the labels that it puts on its recordings. The "majors" own many different labels.

Landmark Digital Services—The wholly-owned subsidiary of BMI that monitors airplay of BMI songs for the purpose of determining how much to pay BMI writers and publishers for public performances.

Leisure-time activities—Those things that people do that are not required by work or normal day-to-day activities such as sleeping or eating.

Librarian of Congress—The appointed head of the Library of Congress, this person has important administrative duties for a number of the compulsory licenses in copyright law. The Librarian is the ultimate overseer of the

Copyright Office, which is part of the Library of Congress. The Librarian distributes the royalties collected through the Copyright Office and is also responsible for convening certain proceedings relative to the **Copyright Royalty Board** (see above).

License—Permission to use something, such as a song or a recording, for some particular purpose.

Lip-synch—A performer pretends to be singing their song while a recording is being played, most often done in motion pictures or television, though sometimes done at concerts as well.

Liquidate reserves—A recording contract term meaning the label must pay out any reserves for returns that have not been accounted for with actual returns.

Listening station—A kiosk or manned listening area in a record store where consumers can hear all, or samples of, selections from albums or singles.

Local (union)—The organizational unit of a labor union that covers a particular city or geographic area.

Logging—The practice of keeping track of how many times individual songs or recordings are played or performed, usually for the performing rights organizations.

Long form video—Usually a video recording of a concert, that would include a significant number of songs.

Loss leader—Any product sold below cost in order to attract customers into a store. Some "big box" stores use recordings this way.

LP—The "long playing" 33 1/3 rpm 12-inch disc phonograph recording, introduced in 1948. It usually contained eight to ten songs.

Major label—A term, probably somewhat out of date, used to refer to a label owned by one of the big four which had its "own" distribution system. Now many small labels are owned by the big four and, therefore, technically have their own distribution because the same corporate parent owns the distribution system.

Majors—The "majors" refers to the four main recording/entertainment conglomerates.

Manufacturing clause—A part of the copyright law that prohibits copies of recordings made outside of the United States for sale outside of the United States from being sold in the United States unless the US copyright owner has given specific permission to import.

MAP (Minimum Advertised Price)—A price established by a label to discourage retailers from selling recordings below cost. The labels attempted to cut off some advertising funds for a retailer that advertised albums below that label's MAP. The Federal Trade Commission found this to be an illegal restraint of trade and the labels entered into a consent decree to stop the practice.

Margin—The amount of revenue left from the sale of a product after deducting the cost of the item sold.

Marketing concept—The creation and delivery of a product or service that will satisfy consumer needs and allow a profit to be made.

Masters—The recordings from which other recordings are later going to be made or duplicated. May refer to a multitrack master, a stereo master, or a duplicating master.

Mastertone ring tone—A ring tone which is an edit of an actual original master recording of an artist and label. Compare that to a "ring tune" which is a recording of the song, but probably with synthesizers playing the parts.

Mechanical license—Permission from the copyright owner of a musical composition to manufacture and distribute copies of the composition embodied in phonorecords intended for sale to the public.

Mechanical royalties—Payments made from record labels to music publishers for the right to reproduce copies of songs (non-dramatic musical compositions) in the recordings made by the labels. The term relates back to the 1909 Copyright Act, when Congress was creating a new right for music publishers that would give them the right to control recordings of their compositions in piano roll or recorded form. Player pianos and "talking machines" (phonographs/gramophones) were primarily regarded as mechanical devices upon which the composition could be reproduced or performed. The term still applies to such rights, even though new devices may be less mechanical and more electronic in nature.

MediaGuide—The wholly-owned subsidiary of ASCAP that monitors airplay of ASCAP songs for the purpose of determining how much to pay its members for performances.

MEIEA (Music and Entertainment Industry Educators Association)—An organization of people who teach audio and music business courses, mostly at colleges and universities, but does include some trade school teachers and related professionals.

Merchandisers—Retailers that sell to the public.

MIDI (Musical Instrument Digital Interface)—A computer communications protocol designed to let synthesizers, controllers, and sequencers from different manufacturers communicate with each other. Now also used as a control language for lighting and other equipment as well.

Mid-line—A label's record albums that have an SRLP of 66 2/3 to 75 or 85 percent of the SRLP of front line albums. (See also **Budget line**.)

Mom and pop store—A single store, usually a sole proprietorship, that is not part of a chain.

MOR (Middle-of-the-Road)—Refers to pop music aimed at older audiences. May specifically refer to recording artists popular in the 1940s and 1950s who were not rock, R&B, or country, or a radio format playing recordings by those performers.

MP3 (Abbreviation for MPEG-1 Audio Layer-3)—A file compression standard developed by the motion picture industry to make audio files smaller and therefore easier to transfer and store in computers and other devices.

MPA (Music Publishers' Association)—An early trade organization for music publishers that primarily emphasized issues relative to print music for education and concerts.

MPAA (Motion Picture Association of America)—The trade association (founded in 1922) that represents the producers and distributors of motion pictures, home video, and other television and cable entertainment programming. (See also **RIAA**.)

MSRP (Manufacturer's Suggested Retail Price)—A term often used in contracts as a basis for computing a recording artist's royalties as a percentage of MSRP as opposed to wholesale price.

MTV (Music Television)—The music video cable television channel launched in 1981 by Warner Communications.

Music director (MD)—The person responsible for a radio station's playlist of songs.

Music Performance Trust Fund (Phonograph Record Trust Agreement)—An agreement between the AFM and labels that requires labels to contribute a small amount per copy of each recording sold (about 0.3 percent) to a fund that is used to pay musicians to put on concerts that are free to the public.

Music publisher—A business that owns and/or administers copyrights in musical compositions.

MySpace—A social network community/site on the Web.

NAFTA (North American Free Trade Agreement)—A treaty among nations in the northern part of the western hemisphere that promotes free trade among these nations by reducing tariffs, quotas, and other trade barriers.

NAMM (National Association of Music Merchants)—The trade organization for music store owners. Music instrument manufacturers are associate members.

NARM (National Association of Recording Merchandisers)—The trade association for all record retailers and distributors. The labels are associate members.

Niche marketing—Finding a small group of people who will purchase the product you are selling rather than trying to sell to a mass market of a significant percentage of all consumers. For example, a record store selling only jazz recordings is niche marketing.

NMPA (National Music Publishers' Association)—A trade organization for music publishers; formerly known as the Music Publishers Protective Association.

Nondramatic performance—Performance of a single song in such a way that it does not tell any particular story; usually any performance of a single song that is not part of an opera or musical is nondramatic unless it tells a story accompanied by action or visuals. Nondramatic performances are the only kind licensed by the performing rights organizations (ASCAP, BMI, and SESAC).

Nonexclusive license—Permission to use a work, such as a song or recording, where that same permission may also be given to other users. Performance licenses and mechanical licenses are nonexclusive.

Nonreturnable—A term usually applied to an advance, meaning the advance does not have to be given back to the provider, even if no royalties are ever earned. The advance is therefore not a debt. Advances are usually recoupable, but nonreturnable.

Notice—In copyright law, the copyright notice placed on published copies of works. The © is used for most works and the ℗ for sound recordings.

Oligopoly—A market condition in which there are only a few firms competing in the market. A "few" is typically somewhere between two and twenty.

One-nighter—A performance engagement for only one night. Also known as a "one night stand."

One-stop—A kind of distributor that sells all records from all labels to retailers.

Open system—An organization that receives input from its external environment and interacts with that environment.

Option—Usually refers to a label's right to extend the recording agreement for an additional album; but this term generally refers to the company's right to keep the writer or artist under contract for some additional period of time.

Out-of-the-box—A radio term for adding a record to a playlist as soon as it is received, usually reserved for new releases by hot artists.

Outsourcing—A situation where a business hires another firm to perform some function that had previously been performed "in house."

Overdub—An audio engineering term meaning to record an additional part along with a previously recorded part.

Packaging deduction (see **Container charge**).

PACTS—The organizations and agreements set up to fund the production of major motion pictures.

Papering the house—A practice in the live entertainment business of giving away tickets so that the audience will be large enough to please the performer.

Parallel imports—Copies of works lawfully made outside of a country for distribution outside of that country but then imported back into the country of origin and sold alongside of copies manufactured in the country of origin.

Pay-for-play—Refers to the practice of some popular clubs, particularly in Los Angeles, of having the performer pay to use the facility. The performer hopes to attract attention from label and other music industry professionals.

Payola—The practice of paying someone to perform a particular song or recording. Historically, music publishers paid performers to sing their songs. More recently it refers to attempts by labels to make undisclosed payments to radio stations or disc jockeys to play their recordings. The latter practice is illegal.

PBS (Public Broadcasting Service)—The television network established to produce and distribute programming to noncommercial television stations.

Perform publicly—A term of art in the Copyright Act meaning to perform a work at a place open to the public, or at a place where a substantial number of people outside the normal circle of a family and its circle of social acquaintances is gathered, or to broadcast a performance of a work for public reception.

Performance right—The right to perform a work publicly. Usually the right to perform a song, but the term can also apply to limited situations in which sound recordings are digitally transmitted via the Internet, satellite, or by background music services. See **Digital performance of sound recordings**.

Performance royalty—The royalty paid to songwriters and music publishers for public performance rights. May also apply in limited situations to royalties paid to record companies for the public performance of sound recordings by digital audio transmission. See **Digital performance of sound recordings.**

Per-program use (or license)—Permission to use a single recording or song on a one-time basis, as compared to a blanket license.

Personal manager—An artist's representative who works closely with the artist at all stages and usually for all purposes to develop the artist's career.

Personality folio—A songbook featuring songs as recorded by a particular artist or writer.

Phonogram—The term most often used internationally for sound recordings.

Phonorecords—Tangible objects such as tapes, compact discs, or vinyl discs in/on which a sound recording is embodied. The term also applies to a digital file containing a recording.

Piracy—The IFPI calls piracy, "The deliberate infringement of copyright on a commercial scale." It includes physical piracy, which is the unauthorized duplications of sound recordings where the person or organization literally dubs a copy of the recording and sells a copy with identical sounds on it. **Counterfeiting**, **bootlegging**, and Internet piracy are three other forms. Internet piracy may not be "commercial" from the point of view of an individual unauthorized file sharer, but the overall magnitude of the activity has tremendous commercial impact.

Pitch—To promote a song to a music publisher or producer, or an artist to a label.

Platinum award—The RIAA certified sales at the wholesale level of 1,000,000 copies of a recording, or sales of 100,000 units or $2,000,000 at SRLP of music videos, and for each equal amount after that. Thus an album selling more than 2 million copies is "multi-platinum" or "double platinum."

Play or pay (also, **pay or play**)—A clause in a recording artist's contract meaning the label can either have the artist play for a recording session, or simply pay them scale wages as if a session were held and fulfill their entire obligation to the artist. Not to be confused with pay-for-play.

PMRC (Parents' Music Resource Center)—An organization dedicated to getting record labels to identify content of their music as potentially harmful to minors.

Point-of-purchase (POP) materials—Advertising and display materials intended to be used/displayed in a retail location that sells the merchandise advertised. A poster for a record album is POP material distributed to record stores.

Point-of-sale—Literally the cash register or other device where the sale of an item is recorded and the payment made.

Poor man's copyright—A term meaning to try to protect works without registering them with the US Copyright Office. Some people tried mailing copies to themselves registered mail, or depositing copies with writers' groups to provide evidence of the creation of the work. (See also **Common law copyright** above.)

Power of attorney—A contractual right to act on someone's behalf in a way that legally binds that person to obligations entered into by the "attorney" on behalf of the person represented.

PPD (Published Price to Dealers)—The price a label charges a distributor or major retailer, close to, but not really the same as "wholesale" price.

Press kit—An assemblage of photos and other information that provides background on an artist.

Press release—A formal printed announcement by a company about its activities that is written in the form of a news article and given to the media to generate or encourage publicity.

***Prima facie* evidence**—A legal term meaning evidence that is sufficient on its face to make a case or prove a point. A copyright registration is *prima facie* evidence of the validity of the copyright and other information on the registration form. It would then have to be up to the other party to prove otherwise.

PRO (Performing Rights Organization)—A generic term, not a formal term, used for convenience in discussing any or all such organizations that license performance rights and pay performance royalties to songwriters, music publishers, and record labels. For example, ASCAP, BMI, SESAC, and SoundExchange.

Producer—In recording, the person in charge of all aspects of the recording process. May also be used to refer to a concert producer of a live event.

Professional manager—The person at a music publishing company who is in charge of finding new songs and songwriters. They may also negotiate special uses of songs such as commercials or motion pictures.

Program director (PD)—The person at a radio or TV station in overall charge of all programming for the station. May make music programming decisions if there is no separate music director. This person has authority over everything that goes out over the air.

Progressive—A radio format, initially rock, playing longer versions of records and other records and artists not usually heard on Top 40 formats. Now more likely known as alternative.

Project studio—A recording studio, usually owned by an artist or producer, which is used mainly to make recordings for that particular artist or producer and is not rented out to outsiders.

Promoter—The person or organization in charge of arranging all aspects of a live performance.

Promotion person—Term applied to record label person or independent contractor whose job it is to get radio stations to play records released by the label.

Promotional copies—Copies of a recording given away to radio stations for the purpose of airplay or for giveaways to listeners, or given to album reviewers to expose the record to the public.

Public domain (PD)—A term of art regarding the status of works whose copyrights have expired or that were not subject to copyright protection. Public domain works may be used by anyone without obtaining licenses or clearances because PD works have no copyrights.

Public performance (see **Perform publicly**)

Publicity—Getting media exposure for an artist in the mass media that is not in the form of paid advertising.

Publishing administration—A deal in which one music publisher, usually a small artist or producer owned company, has a larger music publisher issue licenses and collect royalties in exchange for a percentage of the money collected.

Rack jobber—A distributor who buys records from branches or independent distributors and services the record departments in mass merchandiser stores or other non-record stores.

Rack locations—Those stores that have rack jobber-serviced record departments.

Rating—A radio station's percentage of the total available listeners at any given time or over a given time span (cf. share).

Recording Academy (aka NARAS (National Academy of Recording Arts and Sciences))—The organization for creative people associated with the production of recordings, including performers, engineers, producers, graphic designers, and more. The Recording Academy gives the annual Grammy Awards to recognize excellence in creative achievement in recordings.

Recording artist—A person who makes phonograph recordings under a contractual arrangement with a record label whereby the label pays the performer a percentage royalty based on sales of the recordings; to be distinguished from a side musician or background vocalist who does not receive a royalty.

Recording Artists Coalition (RAC)—A nonprofit organization that represents the interests of recording artists in legislative and public policy questions when the artists' interests conflict with those of the record labels.

Recording engineer—A type of audio engineer whose job it is to operate equipment in a recording studio to capture and reproduce sounds being made for a recording.

Recording fund—A kind of advance where the record label designates a fixed amount of money available to produce a master recording. Usually the artist and producer are allowed to keep any money that has not been used to create the finished master.

Recording Trust Fund—Also called the Music Performance Trust Fund, this fund was established by the AFM. The labels pay a small percentage of the list price of all recordings sold into the fund. The fund is then used to pay musicians who perform for free concerts for the general public. The idea of the fund is to make more live music available to more people.

Recoupable—Recoverable out of royalties actually earned or otherwise due. Advances are usually recoupable but nonreturnable, meaning that they are not a debt that would have to be repaid.

Recurrent—A radio programming term for a "recent current hit." A recurrent is not a hit at the present time, but is still popular enough to play fairly regularly, compared to a current hit, or an "oldie."

Release—A recording made available to the public, or to make a recording available to the public.

Release date—The day designated by the record label when a recording is available to the public. May also be known as the "street date."

Remaster—Take a previously completed and mastered recording and mix the sounds down to a new master, or take the completed master and tweak the sounds, say for CD or MP3 release.

Renegotiate—A term used in the recording industry to refer to the practice of artists who are under recording agreements but who use their substantial success as an opportunity to redefine the terms of the agreement before it would otherwise end.

Renewal term—The second term of duration of copyright for works published prior to 1978. There was only one renewal term for pre-1978 copyrights.

Reserve for returns—An amount of royalties, or the royalties that would be paid for a certain amount of sales, that are not paid to a recording artist because records are shipped to retailers and wholesalers subject to being returned at a later date. Artists are not paid for recordings that are returned. (See also **Liquidate reserves**.)

Returns—Records sent back to the distributor or label because they have not been sold at the retail level. Returns may include defective merchandise as well as simple overstock.

Revenue stream—The path through which money flows. In the music business these paths are from consumers back to the creators of musical compositions, live performances, and recordings.

Reversion—A term usually seen in songwriter-publisher agreements referring to the writer's right to recapture the copyrights in the songs. There is a statutory reversion right called the Termination Right in the Copyright Act. The reversion may also be strictly contractual.

RIAA (Recording Industry Association of America)—The trade association for record labels and manufacturers.

Rider—An attachment to an agreement. In concert promotion, the rider is where the artist spells out specific requirements for the performance, such as sound, lights, size of stage, power requirements, kind and amount of food, and other considerations. There may be a technical rider and a separate food rider with requirements that the promoter is expected to meet.

Right to work—Provision of the laws of some states, particularly in the South, that prohibits unions from requiring that all employees of a particular firm belong to that union.

Rotation—Radio programming term referring to a group of records that is played through in a certain period of time. A station may have several rotations, such as a "power rotation" that is played through entirely every couple of hours and an oldies rotation that is played through every few days. Also refers to video programming.

Royalties—Payments to writers or performers due from the sale of copies, performances, or other uses of their works.

Sampling—Commonly understood as the process of capturing a portion of a recording via some digital recorder so that the sound from the previous recording can be used to create part of a new recording. The sampled signal is manipulated through signal processing or computer sequencing to form an integral part of the rhythm, melody, lyrics, or overall production of the new recording. The process of sampling is important because the digital sounds can be manipulated much more than an analog recording. (See also **Digital sampling**.)

Scale wages—Payments to musicians or vocalists for live or recorded performances at the amount (scale) required by the union.

Self-contained—Usually refers to performing artists who write their own material, but may also refer to a band that does not require any additional musicians for their performances.

SESAC—SESAC, Inc. is the smallest of the three main performing rights organizations in the United States. SESAC used to stand for Society of European Stage Authors and Composers, but now does not have any particular meaning beyond its letters as the name of the organization.

Share—The percentage of people actually listening to any radio station that are listening to a particular station. Thus, if a station has a 15 percent share, 15 percent of the people listening to radio at that time are listening to that station. The other 85 percent are listening to other radio stations.

Shed—Another term for an outdoor amphitheater.

Shelf price—The usual price at which comparable albums are sold in a given store. This is usually not the SRLP but is typically below that; to be distinguished from a sale price.

Short form video—A music video, usually just containing one song.

Shortfall—A kind of tour support, with the label making up any difference between an agreed-upon amount per performance and the amount the artist actually makes per performance.

Showcase—A performance, usually in a small club, designed to promote a performer to radio programmers, label A&R people, music publishing people, or some other industry audience, as opposed to the general public.

Shrinkage—Loss of inventory due to factors not accounted for, such as theft, damage, or accounting errors.

Side—A term in recording contracts referring to a recording of a single song. It may also be used in a non-legal sense to refer to all of the songs on one side of an LP, cassette, or single.

Single—A recording of a single composition released by itself, or with only one other composition. CD-5 or maxi singles usually have four or five cuts on them.

Small rights—Nondramatic public performance rights, i.e. the kind licensed by ASCAP, BMI, and SESAC.

SMPTE (Society of Motion Picture and Television Engineers)—An organization for the technical people associated with the production of television programs and motion pictures. It includes people in multimedia productions. Audio engineers often belong to this and AES.

Social network sites—An Internet-based network such as Facebook, MySpace, or LinkedIn that allows users to define a group of "friends" and to connect to each other and follow each other.

Soft tickets—Tickets for an event that are not printed in advance of sale, but are printed by a computer at the time of sale. Also refers to tickets printed on the purchaser's computer.

Song plugger—A person who works for a music publishing company whose job it is to get the song recorded, performed, and used in other ways.

Songfile—The Harry Fox Agency's online licensing system for mechanical licenses.

Sound-alike—A recording made to sound as much like the one by the original artists as possible. It is a new recording, but the musicians and singers imitate the sounds on the previous recording.

SoundExchange—The organization formed by the RIAA that is in charge of distribution of royalties collected for the digital performance of sound recordings. It also negotiates royalty rates for Webcasters and others not subject to the compulsory license for digital audio performance of sound recordings.

Sound recording—A kind of copyrightable work in which sounds created by various sources are captured, or "fixed," in some tangible medium such as tape or disc. These works are to be distinguished from the underlying works such as musical compositions or dramatic works which are recorded, and the material objects or "phonorecords" in/on which the recordings are fixed. Sound recordings do not include sound accompanying motion pictures; those recordings are part of the motion picture copyright.

SoundScan—The company that collects point-of-sale information from the UPC bar code scanners at a variety of record retail outlets and sells sales pattern information to the labels or other parties; now actually Nielsen SoundScan, a division of Nielsen Retail Information.

Soundtrack—The audio accompaniment to a motion picture or television program.

Soundtrack album—An album consisting of a collection of the musical works, and sometimes other sounds, in a motion picture or television program.

SPARS (Society of Professional Recording Services)—A trade organization for recording studio owners, and tape and CD replicators.

Special payments fund—A trust fund administered by the AFM composed of payments from record labels based on a small percentage of the price of recordings sold. The fund is distributed to musicians on an annual basis based on the number of master recording sessions on which the musician had played over the previous year.

Spin count (also called simply spins)—The number of times a particular recording has been played over the radio, as recorded by a tracking service such as BDS.

Sponsored tour—A live appearance tour where part of the costs and probably some advertising is underwritten by a third party who uses the appearances of the artist to promote and sell non artist-related merchandise, such as soft drinks or clothing.

SRDS (Standard Rate and Data Service)—A series of publications that lists media outlets, their facilities, policies, and advertising rates.

SRLP (See MSRP)

Staff producer—A producer who works on a salaried basis for the label (and probably a small royalty, too). Currently such persons are likely to be label executives who also happen to be producers. Most producers are now independent producers.

Staff writer—A songwriter who works under an exclusive agreement with a music publisher, usually on a weekly or monthly advance.

Statutory rate—A term usually applied to the compulsory mechanical royalty rate. Originally, the rate was set by Congress in the 1909 Copyright Act and later the 1976 Copyright Act, hence the term "statutory." Now the rate is set by the Copyright Royalty Board, but is still referred to as the "statutory rate."

Stiff—A record that sells badly, or that does not get much radio airplay.

Stockout—A situation where the demand or requirement for an item cannot be fulfilled from the current inventory.

Street date—The date a recording is made available for sale to the public.

Street teams—Local groups of people who use networking on behalf of the artist in order to reach the artist's target market.

Strip center—A shopping center with stores spread out in a row, usually along a main road, with common walls, and no enclosed pedestrian area.

Synchronization right—The right of the owner of a musical composition copyright to use the composition in time relation to visual images, such as in movies or television shows, or perhaps in multimedia.

Syndication (television and radio)—The licensing of programs for use at multiple local stations by independent agencies, not through the major networks.

Synergy—In business, the concept that says the combination of several organizations or systems into one can produce a higher output than they can independently of each other.

Systems theory—A business theory which states that any business organization is a system of converting inputs into outputs and that the organization exists in an environment that influences its processes.

Take—A recorded attempt by the recording artists or musicians at a complete performance of a song.

Talent agent (aka booking agent)—A person who secures employment for performers.

Tear sheets—A page of a publication featuring a particular advertisement or feature and sent to the advertiser or public relations firm for substantiation purposes; or copies of previous articles.

Technically acceptable—In recording contracts, this means that a master is of high enough quality to be suitable for release to the public. This is distinguished from commercially acceptable, which implies a higher standard, and the label's judgment as to whether a particular recording will be successful commercially as opposed to artistically.

Telegenic—Presenting a pleasing appearance on television.

Termination rights—Statutory rights of authors (or certain of their heirs) under copyright law to end transfers of copyrights and non-exclusive licenses during a 5-year period beginning after 35 years from the date of transfer and running through the fortieth year. (If the transfer includes the right to publish, then the 5-year period starts after 40 years after the date of transfer, or 35 years after the date of first publication, whichever is earlier.) Thus, the author can "recapture" the transferred copyrights.

Ticket resellers—These organizations acquire concert tickets from original purchasers who can no longer attend the event, or on their own, or other scalpers, and then sell them to the public, often at inflated prices.

Tight oligopoly—An oligopoly where four firms control 60 percent or more of the market.

TNN (The Nashville Network)—Originally a cable television network devoted to country music and other "country" lifestyle programming. In 2003 it changed to "spike TV" and changed its programming to appeal to 18-to-24-year-old-males.

Top 40—The radio format that plays the 40 most popular recordings in the broadcaster's market. Used generically to refer to any format that plays the most popular recordings, including CHR.

Tour support—Usually monetary support for new recording artists to help them make personal appearance performances. Tour support is often given when the label believes that live appearances will help sell recordings. It is usually a recoupable advance (see **Shortfall**).

Track—A recording of one particular instrument or vocalist that is separate from the other performances on the session for that song, or the process of recording such tracks. Also refers to a segment of a recording medium that can be recorded and played back separately from the others for that song. Also refers to keeping "track" of radio airplay.

Track equivalent albums (TEAs)—A way of equating downloads (which are usually of single tracks) to album sales. Each 10 downloaded single tracks is counted as if it were one album.

Trade advertising—Ads aimed at decision makers in the industry, including people in radio, retail, and booking agents.

Trades—The magazines devoted to a particular business. *Billboard*, *Pollstar*, *Broadcasting and Cable*, and *Variety* are among the important trade publications in the recording industry.

Transcription license—Permission to make a recording of a song where copies of the recording are not intended for distribution to the public. Radio stations frequently receive transcription recordings for broadcast purposes of advertisements or programs.

Transnational—A situation where businesses, culture, and even governance may be shared across many national boundaries.

Triple A format—A radio format, Adult Album Alternative, that plays more than just hits, but other album cuts of "alternative" music, mainly targeted to an audience over 24 years old.

Turntable hit—A recording that receives lots of radio airplay, but does not generate many sales.

UPC (see Bar code).

Unrecouped—A term meaning that an artist, writer, or performer has not earned enough royalties to cover the amount of advance which they have already received. The unrecouped portion of the advance is *not* a "debt."

Upstream deal—A deal where an artist signs with one of the "independent distribution" companies owned by one of the four majors and the major has the option to sign the artist to one of its wholly owned labels if it wishes to in the future, mainly if the artist becomes successful.

Venue—The place where a live performance happens. It could be a club, a theater, an auditorium, a stadium, or an open field.

Vertical integration—A market condition in which a firm owns more than one portion of the total distribution chain from manufacturer to consumer. A record label that owns a pressing plant is an example of vertical integration, as is a distributor that owns record stores.

VH-1—The cable television channel programmed to viewers who prefer a wider range of music and softer music than that programmed by the rock/urban-oriented MTV.

VHS—The home video tape recording format (along with Betamax).

Vicarious infringer—A party who benefits financially from an infringement, and who could control whether the infringement occurred. They do not have to have knowledge of the infringement (cf. contributory infringer).

Videogram—A video recording of a motion picture, music video, or other visual work. Usually the term refers to videograms that are manufactured and distributed for consumer purchase.

Viral video and viral marketing—A video that becomes popular because of Internet file sharing. Viral marketing is using file sharing and social networks to spread the popularity of a product or recording.

Webcasting—Transmitting a performance of songs, recordings, or videos by streaming the performance over the Internet/World Wide Web. Known originally as "Netcasting."

Work dues—Dues paid to the union by performers based on their earnings from live appearances.

Work made for hire—In copyright law, a work made by an employee within the scope of employment, or a commissioned work of certain kinds if the parties agree in writing that the work is to be considered for hire. The employer or commissioning party owns the copyrights in works made for hire.

World Trade Organization (WTO)—The international trade organization created in 1995 by the General Agreement on Tariffs and Trade treaty of 1994. WTO members promise to provide "Berne Level" protection to copyrights and may be subject to trade sanctions from the organization and other members for failure to do so. Major disputes between the United States and China over China's lack of copyright protection for recordings, motion pictures, and computer software prevented China from joining the organization until 2001.

Appendix: Internet Resources

The Internet is a rich source of information about the music and recording business. There are certainly more sites about music and artists than can possibly be listed here. While most students are familiar with artist and commercial label websites, MySpace, and Facebook pages, what *are* here are the inside information sources. As with anything about the Internet, it may be that some of these addresses will change, or have even changed as the book went to print, but these are a good starting place, so surf's up!

Industry Organizations

Acoustical Society of America
asa.aip.org
Alliance of Artists and Record Companies
www.aarcroyalties.com
American Association for Independent Music
www.a2im.org
American Federation of Musicians
www.afm.org
American Federation of Television and Radio Artists
www.aftra.org
American Music Conference
www.amc-music.com
Audio Engineering Society
www.aes.org
Australian Recording Industry Association
www.aria.com.au
Broadcast Data Service
charts.bdsradio.com
Canadian Country Music Awards
www.ccma.org/awards
Canadian Music Trade
www.canadianmusictrade.com
Copyright Agency Limited (Australia)
www.copyright.com.au
Copyright Office
www.copyright.gov
Copyright Royalty Board
www.loc.gov/crb/
Copyright Society of the USA
www.csusa.org
Federal Communications Commission
www.fcc.gov

Future of Music Coalition
  www.futureofmusic.org
Global Alliance of Performers
  www.gap.org
Grammy Awards
  www.grammy.com
Home Recording Rights Coalition
  www.hrrc.org
International Association of Theatrical and Stage Employees
  www.iatse-intl.org
International Bluegrass Music Association
  www.ibma.org
International Federation of the Phonographic Industry
  www.ifpi.org
International Intellectual Property Alliance
  www.iipa.com
Irish Music Rights Organization
  www.imro.ie
IRMA
  www.recordingmedia.com
Mechanical Copyright and Protection Society
  www.mcps.co.uk
Music and Entertainment Industry Educators Association
  www.meiea.org
Music Network USA
  www.mnusa.com
Music Publishers Association (MPA)
  http://mpa.org
National Association of Broadcasters
  www.nab.org
National Association of Recording Merchandisers
  www.narm.com
National Music Foundation
  www.usamusic.org
National Music Publishers' Association
  www.nmpa.org
Nashville Songwriters Association International
  www.nashvillesongwriters.com
Neilsen SoundScan (and other Nielsen services)
  en-us.nielsen.com
North by Northeast Conference
  www.nxne.com
Patent and Trademark Office
  www.uspto.gov
Professional Lighting and Sound Association
  www.plasa.org
Recording Academy (NARAS)
  www.grammy.com
Recording Industry Association of America (RIAA)
  www.riaa.com

Society of Motion Picture and Television Engineers
  www.smpte.org
Society of Professional Audio Recording Services (SPARS)
  www.spars.com
Songwriters Guild of America
  www.songwriters.org
SoundExchange
  www.soundexchange.com
South by Southwest Conference
  www.sxsw.com/sxsw/directory.html
Women in Music
  www.womeninmusic.org
World Forum on Music and Censorship
  www.freemus.org

The Majors (Corporate Sites)

EMI Group
  www.emigroup.com
Sony Corp. (Japan)
  www.sony.net
Sony Music Entertainment
  www.sonymusic.com
Universal Music Group
  www.umusic.com
Vivendi SA
  www.vivendi.com
Warner Music Group
  www.wmg.com

Music Publishing

Cherry Lane Music
  www.cherrylane.com
EMI Music Publishing
  http://emimusicpub.com
Hal Leonard Music
  www.halleonard.com
Music Sales Group
  www.musicsales.com
Sony/ATV Music Publishing
  www.sonyatv.com
Universal Music Publishing
  www.umusicpub.com
Warner/Chappell Music
  www.warnerchappell.com

Performing Rights Organizations

ASCAP
  www.ascap.org
BMI
  www.bmi.com
SESAC
  www.sesac.com
APRA Australia
  www.apra.com.au
BUMA Netherlands
  www.buma.nl
GEMA Germany
  www.gema.de
International Conference of Societies of Authors and Composers (CISAC)
  www.cisac.org
PRS United Kingdom
  www.prs.co.uk
SABAM Belgium
  www.sabam.be

Live Performance

AEG Live
  http://aeglive.com
Live Nation
  www.livenation.com
Music Managers Forum
  www.mmf-us.org

Periodicals

Billboard
  www.billboard.com
  www.billboard.biz
Broadcasting & Cable
  www.broadcastingcable.com
Contempory Christian Music Magazine
  www.ccmmagazine.com
Creative Loafing Magazine
  www.creativeloafing.com
Dealerscope Merchandising
  www.dealerscope.com
Mix Magazine Online
  http://mixonline.com
Music Network USA
  www.mnusa.com
Music Trades
  www.musictrades.com

Music Universe
   www.musicuniverse.com
Music Week
   www.musicweek.com
Nashville Scene
   www.nashvillescene.com
Pollstar
   www.pollstar.com
Pro Sound News
   www.prosoundnews.com
Rock and Roll Reporter
   www.rocknrollreporter.com
Rolling Stone
   www.rollingstone.com
Spin
   www.spin.com
Vibe magazine
   www.vibe.com

MISCELLANEOUS

CD Baby
   www.cdbaby.com
CMT
   www.cmt.com
EMusic.com
   www.emusic.com
Rock and Roll Hall of Fame
   www.rockhall.com

Notes

1 The Entertainment Industry and the Music Business

1 Jay Bryan Nash, *The Philosophy of Recreation and Leisure* (New York: WCB/McGraw-Hill, 2000).
2 *The Harris Poll Different Leisure Activities*, Harris Interactive, www.harrisinteractive.com.
3 John Howkins, *The Creative Economy: How People Make Money From Ideas* (New York: Penguin Press, 2001).
4 Simon Frith, "Popular Music and the Local State," in T. Bennett, S. Frith and L. Gossberg et al. (eds) *Rock and Popular Music: Politics, Policies and Institutions* (London: Routledge, 1993).
5 International Intellectual Property Alliance (2009) "Copyright Industries in the US Economy: the 2003-2007 Report," prepared by Stephen E., Siwek Economists Incorporated.
6 Albert Greco, "Shaping the Future: Mergers, Acquisitions, and the US Publishing, Communications, and Mass Media Industries, 1990-1995," *Publishing Review Quarterly*, 12(3): 5 (1996).
7 *Fact Sheet*, Hoover's A D&B Company, www.Hoovers.com.
8 According to each company's 2008 annual report, revenues are as follows: Time Warner $29.8 billion, Walt Disney $37.8 billion, GE $183 billion, VIACOM $14.6 billion, CBS $14 billion, and News Corp $33 billion.
9 *Survey on Movies and Home Entertainment*, Standard and Poor.
10 *Commercial Piracy Report* (IFPI, 2006), www.ifpi.org/site-content/library/piracy/2006.pdf.
11 *RIAA Gold and Platinum Top 100 Albums*, RIAA, www.riaa.org/goldandplatinumdata.php.
12 As of writing, GE and Comcast are in a partnership in which GE would maintain 49 percent control of the new company, while Comcast would have a controlling 51 percent stake in NBC Universal.
13 *Entertainment Industry Market Statistics* 2007, MPAA, www.mpaa.org/usentertainment industrymarketstats.pdf.
14 National Association of Theatre Owners (2009), www.natoonline.org.
15 Ibid (note 13).
16 "TV Trends in Ownership," *Time Almanac of the 20th Century* (New York: Time, Inc, 1995).
17 Gerald Mast, *A Short History of the Movies*, 2nd edition (Indianapolis, IN: Bobbs-Merill, 1976), p. 315.
18 *Essential Facts About the Computer and Video Game Industry 2009*, Entertainment Software Association (ESA), www.theesa.com/facts/pdfs/ESA_EF_2009.pdf.
19 *Pew Internet and American Life Report 2008*, Pew Research Center, http://pewInternet.org/PPF/r/263/report_display.asp.
20 *MobyStats*, MobyGames, www.mobygames.com/moby_stats.
21 Disney Annual Report, 2004.

2 Understanding the Music and Recording Business

1 Address in Frankfurt, Germany, June 25, 1963. From the *International Thesaurus of Quotations* (New York: Harper and Row, 1970), p. 74.

2 For this and other examples, see Lisa A. Lewis, *Gender Politics and MTV* (Philadelphia, PA: Temple University Press, 1990).

3 Lisa A. Lewis, *Gender Politics and MTV* (1990).

4 Simon Frith, "Critical Response," in Deanna Campbell Robinson, Elizabeth Buck, and Marlene Cuthbert, *Music at the Margins* (Newbury Park, CA: Sage Publications, 1991), p. 287 (emphasis in original).

5 Camelot Music executive Jim Bonk, quoted in Geoff Mayfield, "Camelot Pulls Live Crew," *Billboard*, May 2, 1987, p. 87.

6 Melvin L. DeFleur and Everette E. Dennis, *Understanding Mass Communication*, 4th edition (Boston, MA: Houghton-Mifflin, 1991), p. 475.

7 Peter F. Drucker, *Managing for the Future* (New York: Truman Talley Books, 1992), p. 8.

8 Harold L. Vogel, *Entertainment Industry Economics* (New York: Cambridge University Press, 1986), p. 149.

9 *Broadcasting Yearbook*, 1986 and 1996.

10 Dennis McQuail, *Mass Communication Theory* (Thousand Oaks, CA: Sage Publications, 1994), p. 20.

11 James Lull, "Popular Music and Communication," in *Popular Music and Communication*, 2nd edition (Newbury Park, CA: Sage Publications, 1992), p. 1.

12 Richard Campbell, *Media and Culture*, 2nd edition (Boston, MA: Bedford/St. Martins, 2000), p. 66.

13 Werner J. Severin and James W. Tankard, Jr., *Communication Theories: Origins, Methods Used in the Mass Media*, 3rd edition (White Plains, NY: Longman, 1988), p. 43.

14 Alan B. Albarran, *Media Economics* (Ames, IA: Iowa State University Press, 1996), p. 6.

15 Raffaelo Quipino, *Ani DiFranco: Righteous Babe Revisited* (Los Angeles, CA: Fox Music Books, 2004).

16 Bo Burlingham, *Small Giants* (New York: Penguin, 2007).

3 Copyright Basics in the Music Business

1 *Mazer v. Stein*, 347 US 201, 218 (1954).

2 17 U.S.C. §106.

3 17 U.S.C. §§301, *et seq*.

4 17 U.S.C. §§401, 402.

5 17 U.S.C. §101 definition.

6 17 U.S.C. §101 definition.

7 *Community for Creative Non-Violence v. Reid*, 490 US 730 (1989).

8 17 U.S.C §203, and 304(c), and (d).

9 17 U.S.C. §107.

10 *Campbell v. Acuff-Rose Music, Inc.*, 510 US 569 (1994).
    All titles have sections represented by a § (from wikipedia)!

4 Music Copyrights ©

1 *Woods v. Bourne Co.*, 841 F.Supp. 118, 121 (S.D.N.Y. 1994).

2 Herbert v. Shanley, 242 US 591, 592 (1917).

3 *Bright Tunes Music Corp. v. Harrisongs Music Ltd*, 420 F.Supp. 177 (S.D.N.Y. 1976).

4 Although there are earlier claims to the Chinese invention of moveable type, with all due respect to Chinese inventiveness, there was no interest in the mass reproduction and distribution of works in China, and hence no development of copyright law. In fact, there was no copyright law in China until a desire to participate more broadly in international trade in the early 1990s motivated the Chinese to pass a copyright law so they could join the Berne Convention for the Protection of Literary Property. At any rate, it was Gutenberg's press that was imported into England and which gave rise to the copyright laws we inherited from England.

5 John V. Pavlik, *New Media and the Information Superhighway* (Needham Heights, MA: Allyn & Bacon, 1996), p. 125.

5 Sound Recording Copyrights Ⓟ

1 Warner Communications, Inc., "The Prerecorded Music Market: An Industry Survey", *NARAS Institute Journal* 2(1): 78, 1978.
2 Maverick Recording Company v. Harper, 2010 US App. LEXIS 3912, February 25, 2010. US Court of Appeals, 5th Circuit.
3 "64 Individuals Agree to Settlements in Copyright Infringement Cases," September 29, 2003. Retrieved March 15, 2010 from www.riaa.com.
4 David Kravets, "Former Teen Cheerleader Dinged $27,750 for File Sharing 37 Songs," February 26, 2010. Retrieved from www.wired.com, March 15, 2010.

6 Music Publishing: The First Stream

1 Slogan of the Nashville Songwriters Association International.
2 A quote attributed to publisher Lou Levy, founder of Leeds Music, who died in 1995. Irv Lichtman, "Publishing Legend Lou Levy Dies at 84," Billboard, 11 November, 1995, p. 8.
3 Warner/Chappel Music creative VP, John Titta, quoted in Melinda Newman, "The A&R Angle," *Billboard*, June 3, 1995, p. 53.
4 Irv Lichtman, "Strong NMPA Stats in Past Indicate Happy Times Now," *Billboard*, December 25, 1993, p. 24.
5 Al Kohn & Bob Kohn, *Kohn on Music Licensing*, 2nd edition (1996), p. 111.
6 *Broadcast Music, Inc. v. Columbia Broadcasting System, Inc.*, 99 S. Ct. 1551, at 1562–1563 (1979).
7 Bill Lowery was the owner of Lowery Music Group in Atlanta, GA and a past president of the National Academy of Recording Arts and Sciences. This is something that the author heard him say publicly on a number of occasions. He died in 2004. Lowery Music was purchased by Sony/ATV Music prior to his death.
8 Quoted in Tom Roland, "It's Not Easy to Make a Buck," *The Tennessean*, January 5, 1995, p. E1.
9 Gail Mitchell, "They Write the Songs," *Billboard*, June 19, 1999, p. 28.

7 Live Entertainment: The Second Stream

1 Quoted in Bill Flanagan "We Three Kings," *Musician*, April 1991, pp. 52, 59.
2 Quoted in Zenon Schoepe, "Management Maven," *1996 Performance Guide: Talent/PM* (1996), p. 6.
3 Regional promoter Philip Lashinsky, speaking in a concert promotion class at Middle Tennessee State University, September 20, 1994.
4 Chuck Taylor and Melinda Newman: "SFX buys promoter Delsener/Slater," *Billboard*, 26 October, 1996, p. 1.
5 House of Blues Executive Vice President, Alex Hodges, quoted in Ray Waddell, "Concert Outlook Bright as Biz Weighs Mega-Merger," *Billboard*, March 11, 2000, p. 1.
6 Quoted in Ray Waddell "NIPP settles lawsuit: Promoter claimed Clear Channel ran a monopoly," *Billboard*, 12 June, 2004, p. 5.

8 Recordings: The Main Stream

1 Waller, Don. "About LaFace: The Hits Keep Coming," *Billboard*, December 11, 1999.

9 The A&R Function

1 The information in this section is gleaned from personal experiences of the authors and many other sources. Some of the best sources for more information on recording agreements are listed here.

Jeffrey Brabec and Todd Brabec, *Music, Money and Success*, 6th edition (New York: Schirmer Books, 2008).

Mark Halloran, *The Musician's Business and Legal Guide* (Upper Saddle River, N.J.: Pearson/Prentice Hall, 2008).

Donald S. Passman, *All You Need to Know about the Music Business*, 6th edition (New York: Free Press/Simon and Schuster, 2006).

William Krasilovsky and Sidney Shemel, *This Business of Music*, 10th edition (New York: Watson-Guptill, 2007).

2 Primary source material is *T.E.A.M. Entertainment, Inc. v. Douglas*, 361 F. Supp. 2d 362 (S.D.N.Y. 2005).

Secondary sources include:

"Ashanti: Breached Contract," Boggietonight.blogspot.com, July 22, 2005, retrieved March 17, 2010.

"Ashanti Files Lawsuit," www.contactmusic.com, February 1, 2006, retrieved March 17, 2010.

"Ashanti Files Lawsuit over Early Demos," *Billboard.com*, retrieved March 17, 2010.

Moses Avalon, "Getting Inside the Ashanti Lawsuit," *Royalty Week*, March 27, 2007, p. 6.

Elena Grogan, "Ashanti Settles Lawsuit with Former Producer," News.softpedia.com, September 20, 2006, retrieved March 17, 2010.

3 Moses Avalon, "Getting Inside the Ashanti Lawsuit," *Royalty Week*, March 27, 2007, p. 6.

10 The Production Function

1 Simon Frith, "The Industrialization of Popular Music," in James Lull (ed.) *Popular Music and Communication*, 2nd edition (Newbury, CA: Sage Publications, 1992), p. 50.

2 Daniel Marty, *The Illustrated History of Talking Machines* (Lausanne, Switzerland: Edita, 1981), p. 146.

3 Chris Steinwand, "An Industry in Transition, Part I," *Pro Sound News*, October 2001, p. 26.

4 World Studio Group and Record Plant founder, Chris Stone, quoted in Christopher Walsh, "Recording Studios Squeezed as Labels Tighten Budgets," *Billboard*, February 15, 2003, p. 1.

5 Dan Daley, "Studios Develop Coping Skills As Margins Shrink," *Pro Sound News*, February 1996, p. 14.

6 Thomas W. Hutchison and James A. Progris, "Study Shows Music Biz Graduates are Given Top Priority," *NARM Sounding Board*, November 1996, p. 8.

7 NARAS (the Recording Academy), formerly the National Academy of Recording Arts and Sciences, is still called NARAS by many people in the industry.

8 Sasha Frere-Jones, "The Timbaland Era," *The New Yorker*, October 6, 2008, p. 82.

9 Retrieved from www.timbalandmusic.com, January 13, 2010.

10 See note 8 above.

11 The Marketing Function: Product and Price

1 Committee on Definitions, *Marketing Definitions: A Glossary of Marketing Terms* (Chicago, IL: American Marketing Association, 1960).

2 T. Hutchison, A. Macy, and P. Allen, *Record Label Marketing*, 2nd edition (Oxford: Focal Press, 2009).

3 P. Kotler and G. Armstrong, *Marketing: An introduction* (Upper Saddle River, NJ: Prentice Hall, 1996).

4 *Billboard* magazine. Issues selected at intervals.

5 SoundScan sales data.

6 T. Hutchison, A. Macy, and P. Allen, *Record Label Marketing*, 2nd edition (Oxford, UK: Focal Press, 2009).

7 Karl F. Schuessler, "Social Background and Musical Taste," *American Sociological Review*, 13: 330–335 (1948).

8 R.D. Dixon, "Music Taste Cultures and Taste Publics Revisited: A Research Note of New Evidence," *Popular Music and Society*, 8(1): 2–9 (1981).

9 George H. Lewis, "Cultural Socialization and the Development of Taste Cultures and Culture Classes in American Popular Music: Existing Evidence and Proposed Research Directions," *Popular Music and Society*, 4(4): 226–241 (1975).

10 Thomas Hutchison, "For the record: An exploratory study of the role of interactive kiosks in information-seeking behavior by consumers of recorded music, Doctoral dissertation, Florida State University, Tallahassee, FL, 1995. digitool.fcla.edu/dtl_publish/32/120118.html.

11 Edward Wallerstein (date unknown). Narrative told by Edward Wallerstein (1891–1970) about the development of the LP record in 1948, www.classicalmusiccd.com/audiohistoryLP.html.

12 IEEE Global History Network, "LP and 45RPM Records," www.ieeeghn.org/wiki/index.php/LP_and_45_RPM_Records.

13 Krzys Wasilewski, "Short History of Cassettes. News, Interviews, and More" (2007), http://thesop.org/technology/2007/08/02/short-history-of-cassettes.

14 History of Dolby, www.dolby.com/about/who-we-are/our-history/history-2.html.

15 "Downloading Increases while CD Sales Decline," *Pollstar*, March 18, 2009. www.pollstar.com/blogs/news/archive/2009/03/18/655077.aspx.

16 The original players were more of a novelty than a practicality: For a mere $200, you could listen to 60 minutes of CD-quality music in MP3 audio format. Users had to return to their computers and reload the player to listen to more songs, or use removable media such as SmartMedia cards to hold additional music. By 1999, portable MP3 players from a number of manufacturers were popular, and other software developers, such as Liquid Audio and a2b, scrambled to develop audio compression formats that were more secure and would appeal to piracy-conscious record labels.

17 Janelle Brown, "MP3 Crackdown: As the Recording Industry 'Educate' Universities about Digital Music Piracy, Students Feel the Heat," November 17, 1999, Salon.com, www.salon.com/tech/log/1999/11/17/riaa/index.html?source=search&aim=/tech/ log.

18 Sites + Sounds: "Billboard Spotlights the Digital Music Revolution—Downloading: Who's Doing What?", *Billboard*, November 18, 2000.

19 Thomas Hormby, "History of iTunes and iPod," *The iPod Observer*, May 10, 2007, www.ipodobserver.com/story/31394.

20 Justin Oppelaar, "Apple Wants Big Bite of Music Downloads," *Daily Variety*, April 29, 2003.

21 J. Silverstein, "iTunes: 1 Billion Served," *ABC News*, February 23, 2006, http://abcnews.go.com/print?id=165881.

22 Ed Christman, *Billboard*, January 4, 2007.

23 Craig Rosen, "CD Singles Spurred by Addition of Non-Album Cuts," *Billboard*, 30 March, 1996, p. 5.

24 Geoff Mayfield, "A New Billboard Hot 100 Reflects Changes in Music Business," *Billboard*, December 2, 1998.

25 Matthew Benz, "SoundScan Adds Download Data," *Billboard*, July 12, 2003, p. 5.

26 Brian Garrity and Ed Christman, "Digital Sales Spur Chart Debate," *Billboard*, November 15, 2003. www.billboard.biz/bbbiz/search/article_display.jsp?vnu_content_id=2021078.

27 A. Elberse, "Bye Bye Bundles: The Unbundling of Music in Digital Channels," Harvard Business School, Academic Paper (2009). www.people.hbs.edu/aelberse/papers/Elberse_2010.pdf.

28 IFPI *Digital Music Report*, 2009, www.ifpi.org.

29 C. Morris, "Labels Search for New Ways to Jump Start Catalog Sales," *Billboard*, December 11, 1999.

30 C. Phillips, "Record Label Chorus: High Risk, Low Margin," *Los Angeles Times*, May 31, 2001.

31 From an accounting perspective the production costs are fixed because they do not vary with the number of units sold. If recording costs are $250,000 for an album, they remain that way whether none is sold or a million are sold. However, some label executives refer to production costs as "variable" because they have some control over these costs. "Per-unit" costs would be the true variable costs in the accounting sense.

32 Amy Harmon, "Universal to Cut Prices of Its CDs," *New York Times*, September 4, 2003, p. 1.

33 JumpStart Retail Customer Letter, Universal Music and Video Distribution (2003).

34 One of the effects of this new plan is that artist royalties are generally set as a percentage of retail or wholesale price. By lowering both, Universal would be reducing royalty payments to artists.

35 E. Christman, "Retail Track: Consolidation Hits Distributors; Pricing Changes Prevail," *Billboard*, December 25, 2004.

36 E. Christman, "Retail Track: BMG Discount Program Close to Hatching," *Billboard*, August 14, 2004.

37 E. Christman, "Billboard Exclusive: Wal-Mart Stirs Pricing Pot," *Billboard*, March 8, 2008.

38 E. Christman, "Cashing in: Best Buy's $9.99 Price Experiment," *Billboard*, October 25, 2008.

39 E. Christman, "Priced to Move," *Billboard*, June 20, 2009.

40 E. Christman, "MAPing the Route to Consistent Pricing," *Billboard*, March 30, 1996, p. 59.

41 E. Christman, "MAP Policies Bring Price War Cease-fire," *Billboard*, June 1, 1996, p. 3.

42 "SoundData Consumer Panel," NARM Sounding Board, June 1996 (online version; URL extinct).

43 E. Christman, "FTC Broadens its Biz Inquiry into Major's Ad Policies," *Billboard*, October 23, 1993, p. 43.

44 E. Christman, "FTC Tips Hand on Its MAP Ruling," *Billboard*, January 29, 2000, p. 5.

45 Federal Trade Commission, "Record Companies Settle FTC Charges of Restraining Competition in CD Music Market," FTC press release, May 10, 2000, www.ftc. gov/opa/2000/05/cdpres.htm.

46 Tamara Conniff, "CD Price-fixing Suit Settled: Labels, Chains to Compensate States to Tune of $143 mil", *Hollywood Reporter*, October 1, 2002, p, 1; "Settlement OK'd in CD Price-fixing Suit," *Billboard*, June 17, 2003, p.1.

47 *United National Records, Inc. v. MCA, Inc.*, No. 82 C 7589 (N.D. Ill. 1985) (Notice of hearing on proposed additional settlements, proposed plan of distribution and allowance of expenses and attorneys' fees.)

48 Don Jeffrey, "Embattled Majors Act to Protect Music Stores," *Billboard*, December 23, 1995, p. 67.

49 Bill Holland, "Justice Dep't Investigating Music-Video Fee Collusion," *Billboard*, March 2, 1996, p. 1.

50 "NARM Withdraws Anti-Trust Suit vs Sony Music," *Daily Music News*, Billboard.com, December 4, 2001.

51 *Starr v. Sony/BMG.* 2010 US App. LEXIS 768 (2d Circuit).

52 "Sony and Emi Offer Downloads through Online and Physical Retailers," *Music & Copyright*, June 7, 2000.

53 Justin Oppelaar, "Apple Wants Big Bite of Music Downloads," *Daily Variety*, April 29, 2003, p. 7.

54 Brian Garrity, "Seeking Profits at 99[cents]," *Billboard*, November 25, 2003.

55 Business Week, "Universal Music Takes on iTunes," (2007), www.businessweek. com/print/magazine/content/07_43/b4055048.htm?chan=gl.

56 This new model called for hardware makers to add the $5 monthly subscription cost (for 18 months) to the price of the hardware, increasing the retail price by $90, so ultimately the consumer is paying for the subscription service.

57 "The Emi/Apple Deal: Apple and EMI Herald a DRM-free Future," *Music Week*, April 14, 2007, p. 4.

58 M. Mugrove, "iTunes to Sell Songs without Restrictions; Four Record Companies Back Tiered Pricing Plan," *Washington Post*, January 7, 2009, p. D01.

59 A. Bruno and G. Peoples, "The Price You Pay," *Billboard*, June 27, 2009.

60 Marc Graser, "Amazon's Music Bid," *Daily Variety*, May 17, 2007, p. 5.

12 The Marketing Function: Promotion and Price

1 Merriam-Webster dictionary online, www.merriam-webster.com/dictionary/promotion.

2 D. Hinckley, "New Listening Habits Alter Playing Field," *New York Daily News*, July 28, 2008.

3 T. Hutchison, *Web Marketing for the Music Business* (Oxford: Focal Press, 2008).

4 Airplay Specialists, www.airplayspecialists.com/radioterms.htm.

5 B. Farrish, Radio Airplay 101, www.radio-media.com/song-album/articles/airplay33.html.

6 T. Hutchison, A. Macy, and P. Allen, *Record Label Marketing*, 2nd edition (Oxford: Focal Press, 2009).

7 M-Metrics research press release (2008) "With Massive Growth in Musicphones, as Many as 20 Percent of Mobile Subscribers Are Listening to Music on Their Mobile Devices," www.marketwire.com/press-release/M-Metrics-Reports-Growth-in-Mobile-Music-Adoption-810258.htm.

8 J. Horrigan, "Wireless Internet Use," July 22, 2009, Pew Internet and American Life Project, http://pewInternet.org/Reports/2009/12-Wireless-Internet-Use.aspx.

9 IFPI *Digital Music Report*, 2008, www.ifpi.org.

10 J. Ankeny (2009) "Ringtone Sales Fall 24 Percent in 2008," FierceMobileContent.com, www.fiercemobilecontent.com/story/ringtone-sales-fall-24-percent-2008/2009-08-05.

11 W. Holden (2008) "Mobile Music Adoption Passes Tipping Point with Revenues Set to Reach $17.5bn by 2012, whilst Ringtones Revenues Begin Rapid Decline," Juniper Research press release, http://juniperresearch.com/shop/viewpressrelease.php?pr=80.

12 W. Holden (2009) "Streamed Mobile Music Services to Remain Strong as Revenues Approach $5.5bn by 2013, Whilst Those Reliant on Ad-Funding Face Shortfalls," Juniper Research press release, www.juniperresearch.com/shop/viewpressrelease.php?pr=141.

13 IFPI *Digital Music Report* (ibid., n. 9).

14 H. Leggatt (2007) "British Teens Have Mobile Ad Preferences," BizReport.com, www.bizreport.com/2007/04/british_teens_have_mobile_ad_preferences.html.

15 A. Semuels, "Companies C Txt Msgs as a Gr8 Way to Reach Teens. Youths Are Signing up to Have Pitches, Photos and Links to Websites Sent to Cellphones," *Los Angeles Times*, May 23, 2008.

16 M. Hesse, "It's Hannah again. Should We Take This?" *Washington Post* online, Friday, August 1, 2008, www.babble.com/CS/blogs/strollerderby/archive/2008/08/01/Wal-Mart-presents-hannah-montana-wake-up-calls.aspx.

17 W. Holden (2010) press release, "15bn Tickets to be Delivered via Mobile Phone by 2014," Juniper Research, www.juniperresearch.com/shop/viewpressrelease.php?pr=175.

18 Adapted from Jayvee (November 28, 2006) "How to Make Viral Marketing Appealing for Phones," www.everyjoe.com/cellphone9/how-to-make-viral-marketing-appealing-for-phones.

19 IFPI (ibid., n. 9).

20 IFPI (ibid., n. 9).

21 A. Macy, in T. Hutchison, A. Macy, and P. Allen, *Record Label Marketing,* 2nd edition (Oxford: Focal Press, 2009), p. 214.

22 T. Hutchison, A. Macy, and P. Allen, *Record Label Marketing*, 2nd edition (Oxford: Focal Press, 2009), p. 214.

23 NPD Group (2009) press release, www.npd.com/press/releases/press_090818.html.
24 CD Universe, www.cduniverse.com/productinfo.asp?pid=7766579. Amazon.com, www.amazon.com/Fame-Lady-Gaga/dp/B001GM28HO/ref=sr_1_1?ie=UTF8&s=music&qid=1267197529&sr=8-1.

13 The Global Music and Recording Business

1 PricewaterhouseCoopers, *Global Entertainment and Media Outlook: 2009–2013*, www.pwc.com.
2 UNCTAD "Report, Debate, Show of African Art and Music to Highlight Development Promise of Creative Economy," press release, 20/04/2008, www.unctad.org.
3 IFPI, *Recorded Music Sales 2008*, www.ifpi.org/content/section_statistics.
4 IFPI, *The Record Industry 2006 Piracy Report: Protecting Creativity in Music*, www.ifpi.org.
5 Ibid. (n. 4).
6 United States Patent and Trademark Office, www.uspto.gov.
7 WIPO.
8 Country Reports on Economic Policy and Trade Practices, US Department of State, www.state.gov.
9 Edward Mansfield and Helen Milner, *The Political Economy of Economic Regionalism* (New York: Columbia University Press, 1997).
10 Adam White, "BMG Addresses Realities of a Shifting Europe, *Billboard*, 109: 1-2 (2007).
11 *List of Societies*, www.BIEM.org.
12 Copyright Board of Canada, *Copyright Regulations*, www.cb-cda.gc.ca/act-loi.
13 IFPI Statistics, www.ifpi.org.
14 PricewaterhouseCoopers, *From Sao Paulo to Shanghai*, www.pwc.com.
15 Ibid. (n. 14).
16 IFPI, *Recorded Music Sales 2008*, www.ifpi.org/content/section_statistics.
17 Ibid. (n. 16).
18 *Information about Licensing*, www.prsformusic.com.
19 Andre Paine, "Line in the Sand," *Billboard*, 121: 11 (2009).
20 Press release, www.prsformusic.com.
21 Ibid. (n. 13).
22 Population Division of the Department of Economic and Social Affairs of the United Nations Secretariat, *World Population Prospects: The 2008 Revision. Highlights* (New York: United Nations, 2009), www.un.org.
23 *IIPA Special 301 Report* (2009) www.iipa.com/special301.
24 RIAJ *Yearbook 2009*, www.riaj.or.jp.
25 *IIPA Special 301 Report* (2009) www.iipa.com/special301.
26 Rob Schwartz, "Digital Makes Inroads in Japan," *Billboard*, 121: 38 (2009).

Index

Page numbers referring to illustrations are indicated in *italic* type.

eBooks – at www.eBookstore.tandf.co.uk

A library at your fingertips!

eBooks are electronic versions of printed books. You can store them on your PC/laptop or browse them online.

They have advantages for anyone needing rapid access to a wide variety of published, copyright information.

eBooks can help your research by enabling you to bookmark chapters, annotate text and use instant searches to find specific words or phrases. Several eBook files would fit on even a small laptop or PDA.

NEW: Save money by eSubscribing: cheap, online access to any eBook for as long as you need it.

Annual subscription packages

We now offer special low-cost bulk subscriptions to packages of eBooks in certain subject areas. These are available to libraries or to individuals.

For more information please contact webmaster.ebooks@tandf.co.uk

We're continually developing the eBook concept, so keep up to date by visiting the website.

www.eBookstore.tandf.co.uk